An **age-grade** is one of a finite collection of not less than two rule-sets. The rule-sets are all different from one another, and the collection is totally ordered, say $G_1, G_2, \ldots, G_n$. The rule-sets are assigned and disassigned to persons by rules that meet the following constraints:

1. **The first-grade constraint.** No set is assigned to a person before G_1.
2. **The last-grade constraint.** No set is assigned to a person after G_n.
3. **The sequential-assignment constraint.** If the highest set a person has been assigned is G_i ($i = 1, 2, \ldots, n-1$), and that person is assigned another set, then the set assigned is G_{i+1}.
4. **The whole-sequence constraint.** An individual who has been assigned some G_i ($i = 1, 2, \ldots, n-1$) will eventually be assigned G_n if (but not only if) he survives to the maximum life span.
5. **The unique-assignment constraint.** No person is at any time assigned more than one set.
6. **The no-interval constraint.** If a person who is disassigned a set is assigned another, then the two events occur simultaneously.

FUNDAMENTALS OF AGE-GROUP SYSTEMS

STUDIES IN ANTHROPOLOGY

Under the Consulting Editorship of E. A. Hammel,
UNIVERSITY OF CALIFORNIA, BERKELEY

FUNDAMENTALS OF AGE-GROUP SYSTEMS

Frank Henderson Stewart

Trinity College

Oxford, England

ACADEMIC PRESS New York San Francisco London

A SUBSIDIARY OF HARCOURT BRACE JOVANOVICH, PUBLISHERS

ACADEMIC PRESS, INC.
111 Fifth Avenue, New York, New York 10003

United Kingdom Edition published by
ACADEMIC PRESS, INC. (LONDON) LTD.
24/28 Oval Road, London NW1

Library of Congress Cataloging in Publication Data

Stewart, Frank Henderson.
　　Fundamentals of age-group systems.

　　(Studies in anthropology)
　　Bibliography:　　p.
　　Includes index.
　　1.　　Age groups.　　2.　　Ethnology—Africa, Sub-Saharan.
3.　　Indians of North America—Great Plains—Social life
and customs.　　I.　　Title.
GN490.5.S73　　　　　301.2'1　　　　　76-2950
ISBN 0–12–670150–4

For Kate

Contents

*Sections marked with asterisks can be skipped by the reader who is only interested in the main ideas of the book.

APPENDICES

MAPS

Acknowledgments

My first thanks must go to Rodney Needham and Martin Southwold. It was Dr. Southwold's lectures on East African age-group systems that first aroused my interest in the subject, and it was with his encouragement, and under his supervision, that the work on this book began. Professor Needham was an unfailing source of aid and advice throughout the book's long gestation; I do not know whether it would have seen the light of day without his support.

Many people commented on parts of this book in one or other of its drafts—too many, in fact, for me to name them all. I should like to thank them for the numerous improvements they proposed. I hope it will not be invidious if I mention here one person in particular, Michael Cook, who alone read all the various versions in full and whose many creative suggestions I adopted wholesale. He also weeded out innumerable logical errors; the number that remains, large though it may be, gives a wholly inadequate idea of my productivity in that line.

I have benefited greatly—far more than the exiguous mathematical apparatus of the book suggests—from conversations with patient mathematicians, above all Michael Broido and Michael Singer. The latter, indeed, contributed directly to the book: he wrote, or rewrote, all the proofs in Chapter I, Section 1.2.2, and he saved me from various blunders elsewhere in the text.

In the course of the work, I approached a number of scholars with requests for information to supplement what had appeared in their published works. They responded generously, and I am much in their debt. The names of all of them appear at the appropriate points in the text. What is not apparent from the text is that several of them—Christopher Hallpike, John Lamphear, Richard Lowenthal, Denise Paulme, and Paul Spencer—also helped me by supplying proof copies of their publications.

I have had the good fortune, in carrying out this work, to have been given ideal conditions for research by all the institutions that supported it. The first draft was written while I was in the Department of Social Anthropology of the University of Manchester; the main body of the work was done at Merton College, Oxford; and the last revision of the text took place at Trinity College, Oxford. I am deeply grateful to the many who helped me, in one way or another, at all these places.

I must thank S. E. Mann for his notes to Appendix 1 and Sung-hsing Wang for translating some articles in Chinese. The Anthropological Department of the American Museum of Natural History (New York) kindly allowed me to see the unpublished field notes of G. L. Wilson on the Hidatsa, and the International African Institute (London) generously made available various manuscripts in their collection.

Of the libraries I worked in, I should particularly like to mention that of the Royal Anthropological Institute. I can hardly imagine having written this book without it. Its staff, under Miss B. Kirkpatrick, provided unfailing assistance. Both while he was at the library, and subsequently, Jim Urry supplied me with many useful references.

Last, but far from least, I must acknowledge my debt to my first teacher in anthropology, Ward Goodenough. Many of the basic ideas of this book—for example, the importance it attaches to the development of cross-cultural concepts, the central role it allocates to the notion of a rule, and its stand on the relationship between the theorist and the ethnographer—derive from his views.

List of Symbols

a_S	Maximum possible age-range of age-group S
c_S	Cessation interval of age group S
d_S	Duration of age-group S
E	Enrolment age
F	An age-group in a paternal linking system
G	An age-grade
g_S	The f-s inauguration interval of group S
M	Maximum life span
p_S	Progenitive period of age-group S
r_S	Recruitment period of age-group S
S	An age-group
v_S	Inauguration interval of age-group S

FUNDAMENTALS OF AGE-GROUP SYSTEMS

Introduction

1 AIMS

This book is primarily a contribution to the theory of age-group systems, but it can also serve as an introduction to the topic. It is intended to be comprehensible to those who have no knowledge of sociology or anthropology. Such readers may find it useful if I begin by offering a brief account of the subject matter of the book. The two basic notions to be dealt with are those of an age-set (which is the main kind of age-group) and of an age-grade (which is not a kind of age-group).

Radcliffe-Brown, in a letter that will be discussed more fully later, defined an age-set as "A recognised and sometimes organised group consisting of persons . . . who are of the same age. . . . Once a person enters a given age-set, whether at birth or by initiation, he remains a member of the same set for the remainder of his life." This book is mainly concerned with age-set systems, rather than individual age-sets. The notion of an age-set system is explicated at length later; for the moment it is enough to say that, roughly speaking, a society

1

has an age-set system when it has a number of age-sets with no members in common and distinct mean ages. Until the time comes to distinguish between the two terms, this can also be taken as a definition of an age-group system.

Quite often, age-group systems are found in conjunction with age-grades, defined by Radcliffe-Brown as "recognised divisions of the life of an individual as he passes from infancy to old age . . . [for instance] infant, boy, youth, young married man, elder, or whatever it may be." The notion of an age-grade will also be explicated later; one of the points that will be added to Radcliffe-Brown's definition is that the grades are clearly demarcated, that is, transition from one grade to another takes place at a definite point in time, and there is never any doubt about which grade an individual is in. (Our own society does not have age-grades of this kind for adults.) I shall refer to an age-group system that is combined with an age-grade system as a graded age-group system.[1]

Though age-group systems are described in innumerable ethnographies, and sometimes very fully, they have received scant attention elsewhere in the literature of social anthropology.[2] Almost every textbook mentions them, but generally they are allotted no more than a paragraph or two; the few that treat them at some length are all, for a variety of reasons, decidedly misleading. General works on social organization, such as Murdock (1949) or Buchler and Selby (1968), which might be expected to devote a chapter to them, ignore their existence.[3] Even Textor's massive compendium (1967) has nothing to say on the subject. Yet age-group systems are quite common,[4] and not infrequently they play an important part in

[1] To be exact, the term "graded age-group system," as defined later, covers only cases where age-groups and age-grades are combined in a particular way; but the number of societies in which age-groups and age-grades are combined in some other way is so small that we can for the moment ignore this nicety.

[2] And have remained correspondingly unknown to scholars in allied fields. "Age-grading, the insistence that biological age set the lock step in which all youth will march, seems a relatively new invention of the increasingly mechanized and mechanical West [Mazlish 1975: 181]."

[3] Actually, Buchler and Selby do at one point mention a particular type of age organization, that found among the Galla of Ethiopia (1968: 61 ff.). Their purpose in doing so, however, is not to analyze age-group systems but simply to illustrate, on the basis of Hoffmann's paper (1971), the "application of Markov chains to the problem of cultural stability and change."

[4] Hoebel's claim that they are rare (1972: 480) is based on a misunderstanding of his source (for details, see Stewart 1972: 27 f.). The distribution of age-group systems is dealt with in Section 3 of this introduction.

people's lives. Ethnographers have described them as being the central institution of many tribal societies in Africa and in Taiwan. I think the reason why they are neglected by textbooks and other general works is that there is very little theoretical literature about them, and that such theoretical literature as exists has (with one exception) not produced any generally accepted results (see the survey in the following section).

It is because of this lack of generally accepted results that the present work can serve as an introduction to the subject as well as a contribution to theory. It has been necessary to start from first principles. However, the range of questions that will be dealt with is limited, and the newcomer to age-group systems who wants to form a rounded picture of their workings should also look at a few of the more recent ethnographies (some are listed on pp. 13 f.).

To say that a book is a contribution to the theory of a particular subject in sociology is not, as things stand, to characterize it with much precision, for there is no consensus about what a theory should look like or about what a theorist can profitably attempt. I shall therefore begin by explaining what I have tried to do and why.

My main purpose has been to develop a set of concepts that can be used cross-culturally in describing certain features of age-group systems. The kind of ideal I have had in mind is this: to create an array of clearly defined[5] concepts so comprehensive that the ethnographer can describe every feature of a given age-group system purely in terms of those concepts. He should not, in other words, find it necessary to use any concepts not drawn from this central stock, whether they be concepts employed by those who operate the system or concepts invented ad hoc by the ethnographer himself.[6] It goes without saying that this ideal is nowhere remotely near being realized at the moment; the present work, as we shall see, only makes some initial contributions toward it.

What is the point of attempting to develop a set of notions of this sort? A number of answers can be given. In the first place, such

[5] Cf. p. 27.
[6] Contrast the view that two distinct sets of concepts are needed, those for describing particular cultures (ethnographic, etic), and those for cross-cultural comparison (ethnological, emic). This is expressed with great clarity in, for instance, Keesing (1966: 346, 350 f.), with references to works by Goodenough. (Goodenough 1970: 98 ff. adopts what seems to be a more subtle position.) The view that these two "levels of discourse" must be kept distinct is supported by an analogy with certain linguistic theories that are no longer current; modern work in linguistics does not suggest that the distinction is necessary.

notions are a great help to the ethnographer. The main achievement of social anthropology has been to raise very considerably the quality of descriptions of particular societies. This has occurred in large part because successive generations of ethnographers have gone into the field with concepts better and better adapted to the phenomena they encounter. The precise details of this process would be difficult to elucidate and need not concern us here; but it is worth noting that in general the ethnographer has probably learned his trade more from ethnographies than from textbooks or theoretical treatises. In part, this is because much of what he has to learn cannot profitably be formulated in general terms; but in part it is also because theorists have usually been interested in quite other things than in helping the man in the field to give a full and clear account of the culture he is attempting to describe. If, however, they do turn their attention to the matter, there are a number of ways in which they can help him, and one of the main ones is certainly by developing the type of concept with which we are here concerned. In age-group studies, the most important examples of this sort of notion are the concepts of age-grades and age-sets; anyone who tries to make sense of the works of ethnographers unfamiliar with the distinction between the two will quickly appreciate the increase in descriptive power that it brings with it.

Another reason for producing the kind of concepts I have mentioned is that they are needed for cross-cultural theories. Such theories aim to produce interesting generalizations about cultural phenomena that exist in many different societies, and so they must be phrased in terms of concepts that pick out those phenomena, that is, cross-cultural concepts.[7]

It was not my purpose in writing this book to produce cross-cultural theories, but inevitably hints of such theories have crept in. In practice, the formation of cross-cultural concepts cannot be entirely divorced from generalization. For one thing, any at all elaborate structure of such concepts will, if it is to be useful, have to incorporate insights about the functioning of the institutions (or whatever) to which it relates. The central feature of this book is an age-set system model that is used not merely to describe age-set systems but also to demonstrate the implications of certain features that all such systems possess. Furthermore, it is used to elucidate the nature of certain age-group systems that differ from age-set systems, and it has been possible to show in these cases that even the best

---

[7] This is not intended as a definition.

ethnographers have produced descriptions that are internally inconsistent or incomplete, or have reported facts whose significance they have not appreciated.

Last, but not least, the attempt to develop cross-cultural concepts has the merit of forcing us to think about certain very general sociological problems. We must decide on the constituent elements in terms of which the institution we are concerned with is to be analyzed. Do we characterize an age-set system as a collection of roles? Or do we describe it—as Weber might suggest—in terms of the probabilities of certain actions? Do we perhaps make function the basic notion of our model? Or do we use concepts like "power" and "involvement" (cf. Etzioni 1961)? The possibilities are endless. There is absolutely no agreement among sociologists on these fundamental questions, and purely general discussions of them are unlikely to be fruitful. For the moment the most sensible thing is to try to demonstrate the usefulness of a particular notion by using it in dealing with a particular problem.

In this book the fundamental notion employed is that of a rule, and I have characterized both age-set and age-grade systems as sets of rules. I was encouraged to use this concept mainly by the fact that it has been so successfully employed in linguistics. This fact does not of course show that the concept is a useful one in other social sciences, but I hope that the present work will constitute some evidence in that direction.

The extensive use I have made of the notion of a rule may give an exaggerated impression of the importance that I attach to it. I should therefore make it plain here that I do not consider that either age-group or age-grade systems can be wholly characterized as sets of rules. Nor do I wish to make any claim as to the extent to which they can be characterized in these terms. All I want to say is that some fundamental features of these—as of many other—social systems can be described in terms of rules.[8]

There is also a purely practical reason for concentrating on rules: they are relatively accessible and clear-cut. As a result, ethnog-

---

[8] Contrast Weber's view that "the belief that a particular type of behavior is enjoined by law or convention is, from a sociological point of view, in the first instance merely a superaddition, which increases the degree of probability with which the actor can rely on certain *consequences* following his action [Weber 1964: 247; my translation]." (The corresponding passage in the English version—which in this case is fairly accurate but which is often misleading—is 1968b: 327.) Weber discusses rules at length in his essay *R. Stammlers "Uberwindung" der materialistischen Geschichtsauffassung* (1968a: 322–359).

raphers usually report them more fully and reliably than other, murkier but not necessarily less important, aspects of age organization. Equally, the rules of a system are the easiest thing for a cross-cultural theorist to deal with in a fairly rigorous way. But of course an age-grade (say) may carry with it a whole ethos, a whole style of life (see, for instance, Spencer's fine description of the young Samburu "warriors"); and some interesting insights might be derived from a comparative study using the data on such subjects provided by the more sensitive ethnographers.[9] Yet, both because of lack of data and because of the inherent difficulty of the problems involved, it does not seem possible at the moment to produce a systematic cross-cultural analysis of such variations of ethos. I have therefore ignored this and similar matters. But the last thing I wish to imply is that I think them unimportant.

The concept of a rule is still far from having been adequately investigated,[10] and in deciding what is and what is not a rule I have used unspecified and fairly liberal criteria. When it has seemed that the term could be stretched no further I have used other, equally undefined, terms, notably "desire" and its synonyms.

Something should now be said about the limitations of the present work. Some of them are of a kind familiar in modern sociological literature. Of these, perhaps the most important is the absence (in Part One) of any historical perspective, a gap which is in itself enough to preclude full consideration of the question of why age-groups exist in some areas but not in others. One reason for this gap is that there are very few age-group systems about whose history much is known; but historians of Africa are becoming increasingly interested in age-groups,[11] especially as an aid in establishing chronologies, and may well provide much new information on the subject. I hope this book will be of some help to them, even though I

---

[9] Such a study would take its author far beyond the bounds of age-set and age-grade systems. Indeed, it might well take him beyond the bounds of human societies. The following comments on primates indicate a very familiar situation: "The age class of subadult males tends to become socially isolated. . . . In many species the male subadults live on the periphery of the group and may even leave it. . . . Young male monkeys of many species have a stronger tendency to associate with their own sex than have females [Kummer 1971: 34 f.]."

[10] Even though it is dealt with extensively in the literature of sociology, social psychology, jurisprudence, and philosophy. Raz (1975) gives the necessary references to publications in the last two of the fields mentioned.

[11] See, for instance, Person (1963), Jacobs (1968), Muriuki (1974), and Lamphear (1976).

have generally allowed myself the idealizations involved in treating systems purely synchronically.

Other limitations are less familiar, and two of them deserve particular emphasis.

The first is inherent in the objectives: I have not attempted to discuss systematically the relationship between age-group systems and other culture elements. That there is a relationship seems certain, since age-group systems of the kind that are central to this book (i.e., graded systems involving adults) exist only in what are loosely termed primitive societies; and societies that in the past operated age-group systems have frequently abandoned them under the impact of modern conditions. (On these points see the brief but stimulating remarks in Simmel 1908: 408 f.)

The second limitation is connected with the first. It is that I have not (except in Part Two) considered the uses to which different societies put their age-group systems. The variety here is enormous: in some places the ethnographers say that the age-group system is primarily a political institution, in others that it is primarily a religious one, in others that it is economic, in others educational, in others recreational, and so on. There are age-groups that fight wars, age-groups that have wives, age-groups that own property, and age-groups whose members merely help one another in daily life.

But it is not simply the variety that makes it difficult to generalize about the functions of age-groups. The real trouble is the inadequacy of our conceptual apparatus. Useful though they are for many purposes, notions such as "religious" or "political" have only a limited scientific value at the moment. To categorize an age-group system in these terms is a good way of giving a rough idea of what it is like, but no more than that. It seems to me that these concepts are too vague for it to be possible to build any solid theoretical structure out of them.

Now, the solution to the problem of vagueness is, of course, to refine existing concepts and create new ones. But consider, for instance, the notion "political." Any serious attempt to refine and develop it would have to go far beyond the boundaries of a discussion of age-group systems. I have not made such an attempt or anything like it. Instead, I have tried to clarify a few basic concepts relating solely to age-group (and age-grade) systems. I have tried to give partial answers to questions like, What kind of thing is an age-set system? What are its constituent elements? and How do age-grade systems differ from age-set systems and how do they resemble them? I have also tried to suggest means by which it is possible to obtain definite and consistent answers to the question, Is there an age-set system in this society? The problems raised by such questions seem to me fundamental, not in the sense that they are the most important problems of age-group systems but in the sense that until at least provisional solutions have been found for them, it will not be possible to solve any of the deeper problems.

Lastly, some remarks on the way this book is organized. The main ideas are set out in Part One; in Part Two the concepts there developed are applied in an analysis of certain North American Indian systems of age organization. I chose to consider these systems at length because they possess a combination of attributes that to my knowledge is unique: they are well documented, and yet it is not immediately obvious what their relationship is to the kinds of systems described in Part One. There are, to be sure, other systems with the second of these attributes, e.g., the age villages of the Nyakyusa or the urban "age-grade associations" of the Nupe (Nadel 1942: 383 ff.); but it seemed to me that the data on these other systems had too many gaps to make extended analyses worth while. Fortunately the possibility still exists for most of them of collecting fresh information in the field.

Many sections of Part One, and the whole of Part Two, are marked in the text, and in the Table of Contents, with an asterisk. This is to indicate that they can be ignored by a reader who is only interested in the main ideas of this book. The asterisked sections deal either with matters of secondary importance, or else are extended analyses of the age organization of particular tribes in Africa and America.

A draft of Part One was submitted as a doctoral thesis at Oxford at the end of 1972 and was circulated fairly widely in mimeographed form. I occasionally refer to the thesis in this book, though I now disagree with some of what was said in it.

The bibliography contains all the works cited in the text. It is not intended as an exhaustive guide to the subject, nor as an indication of all the works I consulted.

2 *SURVEY OF THE LITERATURE

In this section I shall survey only the best-known theoretical discussions of age-group systems; those interested in less prominent works of this kind will find many of them referred to in Eisenstadt (1956). Articles of a general or theoretical nature that have appeared subsequently include Levine and Sangree (1962), Legesse (1963), Gulliver (1968), Paulme (1968, of which Paulme 1973 is a translation), and the introduction to Paulme (1971a). See also the references given on p. 76 n. 58 below. A quite lengthy early work not mentioned by Eisenstadt is Visscher (1911: 406–447). Among the unpublished studies that I have seen are Abou-Zeid (1953), Fleming (1965), and Sanders (1968).

The first modern writer to deal at length with the theory of age organization was Heinrich Schurtz. His book *Age-Classes and Men's Associations* appeared in 1902, and, as the title indicates, it covers a wide range of topics. A full account of the author's theories would, in fact, take us far beyond the confines of age-group systems; for a convenient summary the reader is referred to Lowie (1947: 297 ff.). Schurtz had at his disposal data from only a small number of age-group systems: half a dozen in Africa, one in India, and three or four in North America. His information on Taiwan, one of the major areas of concentration of age-set systems, was not good enough even to reveal their existence (Schurtz 1902: 274 f.). Under these circumstances it is hardly surprising that his ideas do not throw much light on the problems of which we have since become aware. His central thesis about age divisions is that the men of a tribe are initially divided into three groups—boys, bachelors, and married men—and that any further age-classes derive from these three original ones (Schurtz 1902: 125).

Schurtz's book was generally well received and for many years often cited with approval. Even soon after its publication, however, there were dissident voices. Mauss in 1906 referred to it as "trop tôt devenue classique [Mauss 1969: 59]," and its evolutionary and generalizing approach was above all unacceptable to the new school of American anthropologists. The work came under heavy attack from Lowie, who had personally collected data on the age organization of several Plains Indian tribes. Lowie discussed age organization in general in a number of his works, most extensively in the comparative sections of "Plains Indian Age-Societies" (1916) and in *Primitive Society* (1947: 257–337). A good deal of his energy was devoted to demolishing Schurtz's theories, but this was by no means an entirely negative enterprise; in the course of it he was—as might be expected from a student of Boas—at great pains to bring out the individual character of the various systems he considered, and to demonstrate the profound differences that may lie beneath superficial similarities. Given this approach, it is not surprising that he put forward no general theories of his own.

Since World War I the main ethnographic works on age-groups have come from Africa, and the Africanists have in general ignored Lowie. Instead they have turned to Radcliffe-Brown, who in 1929 sent an unpretentious letter to *Man* which is undoubtedly the most influential single contribution to the theory of age-set systems. [12] Radcliffe-Brown wrote that he wanted to "draw attention to the need of somewhat more exact terminology in the sociological description of age-organization," and he proceeded to give the definitions of the terms "age-set" and "age-grade" quoted earlier.

It is important to understand just what Radcliffe-Brown is doing in this letter. He is not simply making a terminological innovation, suggesting, say, that what used to be called "age-classes" should now be known as "age-grades." The significance of his letter is that it makes a conceptual distinction which is of great importance, but which, as he points out, had hitherto often been neglected: he is saying that age-grades and age-sets are two quite different things and that they should not be lumped together.

Radcliffe-Brown was undoubtedly correct in claiming that they often were lumped together; he cites as an example Rivers (1924), and there are plenty of other instances. On the other hand, the two concepts were not new. In the ethnographic literature, for instance, Merker (1910) distinguishes with perfect clarity between grades (*Altersstufen*) and sets (*Altersklassen*), and in the theoretical literature Lowie (1916: 968, 975, cf. 977) attacks Schurtz for failing to make this kind of distinction.

Then why is Radcliffe-Brown's letter so important? Partly, perhaps, it is a matter of chance; the best ethnographic works on age-set systems published in the last 50 years have mostly been written by Africanists, many of them British trained, who were weaned on Radcliffe-Brown. But there is more to it than that. In the first place, there can be no doubt that Radcliffe-Brown recognized the importance of this distinction in a way that Lowie did not. Lowie made no attempt to develop a consistent terminology, and when treating the question of age organization fairly briefly (1930,

---

[12] Its influence no doubt also made itself felt through *Notes and Queries on Anthropology*, in which the section on age organization is extremely similar in its approach to the 1929 letter.

1950: 303 ff.) simply did not bother to distinguish between grades and sets.[13]

In the second place, Radcliffe-Brown was breaking new ground in attempting to specify in general terms the nature of the two phenomena in question. The present work continues that attempt, and in the course of it we shall find our advance checked by a number of obstacles that Radcliffe-Brown either ignored or was not conscious of. So, for example, Radcliffe-Brown is content to state that "once a person enters a given age-set . . . he remains a member of the same set for the remainder of his life." Yet a reference cited by him in his letter (Seligman 1910: 470 ff.) gives a clear instance of inidviduals shifting their age-set affiliation (see p. 116). But whatever the weaknesses of Radcliffe-Brown's definitions, they have certainly not been improved on to date.

Naturally enough, Radcliffe-Brown's proposals did not meet with universal acceptance. Richards (1929) objected to the terminology, while accepting the concepts. Lehmann (1943) proposed a much more elaborate typology of age groupings, and a correspondingly elaborate terminology; but his suggestions were not accompanied by analyses of actual systems, and they have not been taken up. Bernardi, in his article "The Age-System of the Nilo-Hamitic Peoples" (1952), rejected Radcliffe-Brown's proposals on the grounds that they "do not seem clear enough for describing the real nature of the various age-associations found in Nilo-Hamitic societies"; but Bernardi's counterproposals have not been adopted, and ethnographic work on these societies continues to be largely influenced by Radcliffe-Brown's ideas.

The 1950s saw the appearance of two theoretical monographs on age-group systems, both of which accepted Radcliffe-Brown's scheme, while supplementing it with additional notions of their own. The first of these was *East African Age-Class Systems* by A. H. J. Prins (1953). The author says that his "aim is to make a first contribution only towards a full description and interpretation of the various East African systems [Prins 1953: 12]." The main body of his book is an analysis of the age organization of three tribes, the Galla, the Kipsigis, and the Kikuyu. In each case he takes an inadequate ethnographic literature and tries to make sense of it. Prins's

---

[13] He is not alone in this. Many textbooks, including recent ones that devote some space to age organization, follow his practice, e.g., Salzmann (1969: 164–166) and Hoebel (1972).

accounts have the great merit of being coherent—of recognizing what the major components are and fitting them together in a consistent fashion—even though in the case of the Kikuyu at least his conclusions cannot be accepted (see Chapter II, Section 4.4.1).

Prins's main conceptual innovation is the notion of an "age-class," which he defines as "the total of persons occupying a given grade" (1953: 49, cf. 10). He also uses the specialized notions of "ultra-senectation" and "infra-puerilization" for describing the age organization of the Galla (1953: 65). These concepts derive from the work of A. E. Jensen (who used the more euphonious terms *Über-alterung* and *Verjüngung*) and are further developed in the present work, where they appear as "overaging" and "underaging."[14]

The most recent treatise, and the most ambitious since Schurtz, is Eisenstadt's *From Generation to Generation* (1956). This book does not limit itself to age-group systems—though it devotes a great deal of space to them—but considers all kinds of groups consisting largely of coevals, including, for instance, youth movements. Eisenstadt asks the question, What kind of society gives rise to "age-homogeneous groups"? His answer is that there are two types of society in which such groups arise. The first, and most important, is what he calls the "universalistic society." In establishing this category—and indeed in the way he approaches his problem in general—Eisenstadt uses the conceptual scheme established by Talcott Parsons and E. A. Shils. Universalistic societies, according to one of the definitions given, are societies with "social systems in which the allocation of roles, facilities and rewards is not based on membership in kinship—or otherwise particularistically defined—units and criteria [1956: 54]." The second type of society that Eisenstadt isolates is the "familistic society," defined as one in which "the structure of the family or descent group blocks the younger members' opportunities for attaining social status within the family because (a) the older members block the younger ones' access to the facilities which are prerequisites of full adult roles, and/or (b) the sharpening of incest taboos and restrictions on sexual relations within the family unit postpones the young members' attainment of full sexual maturity [1956: 248]." Eisenstadt goes on to suggest that while both these types of society give rise to "age groups," the kinds of age group that arise in universalistic societies differ from the kinds

[14] The terms "overaging" and "underaging" first appear in print in Hallpike (1976), where they are taken from Stewart (1972). Cf. *Africa* (1976) **46**: 246.

that arise in familistic societies. "In the latter type the extent of general, society-wide age identification is relatively weak as a criterion of membership, the span of their activities is usually limited to the limits of particularistic units (family and lineage), and their main function seems to be the easing of tensions between the different generations [1956: 267]."

The main difficulty in assessing Eisenstadt's theories lies in the fact that it is not clear exactly what he is asserting. For one thing, the terms in which the theory is couched—"age groups," "universalistic societies," and "familistic societies"—are so vaguely defined that there are innumerable cases where there would be no general agreement as to which (if any) of his categories a particular phenomenon belongs to. Furthermore, even if we understood exactly what these terms meant, it would still not be clear precisely what Eisenstadt is claiming. In certain places he writes that "age groups exist in universalistic [and also, presumably, familistic] societies [1956: 17]," in others that they "tend to arise" in these types of societies (1956: 54). It may be that he means that age groups *only* exist in these two types of societies, but that they do not exist in *all* societies of these types. Other interpretations of his claims are, however, possible. Until these and similar matters are clarified it will be impossible to evaluate Eisenstadt's theories.

A useful test of the importance of any theoretical work in social anthropology is the degree to which its ideas affect the subsequent ethnographic literature. Of the works we have just been looking at, the only one that can be called important by this criterion is Radcliffe-Brown's. His distinction between age-grades and age-sets has been widely adopted and lies also at the foundation of the present book.

To say this is not to say that our understanding of age-group systems has remained at the same level as it was in 1929. Since then there has been a great increase not only in the quantity but also in the quality of the ethnographic literature, and the more recent contributions have often made it possible for the first time to understand earlier reports. A striking example of this is the way in which Dyson-Hudson's account of Karimojong age organization (1966) clarified obscurities in the descriptions of several similar systems, notably that of the Kikuyu.

Among the best and most accessible of the recent ethnographies are Gulliver (1963), Spencer (1965), Maybury-Lewis (1967), and Ottenberg (1971), all describing graded age-group systems; Dyson-

Hudson (1966) and Bischofberger (1972) on generation-groups; and Evans-Pritchard (1940) and Gulliver (1958) on age-sets without age-grades. Denise Paulme has edited a valuable collection of papers, in which over a dozen different West African systems are described (1971a). A similar collection, but dealing with East Africa, is to appear under the editorship of P. T. W. Baxter and U. Almagor.

I end this section with some simple methodological remarks directed at ethnographers. The modern ethnographer is usually studying a culture (or some features of a culture) on which there is some earlier literature. It is his job to establish the relationship between his findings and those of the earlier investigators. This means that unless something of the sort already exists he should provide a comprehensive bibliography of the existing literature (cf. p. 147, n. 15). Furthermore, he should comment on the information in that literature. Sometimes it happens that an earlier writer gives a description so inaccurate that it can be dismissed out of hand; if this is the case, then the ethnographer should say so. Often enough, however, earlier writers will make statements that look quite trust-worthy. The ethnographer should investigate all such statements, and he should report the results of his investigations. Above all, he should always indicate whether the information he gives was collected in the field or whether it derives from the earlier literature.

These injunctions are banal in the extreme, but anyone who has attempted a critical evaluation of a good number of modern ethno-graphic writings will know how often they are neglected. This sort of neglect can considerably reduce the value of an ethnography; it may cast doubt both over the ethnographer's own work and over that of his predecessors. Let me give some examples of typical problems. Imagine there are two sources, an early one, Captain Arbogast, and a recent one, Professor Zylinder. Arbogast describes something that Zylinder does not mention. We wonder whether this means that Arbogast made a mistake. If only Zylinder had said something about it we would know where we stood. Or, Zylinder says something that agrees with what Arbogast wrote. Did Zylinder copy from Arbogast, or did he discover it independently? Or, Zylinder differs from Arbo-gast about something. Is it because he is writing at a later date and things have changed? Is it that their information refers to different localities? Or is it just that one or other of them is wrong?

It is natural enough that problems of this sort should arise when one is dealing with the casual observations of early travelers. It is inexcusable when they arise in relation to the work of a professional ethnographer.

There is also a less banal methodological point that deserves mention. It often happens that within a certain area there exist a large number of rather similar age-group systems. It may be, for instance, that the members of a tribe are distributed among a number of villages, and that each village has its own age-group system, which differs only in relatively minor ways from the age-group systems found in other villages. In such cases there are a number of courses open to the ethnographer. One is to produce a kind of generalized description that represents a synthesis of practice in a number of different areas; another is to give very brief descriptions of a number of systems; yet another is to break down the notion of an age-group system into a number of component elements and then to describe in turn the local varieties of each component. All these practices are quite common among modern ethnographers, and *mutatis mutandis* they exist equally in the description of other phenomena than age-groups. My experience in writing the present work was that these practices produce descriptions that have little or no value for theoretical purposes; and I strongly suspect that even theorists who are not dealing with the type of question considered in this book, or who are dealing with other subjects than age-group systems, will also usually find this to be the case. Given the kind of situation outlined at the beginning of this paragraph, the proper method, I would suggest, is to produce the most detailed possible description of the system in a single locality and then, to the extent that it is practicable, to indicate how systems in other localities differ. Even this approach may involve some distortion, but I feel certain that it is the one which will lead to most insight.

3 *DISTRIBUTION

In this section I have indicated the locations of all tribes mentioned elsewhere in the book and have tried to mention all the regions of the world where there are age-group systems (though without listing all the tribes that have systems within each region).

Although graded age-group systems exist in most parts of the world, there are only two regions where they are both numerous and frequently a major feature of social organization: Africa and Taiwan. Of these, Africa is much the most important to us. It harbors a far greater number and variety of systems, and the systems are on average better documented.

Most of the African tribes mentioned in this book appear on the maps at the end. In a rough-and-ready way they can be divided into four groups: East, West, South, and Central.

The East African systems are the ones that will concern us most, partly because of certain special problems they present, and partly because the ethnographic literature on them is exceptionally good. The reader who is unfamiliar with the area may find it useful to have some kind of framework into which to fit the various tribes to be mentioned in the text. Solely to provide such a framework, and without using any criteria consistently, these tribes can be divided into the following groups.

The Gada area. There exists a group of tribes, living mainly in southern Ethiopia, that possess age-group systems of a type generally referred to as Gada systems. The biggest of these tribes is the Galla.[15] Estimates of the number of Galla vary widely, but there are certainly several million of them, and they constitute a large proportion—some say as much as one-half—of the population of Ethiopia. They are divided into many groups and subgroups. Among the major groups that make up the tribe, we shall encounter the Borana, the Guji, the Arussi, the Shoa (or Tulama), and the Machcha. Of these, the Borana are the ones who will concern us most. They are seminomadic cattle herders living in the extreme south of Ethiopia, with some outliers in northern Kenya. The other Galla groups are now primarily farmers but were all, in the more or less recent past, mainly pastoralists.

Gada is a Galla word whose meaning varies somewhat from one subtribe to another. In some it means "age-group," elsewhere it is the name of a particular age-grade. The term "Gada system" is usually applied not only to the age-group systems of the Galla, but also to the systems of certain neighboring tribes, since these systems have some important (and idiosyncratic) features in common with the Galla ones. Some, but by no means all, of these neighboring tribes also use the word *gada.* In this book the term **Gada system** will be used in

[15] The best general work on the Galla is Haberland (1963), which contains, among other things, an extensive bibliography. Haberland gives information on the Gada systems of a number of Galla subtribes, virtually all of it collected at first hand. Michels (1941: 80—185) gives a careful and comprehensive survey of the older literature on the Gada systems of the Galla.

this customary fashion, and I shall refer to the region where Gada systems exist as the **Gada area.**

The notion of a Gada system has never been carefully defined (and is not so defined here; cf. p. 88). But in spite of this there appears to be general agreement as to what are, and what are not, Gada systems. With negligible exceptions, they are found only in southern Ethiopia, mostly among tribes speaking Cushitic languages.[16] Of the non-Galla tribes with Gada systems, the one that will concern us most is the Konso, a people of some 60,000 souls, who live in a mountainous region just north of the Borana and practice intensive agriculture with the aid of terraces. Rather more briefly we shall encounter two other agricultural tribes, the Sidama (who are divided into various subtribes) and the closely related Darassa; and we shall also mention the Dassanetch (also called Murille, Geleba, or Reshiat), a hitherto little known pastoral tribe. There will be brief references to the age organization of two Cushitic speaking peoples who do not (at least nowadays) have Gada systems: the Somali, a large nation divided into innumerable smaller groups, and the Tsamako, who evidently number only a few thousand.

Southern Sudan. To the West of the Gada area, in the southern part of the state of Sudan, lie several tribes that make brief appearances later. In the north are the Nuba, a congeries of tribes speaking a number of languages and living in the Nuba Mountains. Further south are the Shilluk, a basically agricultural people living on the west bank of the Nile. They have as neighbors two large, related, pastoral tribes, the Nuer and the Dinka. East of the Nile and south of the Sobat lie many other tribes with age-set systems; those mentioned in this book are the Anuak, the Murle, and the Longarim (these last two being linguistically related), and the Bari. (The Bari also have representatives on the west bank of the Nile.)

The Karimojong cluster. This name was given by Gulliver (1952) to a group of seven tribes that straddles the border between Uganda and Kenya north of Mt. Elgon and extends slightly into the Sudan.[17] The tribes are largely pastoral and speak mutually intelli-

---

[16] The view that they are found only among speakers of East Cushitic languages (Haberland 1963: 169) needs to be modified, since it is doubtful whether Dassanetch is Cushitic, and the status of Konso is unclear (Tucker and Bryan 1966: 56; Tucker 1967: 660, 678).

[17] See the map in Gulliver (1952). Lamphear (1976) gives an up-to-date bibliography. Lamphear objects to the term "Karimojong cluster," on the

gible dialects.[18]   Three of the best studies of age-group systems have
been carried out among tribes from this group: the Turkana, the Jie,
and the Karimojong (the tribe that gives its name to the whole
cluster). The last two of the tribes mentioned have particularly
interesting systems and will figure prominently in the pages that
follow. Of the other members of the cluster, we shall mention briefly
the Dodoth and the Topotha.

Several small, mainly agricultural tribes live next to or amidst
the tribes of the Karimojong cluster but continue to speak languages
that are (at least) not closely related to those of the cluster. Two of
these tribes will appear briefly in this book: the Labwor (or Tobur)
and the So (or Tepes).

Bantu tribes to the east of Lake Victoria.   These tribes, primarily farmers, are found on both sides of the Kenya–Tanzania border.
They include the congeries of tribes now known as the Abaluyia
(dealt with in Wagner 1949, Sangree 1966), and, further south, the
Gusii, the Kuria, the Zanaki, and some other groups listed on p. 70.

The Kalenjin speakers.   To the east of these Bantu tribes lie the
territories of a number of tribes that speak closely related languages
belonging to the group now generally referred to as Kalenjin (which
in turn constitutes a subdivision of what Tucker and Bryan, 1966,
call the Paranilotic languages). From the point of view of their age
organization (and also, as it happens, from a linguistic point of view),
the Kalenjin tribes mentioned in this work fall into three subgroups.

  (i)   In the north are the Pokot (or Suk), whose age organiza-
        tion has been strongly influenced by the Karimojong.
  (ii) Further south lie four closely related tribes that speak
        mutually intelligible dialects: the Tugen, Keyo, Nandi, and
        Kipsigis.
  (iii) In the extreme south are a group of tribes known as the
        Tatoga, the most important of which are the Barabaig.

---

grounds that it gives undue prominence to the Karimojong tribe, and he refers to
these peoples as the Central Paranilotes. (Tucker and Bryan 1966: 442 ff.
propose the term Paranilotic to replace the term Nilo-Hamitic.)

[18] So, at least, Gulliver (1952:1). Tucker and Bryan (1956) classify Kari-
mojong, Jie, and Dodoth as belonging to a single dialect cluster but regard
Topotha and Turkana as languages distinct both from each other and from the
Karimojong dialect cluster.

Originally all the Kalenjin speakers were primarily pastoralists, though in recent times there has been an increasing tendency toward agriculture. (There are, however, great differences between the tribes in this respect.) To group (ii) may be added the Dorobo, originally a purely hunting people, who speak Nandi and have adopted Nandi age organization. There exist fairly good studies of the age-group systems of all these tribes, except those of the Tatoga group.

The Masai group. To the east of the Kalenjin speakers is a long strip of territory that we may distinguish as belonging to the Masai group. It runs from the southern end of Lake Rudolf due south to central Tanzania. In this group I include, first, the Masai-speaking tribes. Following Jacobs (1965a) these may be divided into two subgroups: the Masai proper (or pastoral Masai), consisting of a number of subtribes, mostly in Tanzania, and the others: the Samburu, in the area south of Lake Rudolf, the Baraguyu, spread thinly among Bantu tribes to the south of the Masai proper, both of whom are pastoral, and the Arusha of Mt. Meru, who are farmers. The age-group systems of these tribes—which have all been well described—are very similar to one another. Second, I include in this group certain non—Masai-speaking peoples who live close to the Masai and are to a greater or lesser degree influenced by them: in the north, near the Samburu, are the Rendille, a pastoral tribe speaking a language close to Somali (Fleming 1964: 60); in the south, two Bantu-speaking agricultural tribes, the Sonjo, a small people who live just east of Lake Natron, and the Chagga of Mt. Kilimanjaro.

The Kikuyu tribes. These constitute one of the largest East African peoples, numbering well over a million, and divided into many groups and subgroups (see further Chapter II, Section 4.4.1). They are Bantu-speaking farmers who live to the south and east of Mt. Kenya. Their age organization, which was of major importance in their society, varied considerably from one area to another. In most parts of the country it has either completely vanished, or else radically changed, since the imposition of British rule at the turn of the century. The loss is great, for many of the Kikuyu tribes shared a system of age organization that is perhaps the most complex on record; and the available accounts of it are decidedly imperfect.

The Nyakyusa. The most idiosyncratic of all systems of age organization on which there is a reasonable amount of information belongs to the Nyakyusa, Bantu-speaking farmers who live at the northern end of Lake Malawi. For the reason mentioned on p. 8, I have not attempted an analysis in this book. There is at present a controversy in progress about the social organization of the Nyakyusa; a recent contribution to it (Wilson 1975) gives all the necessary references to the earlier literature.

I turn now to West Africa. Age-group systems are widespread in this region,[19] and they are often a major feature of social organization; but the ethnographic sources are in general much less satisfactory than for East Africa. Broadly speaking, the systems that have been best described are the simple ones, which are not of great importance in the social structure; the more complicated and important systems—those of the Edo speakers, for instance—remain largely unknown.

The West African tribes mentioned in this book are dispersed over a much larger and more densely populated area than those of East Africa, but they figure less prominently in our text. I shall therefore deal with them here in an even more cursory fashion.

Many of the tribes we shall meet live on the coast or in the forest belt immediately behind it. Beginning in the east, we shall encounter the Douala, a fishing tribe of Cameroun. We then come to several very large peoples—each numbers its members in millions—in southern Nigeria: the Ibibio, the Ibo, the Edo (whose best-known representatives are the peoples of Benin), and the Yoruba, famous above all for their cities. All these peoples are divided into many subgroups. The only ones who will concern us much are the Ibo (Izi, Afikpo, and Asaba subtribes).

We shall also mention three relatively small tribes in this area—each with some tens of thousands of members—who live on the middle and upper reaches of the Cross River: the Yakö, the Mbembe, and the Banyang. These three all have ungraded age-set systems that have been well described, as do also the Tiv, from whom the Yakö and Mbembe are divided mainly by the Ibo.

Moving west again, we come to the Gã, on the coast of Ghana, and then to a cluster of small tribes on and near the shores of Ivory Coast. These are the Lagoon tribes, so called because they live around the lagoons that stretch along the shores to the east and west of Abidjan. We shall mention the Abouré, the Mbato, the Atié, the Ebrié, the Alladian, the Abé, and the Adioukrou. Age-group systems

[19] The index to Aghassian's valuable, though far from exhaustive, bibliography (1971) lists over 60 tribes; and some of these are large peoples among whom a number of different age-group systems exist (or existed).

were an important feature of the social structure of several of these tribes, and the ethnographic literature is relatively extensive. Once again, however, the information on the most interesting systems is unsatisfactory. In particular, there are many contradictions in the sources, in part probably because there were important differences between the age organizations of different villages of even the same tribe.

Directly to the west of the Lagoon tribes, in Ivory Coast and Liberia, are the Kru people. We shall briefly encounter two Kru tribes, the Dida and the Godie. The last coastal tribe to be mentioned lies much further north, at the mouth of the Casamance River, in Senegal; this is the Bainouk, a small people living among the Diola.

I turn now to the West African tribes that lie inland, in the savannah belt to the north of the forests. We have several good studies of age organization from the Kédougou region of south-east Senegal, thanks to the investigations carried out there by the Centre de Recherches Anthropologiques of Paris. Perhaps the most remarkable of these relates to the Bedik, a tribe of some 1500 souls, belonging to the Tenda, a small group of peoples in that area.

We shall also mention the Kédougou Mandinka. The Mandinka are a large and famous tribe, the founders of the great medieval empire of Mali, and their representatives are to be found in a number of West African states.[20] Their age organization evidently varies a good deal from place to place; certainly the other Mandinka we shall mention, those of the Gambia, have a system that is quite different from that of the Kédougou Maninka.

Two tribes related to the Mandinka will also be mentioned, though briefly. One is the Soninké, whose ancestors are believed to have been the main tribe in the first of the medieval West African empires that we know of, Ghana, and who speak a language which is fairly remote from that of the Mandinka. The other is the Bambara tribe, linguistically very close indeed to the Mandinka, but rather different in culture.

To the east of the Bambara, mainly in the state of Upper Volta, lies an unrelated tribe, the Bobo, whose age organization we shall consider in some detail.

---

[20] The distribution and nomenclature of the Mandinka and related tribes is discussed in an admirable paper by Dalby (1971). The volume in which Dalby's paper was published (Hodge 1971) contains several contributions that refer briefly to age organization.

Another large tribe, even more widely dispersed than the Mandinka, are the Fulani, some of whom are pastoralists. A number of
Fulani groups have some type of age organization (Dupire 1970: 450
ff.), but the only ones we shall have occasion to refer to are those in
northern Dahomey and those in the region of Labe, in Guinea, not
far south of Kédougou.

From northern Togo and north-east Ghana we have a number
of useful reports of the age organization of several relatively small
tribes: the Konkomba, the Nawdeba, the Kabré, and the so-called
Somba.

Lastly, there will appear some of the inhabitants of Timbuctoo:
the Bela, a Tuareg speaking group in that city, and the Songhoi who
live there, representatives of an important tribe in the region of the
great bend of the Niger.

Data from South and Central Africa are very little used in this
book. Age-group systems are widespread among the South African
Bantu, but they are much less varied and complex than those found
in the north. They are typically not associated with age-grades but,
rather, with centralized political systems whose rulers use the age-sets
as laborers and warriors. We shall briefly mention the Tswana and the
Ngoni, the latter being a South African people who migrated to
Malawi in the nineteenth century.

In what may loosely be called Central Africa, age-group systems
seem to be uncommon. The only ones we shall come across are those
of the Ila, in Zambia, and the Lele, in Zaire. The Lele system is a
prominent feature of the social organization of the tribe, and is
remarkable in a number of respects.

The existence of age-set systems among the aborigines of Taiwan has not hitherto been noted in the Western literature on the
subject (see, for instance, Gulliver 1968: 159). The total aboriginal
population is about 200,000 (Kokubu and Kaneko 1962), and it
would appear that a majority live in villages which have, or until
recently had, graded age-set systems that were a major feature of
their social structure. Chen (1965) gives a useful survey of the quite
extensive literature, virtually all of it in Chinese or Japanese. Because
I do not know these languages, I was unable to make anything like
proper use of all this material. For what it is worth, my impression is
that for the limited range of questions discussed in this work the
information available in the literature on Taiwan would not have
been of critical importance. As regards many other problems this
might well not be the case, and it is to be hoped that more of these
data will become available in European languages. Since aboriginal

culture is changing rapidly through contact with the Chinese, field-work in Taiwan is undoubtedly the most urgent task facing age-group studies.

It may be that graded age-set systems were at one time common also in Japan. Norbeck (1953) gives a survey of the literature (all of it in Japanese). See also Sofue (1962: 185 f.) and Befu (1968: 312 f.). To judge from the entries in recent issues of the *International Bibliography of Social and Cultural Anthropology*, a good deal has been published on the subject. My ignorance of Japanese has prevented me from making any use of these data, and indeed I cannot be certain that these systems were of the type discussed in the present work.

At least one article has been written on age organization in ancient China (Quistorp 1915), but the data seem too scanty for it to be possible to decide exactly what the nature of the "age-classes" was. On the other hand, imperial China certainly did have age-sets of a type similar to, but much more highly developed than, the groups that are formed in many North American universities and consist of all those who graduated in a given year (Ho 1962: 99).

There are (or were) several Brazilian tribes of the Gê group that possessed graded systems, but the evidence is at present inadequate. The only good description of such a system is in Maybury-Lewis (1967), which deals with the Akwe-Shavante. It is clear also that the Apinayé (Western Timbira) had such a system (Nimuendajú 1939). The Canella (Eastern Timbira) had an age-set system, but it could only be considered graded in the most limited degree (Nimuendajú 1946; cf. Lave 1971: 344). The Sherente may once have had an age-set system, but no longer possessed it when visited by their ethnographers (Nimuendajú 1942; cf. Maybury-Lewis 1971). The Northern Kayapó evidently have only an age-grade system (Banner 1952; Dreyfus 1963; Turner 1971; Dreyfus gives a survey of the material on the age organization of the Gê). Outside the Gê group we also find age-grades without sets among the Karajá (Dietschy 1964). The Tapirapé had age-groups of some kind, but their exact nature remains unclear (see Baldus 1970: 320 ff., which gives references to all the earlier literature and also to some comparative material from the same area).

The evidence relating to North America is examined in Part Two, to which the reader is referred for further information.

Age-set systems almost certainly existed, and were conceivably even widespread, in Central Asia, but the ethnographic record is thin. Far and away the most important source is Snesarev (1963), which, despite its title, concentrates mainly on the Uzbeks of Khorezm. (Snesarev 1967 has a few data in English.) Nevertheless, it includes comparative material from other areas and a good general bibliography. Although Snesarev's article is full and informative on many points, it has almost nothing to say about just those topics that are central to this treatise. It is because of this that I am not certain that the groups he discusses were in fact age-groups in the sense defined below. In Appendix 3, I have translated two passages that make it seem highly probable that this was so. Mirkhasilov (1963) contains a few additional data. I was able to consult most of the works Snesarev lists, but only one of them (Nurdzhanov 1956: 56–68, 61) had anything to add on the subject of age-groups. A more recent book on the Uzbeks contains a chapter by Snesarev (1969: 273 f.) in which he mentions the topic but without adding anything to his earlier work.

In Europe, I have noted age-set systems in Switzerland and some surrounding regions, and in Albania (Appendices 1 and 2). See the notes to Appendix 1 on the possibility of age-sets in antiquity. The data and references in Kramer (1964) relate to associations of young people, and not to age-group systems.

An area that may contain a fair number of age-group systems, but mostly ungraded ones, is New Guinea. From the region of Goodenough Bay there is a useful account in Seligman (1910: 470 ff.), and from the Highlands come data on the Gama (Read 1951, 1952, 1965) and the Fore (Lindenbaum and Glasse 1969). Two other tribes that I know of apparently had some kind of age organization, though the details remain obscure: the Kwoma (Whiting 1941; Kaufmann 1972; the latter gives additional references) and the Iatmül (Bateson 1932: 432–435, 1958: 244 ff.).

Finally, some scattered instances: a well-attested graded system among the Ao Nagas of north-east India (Mills 1926: 177 ff.) and a rather less well-attested graded system on the Indonesian island of Tanimbar. Drabbe (1940: 23 ff.) comments on the original description by van der Kolk (1924) but unfortunately discusses only the age-grades, while ignoring the age-sets that van der Kolk mentions. Pukapuka, in the Cook Islands, had an age-set system which may have been graded (MacGregor 1935; Beaglehole and Beaglehole 1938).

PART ONE

Age-Group Systems

1 A MODEL OF AGE-SET SYSTEMS

1.1 The Model

In general, the concepts sociologists possess for discussing the various kinds of human group—families, states, clans, organizations, and so on—have not been clearly defined. In saying that a sociological concept has not been clearly defined, I mean that there do not exist criteria such that, given the relevant data about something that exists, it is possible in at least the overwhelming majority of cases to decide, without leaving room for dispute, whether or not that thing falls under the concept in question. Attempts have been made to develop criteria of this sort for the notions relating to groups, but none has yet led to generally accepted results. It looks as if a lot more work will be necessary before there is any large number of these well-defined concepts in sociology.[1] Yet for all the difficulties,

[1] See, for instance, Goodenough (1956), which shows how inadequate our criteria are even for classifying something as apparently simple as the pattern of marriage residence in a given society.

attempts to find clear definitions are well worthwhile. If we are to produce interesting theories, then by and large we are going to have to operate with clearly defined notions. Furthermore, the search for clear cross-cultural concepts has a heuristic value: the concepts are likely to be complex, and the step from a complicated concept to a theory is short.

I shall begin by presenting what I hope is a clearly defined cross-cultural concept, using for this purpose what I shall call the age-set model.[2] I shall then say something about the nature of the model and the uses to which it will be put.

I shall say that a collection of groups[3] in a society[4] constitutes an **age-set sequence** when the groups are governed by rules which are such that in that society they generate an unbounded number of groups with the following characteristics:

(i)   There is a total ordering on the groups given by the order in which they begin recruiting.[5] This is the **ordering characteristic**.

(ii) Each group ceases permanently to recruit members before the next one starts (the **no-overlapping characteristic**).

(iii) There are always at least two groups in existence[6] (the **two-group characteristic**).

(iv) No group dissolves[7] before one which began recruiting before it.[8] This is the **dissolution characteristic**.

---

[2] A stimulating article on models is Hagen (1961), reprinted, with minor revisions, in Hagen (1964).

[3] The meaning of this term is discussed in Chapter IV, Section 1.

[4] The notion of a society is left undefined, but the model assumes that it is always possible to identify the set of individuals that constitutes all and only the members of a given society. This is clearly not so, but in relation to this model the matter of identifying the members of a given society does not in practice seem to present significant problems.

[5] In other words, the groups begin recruiting one after another—it never happens that two (or more) groups begin recruiting simultaneously.

[6] Roughly speaking, a group exists if it has members. For a more accurate definition, see Section 1.2.1 of this chapter.

[7] A group is said to **dissolve** if it becomes extinct for some other reason than that all its members have left the society. (For our purposes, we can say that a group becomes extinct when, having once had members, it no longer has any.) In most cases an individual leaves the society by death or by emigration, but it is possible also for a person who is physically present to be deemed no longer a member of the society.

[8] So, given the ordering characteristic, if groups dissolve, then they do so in the order in which they began recruiting.

(v)   There is a certain age[9] (the **enrolment age**) which has the following properties:
1. No individual joins a group before reaching this age: it is the **minimum enrolment age.**
2. Any individual who has not yet joined a group, but who is going to join one, and who has reached this age, joins a group as soon as there is one recruiting members: it is the **basic enrolment age.**

This is the **enrolment characteristic.**[10]

(vi) No individual is at any time a member of more than one group (the **single membership characteristic**).

(vii) A member only leaves a group under one of the following circumstances:
1. When he leaves the society, or
2. When the group is dissolving.

This is the **no-resigning characteristic.**

(viii) A member who has left a group because he has left the society or because the group is dissolving does not again join a group. This is the **no-rejoining characteristic.**

The groups in an age-set sequence will be referred to as age-sets.[11] An **age-set system** consists of all the age-set sequences of the same kind in a given society. Very often there is only one sequence, so that the system and the sequence are identical. (For cases where there is more than one sequence, see Section 6 of this chapter.)

The model is formulated in terms of constraints on rules, and I shall refer to the eight items in it interchangeably as characteristics or as constraints.

[9] Here and elsewhere, an individual's age is simply the length of time that has elapsed since his birth. Some authors refer to this as his "chronological age."

[10] A slightly revised version of this characteristic is presented in Chapter III, Section 1.

[11] A word about the relationship between the notion of an age-set and the notion, used by demographers, of a cohort. Given a set of individuals, a cohort is the subset of those who did something (or to whom something happened) within a given period of time. So, for example, there is the cohort of British women who married in 1969, the cohort of Americans who entered university between 1950 and 1955, and the cohort of those born between 1880 and 1882. This last is an instance of a **birth cohort.** By our definition, all age-sets are cohorts. (Indeed, they are all birth cohorts; but in Chapter III, Section 1, the enrolment characteristic will be revised in such a way that, while they remain cohorts, they are no longer necessarily birth cohorts.) But not all cohorts are age-sets, for an age-set—in contrast to a cohort—is *by definition* an entity created and recognized by the society in which it exists.

We can use this model to define two large classes of age-group systems: on the one hand, those systems that correspond exactly to the model (the age-set systems), and on the other, those systems that meet some, but not all, of the constraints of the model—the deviant (age-group) systems. All age-group systems fall, by definition, into one or other of these two classes.

For a number of reasons, it would be unprofitable to try to determine exactly what proportion of age-group systems is found in each class.[12] My guess is that most attempts at a count would suggest that there are more age-set systems than deviant systems.[13] This is worth bearing in mind, since it is the deviant systems that will figure most prominently in the pages that follow.

The main thesis advanced in this book is that all age-group systems are best understood in terms of their relationship to a structure of the kind defined by the age-set model. I shall discuss all types of deviant system for which I have adequate data, and will try to show that most of them can best be understood as differing from the model as a result of specific forces. My view, in other words, is that a structure of the type defined by the model in some sense also underlies systems which do not possess precisely that structure (see Chapter IV, Section 2). I hope, however, that even readers to whom this idea is unacceptable will find that the model is a useful tool for showing how a large number of systems resemble each other or differ from each other with regard to certain of their basic properties.

[12] The difficulties involved in counts of this type are numerous and familiar. Among the most important in this instance are the following. A conceptual problem arises because the notion of a deviant system (in contrast to the notion of an age-set system) is not clearly defined. Factual problems arise because the ethnographic literature is by no means evenly distributed over the world's age-group systems, and because the deficiencies in the ethnographies are such that, while one can often make a plausible guess, the data necessary to attain certainty in categorization are often lacking. A methodological difficulty is presented by Galton's problem: if we find a number of instances of a particular phenomenon in a single small area, where they are evidently the result of mutual contacts of one kind or another, are they to be ascribed the same numerical weight as an equal number of instances scattered widely over the whole world in such a fashion that independent origins seem indicated? Lastly, my ignorance of the relevant languages would make it impossible for me to deal properly with the age-group systems of Taiwan.

[13] Provided, that is, we accept certain suggestions relating to the model, which are advanced in Chapter III, Sections 1 and 2; and perhaps also counting as age-set systems systems that are deviant only by virtue of secondary rules (see Section 5 of this chapter).

1.2 Implications of the Model

Although there is an indefinite number of possible types of age-set system, all of them will necessarily have certain features in common in addition to those specifically mentioned in the model, these additional features being more or less direct consequences of the ones explicitly mentioned. Some of them are noted in the pages that follow. The reader may find it easiest simply to glance through this section and then refer back to it as the need arises in reading the rest of the book.

1.2.1 Levels

The first feature that must be mentioned amounts to little more than a notational point—though a very important one. It derives from item (i) of the model, the ordering characteristic. If a system has this characteristic, then it will be possible to rank the sets according to when they were inaugurated (i.e., began recruiting). It is often necessary to refer to this order, and in doing so I shall employ the following conventions. The rank of an age-set will be referred to as its level. The set most recently inaugurated will be said to be at the first level, or to have the level number 1; the set inaugurated immediately before will be said to be at the second level, or to have the level number 2; and so on. It will be seen that whenever a new set is inaugurated, the level number of each other set in the system rises by one.

It is often useful to be able to refer to the relative level of sets; so, for instance, I shall use the form $S - 5$ to refer to the fifth set to be inaugurated after some set S, or $S + 1$ to refer to the set inaugurated immediately before set S. As a mnemonic device it may be remembered that a minus sign indicates a junior set, and a plus sign indicates a senior set.[14]

Usually the point in time at which a set is inaugurated is also the point at which one or more individuals join the set. But this is not necessarily the case. I shall take it that an age-set is **inaugurated** (= comes into existence = begins recruiting) at a given point in time if anyone who is qualified to join a set can join that set at that point in time. There are a few cases where there may be a short interval between the inauguration of a set and the enrolment of its first

---

[14] Notation of essentially this type was already used by Lowie (1916: 932).

member (see p. 207). In the nature of things, there is hardly likely to be a long interval, except perhaps in a system on the verge of collapse. Still, strictly speaking some clause should be added to exclude the possibility of sets which no-one ever joins.

The implication of this definition is that an age-set can exist and yet have no members. This may seem odd, but the analysis later in the book should make the idea more acceptable (see Chapter IV, Section 1). The reader may also find it reassuring that in English law there are circumstances under which a corporation is said to exist even though it has no members (Dias 1970b: 315).

1.2.2 Recruitment Period, Duration, and Inauguration Interval

An item of the model that has some significant consequences is the two-group characteristic. Taken in conjunction with some of the other constraints, it entails that the recruitment period[15] of age-sets cannot average out at more than marginally above one-half of their total average duration.[16] It also entails that the duration of a set can be no more than twice the maximum life span of an individual; and that the interval between the inauguration of successive sets (the inauguration interval) cannot be greater than the maximum life span of an individual.

*There are, as we shall see, some real systems where most of the time only two age-groups are in existence. At this point, however, the subject will be discussed in general terms. In demonstrating the propositions that have just been advanced, and also elsewhere in the book where the question arises, I shall assume that an individual is enrolled in his group at a single point in time. This is something of an idealization—in some systems, for instance, the ceremony of enrolment is spread over a number of days—but it will simplify the exposition without leading to any significant inaccuracies.

I shall further assume, in the proofs in this section, that the point in time at which a set is inaugurated is also always the point in

---

[15] The **recruitment period** of an age-set is the period of time between the inauguration of the set and the point in time after which no one else is allowed to join the set. In some systems the rules demand that all members of a set be recruited simultaneously, in which case the recruitment period is just a point in time.

[16] The **duration** of an age-set is the length of time that passes between its inauguration and its extinction.

time at which it enrols its first member. As has been mentioned, this assumption is incorrect, and partly for this reason the recruitment period of a set does not necessarily coincide with the length of time between the enrolment of the first member to join the set and the enrolment of the last member to join the set. On the other hand, even in those rare systems in which it is possible for there to be an interval between inauguration and the enrolment of the first member, that interval is always in practice very short (never, I think, more than a matter of a few months). So I have not felt it necessary in setting out these particular propositions to distinguish between these two points in time.

(i) *The recruitment period of age-sets cannot average out at more than marginally above one-half of their average duration.* Assume that the inauguration interval between set S and set S − 1 is v_S years, and that the interval between S − 1 and S − 2 is v_{S-1} years. Now, for there always to be at least two sets in existence, set S must continue to exist at least until S − 2 is inaugurated.[17] Set S therefore exists a minimum of v_S years (during all of which it may be recruiting) plus v_{S-1} years (during which it must not recruit). Now let us begin by considering the simple cases where the inauguration interval is constant; in such cases $v_S = v_{S-1}$, and a given set S cannot recruit for more than one-half of its duration.

Though there are many systems in which the inauguration interval is constant, there are also many in which it varies somewhat (see Chapter III, Section 3). In these cases it can be said that the mean recruitment period of sets will not be more than marginally above one-half of their mean duration. The margin can be made as small as we please by averaging over a sufficiently long period of time.

Proof. Suppose that age-sets S − 1, S − 2, . . . have recruitment periods $r_1, r_2, \ldots$, and durations $d_1, d_2, \ldots$ respectively.

It was mentioned earlier that in an age-set system set S must continue to exist at least until S − 2 is inaugurated. It follows, then, that

$$r_i + r_{i+1} < d_i \qquad i = 1, 2, \ldots$$

[17] I am assuming that the age-sets become extinct in the order in which they were formed. In practice this presumably is normally, but not invariably, the case. The proposition advanced here could be proved without making this assumption, but the proof would be more difficult to a degree not commensurate with the gain in generality.

Summing for $i = 1, \ldots, n$ (say), and rearranging terms:

$$2(r_1 + \cdots + r_n) < d_1 + \cdots + d_n + (r_1 - r_{n+1})$$

Let M be the maximum life span of an individual. We show below that all $r_i \leqslant M$. Now we have

$$\frac{r_1 + \cdots + r_n}{n} < \frac{1}{2}\frac{d_1 + \cdots + d_n}{n} + \frac{1}{2}\frac{M}{n}$$

By taking n large enough—that is, averaging over a sufficiently long period,—M/n can be made as small as we like. The other two expressions are clearly the averages in which we are interested.

(ii) *The duration of a set can be no more than twice the maximum life span of an individual.* To establish this, it is enough to show that the maximum recruitment period of set S is no more than the maximum individual life span (M).

Suppose otherwise. Then during the recruitment period of S, all sets $S + i$, $i \geqslant 1$, must die out completely, and S is left as the only extant set, violating the two-group constraint.

(iii) *The inauguration interval cannot be greater than the maximum life span of an individual.* The argument is very similar. Suppose the length of the inauguration interval between S and $S - 1$ is v_S, with $v_S > M$. At time M after the inauguration of S, all $S + i$, $i \geqslant 1$, have died out. So between times M and v_S after the inauguration of S, S is the only extant set.

1.2.3   The Age-Range of an Age-Set

This section considers the question of what it is that determines the maximum possible age-range of an age-set. It will simplify our presentation if we introduce some symbols.

v_S is the length of the inauguration interval of some set S, i.e., the length of the interval between the inauguration of S and the inauguration of $S - 1$.

r_S is the length of the recruitment period of some set S.

a_S is the maximum possible age-range of some set S. By this, I mean the maximum difference between the age of the oldest and the age of the youngest member of the set that is permitted by the rules. If the rules have been obeyed, then the *actual* age-range of S will usually be less than a_S.

Now what is it that determines a_S? An examination of Figure 1.1 supplies the answer. In that diagram the line marked t represents

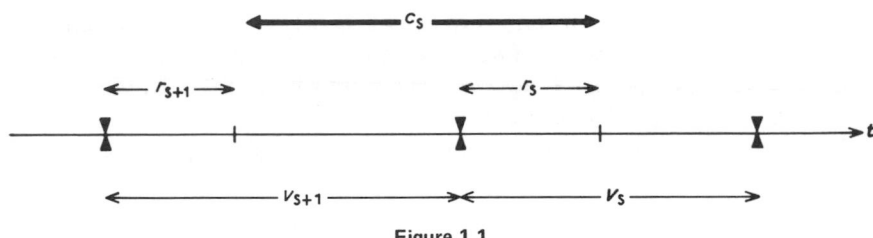

Figure 1.1

time. Three points on the line are marked by solid arrowheads above
and below the line. These are the points at which new age-sets are
inaugurated, the age-sets being, respectively, $S + 1$, S, and $S - 1$.
Below the time line are arrows that indicate the lengths of v_{S+1} and
v_S. Immediately above the time line are two-headed arrows indicating the lengths of r_{S+1} and r_S.

It will be evident from the diagram that the people who join set
S must all have reached the enrolment age between the end of the
recruitment period of $S + 1$ and the end of the recruitment period of
S. I shall refer to this interval as the **cessation interval** of set S. The
length of the cessation interval of set S will be symbolized as c_S.[18]

If anyone who reaches the enrolment age during the cessation
interval of S is allowed to join an age-set, then the maximum possible
age-range of S will be the same as the length of the cessation interval
of S, that is, $a_S = c_S$. This is an important equation, to which we
shall return more than once.

It is not necessarily the case, however, that $a_S = c_S$. It will be
observed that the cessation interval of S can be divided into two
parts: the part that overlaps the recruitment period of S and the part
that does not. By definition, someone may join at the beginning of
the recruitment period and someone may join at its end. We know,
therefore, that the value of a_S cannot be less than the value of r_S. On
the other hand, it would be possible to exclude individuals from the
system on the grounds that they reached the enrolment age during
some, or all, of the period between the end of the recruitment period
of $S + 1$ and the beginning of the recruitment period of S. If they
were excluded for the whole of this period, then the maximum
possible age-range of set S would be the same as the length of its
recruitment period, that is, $a_S = r_S$.

[18] It will be noted that c_S is a length of time—say 5 years. But the period of
which it is a measure has to fall during a particular period of time. If some set $S
+ 1$ ends recruiting in 1950 and set S ends recruiting in 1955, then the cessation
interval of S falls between 1950 and 1955.

In sum, then, for any given set S in an age-set system, the maximum possible value of a_S is c_S, and the minimum possible value of a_S is r_S, that is, $c_S \geqslant a_S \geqslant r_S$. We may say at once, however, that there are no known systems in which the value of a_S is ever less than the value of c_S for any S, so that for all practical purposes the reader need only bear in mind the equation $a_S = c_S$ (for all S).

1.2.4 Age Ordering of Age-Sets

We shall see later (Chapter III, Section 1) that the equation $a_S = c_S$ (for all S), though useful, is not, in fact, an exact representation of the state of affairs that obtains in most age-group systems. But there is a related feature of any system that conforms to the model which is both very important and well-nigh universal among age-group systems. It is that the further back in time a group was inaugurated, the older its members will be, and the more recently a group was inaugurated, the younger its members will be. In other words, the ordering of mean ages is the same as the ordering of levels.

To show roughly how the items in the model give rise to this feature, I shall list the ones in whose absence the remaining constraints would not necessarily lead to an age ordering coinciding with the level ordering.

(i)   If the ordering characteristic were eliminated, several sets could start (and end) recruiting simultaneously and might therefore have the same mean age.

(ii)   If the no-overlapping characteristic were rejected, then we might find the following situation: set S ceases to recruit and set $S-1$ starts recruiting; then set $S-1$ stops recruiting and set S starts again, ending up, perhaps, with a lower mean age than set $S-1$.

(v)   Without the enrolment characteristic, individuals could join at any age, and there might cease to be an exact coincidence between the two orderings that concern us.

(vi)   If we drop the single membership characteristic, then we may find, for instance, that each individual joins all the groups, so that they all have the same mean age.

(viii) Without the no-rejoining constraint a number of old men might join an age-group S during its recruitment period and thus give it a higher average age than group $S+1$ (or even than more senior groups still).

Given the model as it stands, the remaining constraints could be eliminated without any effect on age ordering. However, in Chapter

III, Section 1, a weaker, but more realistic, version of the enrolment characteristic is introduced. There are many systems that conform to the model with the weak enrolment characteristic, but not with the strong one. In such systems there can be some overlap of the age-ranges of successive age-sets (though in practice they always retain distinct mean ages). In a system of this kind, under the following bizarre circumstances, the age ordering might cease to coincide with the level ordering. Imagine sets S and S − 1 have somewhat overlapping age-ranges. All the older members of S die or leave the society, as do all the younger members of S − 1. As a result, the mean age of members of S − 1 is higher than the mean age of members of S.

1.2.5 * Cessation Interval and Inauguration Interval

In this section, I shall consider the relationship between the length of the cessation interval of a set (c_S) and the length of its inauguration interval (v_S).

The first and most important point to note in this context is that over a given period of time the average value of c_S will be the same as the average value of v_S (excluding end effects).

The second point is that the cessation interval of set S can never fall after the inauguration interval of S and can never fall before the inauguration interval of S + 1. In other words, the cessation interval of a given set and its inauguration interval always fall at roughly the same time. Let us see why this is so.

Given a particular inauguration interval, when the cessation interval of some set S falls depends on the values of r_{S+1} and r_S. There are two extreme possibilities, represented on Figures 1.2 and 1.3 respectively. Consider first 1.2. The maximum possible value of r_S in any system is v_S, and Figure 1.2 assumes a system in which $r_S = v_S$ for all S. Under these circumstances, $c_S = v_S$, and the cessation

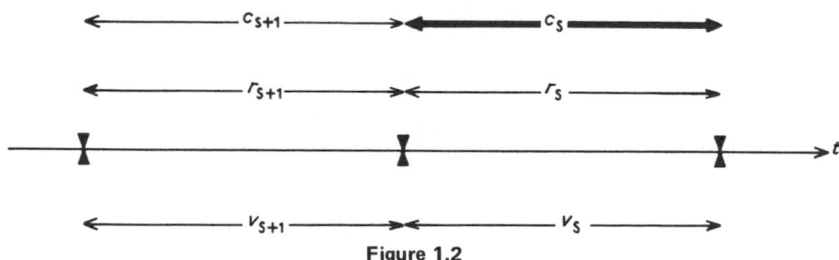

Figure 1.2

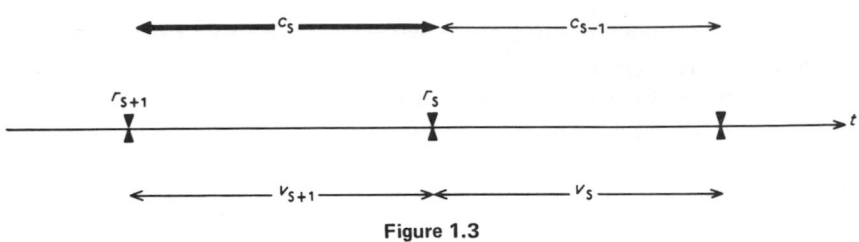

Figure 1.3

interval of S and its inauguration interval fall at the same time (for all S).

Now look at Figure 1.3, which represents a system in which r_S has its minimum value, zero, for all S. For this reason the recruitment period of each set is not represented as having any extension on Figure 1.3; it is simply a point in time. As may be seen, in this case c_S and v_{S+1} have the same value and fall at almost exactly the same time. (Not quite the same time, because though r_S has zero value, it is a point in time that falls within the limits of v_S.)

Between these two extremes lie intermediate cases of the kind represented on Figure 1.1, where r_S is greater than zero but less than v_S (for all S). In the real world there are systems that approximate to both the extremes, and systems of the intermediate kind; none are particularly uncommon.

The third, and last, point to note about the relationship between c_S and v_S concerns their relative values. The maximum possible value of c_S is $v_S + v_{S+1}$ minus the possibly very short length of time during which S + 1 recruits its members (Figure 1.4). The minimum possible value of c_S is the same as the minimum possible length of the period of time during which S recruits its members; see Figure 1.5, where r_S and hence c_S are again simply points in time.

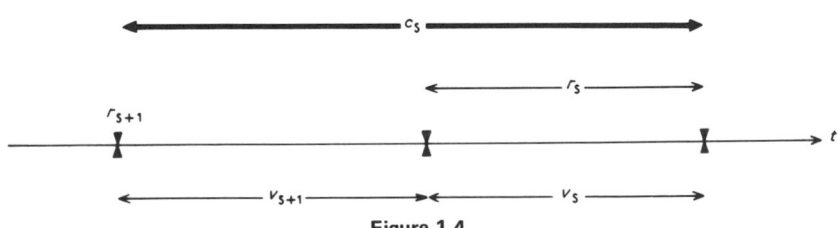

Figure 1.4

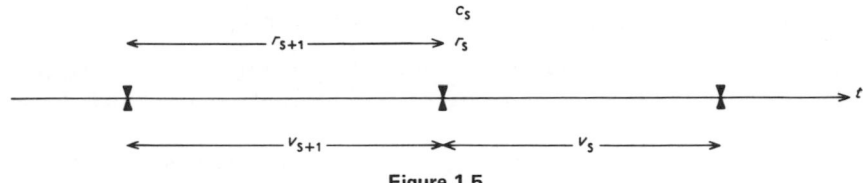

Figure 1.5

1.3 *Using the Model

Why is it that the model assumes just the form it does and no other? This question really has to be broken down into (at least) three others. First, why is it that the model circumscribes just this particular structure of groups, with just these relations between them, and no other? Second, given that it circumscribes just such a structure, why does it do so in terms of constraints on rules, and in no other way? And third, given that the model circumscribes just this structure, and given that it does so in terms of constraints on rules, why is it that the constraints are formulated in just this way and no other?

To a large degree, all these questions are only answered by this book as a whole; the model justifies itself to the extent that, by using it, we gain new understanding of how different kinds of age-group system are related to one another, and how individual ones work. But rather more specific answers can also be given. The first question is dealt with in Chapter IV, Section 2, and the second (implicitly) in Section 1 of the introduction. I shall say something here about the third one.

A number of models can be produced that circumscribe the same structure as ours does, but which use different constraints. For example, the ordering characteristic and the no-overlapping characteristic could be replaced by

(i)*   At any given point in time not more than one group is recruiting members.

(ii)* If a group M is, or has been, recruiting members, and a group N starts recruiting, then
1. N is a group that has not hitherto recruited any members, and
2. M recruits no further members.

Equally, the single membership characteristic and the no-rejoining characteristic could be replaced by (iii)*   No individual joins more than one group.

There are, however, definite reasons for having chosen the present constraints, rather than any of the alternatives of which I was aware.

The purpose of the age-set model is not merely to define a particular structure but also to show its relationship to certain others—the deviant systems—and their relationships to each other. This is why the characteristics are formulated as they are, and in particular why they are all logically independent of each other (except that the ordering characteristic is presupposed by the no-overlapping characteristic). As the model stands, it is possible to say things like "This deviant system differs from an age-set system in that it lacks characteristic A of the model, whereas that one differs in that it lacks characteristic B." But now imagine that we revise characteristics A and B in such a way that, though the structure defined by the model remains unchanged, any system that has characteristic $A*$ (the replacement for A) also, by logical necessity, has characteristic $B*$ (the replacement for B), and vice versa. Both deviant systems would now differ from an age-set system by virtue of lacking both $A*$ and $B*$; the model would not supply concepts for indicating with the same precision as before how they differ from each other, or for characterizing the relationship of each of these systems to the structure defined by the model.

Apart from being largely independent of each other, the characteristics in the model have to be relevant to the deviant systems that actually exist. Items (i) and (ii) are worth distinguishing because there are many systems that lack the no-overlapping characteristic but possess the ordering characteristic. The fact that (ii) is logically dependent on (i), that is, that a system cannot be said to have the no-overlapping characteristic and yet lack the ordering characteristic, does not matter in practice, since few, if any, systems lack the ordering characteristic (cf. Chapter II, Section 4.5.2). In contrast, characteristics (i)* and (ii)* are logically independent of each other, but there is actually little point in distinguishing them, since (as far as I know) all the real systems either possess both these characteristics or neither of them.

Item (iii)* has similar disadvantages. In the real world two distinct phenomena are to be found. Relatively often a system allows a person to leave one age-group and join another; such a system may lack only the no-resigning characteristic. Very occasionally a system allows a person to belong to two groups at once (Section 5.4 of this chapter); in this case it may only be the single membership constraint that is violated. If, however, we introduced (iii)* to replace the single membership characteristic (and the no-rejoining characteristic), then systems of both these kinds would be violating the new constraint. The model would be a less discriminating device for showing the relationship between different sorts of system. Dropping the no-rejoining characteristic would be undesirable for much the same kind of reason.

These examples—which could, of course, be multiplied—should give some idea of the kind of considerations that led to the present formulation of the model. As it stands the model is still very crude. Imagine that we are faced with an age-group system and want to use the model to describe it. It seems that all we can do is to run through the eight constraints and say in each case that the system does or does not meet that constraint. If it meets all the constraints it is an age-set system; if not, a deviant system.

But would this produce an adequate description even of those aspects of a deviant system that are explicitly referred to in the model? To say that a system violates a particular constraint may be to say very little about it. It would not be enough, for instance, simply to say of a system that it lacked the single membership characteristic. We would demand an account of just what groups an individual *is* able to join. As things stand, this account would have to be ad hoc in nature; but ideally we want every ethnographer's description to be couched in terms of a single rigid conceptual scheme.

Similarly, it may not be very informative to say that a system possesses a particular characteristic. Consider the two-group constraint. In describing a particular system we should (if possible) say just how many age-sets are in existence at any point in time, and not be content merely to say that there are two or more. In dealing with this matter we would generally have to take into account not only the rules of the system but also (for instance) the demographic structure of the people among whom the system exists.

It looks as if an improved model would be far more complicated and more flexible, and it also seems that it would not be phrased entirely in terms of constraints on rules.

Let me conclude with a brief conspectus of the main types of deviant system that will appear in this book.

    (i)   There are certain systems—mostly in East Africa—which in one way or another incorporate the father—son relationship into their rules. Mostly they lack the no-overlapping characteristic and the enrolment characteristic. These systems are examined in Sections 2 and 3 of this chapter.

(ii)   There are systems in all parts of the world which differ from the model in rather minor ways, for instance by allowing a few people to change their age-group affiliations. These systems are mostly examined in Sections 4 and 5 of this chapter.

(iii) There are a number of systems which, though conforming in other respects, lack the enrolment characteristic. They are examined in Sections 4 and 5 of Chapter III.

(iv)   There are three rather enigmatic North American Indian systems which are examined in Part Two, Chapters II and III.

The discussion of deviant systems will mostly center round three items in the model: the no-overlapping characteristic, the enrolment characteristic, and the no-resigning characteristic. Instances of systems that lack any of the other characteristics of the model are rare.

2 GENERATION-GROUPS

Among a number of tribes in East Africa there is to be found a form of social organization that I shall refer to as a generation-group system. The groups generated by these systems—known variously as "generations," "generation classes," "generation-sets," and so on— have puzzled scholars for some time. It has not been clear whether generation-groups (g-groups for short) are a form of social organization entirely *sui generis*, whether they are a type of descent or kinship group, or whether they are a type of age-group organization. The prevalent view is perhaps that they represent an intermediate form between age-groups and descent groups. In this section, I shall use the age-set model to show something of how g-group systems work, and in Chapter IV, Section 2, I shall give reasons for looking on them as distorted age-set systems.

2.1 The Jie

Generation-groups have cropped up in the literature on East Africa for well over half a century, but the first extended description

appeared only in 1951, when Peristiany published a long article on
the age organization of the western pastoral Pokot. Because it is a
recent innovation, the g-group system of these people presents some
special problems. Peristiany's description contains valuable information, and, as he himself predicted (1951: 300), subsequent ethnographic work among other tribes of the same region has made
possible a better understanding of his data; but without the comparative material his account remains rather obscure, as may be seen, for
instance, from a summary of it originally published in 1953 (Huntingford 1969: 84 f.).

Two years after the publication of Peristiany's article, there
appeared Gulliver's work on the Jie g-groups. This lucid and comprehensive description provides a good starting point for our discussion,
and I shall begin by recapitulating the relevant data.

The Jie g-groups, in Gulliver's account, are age-groups with very
long inauguration intervals[19] —a matter of 20 or 30 years (Gulliver
1953: 148, 157 f.). As a result, he tells us, most of the time only two
of these groups are in existence, though the number can for short
periods rise to three.[20] This long inauguration interval is related to a
rule which says that if a man joins some group F, then $F - 1$ is the
group that all his sons must join.[21] Group $F - 1$, we are told, will
only start recruiting when all the sons of men in $F + 1$ have joined F

---

[19] Strictly speaking, the term "inauguration interval" has only been defined
for age-sets, not for other kinds of age-groups. A new definition would simply
substitute the term "age-group" for "age-set" in the original one. In what
follows, I shall regularly extend the meaning of previously defined terms in this
way, but without explicitly noting the fact unless there seems some possibility
of misunderstanding.

[20] The rules are such that there should never be less than two: a new group
$S - 2$ must be inaugurated by the surviving members of S. When Gulliver was in
the field, the most junior g-group was Ngimugeto, which for present purposes we
may call $S - 2$. Gulliver states that when it was inaugurated "only one very old
man" survived from g-group S in the whole of Jieland, though according to
another source there was "a handful of survivors" (Lamphear 1976: 40). At any
rate, the Jie system provides a nice limiting case of the two-group characteristic:
if the last member of S were allowed to die before the inauguration of $S - 2$,
then for a time $S - 1$ would be the only group in existence—thus violating the
two-group constraint. Conceivably this may happen in practice (cf. Gulliver
1965: 193 n. 5), but it is against the rules.

[21] We shall encounter many more rules of this sort. In stating them, I shall
use a notation in which F stands for the father's age-group. This makes it
possible to state the rule briefly: in this case, for instance, it is that sons join
$F - 1$.

(Gulliver 1953: 148; 1965: 182). The minimum enrolment age appears to be in the late teens (see further Chapter III, Section 5).

The Jie g-groups have recently been described again in Lamphear's remarkable history of the tribe (1976). In what follows I shall take Gulliver's account as my starting point, but in the course of the discussion will modify it in certain respects in the light of the new facts supplied by Lamphear.

The easiest way to analyze this sort of system is to view it in relation to an extended version of the age-set model. Let us add to that model two further constraints, which between them cover the rule that Gulliver ascribes to the Jie system: that sons join $F - 1$.

(i) Every son of a member of a group himself joins a group, if (but not only if) he survives to the maximum life span. This is the **no-shrinking characteristic**.

(ii) A man who joins a group, and whose father joined a group, joins the first group to begin recruiting after the one that his father joined (the **generation-linking characteristic**).

An age-set system that also meets these additional constraints will be referred to as a **generation-set system,** and we can call this augmented age-set model the **generation-set model.** The type of age-set generated by a generation-set system will be called a **generation-set**.

The g-set model will be useful in a number of ways, but it is most unlikely that any g-set systems have ever existed in the real world. We therefore need an additional term that will cover the systems that do exist. I shall call them **generation-group systems,** and I shall take this term to include both g-set systems and systems more or less like g-set systems.[22]

Now according to Gulliver's account, the Jie g-groups differ from generation-sets only in one respect: the Jie system lacks the enrolment characteristic. A man can only be enrolled in his g-group after it has been inaugurated, even if that is long after he has passed the minimum enrolment age. "Thus, the older sons of older men of a generation have to wait until they are forty or more years of age, and in exceptional cases they may be old men [Gulliver 1953: 148]." Gulliver does not explicitly state that any man who survives to the maximum life span will join a group, but this seems to be implied by

[22] The notion of a **g-group** stands in the same relation to the notion of a g-set as the notion of an age-group does to the notion of an age-set. A g-set is a particular type of age-set, and g-sets, age-sets, and g-groups are all particular types of age-group.

the sentence just quoted. So it appears that he viewed the system as possessing the no-shrinking characteristic, or, at the very least, as coming extremely close to possessing it.

It is important to understand the workings of the kind of system the g-set model defines. For this reason, rather than examine merely the implications of the system that Gulliver ascribes to the Jie, I shall examine the implications of any system that conforms to the g-set model, while at the same time indicating the relevance of these implications to Gulliver's data. Because the system Gulliver describes is so close to the g-set model, there is no difficulty in carrying out this double undertaking.

In order to test the implications of the g-set model in a simple way, we need to make some assumptions about the demographic structure of the population in which the system operates.[23] Take it that each man has three sons: one when he is 20, one when he is 30, and one when he is 40. In Figure 1.6 I have represented some of the descendants of one man. The numbers on the extreme left and right of the diagram stand for years. The position of each man (triangle) on the diagram indicates when he was born; the number beside each man is his generation, counting that of the founding father as zero. [24] The line of men on the left of the diagram are the eldest sons of eldest sons: the interval between generations is only 20 years. The line of men in the middle are the middle sons of middle sons, with a 30-year generation gap. The men in the right-hand column are the youngest sons of youngest sons, with a 40-year generation gap. In this form, naturally, the lines of descent are quite unrealistic. But

[23] We do not have the relevant demographic information for the Jie, so we are in any case debarred from using authentic data. But even if we were not, simplified assumptions would be preferable for purposes of exposition. At the end of the section I consider such demographic data on the Jie as we do have in relation to the assumptions made here.

[24] I am using the term "generation" in a sense that is familiar, but that is also different from the sense in which sociologists (and demographers) normally use it. The term usually means a cohort, particularly a birth cohort (see, for instance, Carlsson and Karlsson 1970), though other definitions have been proposed (e.g., Buchhofer, Friedrichs, and Lüdtke 1970: 308; this article, together with Spitzer 1973, gives all the necessary references to the literature on generations). In this book a generation is the set of individuals who are the offspring of a given birth cohort, or the set of individuals who are the offspring of the offspring of a given birth cohort, and so on. This distinction between the two main senses of the word "generation" has of course been made before, e.g., by Needham (1966:4), who uses the term "genealogical level" for what I call a "generation."

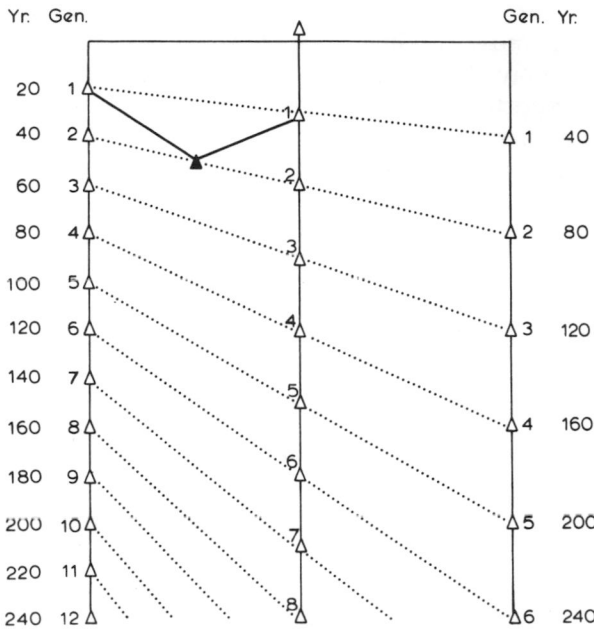

Figure 1.6

they have a purpose: the two extreme ones, the left- and right-hand lines, indicate roughly what the age-range of each generation would be in a large population with the demographic structure that has just been specified. Consider the third generation (i.e., the generation labeled 3). From the left-hand column we see that its oldest representative was born in the year 60; and from the right-hand column we see that its youngest representative was born in the year 120. We can draw a straight line between the oldest and the youngest representative and say that all other men in this generation would (by the conventions of our diagram) be born at some point on that line. To illustrate this, two sons of members of the first generation have been drawn in (they occupy the same space on the diagram): the second son of the oldest member of the first generation and the first son of the middle member of the first generation.

In a diagram of this kind—there will be several more like it—the lines representing generations are necessarily always straight, but it is possible for them to cross, as will appear from the following considerations. Given two adjacent generations, the older n, the younger $n + 1$, it must always be the case that the oldest member of generation n was born before the oldest member of generation $n + 1$. This means that on the left-hand side of this kind of diagram the point at which line n begins will always be higher than the point at which line $n + 1$ begins. On the other hand, the youngest member of generation n may be born after the youngest member of generation $n + 1$. (For that matter, he could even be born later than the youngest member of some more junior generation.) In principle, then, the point at which line n ends on the right-hand side of the diagram may be lower than the point at which line $n + 1$ ends, so that the two lines cross. This does not, however, occur in any of the diagrams in this book.

Now, what will happen if we attempt to introduce a g-set system among the population of Figure 1.6? There are three main possibilities, depending on the length of the inauguration intervals. (I shall ignore the highly unrealistic cases where the intervals are very short or very long.) In each instance the first group will be assumed to begin recruiting in the year 0, which is also the year in which the founding father is born. For the sake of simplicity I shall assume that the enrolment age is 0, though it would make no real difference to assume some other enrolment age (unless it were excessively high). The founding father therefore joins the first group at birth.

First, there is the case of a fairly short interval—to make things easy, say 20 years. Clearly this interval will fit very well for the people in the left-hand line of Figure 1.6, that is to say, for people who are the oldest representatives of their generation. Each of them joins his proper group as soon as it is inaugurated. But consider the youngest members of each generation, represented schematically by the right-hand column. The individual in the first generation must join $F - 1$ (the founding father's group being F). Let us assume he succeeds in this: $F - 1$ continues to recruit throughout its inauguration interval, he is born early in the year 40, and group $F - 2$ is not inaugurated until later that year. So far the system conforms to all the constraints of the g-set model. But what about $F - 2$? According to the rules, the youngest member of the second generation, born in the year 80, is supposed to join it. This means that some constraint of the system is going to be violated. There are a number of possibilities, several of which we shall encounter later in this work. For the moment I shall only consider one: the no-overlapping characteristic. I choose this because it is a characteristic lacking in almost all g-group and Gada systems, and because Lamphear (1976: 45), in contrast to Gulliver, states that it is also lacking in the Jie system.[25]

We take it, then, that **overlapping** is to be permitted. If $F - 2$ is to take in all the members of the second generation—as it must according to the remaining constraints—then it will have to continue recruiting members for 40 years, from the year 40 to the year 80. As a result, it will overlap with $F - 3$, which is inaugurated in 60. The case of $F - 3$ is still more extreme: it continues to recruit for 60 years, and overlaps with $F - 4$ and $F - 5$.

The demographic process that in this instance has led to overlapping will be referred to as **underaging**. Roughly speaking, we say that a system suffers from underaging when individuals who are supposed to join a given g-group (or similar entity) are reaching the minimum enrolment age at a point in time when some more junior group has already been inaugurated.[26] The main points to remember about underaging are that it affects the younger members of each generation, and that it often manifests itself by producing more and more overlapping.

Let us imagine that the people in our society are distressed by the effects of underaging, and try to eliminate them by doubling the inauguration interval. This gives us our second case—the fairly long interval. An interval of 40 years will suit the right-hand descent line (the younger representatives of each generation) very well. But as time goes by the left-hand line will find it increasingly unsatisfactory. Once again, some constraint of the g-set model is going to be violated. Among the various possibilities, I choose the one which accords best with what both Gulliver and Lamphear say about the Jie: I take it that the enrolment characteristic is abandoned. Let us follow, then, what happens to the people in the left-hand line. $F - 1$ is inaugurated in the year 40, so the representative of the first generation will be able to join it at the age of 20 (already 20 years above the minimum enrolment age); but the representative of the second generation will be 40 before he can join $F - 2$, and it is clear

_____

[25] The only characteristic whose absence can be inferred with certainty from Gulliver's account—the enrolment characteristic—is irrelevant in this context: to violate this constraint would not help solve the problem of enrolling all the members of the second generation in $F - 2$.

[26] It would be easy enough to define the term "underaging" rather more sharply than has been done here, but I think that in the present state of our knowledge this would only lead to an increase in the number of technical terms, without any corresponding increase in understanding.

that by the time F − 5 is inaugurated (in the year 200) the oldest members of each generation will have died before their group begins recruiting.

We call this process—one that affects the older members of each generation—**overaging**. Roughly speaking, a system suffers from over-aging when individuals who are supposed to join a given g-group (or similar entity) are reaching the minimum enrolment age at a point in time when (*a*) the given group has not yet started recruiting, and (*b*) some other group is recruiting, or will be before the given group starts doing so.

In this example, overaging led to two deviations from the g-set model. First, the system ceased to possess a basic enrolment age. A system that deviates from the model in this respect will be said to be characterized by **waiting**. Both Gulliver and Lamphear report waiting among the Jie. Second, the system lost the no-shrinking charac-teristic. Gulliver perhaps implies that the Jie system does not suffer from shrinking (p. 44), but Lamphear says that some men die of old age before their group is inaugurated (1976: 35 f.).

The third case is a compromise between the other two—a moderate inauguration interval, in this instance, let us say, 30 years. Here, in the course of time, the system suffers both evils. The oldest members of each generation will be unable to join their proper group because they will have died by the time it starts recruiting; and, if the youngest members are to join, then the recruitment period of suc-cessive groups will have to grow longer and longer and the degree of overlapping more and more pronounced.[27]

Such are the short-term implications of the system. Now con-sider the long-term ones, represented in Figure 1.7. The conventions of this diagram are essentially the same as for Figure 1.6, the main difference being that individual men are not marked. We shall now make rather different demographic assumptions. As in Figure 1.6, we shall assume that the left-hand side of the diagram represents a line of fathers and sons separated by only 20 years, and that the right-hand side represents a line separated by 40 years. But we shall ignore for the moment the distribution of individuals along the line that represents the age-range of each generation. We shall also, for the sake of exposition, make a wholly implausible assumption: that

[27]The first (and almost the only) writer to perceive the problems of over- and underaging with some clarity was A.E. Jensen (see especially 1936: 319). He does not, however, appear to have realized that the two problems are not mutually exclusive.

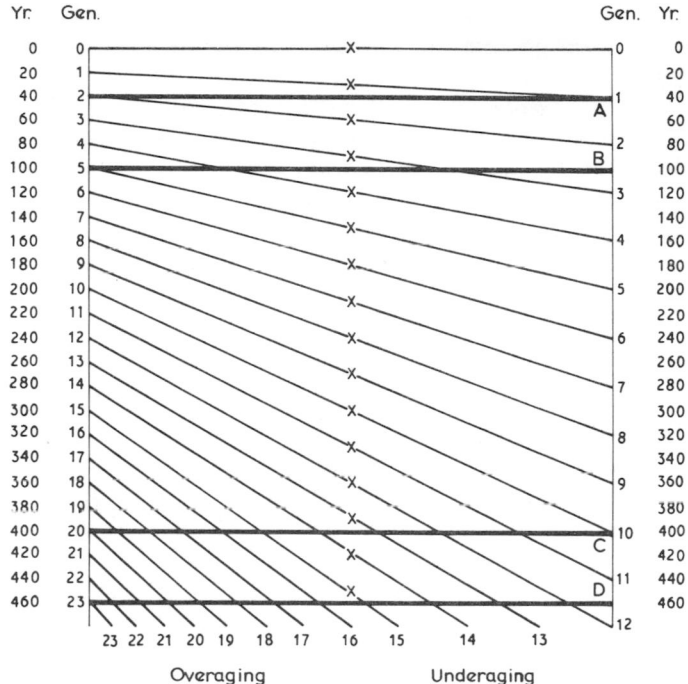

Figure 1.7

everyone lives to the age of 60. This means, for example, that in the year 100 the living men will be all the men born between the years 40 and 100. In terms of the diagram, these are the men whose birth is marked on the section lying between line A and line B.

As far as the g-group system is concerned, let us assume that it violates just those constraints that have been mentioned: that is, it deals with underaging by permitting overlapping, and it deals with overaging by permitting waiting and shrinking. We assume further that the minimum enrolment age is 0 and that the inauguration interval is 30 years. The crosses down the center of Figure 1.7 mark the points at which new g-groups are inaugurated. Each cross is placed on the line which represents the generation which must join that particular g-group. Those members of the generation to the left of the cross have a problem of overaging; those members to the right have a problem of underaging.

Consider first the situation in the year 100. Things are very much as Gulliver represents them as being among the Jie. There are two g-groups with living representatives, $F - 2$, which was inaugurated in the year 60, and $F - 3$, which was inaugurated in the year 90. The more junior of these, $F - 3$, is still recruiting new members; but the more senior one, $F - 2$, has ceased to recruit, since the youngest member of the second generation was born, and enrolled in his group, in the year 80. In addition, there is a certain number of men who have not yet joined an age-group: they are the members of the fourth generation, who will eventually be enrolled in $F - 4$.

Now look at the situation in the year 460. The living men at that time are those whose births are indicated on the diagram between lines C and D. A number of changes have occurred. First, instead of two g-groups being in existence, there are now five. The most senior of them is $F - 11$, and the most junior is $F - 15$, which started to recruit members in the year 450.

Second, there is a considerable amount of overlapping (there was none in the year 100). $F - 11$ has ceased to recruit, but $F - 12$, $F - 13$, $F - 14$, and $F - 15$ are all recruiting simultaneously.

Third, the proportion of those who do not belong to any g-group has greatly increased: none of the representatives of generations 16 to 22 belong to groups.

Let us see what would happen if the inauguration interval were not 30 years. Consider first the short interval, 20 years. In effect we are moving the lines of crosses over to the extreme left of Figure 1.7. In the year 460 the last group to have been inaugurated is $F - 22$ (we assume that we are observing early in the year, and that $F - 23$ is only inaugurated late in the year). Everybody belongs to a g-group, 12 g-groups are in existence, and 11 of them are still recruiting.

Now consider the long interval, 40 years. Here the line of crosses is moved to the extreme right of the diagram. The last group to have been inaugurated is $F - 11$, which recruited all its members in the year 440. At that time one other group, $F - 10$, was still in existence, but it had ceased to recruit, so there was no overlapping. At the moment $F - 11$ is the only existing group, and it will remain so until the year 480. The system therefore lacks the two-group characteristic. Hardly anybody belongs to a group, and hardly anybody is ever going to.

In our discussion so far we have said nothing about an extremely important feature of the situation: the distribution of individuals along each generation line. In considering this question we are fortunately able to draw on the work of the demographers. Although only one or two of them have considered the problem of generations, some interesting results have been achieved. The fundamental paper

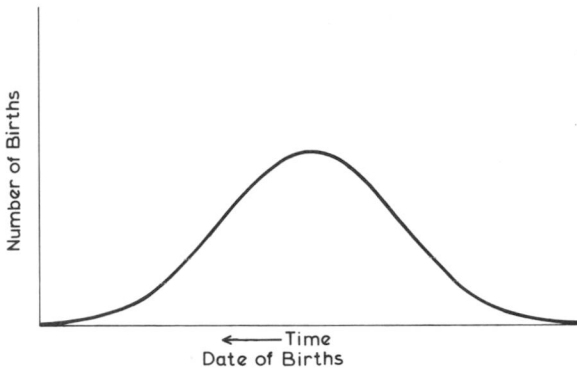

Figure 1.8

on the subject is by A. J. Lotka (1928); his findings are also set out in Lotka (1939) and, in a nonmathematical form, in Lotka (1929). More recently the topic has been taken up again by Keyfitz (1968: 117 ff.). In what follows, I shall summarize those findings that are relevant to the present discussion.[28]

Lotka's main achievement was to show that, even if the distribution of births along the generation line of the first generation differs quite considerably from a normal distribution, later generations will approximate more and more closely to a normal distribution. Figure 1.8 shows a distribution of births, assumed to be all of members of the same generation, similar to a normal distribution.

Figure 1.8 shows the situation in the year in which the last member of the generation was born. If we look at the situation somewhat earlier—say at a point were most, but not all, of them have been born—we can produce something like Figure 1.9. Our main concern, however, is not with the number of members of a given generation who have been born at any given point in time but, rather, with the number of those who are still alive. In general terms, we can say that the curve giving the age distribution of the surviving members of a given generation at a given point in time will resemble in shape the curve of dates of birth. More specifically, imagine that

[28] None of the demographers who have written about generations appear to have been aware of the relevance of their work to age-group studies. Equally, none of the anthropologists who have written about g-groups (and similar systems) have used the relevant demographic literature. The demographers, however, have not made any mistakes that can be ascribed to their ignorance of the anthropological literature.

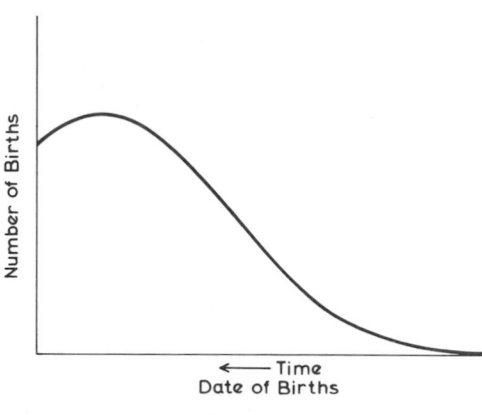

Figure 1.9

the former curve (the survivors curve) is superimposed on the latter cruve (the births curve). The survivors curve will be wholly within the birth curve and will follow a similar contour, subject to being continuously more depressed in the direction corresponding to increasing age. (That direction is the right in our diagrams.)

Now from what was said earlier, we know that the number of generations with living representatives is continually increasing. What happens if we place on a single graph all the generations that have living representatives at a given point in time? The result may be seen on Figure 1.10. In contrast to its predecessors, this particular diagram is not merely an arbitrary construction. It is based on a report by Keyfitz of a "projection of 1000 girl children under five years of age by United States 1964 female fertility and mortality rates, showing distribution by age and generation after 50, 100, and 250 years [1968: 122 f.]." I have represented the situation after 250 years. Nine generations (generations 5 to 13) have living representatives. There is a lot of overlap in the age-ranges of these generations, but each has nevertheless a distinct mean age; so, if there were g-groups, then the higher the level number of the g-group, the higher would be the mean age of its members (see Table 1.1). On the other hand, as the number of living generations increases, so also will the overlap of ages increase and the differences between the mean ages decrease.

The data on Figure 1.10 can also be represented as on Figure 1.11. Figure 1.10 shows the age distribution of each generation; we can see, for instance, roughly how many members of generation 8 are

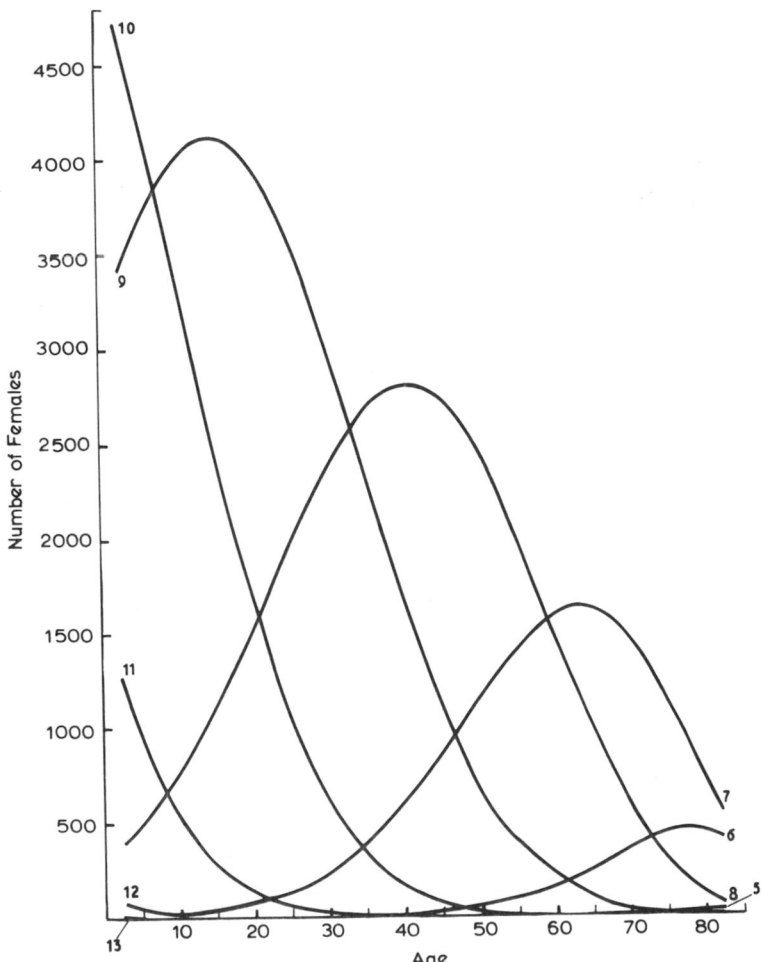

Figure 1.10 [Based on data from Nathan Keyfitz, *Introduction to the Mathematics of Population*, 1968, pp. 122f., Addison-Wesley, Reading, Massachusetts.]

30 years old. What Figure 1.11 shows is the total number of females aged 30 and the contribution that each generation makes to that total. (Generations 5 and 13 are omitted from Figure 1.11 because their contributions to the total population are so small.)

There is one last question we must touch on briefly before we leave this topic, and that is the rate at which the number of generations with living representatives increases. In broad terms,

TABLE 1.1

Generation number	Percentage of total population	Mean age
5	0.046	78.0
6	2.287	71.5
7	13.187	60.2
8	27.759	39.4
9	34.564	21.6
10	18.880	12.0
11	3.140	7.5
12	0.136	5.2
13	0.001	2.5

NOTE: Figures calculated from those given by Nathan Keyfitz, *Introduction to the Mathematics of Population*, 1968, p. 123, Addison-Wesley, Reading, Massachusetts.

Lotka's finding is that "although a considerable number of generations may be existing together, only a few of these are actually represented in considerable proportions; the remainder contribute but little to the total [Lotka 1929: 314]." This can be illustrated from Table 1.1 and from Figure 1.12. Although there are nine living generations, well over 90% of the population are concentrated into only four of those generations.

As already mentioned, we do not have all the demographic information necessary in order to form a clear idea of the generational processes among the Jie (though I imagine that one could combine what we do know about the Jie with data on more or less similar peoples, and produce a hypothetical projection). But there is reason to believe that the rate of **generational spread** (to adapt Lotka's phrase) among the Jie may be considerable. Few Jie men, it is true, marry before the age of 30 (cf. Lamphear 1976: 33); on the other hand, most men who survive past the age of 45 acquire in their later years one or more wives in addition to their first one; and these new wives are young and fertile.[29] This already suggests that the

[29] Gulliver gives extensive numerical data on Jie polygyny (1966: 242). From his figures it can be calculated that about 39% of married men are polygynists (a measure of the incidence of polygyny), and that the average number of wives per polygynist is 2.75 (a measure of the intensity of polygyny). (Gulliver's statistics are based on the assumption that no man marries below the age of 30. As he points out, this is not absolutely correct. The figure for incidence is therefore a little higher than it should be; the intensity figure would be affected only marginally, if at all.) If the studies drawn on by Dorjahn (1959)

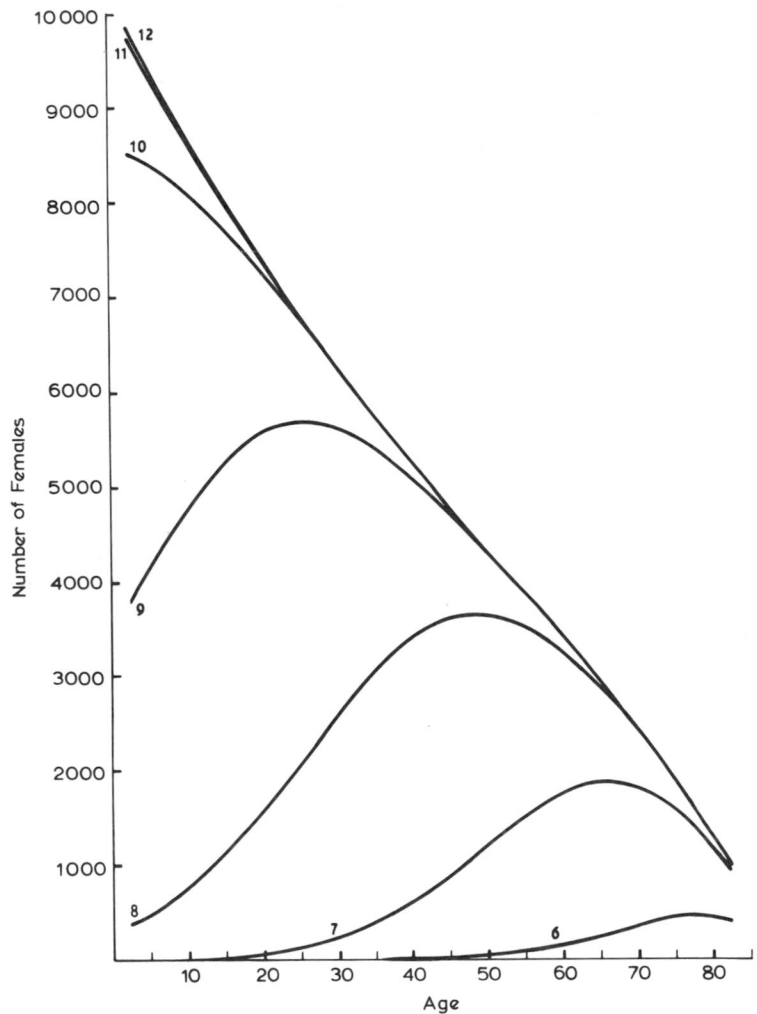

Figure 1.11 [Based on data from Nathan Keyfitz, *Introduction to the Mathematics of Population*, 1968, pp. 122f., Addison-Wesley, Reading, Massachusetts.]

are representative, these figures—especially the intensity figure—are a little above the average for sub-Saharan Africa. It is now generally agreed that polygyny on this sort of scale is usually made possible by a marked disparity between the average age at first marriage of men and women, and there can be little doubt that this is the explanation that applies in the Jie case. We are therefore justified in assuming that the women whom the older men marry are young and fertile, though as far as I know Gulliver nowhere indicates the age at which Jie women usually marry. Gulliver's figures show that the men between 30 and 45 have an average of 1.1 wives, while those over 45 have an average of 2.3 wives.

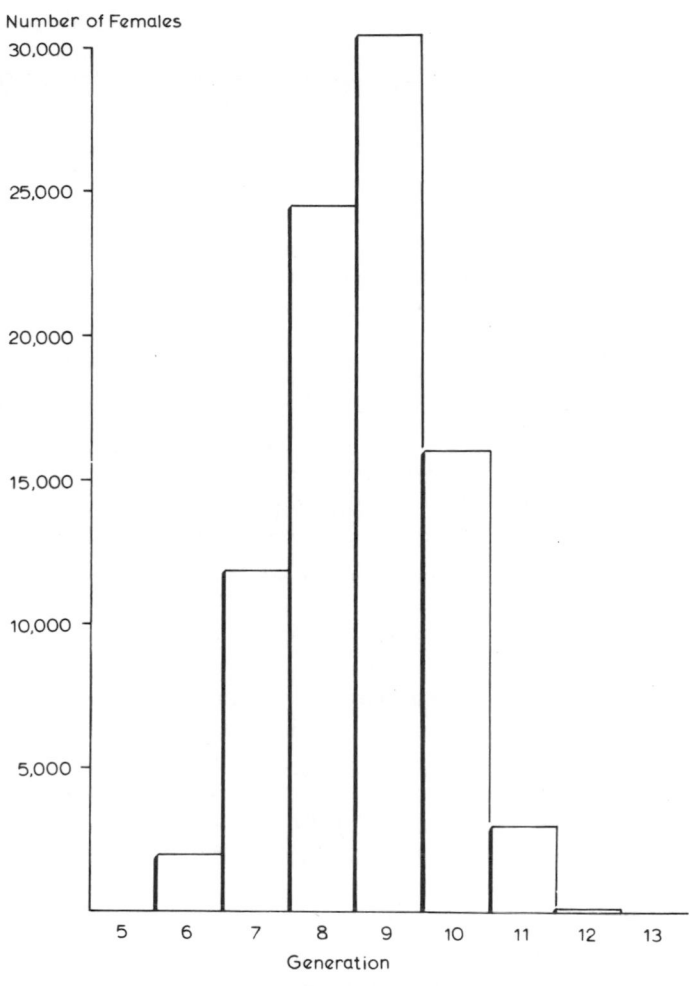

Figure 1.12

period of male fertility may be quite long for quite a high proportion of the male population who survive to produce children.

But it is not merely old men who beget sons among the Jie; even dead men do. Here, as among other peoples of the region, when a man dies his widow becomes a member of the household of some close relative of his and is for most practical purposes treated as if she were a wife of that relative. Her children, however, not only those she has already born, but also any she may bear thereafter, are counted as the offspring of her late husband (Gulliver and Gulliver 1953: 43). In particular, the generation-group affiliation of any boy born to a widow is determined by the g-group affiliation of her deceased husband (the pater), and not by the g-group affiliation of the child's biological father (the genitor) (P. H. Gulliver and J. Lamphear, personal communications). Obviously, this rule, taken in conjunction with the practice of old men marrying young women, must result in the process of generational spread taking place at rather a fast rate.[30]

Lamphear is clearly right in saying that the system is characterized by overlapping and shrinking, and Gulliver (personal communication) accepts that his own account should be modified. Yet even if we make the necessary modifications, the description of the Jie g-groups that results has some puzzling features.

We have just given reasons for believing that generational spread must occur at a fairly fast rate among the Jie; and yet the data supplied by both Gulliver and Lamphear suggest that the process has not really had much effect on the g-group system. Consider first overlapping, a symptom of underaging. According to Lamphear (1976: 45), it only occurs to the extent that a g-group S may continue recruiting members for a number of years after the inauguration of $S - 1$. His account makes it clear that by the time that $S - 2$ is inaugurated, S will have ceased to recruit members. Gulliver was in the field at a time when, in all probability, about 30 years had passed since the last g-group was inaugurated; and it was to be about 12 years before the next one was inaugurated (Gulliver 1966: v; Lamphear 1976: 46–48, *contra* Gulliver 1953: 148; Lamphear 1976: 37). At that time "there was *definitely* no overlapping going on [Lamphear, personal communication]." Gulliver, of course, agrees.

Now consider the symptoms of overaging. Gulliver and Lamphear agree in describing waiting as a prominent feature of the system. But, as we know, waiting alone is not an indication of extensive overaging. It is only Lamphear who says that the system suffers from shrinking, and from both Gulliver and Lamphear it can be inferred that the number of men who reach the maximum life span before their g-group is inaugurated must be small.

It looks, then, as though generational spread is affecting the g-group system much less than one might expect.[31] A possible

[30] I am indebted to Paul Spencer for drawing my attention to the significance of rules of the kind mentioned in this paragraph.

[31] Cf. also Lamphear (1972: 289 n. 1), where he remarks that "in the great majority of cases . . . there is a close correspondence between biological and sociological age," the latter being determined by the g-group system.

explanation would be that the Jie only introduced their g-group system fairly recently; but Lamphear's findings exclude this. He supplies excellent evidence to show that the g-group that was inaugurated in 1963 was at least the seventh one (which by his reckoning means that the first he could trace with assurance was inaugurated in the early eighteenth century). In the course of so many generations, the symptoms of over- and underaging would surely have become more marked than they actually are, unless there were factors at work other than those we have so far taken into consideration.

Unfortunately, these other factors cannot be identified with any assurance. At a later stage (Chapter III, Section 5), I shall offer a guess as to what they may be, but for the moment I want to consider another question: how did Gulliver, and even, as I have just suggested, Lamphear, come to misrepresent the system?

The clearest mistake in these two accounts is Gulliver's statement that there is no overlapping in the Jie system. This mistake did not arise because of some misunderstanding on Gulliver's part but because his informants misled him.[32] But why? Was it just that they were giving him rough-and-ready "rules of thumb" about the institution (cf. Goodenough 1951: 9)? Or was it rather that they presented to him an elaborate, but false, model of how the institution operated,[33] a model based on how they think it ought to work, rather than on how it actually does work?

[32] In a personal communication (1975) Gulliver writes "I did question further [about overlapping] and was then given the folk model which, as you say and as I discovered myself afterwards (but too late to requestion the Jie), is a 'false' one. They did, that is, explicitly deny that two generations could be undergoing initiation at the same time." Even before Gulliver wrote this to me I had assumed that his error was not the product of a mere misunderstanding (Stewart 1972: 56 f.). Such a thing seemed unlikely given the high quality of Gulliver's work in general, the favorable circumstances of his stay among the Jie (Gulliver 1966: 12 f.), and the special interest that both he and the Jie take in age organization. (Lamphear says of the Jie elders that "most seemed to enjoy discussing the generation-sets more than any other subject [1976: 44].")

[33] I am following the usual practice of using the term "model" to refer to a native representation of a system as well as to one created by a sociologist. Examples abound of highly developed native models that nevertheless differ from reality, and they are found as often in our own society as anywhere. It will be observed that I distinguish between the actual rules of a system, the native representation of the system, and the way the system really works on the ground. These three things can be related to each other in various ways. The distinction between them is commonplace and far from sophisticated; but it seems quite useful for present purposes.

Almost all the evidence supports the latter explanation. Gulliver writes that the Jie "produced various supernatural dangers that would occur if this [i.e., overlapping] were to happen: failure of the rains (the great danger for any transgression), illness of the participants, failure to receive the true spiritual force that initiation gives to the initiate, etc. [personal communication, 1975]." Lamphear's data also support this explanation.[34] He makes it evident that, although the Jie do allow overlapping in their system, they are by no means happy about it. During the period immediately before the inauguration of a new g-group (let us call it $S - 1$), an attempt is made to enroll in S the largest possible number of sons of members of $S + 1$; in order to do this "younger and younger boys, well below the 'proper age', [are] initiated [Lamphear 1976: 38]." Equally, when, after the inauguration of $S - 1$, group S is still recruiting, "an effort is usually made to initiate even very young boys of the 'fathers' generation [i.e., prospective members of S] so that initiations into that generation-set can be brought to as rapid an end as possible [Lamphear 1976: 45]." There can be no doubt, then, that the Jie do not like overlapping and that they try to reduce it to a minimum. When it is not actually taking place, they tend to deny that it ever occurs.

What is the Jie attitude to waiting and shrinking? They could scarcely deny that waiting occurs, but almost certainly they would *like* their system to have the enrolment characteristic, or something very similar. This is indicated, for instance, by the fact that there is a " 'proper age of initiation' " (i.e., enrolment) somewhere in the late teens or early twenties (Lamphear 1976: 38; see further, Chapter III, Section 5). *A fortiori*, the Jie can hardly be happy about shrinking, though whether they tend to deny that it occurs is a question the sources do not answer.

In sum, then, there is reason to believe (*a*) that the Jie would like to have a g-set system or something scarcely distinguishable from a g-set system, (*b*) that in describing their system they tend to represent it as being more like a g-set system than it really is, and (*c*) that their system is actually less like a g-set system than even Lamphear's account suggests.

---

[34] I should emphasize, however, that Lamphear himself (in a personal communication) says that he considers this explanation totally out of character for the Jie. Gulliver, of course, disagrees.

2.2 The Karimojong

The years following the publication of Gulliver's work on the Jie saw two other important studies of g-group systems: Lambert's book on the Kikuyu (1956) and Ruel's article on the Kuria (1962). But neither of these cast much light on the problems that Gulliver's description had raised. In 1965 the Italian missionary Felice Farina published a book on the Karimojong; though not entirely oblivious to the problem of generational spread, he nevertheless represents the tribe as having, in effect, a g-set system (1965: 127 ff.). It was only in 1966, with the appearance of Dyson-Hudson's ethnography of this people, that it at last became possible to form a coherent picture of the aspects of a g-group system that interest us here.[35] Dyson-Hudson was especially fortunate in that he was actually in the field at the time when a new g-group was inaugurated.

It seems that the Karimojong, like the Jie, represent their age organization as a g-set system, or something very similar,[36] that is, as containing rules that, in the long run, are not mutually compatible.[37] In the case of the Karimojong, however, we can determine with some assurance just how the real system differs from a g-set system.

The Karimojong system is such that, at any point in time, there are two g-groups in active existence. We may call them the Senior Group and the Junior Group. Each is governed by a particular set of rules, and the Senior Group perform certain tasks that are important to the whole society. When the members of the Senior Group are no longer capable of carrying out these tasks (because of old age and death) a ceremony is held, which Dyson-Hudson calls the Succession Ceremony. Its effects are as follows.

(i) The members of the group which before the Succession Ceremony was the Senior Group (call it S + 1) now retire (and are soon all dead).

(ii) The group which before the Succession Ceremony was the Junior Group (S) is the Senior Group after the ceremony.

[35] Other sources on the Karimojong, including Clark (1950) and Maconi (1973), contain no information that bears directly on the questions considered here.

[36] Dyson-Hudson (1966: 156, 163, 195, 200, and especially 204).

[37] Unless, that is, one introduces certain additional rules of a kind to be described later in this chapter.

(iii)   A new Junior Group (S − 1) is inaugurated and begins recruiting.

Group S was able to recruit members throughout its period as Junior Group. It continues to do so after the Succession Ceremony until all members of S + 1 are dead.[38] The minimum enrolment age appears to be in the early teens (Dyson-Hudson 1966: 204).

Like the Jie, the Karimojong consider it highly desirable that sons should be enrolled in F − 1 (except in certain special cases, which will shortly be mentioned). Furthermore, it seems—though we have no figures on this point—that the proportion of sons who do not join F − 1 is quite small. Now, we know that an attempt to operate a g-group system is liable to run into problems caused by generational spread; and, if Dyson-Hudson is right in saying that the Karimojong "are commonly polygynous,"[39] then generational spread probably occurs at quite a fast rate. How do the Karimojong deal with the difficulties to which it gives rise?

Consider first overaging. This comes to be a serious problem when, for a number of generations back, fathers have been producing sons at an average interval which is less than the average inauguration interval. The Karimojong, however, have a rule that prevents this from happening: a man is not allowed to marry until he has joined his g-group (Farina 1965: 133; Dyson-Hudson 1968: 168, 198 f., 201).[40] Imagine that the inauguration interval is 40 years. A certain man joins group F as soon as it is formed, marries, and promptly produces a son. The son must now wait until F − 1 is inaugurated before he can marry; and so he will be about 40 years old before he can father a son, whatever age his own father may have been when he was born. The rule eliminates the possibility of a line of fathers and sons in which the successive generations of sons are all born to their fathers when the latter are, say, in their early twenties.

Let us look at the effects of this rule in relation to the g-set model. Overaging, it will be remembered, can lead first to waiting, and then to shrinking. Now, the Karimojong marriage rule does not eliminate waiting: though precise data are lacking, there is no doubt that some men have to wait until long after the minimum enrolment

---

[38] It is not clear whether all members of S + 1 in the whole tribe must be dead, or only all members of S + 1 in some section of the tribe.

[39] Dyson-Hudson (1966: 206), *contra* Farina (1965: 165).

[40] The Jie, incidentally, do not have a rule of this kind (Gulliver 1953: 158; 1966: 226), so we know that their system does not work on the same principles as that of the Karimojong.

age before they can join a group; this wait must be a matter of decades in some cases.[41] But the marriage rule does stop overaging giving rise to shrinking.[42] Inauguration intervals in the Karimojong system are certainly long—I think they would probably average out at over 40 years—but they are surely less than the maximum life span.[43] The marriage rule prevents a man from being born before his father's group is inaugurated; if he survives to the maximum life span he will therefore live to see his own group inaugurated.

Some reservations must be made with regard to the account of the marriage rule given in the preceding paragraphs. The Karimojong, in fact, recognize two main kinds of sexual relationship between men and women. In the kind which Farina and Dyson-Hudson call "marriage," and to which the above rule applies, a payment of cattle is made to the woman's close relatives. In this case the man has various rights over his children, and his sons will join $F - 1$ or a more junior group. The other kind is what the two ethnographers call "concubinage," a relationship that Farina (1965: 133) says is looked on as illegitimate, though no such implication appears in Dyson-Hudson's account (1966: 83). Here, no payment is made to the woman's relatives, and rights over the children belong to her brothers. A union of this sort can be entered into before a man is enrolled in his g-group. If the sons produced by this kind of union were supposed to be enrolled in $F - 1$, then overaging could eventually occur. But they are not: the rule is that they join the same g-group as their mother's brothers (Dyson-Hudson 1966: 84, 203 n. 22). (Perhaps, more exactly, they join the g-group immediately junior to the one which their mother's father joined, provided that it is still recruiting when they reach the minimum enrolment age; and the next junior g-group if it is not.)

There is also a further complication. If a woman marries a man of the same g-group as her brothers, then a son previously born by

---

[41] Waiting also occurs for other reasons: see pp. 222 and 224.

[42] A little shrinking does, however, occur for a quite different reason. It appears that occasionally a very poor man is never able to join a g-group because he cannot muster the ox necessary for the initiation (i.e., enrolment) sacrifice (Dyson-Hudson 1966: 205; cf. p. 224 of this book).

[43] See Section 2.5 of this chapter. In Section 1.2.2 it was shown that in an age-set system the inauguration interval *cannot* be greater than the maximum life span. Unfortunately this argument does not apply to the Karimojong system, for though it possesses the two-group characteristic, it suffers from some overlapping.

her in "concubinage" "will be due for membership in the generation-set junior to that of his uncles [Dyson-Hudson 1966: 203 n.
22]." Possibly the true form of this rule is that a boy who is born in
"concubinage" and whose mother marries before he joins a g-group
will be treated by the rules of the system as if he were the son of his
mother's husband. In any case, it is a rule whose effects would be
difficult to analyze in full because of the large number of different
cases that could arise under it. Dyson-Hudson says no more about it,
so I shall not attempt an analysis here. In any event, there is no
reason to believe that it does in fact lead to a significant amount of
overaging. The same is true of the less clearly reported rule relating
to divorced women (Dyson-Hudson 1966: 203 n. 22).

   Another reservation which has to be made is that the marriage
rule is not always obeyed. When Dyson-Hudson was in the field, a
new g-group (call it S) was inaugurated; but a long time had passed
since the inauguration of its predecessor, S + 1, and prospective
members of S were marrying before S was inaugurated (Dyson-
Hudson 1966: 198). In Section 2.5, I argue that the inauguration
interval in this system is in fact normally very long; and if this is
so, then it may well be usual for some of the older future members
of a group to break this rule. But note that these men do not simply
ignore the rule completely and marry whenever they feel like it; they
only break it, apparently, in the period immediately before the
inauguration of their group. (Their breaking it is in fact one of the
pressures that leads to the group being inaugurated.) As far as
generational spread is concerned, the rule has essentially the same
effect if it is broken only in the period immediately before the
inauguration of a new group as it would have if it were strictly
obeyed: it still prevents overaging as a cumulative process.

   Let us now turn to the younger representatives of a generation,
those who pose the problem of underaging. The main method the
system uses for coping with them is simply to allow them to join a
more junior g-group than F − 1. In other words, the system lacks the
generation-linking characteristic, though almost certainly this characteristic is part of the native model of the system. As I have remarked,
however, the proportion of those who join a group other than F − 1
is probably not large. One reason for this is that the inauguration
interval is very long, and, as we know, underaging is a problem
associated above all with a short interval.

   To enrol a son in a group junior to F − 1 is, however, the

method of last resort. In certain cases the Karimojong have another, and less radical, means at their disposal. It was mentioned earlier (p. 63 n. 41) that the Karimojong system usually permits a certain amount of waiting, quite apart from what is necessary in order to ensure that sons do not join F. In other words, the son of a member of F who reaches the minimum enrolment age (which, it will be remembered, is in the early teens) at a time when $F - 1$ is recruiting will, in spite of this, often have to wait. Now, the second expedient that the Karimojong use to deal with the effects of overaging is immediately to enrol any son of a member of F who reaches the minimum enrolment age at a time when $F - 1$ is recruiting, if $F - 1$ is about to cease recruiting. In these cases there is no waiting, since waiting would lead to the boy being enrolled in $F - 2$ (Dyson-Hudson 1966: 204). (As Dyson-Hudson points out, there are also other motives for this action: see further p. 75.)

There is a third feature which—as will be argued in a broader context in Chapter IV, Section 2—is also to be seen as a response to underaging: the rule that allows $F - 1$ to continue recruiting members until all the members of F are dead, even though $F - 2$ has already started recruiting.[44] It is because of this rule that the system lacks another characteristic of the g-set model: it permits some overlapping.

Lastly, we may mention a minor and rather obscure part of the Karimojong system. It will be remembered that in the Jie system, the sources state that if a woman marries a man in some group F, and that man dies, and the woman subsequently bears a son, then that son, whoever his genitor may be, will enrol in $F - 1$. (See p. 58 and p. 221 n. 24). Dyson-Hudson's account of the corresponding rules among the Karimojong (1966: 206) is not entirely clear, and what follows lies somewhere between a guess and a summary of his data. It appears that among the Karimojong, as among the Jie, a widow does not remarry, and any children she produces after her husband's death are in general treated as his offspring, whoever the genitor may be. Now, the effect of strictly observing a rule of the sort that is to be found among the Jie would be to exacerbate the problem of generational spread. The Karimojong, it seems, avoid this by allowing a son born to a widow to join either the g-group immediately junior to that

---

[44] Dyson-Hudson (1966: 203) already suggested that this rule should be looked on in this light, though he also suggested another, quite different (though not incompatible), reason for its existence (1966: 196).

of her late husband (the son's pater), or a g-group immediately junior to that of his genitor,[45] depending on which is recruiting when he reaches the minimum enrolment age or which is first to begin recruiting thereafter. (It seems that if both g-groups are recruiting when he reaches the minimum enrolment age, then he joins the junior of the two.)

We have now noted all those features of the Karimojong system that distinguish it from an age-set system (as defined by our model). It will be evident that the degree of deviation is not great. The system does not possess the enrolment characteristic, but nor, as far as one can tell, does it deviate widely from that characteristic. There is no basic enrolment age, but it seems that a considerable proportion—most probably a majority—of men are enrolled not long after reaching the minimum enrolment age. The second point in which the system differs from the age-set model is in permitting overlapping, but again, the amount of deviation is not striking. Group S will overlap with S + 1 for a while after its inauguration and with S − 1 just before it ceases recruitment; but the period during which S is recruiting simultaneously with some other g-group amounts—at a guess—to only about one-quarter of its total recruitment period.

The system deviates only slightly more from the type defined by the g-set model: in addition to violating the two constraints just mentioned, it also lacks the generation-linking characteristic. As we have seen, however, there is reason to believe that the proportion of sons who join a group junior to F − 1 is small.

2.3   * The Zanaki

Bischofberger's recent study of the Zanaki (1972) makes it quite easy to establish the relationship between their system and the g-set model.

Simplifying matters slightly, we can say that among the Zanaki, as among the Karimojong, there is a Senior Group and a Junior Group, together with a Succession Ceremony that has the same three effects as those listed on p. 61 f.[46] In other respects, however, the system differs from that of the Karimojong.

---

[45] Presumably a posthumously born son, i.e., one whose pater is also (hopefully) his genitor, can only join the g-group junior to that of his late father.

[46] What I here (for the sake of easy comparison with the Karimojong) call the Junior Group is what the Zanaki call the *munyikura;* what I call the Senior Group is what Bischofberger (a little misleadingly perhaps) calls the "retired

Among the Zanaki, the g-group that an individual joins is determined mainly by his father's g-group, his age, the number of brothers he has, and his birth order number among these brothers.[47] The rules involved are rather complicated and evidently allow a certain amount of latitude (Bischofberger 1972: 30 ff.). For present purposes we can largely confine ourselves to considering the simple case where there are only two brothers.

In such a case (and indeed in all cases), the first-born son, whenever he may have been born, joins $F - 1$ as soon as it has been inaugurated and he has reached the minimum enrolment age;[48] and he remains a member of that group for the rest of his life. For the second-born son different rules apply.

(i) If he reaches the minimum enrolment age before $F - 1$ is inaugurated or while $F - 1$ is still at the first level, then he joins $F - 1$; but when $F - 1$ reaches the second level (i.e., when $F - 2$ is inaugurated) he ceases to be a member of $F - 1$ and joins $F - 2$. (A son who has a very high birth order number may even shift g-groups twice: from $F - 1$ to

---

generation class." What I here call the Succession Ceremony is what Bischofberger calls the "handing-over ceremony." It consists, in fact, of two separate, but simultaneous (or virtually simultaneous), ceremonies. One of these, the *kuturya zinzoya*, marks the inauguration of a new g-group; the other, the *kung'atuka*, marks the transition of a g-group from the status of Junior Group to that of Senior Group.

[47] Birth order numbers indicate the order in which some specified set of individuals were born, the first-born having the number 1, the second-born the number 2, and so on. In the course of the present work we shall encounter a variety of rules that are best formulated with the aid of birth order numbers. In all cases, the individuals involved will be the male offspring of some man or woman. We may use the term **paternal birth order numbers** if the individuals involved are the offspring of one man, and **maternal birth order numbers** if they are the offspring of one woman. In the case of the Zanaki, among whom "polygyny is common" (Bischofberger 1972: 31), both the maternal and the paternal birth order numbers seem to be relevant. In all cases mentioned in this book where birth order is significant, the accounts of the rules given by the ethnographers are incomplete. Little or nothing is said about what happens in the case of half-brothers, step-brothers, brothers who die young, adopted brothers, and so on. I mention this here in general terms in order to avoid repeating it in each individual case.

[48] Attainment of the minimum enrolment age is marked by circumcision, which is carried out on a boy of the proper age irrespective of whether $F - 1$ has been inaugurated (Bischofberger 1972: 29). Bischofberger does not say at what age circumcision is performed nowadays, but he writes that "In earlier times the boys were usually older (about eighteen) . . . [1972: 19]."

F − 2 when F − 2 is inaugurated; and then from F − 2 to
F − 3 when F − 3 is inaugurated.)

(ii) If the second-born son reaches the minimum enrolment age
after F − 1 has moved to the second level, then, as far as I
can tell, he does not join F − 1, but some more junior
group, presumably whichever one is at the first level at that
point in time.[49]

The effect of these rules is to counteract underaging. As far as
(ii) is concerned, this is immediately obvious in the light of our
analysis of the Karimojong system. The case of (i), however, is
perhaps not quite so transparent, and the reader may find it useful to
glance for a moment at pp. 99 ff., where there are some remarks on
this kind of downward shift in age-group affiliation.

The use of birth order numbers as an important criterion in
determining who shall shift downward can of course lead to anomalies, but the Zanaki system is fairly flexible and can in some cases
correct such anomalies. For example, if a junior son is forced to shift
down to F − 2 even though his age renders F − 1 a more suitable
group for him, then he can perform a special ceremony later and
shift up to F − 1 again (Bischofberger 1972: 31).

If shifting from one group to a more junior one is to be a
long-term method of controlling underaging, then the g-groups of the
sons of a father who has shifted downward must in general be
determined in relation to the g-group into which the father shifted,
rather than in relation to his original g-group. I assume that such is
the case among the Zanaki, but Bischofberger does not explicitly
state the relevant rules. As a result we can imagine various possible
cases without knowing what rules would apply to them. For example: a man who is a junior son joins F − 1; he has a son who reaches
the minimum enrolment age before F − 2 is inaugurated; what
happens now? Does the son enrol in F − 2, while the father remains
in F − 1? Does the father shift down to F − 2, leaving the son to join

---

[49] See Bischofberger (1972: 30, paragraph beginning "It is possible . . .").
Bischofberger tells us what happens to a first-born son who reaches the minimum enrolment age after F − 2 has been inaugurated, but he does not say what
happens in the case of junior sons; it is clearly implied, however, that different
rules apply. My guess is that junior sons join whichever group is at level 1 when
they reach the minimum enrolment age; in the case of second-born sons, this
must in practice mean that if they do not join F − 1 then they join F − 2; but
sons who are more junior may well join groups that are more junior—at least
F − 3.

F − 3 eventually? Or do they both join F − 2 (very unlikely in view of Bischofberger 1972: 32)?

Bischofberger does not mention any special rule that would prevent overaging. In particular, there is nothing to prevent a man from marrying before he joins his g-group (1972: 82 etc.). In spite of this, overaging does not seem to be a serious problem. There is no indication, for instance, that the system suffers from shrinking. More generally, though no precise data are given, one has the impression that most members of a given g-group fall within an age-range of about the same length as its inauguration interval—though the overall age-range of a group is evidently considerable: at least 60 years in one case (1972: 30). If the system does indeed work fairly well without a rule to check overaging, then the reason may lie in a harmonious relationship between the inauguration interval and the age at which men first marry.

Let us conclude by comparing the way in which the Zanaki system deviates from the g-set model to the way in which the Karimojong system deviates.

(i) Like the Karimojong system, the Zanaki one permits waiting. In both systems it occurs in the case of a boy who reaches the minimum enrolment age before F − 1 is inaugurated.

(ii) Also like the Karimojong, the Zanaki permit overlapping; but whereas, among the Karimojong, there is a definite point in time after which no one may join a given g-group, in the Zanaki system there is no such point in time: first-born sons *always* join F − 1. One can only be certain that recruitment to F − 1 has ended when there remain no more sonless men in F. To join a Karimojong g-group one must have certain qualifications during a certain period of time; to join a Zanaki g-group it is sufficient in some cases merely to possess the qualifications. The Zanaki system allows more overlapping in the sense that there is *always* more than one g-group recruiting members at any given point in time; quite likely there are sometimes three. Among the Karimojong there is usually only one g-group recruiting, and never more than two.

(iii) Another similarity to the Karimojong is that the Zanaki system lacks the generation-linking characteristic—at least, this is so if I am right in assuming that under certain circumstances non−first-born sons may fail to join F − 1. But, once again, the two systems deviate from the characteristic in rather different ways. Among the Zanaki (on my hypothesis) one fails to join F − 1 if one is a non−first-born son who reaches the minimum enrolment age after the inauguration of F − 2. Among the Karimojong one fails to join F − 1, whatever one's birth order number, if one reaches the minimum enrolment age after F − 1 has stopped recruiting (a point in time which comes later than the inauguration of F − 2).

(iv)   The Zanaki system differs from that of the Karimojong in that it permits resigning, which occurs by virtue of the fact that some men shift downward. In the Karimojong system all these men would remain in their original g-group.

The demographic history of a given g-group would evidently be a good deal more complicated among the Zanaki than among the Karimojong, partly because of the difference mentioned under (ii) and partly because of that mentioned under (iv).

2.4   * Distribution

Generation-group systems exist in at least three tribes of the Karimojong cluster: the Jie, the Karimojong, and the Dodoth. Information on the last-mentioned system is very sketchy (E. M. Thomas 1966: 57–59; Lamphear 1976: 107 ff.). There is an obscure reference which suggests that g-groups may exist, or may once have existed, among the Topotha. They no longer exist among the Turkana, but there is some reason to believe that they once did. (On both the Topotha and the Turkana, see further p. 120 n. 105.)

Several tribes bordering on the Karimojong tribe appear to have imitated the Karimojong g-group system: the Labwor, whose age organization is to be described in a forthcoming article by R. G. Abrahams; the So, whose system is the subject of Laughlin and Laughlin (1974); and the Pokot, or rather, certain sections of the Pokot, who seem to have introduced g-groups in the nineteenth century (Peristiany 1951).

Further to the south, on the eastern side of Lake Victoria, are a number of Bantu tribes with g-group systems. The largest of these is the Kuria, with a population of about 100,000; among the smaller ones are the Zanaki, the Kwaya (whose system is briefly described in Huber 1973: 72–76), the Nguruimi (or Ngoreme), the Ikizu, the Sizaki, the Nata, and the Ikoma (Baker 1927; Ruel 1962: 35; Bischofberger 1972: 92 f.). No doubt there are several other tribes whose names could be added to this list.

There are extended descriptions of only two of these systems: that of the Kuria and that of the Zanaki. On the latter, the sole source is Bischofberger (1972), some of whose information has just been analyzed. On the former, the main source is Ruel (1962), but there are additional data in Ruel (n.d.) and Baker (1927, 1953, and especially 1955: 54 ff.). We can tell that the Kuria system differs from that of the Zanaki (see Bischofberger 1972: 89 ff. for a comparison), and even more so from the Karimojong and Jie systems;[50] but its exact nature remains a little obscure.

Further south still, g-groups exist among the Tatoga tribes, though not much is known about them. A good bibliography of the literature on these tribes is to be found in Beidelman (1970). Of the sources he mentions, the only ones with significant information on g-groups are Berger (1938: 190 ff.) and Wilson (1952: 36; 1953: 41 f.). Klima (1964: 17) mentions them in passing.

Finally, traveling north again, generation-groups existed among a number of the Kikuyu tribes, on which see Chapter II, Section 4.4.1.

2.5 * Inauguration Intervals

Judging from the available data, the factors leading to the inauguration of a new g-group are always complicated and vary considerably from one system to another. None of the systems that have been described has a rule which establishes a fixed length of time between inaugurations or which otherwise takes out of the hands of the people involved the decision as to when a new group should start recruiting. In this g-groups differ from many other age-group systems (cf. Chapter III, Section 3). In all the known g-group systems the inauguration intervals stand in some fairly compatible relationship with the age at which men beget sons, and this is why they retain more or less of a resemblance to g-set systems.

There is unusually full evidence on the length of inauguration intervals among the Jie and the Karimojong, and I shall devote the rest of this section to these two tribes. I shall begin with an analysis of the Karimojong system, in which I hope to show that the inauguration intervals in their system are actually a good deal longer than they are reported as being.

In this discussion I shall follow the notation developed by Dyson-Hudson (1966: 158). The names of the Karimojong g-

---

[50] It should perhaps be noted here that all known g-group systems resemble those of the Jie and Karimojong in having only a very small number of groups extant at any given point in time: not less than two, certainly, but in no case, I think, more than four (in one sequence).

groups[51] which had living members while he was in the field will be represented by the letters A, B, and C, A being the most senior and C the most junior. The period during which a g-group recruits its members is divided into five portions. Those recruited during one of these portions form a named group, which I shall call a sub-group. [52] The sub-groups in each g-group will be represented by the numbers 1 to 5, 1 being the most senior sub-group and 5 the most junior.[53] The Succession Ceremony that took place in 1956 retired group A, promoted group B to senior status, and opened recruitment to group C.

There are two questions that should be touched on here: one is what the Karimojong consider the proper length of the inauguration interval; the other is its actual length.

"Ideally, each [sub-group] recruits for five to six years [Dyson-Hudson 1966: 196]" and "each generation-set thus comprises all men of the tribe who have performed initiation within (ideally) the twenty-five to thirty year period covered by its constituent [sub-groups] [p. 156]." Dyson-Hudson's view as to the ideal length of Karimojong inauguration intervals has recently been criticized by Lamphear (1972: 500 f.). Lamphear points to Dyson-Hudson's statements to the effect that g-group B (Ngimoru) was inaugurated "at the close of the last century," and that g-group C (Ngigete) should have been inaugurated "by the late 1930's at the latest [Dyson-Hudson 1966: 191, 197]." From these Lamphear infers—not altogether convincingly—that an inauguration interval "on the order of 43 years was considered 'normal'."

A rather stronger case, however, can be made for the thesis that the *actual* inauguration interval is usually much more than 25 to 30

---

[51] Farina (1965: 128, 130) and Lamphear (1976: 43) disagree with Dyson-Hudson and with each other about the Karimojong g-group naming system. I think Lamphear probably has it right (cf. Peristiany 1950: 290; Laughlin and Laughlin 1974: 270). The matter has no significance for the present discussion.

[52] An age-group is divided into sub-(age-)groups if there is a partition of its members and each of the sub-sets is a group. Correspondingly, age-sets are sometimes divided into sub-(age-)sets. Stewart (1972: 264–267) gives a narrower definition of a sub-age-set, but, as a result, the definition of a sub-age-group there is misleading.

[53] We may mention here a small inconsistency in Dyson-Hudson's account. In his Figure 24 (1966: 158), he lists the most senior sub-group of the Ngigete g-group (C1) as Ngikangaarak, and its most junior (C5) as Ngimeguro. But in his text Ngimeguro is always referred to as the most senior sub-group (1966: 159, 176, 178, 196).

years. Dyson-Hudson points out that, though the ideal recruitment period (and hence inauguration interval) of a sub-group is 5 to 6 years, "in fact, it may recruit for as few as two or as many as eight to nine years [1966: 196]." He mentions as a completely exceptional case the sub-group B5 (Ngirengilim), which began recruiting in 1929 or 1930 and was still recruiting when he left the field in September 1958.[54] Now, one would expect the last sub-group to recruit rather longer than the others, since it has, in addition to the normal recruitment period, also the overlapping period (see p. 65). But even if we leave out of consideration the overlapping period, sub-group B5 still continued recruiting for a remarkably long period of time: something like 25 years, since the Succession Ceremony took place in 1956.[55]

The fact that B5 continued to recruit for perhaps five times as long as it should have is one of many indications that the Succession Ceremony was held much later than the ideal date. If we accept the ideal of an inauguration interval of 5 or 6 years for sub-groups, then we can set the ideal date at about 1936. On this basis we can say that the ceremony took place some 20 years later than it should have, a view subscribed to not only by Dyson-Hudson but also by Lamphear.

The other evidence—that is, the evidence apart from the long recruitment period of sub-group B5—which shows that the Succession Ceremony of 1956 took place much later than was considered proper is collected by Dyson-Hudson (1966: 198 f.). It is entirely convincing, and need not be rehearsed in detail here. There is no question but that the delay in performing the ceremony had set the whole system out of kilter: one of many striking indications is that in certain localities some of the oldest members of the Junior Group had to be initiated a second time and enrolled as members of the Senior Group, the reason being that so few of the original members of the Senior Group survived that they could no longer carry out their duties.

Dyson-Hudson considers

(i) That the lengthy recruitment period of sub-group B5 was "particularly abnormal" (1966: 196);

[54] He expected that it would cease recruiting in about 1960, but was unable to gather any information about the matter after having left the Karimojong (1966: 197).

[55] Dyson-Hudson (1966: 159 (where the month—October—is also given), 197, 205). At two points on p. 180, Dyson-Hudson writes as if the ceremony had not yet taken place in 1957, but this seems to be a mistake.

(ii) That the delay in performing the Succession Ceremony of
1956 is to be explained by economic factors. "From 1939
on, natural conditions made a tribal gathering [necessitated
by the ceremony] difficult; then epidemics of contagious
pleuro-pneumonia and rinderpest caused Administration to
restrict stock movement [necessary for the ceremony];
then conditions were again bad [1966: 197, cf. 196 n.
19.]."

I shall try to show that the lengthy recruitment period of B5 was
probably not "highly abnormal" (1966: 203); and that the delay in
the Succession Ceremony was caused mainly by deep-rooted features
of the whole system, though economic difficulties may well have
played their part.

As regards the first point, it seems likely that the reason
sub-group B5 continued recruiting for so long was in part that
sub-group A5 also continued recruiting for far longer than sub-groups
A1 to A4. In 1956 some members of A5 were still alive, although not
enough of them to carry out the tasks of the Senior Group. That A5
was a large and relatively young sub-group is also indicated by the
fact that, in 1956, B1 had already completely died out. Now, if some
members of A5 were still alive in 1956, it is highly unlikely that
g-group A was really prepared to retire in 1936, or even in 1946.
Dyson-Hudson (1966: 215) implies that g-group A only began to be
too few for their duties in the 1950s (see the comments on the
Freeing of the Cattle ceremonies). It may be that in the case of B5
certain economic factors made the problem even worse, but it is clear
that the imbalance caused by a long period of recruitment to the last
sub-group of the g-group is a problem that also existed in the
previous g-group. Probably it is endemic to the system.

How can it be explained? The rich material supplied by Dyson-
Hudson enables us to give what looks like a satisfactory solution. The
crucial factor appears to be the reluctance of the members of a
Senior Group to surrender their prerogatives and retire. The reasons
for this reluctance are strikingly brought out by Lamphear, who
writes

My Jie research assistant was quite appalled on several occasions
during our interviews among the Karimojong at the lack of respect
shown by even fairly young men to some of the aged "retired"
elders who served as my informants. Even I was keenly aware of this
lack of respect, which was sometimes manifested by open ridicule of
a senile elder. Nothing even vaguely similar was ever encountered

amongst the Jie, where even the most senile elders were held in great
awe [1972: 291 n. 2; cf. 1976: 153 n. 25].

We can isolate two processes that would account for the length-
ened recruitment periods of the last sub-group of each g-group.[56]

(i) A5 members will have no interest in when sub-groups B1 to
B4 cease recruiting, and the latter can be expected to recruit for the
usual length of time. But A5 members want to retain their active role
in society as long as possible, so they have a strong interest in not
allowing C1 to be inaugurated. They will therefore prolong the
recruitment period of B5. From this point of view they will be
interested in the length of time that B5 remains open, not in the
number of persons recruited or their ages. Pressure of this sort will
operate *before* the Succession Ceremony.

(ii) According to Dyson-Hudson (1966: 203 f.), *after* the Succession Ceremony, when g-group B has just become the Senior
Group, the members of B will be interested in ensuring that B5
recruits as many young men as possible, as young as possible, so as to
keep B "in power" for a long time. The length of time B5 continues
to recruit is not of primary interest to them, and indeed, according
to the rules, is not within their control. The interest of, say, B1 and
B2 in this matter will of course be less than the interest of B3 and
B4.

I have no doubt, under these circumstances, that if we had
historical records we would find that the average inauguration interval was very considerably more than the ideal 25 to 30 years
reported by Dyson-Hudson, and perhaps even more than the 40-odd
years suggested by Lamphear (1976: 52) as the actual interval.[57]

A similar disparity between ideal and reality may exist among
the Jie. Gulliver, as may be remembered, thought that the Jie
inauguration interval was somewhere between 20 and 30 years
(1953: 148). But he also reports that "For a Jie man, marriage below
the age of 30 is rare [1966: 242]," a statement confirmed by

---

[56] In what follows the letters A, B, and C refer to any three adjacent
g-groups, and not merely to the three particular ones which had living members
when Dyson-Hudson was in the field.

[57] Lamphear refers to his thesis (1972) for evidence that the Karimojong
inauguration interval was of about this length, but the argument in the thesis
seems to relate to the *ideal* length of the interval rather than its actual length
(see p. 72 of this volume).

Lamphear (1976: 33). If both these data were correct, than we
would expect the system to suffer badly from underaging; but there
is no evidence that it does, so at least one of the data is probably
wrong.

There is no real doubt that Gulliver underestimated the length
of the inauguration interval. Lamphear (1976: 45 ff.) carried out
very careful investigations on this point, and he concludes that "the
span of time between Jie generation-sets is, on the average, approximately 40 years [1976: 52]."

It is certainly curious that both Dyson-Hudson and Gulliver
should have underestimated the lengths of the inauguration intervals
in the systems they were describing. Dyson-Hudson was evidently
misled by his informants; he reports the 5- or 6-year recruitment
period of the sub-groups as the Karimojong ideal. Gulliver may also
have been misled by a native model, in this as in other respects. But
even if we assume that in both systems the actual inauguration
intervals are greater than the native models represent them as being,
we cannot simply infer from this that the reasons for the disparity
are the same in both cases. It would be possible to speculate at some
length about this question, but since both systems are still in existence, it seems best to wait for further data collected in the field.

3 GADA SYSTEMS AND PATERNAL LINKING

Gada systems are a good deal more numerous than g-group
systems, and far more literature, both ethnographic and theoretical,[58] has been devoted to them. If, in spite of this, we began our
exposition with an account of g-group systems, it was for two
reasons: first, because g-group systems pose essentially the same
problems as Gada systems, but in a simpler form; and second,
because there is no account of a Gada system that is quite as good as
Dyson-Hudson's description of the Karimojong g-group system.

The central theoretical problem that has been canvassed in the
literature on Gada systems—often in the form of an historical question—is that of their relationship to age-set systems. No consensus of
opinion on this subject has emerged (the discussion is reviewed in
Haberland 1963: 167 ff.). To judge from the numerous, if imperfect,

[58] The main theoretical works consulted were Michels (1941), Prins (1953),
Jensen (1941, 1954), Legesse (1963), Kalinovskaya (1969, 1972), and Hoffmann (1971).

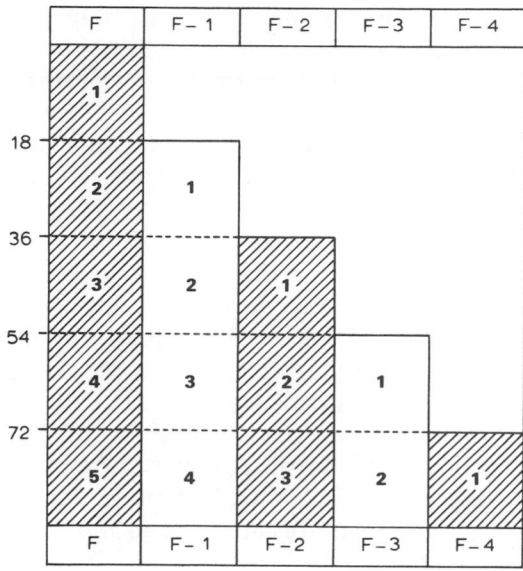

Figure 1.13

ethnographies available, it appears that most (or at least many) Gada systems differ from age-set systems just as the Karimojong g-group system does: that is to say, they permit overlapping and waiting.

The relevant elements of Gada systems can be illustrated from an example. I have chosen a system that operates among the Konso of Ethiopia, because it is quite well described and because (as far as one can tell) it is fairly typical.

3.1 The Konso

3.1.1 Outline

The main features of the system are represented in Figure 1.13. Although this diagram represents a particular system, I should also like to bring it to the attention of the reader as a method of representing age-group systems in general.[59] Diagrams of the same kind will also be used in slightly different ways later in this work.

The numbers in the column on the extreme left of the diagram represent years. The system is assumed to have come into operation

[59] Diagrams of essentially this form were, I believe, first used by Fosbrooke (1948: 24), and, in a somewhat different version, by Pecci (1941).

in the year 0 with the inauguration of age-group F. The history of age-group F is represented in column F. Each box in that column has in it the level number of the group during the years indicated on the extreme left. In the year 18, age-group F − 1 was inaugurated; 18 years later, age-group F − 2 was inaugurated; and so on.

The diagram can be used in two ways. By reading down a column it is possible to follow the history of a given group; for instance, column F − 2 shows that group F − 2 was inaugurated in the year 36, reached level 2 in the year 54, and so on. By looking across the diagram it is possible to see the state of the system at a given point in time. In the year 40, for example, group F was at level 3, group F − 1 at level 2, group F − 2 at level 1, and no groups more junior than that were yet in existence.

As the diagram indicates, the Konso inaugurate a new age-group every 18 years. A man's sons must all join F − 2 (this is why alternate columns are shaded in the diagram). The minimum enrolment age is zero. No man may marry or beget children until his group reaches the second level.

These are the rules of the system as it was found by both of the ethnographers who have described it, Jensen in 1935, and Hallpike 30 years later. Jensen, however, offers evidence (on which see Section 3.1.2.5 of this chapter) which indicates that at some earlier stage there was an additional rule whose effect was to forbid men to beget children after their age-group had reached level 4. In such a system, then, a man would only be able to beget children when his age-group was at levels 2 and 3. Now, since his sons must join F − 2, they will either be born before their age-group is inaugurated, or else when it is at level 1. A system of this kind corresponds almost exactly to the age-set model. It deviates only in that it permits waiting: the minimum enrolment age is 0, but a son who is born when F is at level 2 will not immediately be enrolled in F − 1, even though that group will still be recruiting members; instead he will wait until F − 2 starts recruiting, by which time he may be up to 18 years old.

This deviation has important implications. If the recruitment period of a Konso age-group only extended from the inauguration of that group to the inauguration of the next, then the system would be one that conformed exactly to the model and in which, for all S, $a_S = c_S = 18$ years (see Section 1.2.3 of this chapter). But in a system with Jensen's additional rule, $a_S = c_S + r_{S+1} = 36$ years (for all S).

Whatever the truth about Jensen's additional rule, there is no disputing the fact that it no longer exists and has not existed for at least half a century. As things stand, men continue to father sons even when their age-groups are at higher levels than 3. Let us imagine the case where a man has a son when his age-group is at level 4. The son is still enrolled in $F - 2$, even though that group is now at level 2, since group $F - 3$ has already been inaugurated. Overlapping has occurred.

The Konso system as it now is therefore differs from an age-set system in two familiar respects. First, it permits overlapping (which the system with Jensen's additional rule did not). Second, it permits waiting. The system with Jensen's rule also permitted waiting, but in the absence of Jensen's rule the possible effects are far more striking, since the remaining rules impose no limit on a_S. In practice, however, the age-range of groups is evidently quite moderate (see further the following section).

3.1.2 * Details

I now turn to consider the evidence for some of the statements about the Konso made above. It will unfortunately be necessary here to assume one or two points that are only dealt with later in this work; in particular, the reader may find it easier to return to this section after having read the one that follows. On the other hand, a reader who wants to attempt this section now will not find it impossible.

1. *Sources.* A good bibliography of works on the Konso will be found in Hallpike (1972: 336).[60] The only authors who offer significant information on Konso age organization are Jensen and Hallpike. The system was first described in Jensen (1936) on the basis of fieldwork carried out in 1935.[61] Jensen returned to the field in 1951, and in 1954 published another—this time very brief— account of the system, using information from both visits. These two published accounts are notably clear, but they differ from each other on some important points. Professor E. Haberland informs me that Jensen made a third and last visit to the Konso in 1954 and that he then wrote a third account of their system, which is still in manuscript but which it is hoped eventually to publish. Professor Haber-

---

[60] To it may be added Vicariato Apostolico del Gimma (1938), which I have not seen, Kuls (1958) and Kalinovskaya (1974; based entirely on published sources). There are some references to the Konso in Cerulli (1933; see index s.v. Conso). The linguistic material on the Konso that Cerulli collected, and to which he refers in a number of his writings, has not been published.

[61] Jensen (1942) is essentially just a shorter version of his original report.

land kindly supplied me with some brief extracts from this manuscript, two of which are quoted later.

A more recent description of Konso age organization is to be
found in Hallpike (1972), which is based on fieldwork carried out
between 1965 and 1967. This account differs in a number of ways
from both of those published by Jensen. In evaluating the work of
these two authors, it should be borne in mind that Jensen's visit of
1935 lasted little more than a month and that his subsequent periods
in the field were also very short, whereas Hallpike spent the better
part of a year and a half among the Konso.

The data given in Section 3.1.1 of this chapter are common to
all the publications of Jensen and Hallpike, except where otherwise
indicated.

2. *Local differences.* What I refer to, here and elsewhere, as
the Konso system is in fact only the system found in one section of
Konso territory. Jensen calls it the system of the North Eastern
Konso (1954: 2), or Gamole (1936: 384), while Hallpike refers to it
as the Garati system. Jensen (1954: 2) says that there are altogether
four different types of system among the Konso,[62] while Hallpike
says that there are three (all of which he describes). In his published
work, Jensen only describes one other type of system, and then very
briefly. He calls it the system of the South Western Konso (1954: 8),
or Madjallo (1936: 384). This corresponds to what Hallpike calls the
Takadi system, though the two accounts are decidedly different from
each other (cf. p. 105). The third system described by Hallpike, that
of the Turo region, is mentioned on p. 106.

3. *Age-grades.* Hallpike describes the Konso as having seven
grades, while Jensen (1936: 336, 339) only mentions six. These six
correspond in name and order to the first six mentioned by Hallpike.
(Jensen and Hallpike transcribe the names of the grades rather
differently. I have followed Hallpike in this respect.) I shall refer to
the age-grades by means of roman numerals, the most junior being I.
Grade I is assigned to the group at level 1, grade II to the group at
level 2, and so on.[63] Hallpike represents grade VII as being assigned
to the group at level 7; in fact, I suspect that it is a retirement grade
assigned to the groups at level 7 and all levels higher than that (cf.

---

[62] Though earlier (1952: 61) he had said that there are only three.

[63] This is a simplified description of the way in which the grades are
assigned, but it is adequate for present purposes. A proper analysis would take
into account Hallpike's description of the *harriyada* (1972: 186 f.).

Hallpike 1972: 194 on grade VII of the Takadi system). This is, however, a perfectly academic point, since Hallpike "never found anyone in Ukuda [VII], and only two men in 'Gulula [VI] [1972: 184 n. 1; cf. 1972: 205]." This evidently corresponds to Jensen's experience, for in his 1936 account he is unable to give any information about grades V and VI (1936: 348), in his article of 1942 he only mentions the first five grades (1942: 218), and in his article of 1954 he lists only the first four grades (1954: 4).

This lack of men in high grades is a phenomenon we shall have occasion to refer to again later. For the moment, let us just consider how it may have arisen.

It will be observed that an age-group spends 18 years in each grade (except the last). This means that only 72 years after its inauguration does it reach grade V, only 90 years after its inauguration does it reach grade VI, and only 108 years after its inauguration does it reach grade VII. It follows, then, that these high grades would only have a lot of men in them if men were joining their age-groups when the age-group were at relatively high levels. No one who joins his age-group when it is at level 1 can expect to pass beyond grade V. From the absence of men in high grades we can safely infer that most men join their age-groups when the groups are at low levels. The reasons for the lack of men in the high grades, then, are quite simple; they are (a) that most men join their age-group when it is at a low level and (b) that the age-group only reaches the high grades many decades after its inauguration.

There still remains a problem: if the high grades are of so little practical significance, why is it that they exist at all? Hallpike supplies what is no doubt the correct answer. He suggests that the inauguration interval was probably at one time not 18 years, but 9 years. He points out that

> still today the eighteen-year cycle is also referred to as the "twice-nine years" instead of the "the eighteen years," that a nine-year cycle would have allowed the top grades of 'Gulula [VI] and Ukuda [VII] to be filled, whereas now they are empty, and that according to Garati tradition the cycle was once nine years [1972: 205 f.].

4. *Marriage.* It was stated in the preceding section that among the Konso no man may marry or beget children until his group reaches level 2. The only reservation to be made to this statement is that both Jensen (1936: 338, 377) and Hallpike (1972: 189; cf. 1972: 188, 181 n. 2) note cases where some kind of union with a girl—whether it should be called marriage or not is unclear—is per-

mitted to a man at level 1. Their accounts of this phenomenon differ very widely indeed, but they are agreed on one point: a man at level 1 is never recognized as the father of a child; either it is aborted or paternity is ascribed to someone else. (Jensen mentions abortion in 1954: 6.)

According to Jensen (1936: 197, 337, 346) all men are married immediately upon their age-group reaching level 2, though if a boy is very young, consummation of the marriage and the establishment of a joint household is delayed. Hallpike, however, states that "boys are expected to wait at least another two years (and sometimes four or five)" after reaching level 2 and before marrying (1972: 189).

5. *Jensen's additional rule.* The evidence for the existence at some earlier period of a rule forbidding men to beget children after reaching level 4 is rather complex. It will be as well to begin with the present situation among the Konso. According to Jensen, when an age-group makes the transition from grade III (Kada) to grade IV (Orshada), six priests from the age-group are circumcised and are thereafter forbidden to have sexual intercourse (Jensen 1954: 6). (In an earlier account (Jensen 1936: 348) he mentions only one man as being circumcised.) Hallpike also mentions this ceremony, but he says that three men are circumcised and that the ceremony takes place at the time of the transition from IV (Orshada) to V ('Gurula), that is, when the age-group reaches level 5 (1972: 193). All Jensen's accounts of the system agree, however, that this ceremony is simultaneous with the transition from III to IV.

Now, Jensen reports two further data. First, he states that "The Konso say that it is impossible for a circumcised man to have intercourse with a woman. They say that a circumcised man is in fact himself a woman [unpublished manuscript, p. 30, quoted from a letter from Professor Haberland]." Second, he writes that "According to a great many accounts, all of them in agreement with each other and collected in various villages, until recently all Konso men were circumcised on transition to Orshada (IV), i.e., none of them were thereafter permitted to cohabit with a woman [unpublished manuscript, p. 30, quoted from a letter from Professor Haberland]." In his original (1936) account of the Konso, Jensen did not mention the first of these data, but he did report that some Konso men had told him that originally all Konso men were circumcised on transition to Orshada (IV). He added, however, that this statement should be viewed with some suspicion since "very many old men" knew nothing of such a custom (1936: 348). Nevertheless, after his second visit Jensen accepted this additional rule as fact (1954: 6).[64]

Hallpike does not mention either of these data, but in his account of transition from Orshada (IV) to 'Gurula (V) he does remark that "It is possible that at one time all men entering 'Gurula were prohibited from begetting any more children [1972: 193; cf. also 1972: 142, 149 on the Takadi system]."

What conclusions can be drawn from all this? In the first place, I think we may accept without question that many informants told Jensen that at one time Konso men were circumcised on transition to IV and that thereafter they were not allowed to beget children. Second, I think we can also accept that Jensen is correct in stating that at present the priests are circumcised on transition from III to IV, and not IV to V as Hallpike states. Jensen was clearly interested in this point; his later accounts contain additional information that sometimes contradicts his original report of 1936. It is unlikely that he would make a mistake about this. Third, and most important, there is the question of whether to believe Jensen's informants. On balance, I think we should, because they do not appear to have had any motive for misleading him. Furthermore, the additional rule would have the effect of making it impossible for a father and his son both to beget children at the same time, and this, according to Hallpike, is something the Konso consider desirable (1972: 46, 185 etc.). A final argument in favor of accepting that the additional rule once existed is that it would prevent underaging, a process to which the system might otherwise be susceptible (see later). On the other hand, there is no reason to believe that the rule existed in the very recent past, since, even in his report of 1936, Jensen makes no mention of having encountered any old men who claimed to have been circumcised in this way.

6. *Underaging.* If the Konso system were suffering from underaging, then this would almost certainly manifest itself as a decrease in the average age of the men in high grades and a corresponding increase in their number. There is quite good evidence, however, that no important changes in these directions took place between Jensen's visit of 1935 and Hallpike's investigations some 30 years later. In the first place, both Jensen and Hallpike say that men

---

[64] Indeed, his attitude is already significantly less skeptical in his article of 1942 (230 f.).

are generally to be found in grades that correspond to their ages (Jensen 1936: 337; 1942: 220; Hallpike 1972: 183, 189, 213). Though statements of this sort are rather vague, they are not without significance. Second, both ethnographers seem to have found few men in the high grades (see Subsection 3 of this section).

I believe, therefore, that we are on quite safe ground if we assume that the Konso system does not suffer significantly from underaging. Yet, as we know, there is no rule that obviates the possibility of underaging, and, if such a rule did once exist, it was certainly abandoned long before Jensen's first visit. What is it, then, that accounts for the absence of underaging?

Let us begin by considering in slightly more detail how underaging could occur in the Konso system. In Figure 1.14 I have represented five generations of men. The location of a triangle indicates the time at which a man was born and the age-group to which he belongs. The length of the vertical line beneath each triangle indicates the man's age when his son is born. The shaded areas in each column indicate the period during which a man is not

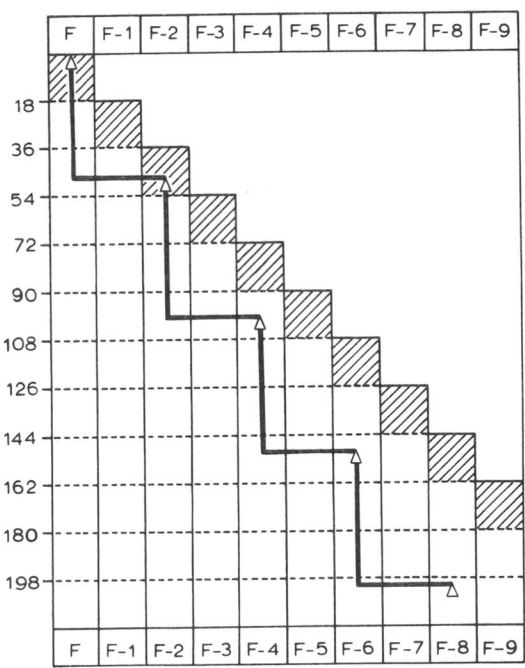

Figure 1.14

allowed to father children. In this diagram, I have assumed an interval of 50 years between each generation. As a result, underaging takes place: the man in the first generation was born when his age-group was assigned grade I; the man in the fifth generation when his age-group was assigned grade IV. In general, if over several generations the age difference between father and son is more than 36 years, then underaging will take place. In this artificial example it occurs at a regular rate of 14 years per generation. There is nothing in the rules of the age-group system that prevents something like this from happening.

Now consider another artificial example. Let us assume

(i)   That there is a certain age (call it m) after which every man marries as soon as the rules of the age-group system permit.

(ii) That the period of male fertility has a certain fixed length (call it f), which is the same for all men, irrespective of when they marry.

Imagine a society in which $m = 18$, and $f = 18$. Furthermore, imagine that each man has three sons who survive to adulthood, that the first of them is born in the year the father marries, and that they are spaced at equal intervals over the 18-year period of fertility. Underaging, it will be remembered, shows itself in its most extreme form among the youngest sons of youngest sons. In Figure 1.15, therefore, I have followed the fate of several generations of such men. Yet, as can be seen from the diagram, this descent line shows no tendency to underaging. In fact the sons of the two older brothers in each generation of this line will be born at precisely the same time as the sons of the youngest brother; but whereas, for example, a youngest brother is 18 when his first son is born and 36 when his last one is born, an oldest brother is 36 when his first son is born, and 54 when his last one is born.

Why is it that underaging does not occur in this society?[65] The answers lies in the relationship between three functions, m, f, and the length of the interval between the inauguration of the father's age-group and the inauguration of the son's. For a given group S, let us define g_S as the length of time between the inauguration of the group to which the fathers of the members of S belong and the

---

[65] In my example I have only considered the case where the founding father is born at the time of the inauguration of his age-group. Even if we assume that the founding father is born at some other time, underaging does not occur. It is unnecessary here to discuss these other possibilities.

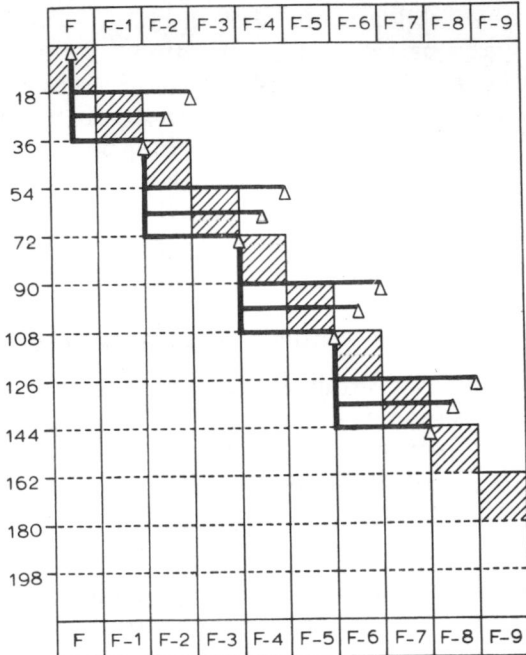

Figure 1.15

inauguration of S. We can now say that underaging will not occur provided that $m + f$ is not greater than the average of g_S.

This formulation suggests why it is that the Konso system is not underaging. Among the Konso, g_S is, as we know, constant at 36 years. Assumption (i) above is not too far from what obtains among the Konso (cf. Subsection 3 of this section). We do not know the minimum age at which men marry but can safely assume that it is not high. If it were true, say, of the Konso—as it evidently is of the Jie—that men rarely marry below the age of 30, then there would almost certainly be underaging.

Assumption (ii) is decidedly artificial: a proper description of the situation would be far more complex, and would take into account, among other things, the fact that the length of a man's period of fertility is related to his age at marriage. In the absence of a proper analysis, the essential point to note is that very long periods of male fertility must be uncommon among the Konso. This is consistent with the limited degree of polygyny found in this tribe—"only about one man in ten or more can afford the expense of a second wife, and fewer still have married three [Hallpike 1972: 105;

cf. 1972: 183.]'' The relationship between polygyny and the age of marriage of men has already been mentioned (p. 56 n. 29).

7. *Hallpike's computer simulation.* In his book on the Konso, Hallpike makes a pioneer attempt to work out the demographic implications of their age organization by simulating it on a computer. (A similar exercise is reported in Legesse 1973.) I have criticized this part of Hallpike's study in detail in Stewart (1972: 83–85); all that need be said here is that none of his conclusions can be accepted, since some of the assumptions on which the simulation is based are grossly unrealistic (e.g., the assumed infant mortality rate), while others are not reported at all (e.g., the initial distribution of the population among the grades).

3.2 Unique Paternal Linking

The Konso system, which assigns all sons to $F - 2$, is obviously similar to the g-group systems, which assign most sons to $F - 1$. All are instance of a type of age-group system which is widespread in East Africa, which has once or twice been reported from West Africa (see p. 103 n. 84), but which is not, to my knowledge, found anywhere else in the world. This type is the **paternal linking (PL) system,** that is, an age-group system whose rules are such that the age-group (or groups) that an individual may join are specified in relation to the group that his (or her) father joined.[66]

There are many different kinds of paternal linking system, some of which are discussed in the next section. For the moment I wish to consider mainly the type that is most characteristic of the Gada area. We can analyze this type by setting up a new model. It consists of the age-set model, plus the no-shrinking constraint, plus the following constraint:[67]

> There is an integer i, $i \geqslant 1$, a function of the system, such that any individual who joins a group, and whose father joined group F, joins group $F - i$.

[66] Among other things, this definition presupposes something we lack: an acceptable cross-cultural definition of the notion of a father. In practice, this particular lack will not cause us trouble (cf. p. 221 n. 25), but it will appear later (p. 111 and Chapter III, Section 5) that paternal linking systems demand to be treated in a larger context; and in that context the whole notion would probably have to be revised.

[67] We assume that the notation for levels has been introduced as part of the ordering characteristic.

I shall call this the **unique paternal linking (UPL) characteristic**, and will refer to the new model as the **UPL model**. A system that conforms exactly to the UPL model will be called a **strict UPL system,** and I shall use the loose term **UPL system** to refer both to systems that conform to the model and to systems that are more or less like the model but do not exactly conform to it.

It will be evident that the generation-set model simply delimits one particular type of strict UPL system, the type in which $i = 1$. Gada systems are UPL systems in which $i > 1$.

As far as their general demographic implications are concerned, all UPL systems are rather similar. Let us take as an example the kind of system that is widespread among the Galla, in which the inauguration interval is 8 years and sons are enrolled in $F - 5$. This entails that the sons' sons are in $F - 10$, and the sons' sons' sons in $F - 15$, and so on. If, on the other hand, the father is in $F - 1$, then the sons are in $F - 6$, the sons' sons in $F - 11$, and so on again. We can continue this until we reach the father who is in $F - 5$, at which point we are back with the "line" that we started with. (I shall use the term **descent stream** to refer to a "line" of age-groups of this kind in a UPL system.) All the men in the system are thus divided among five descent streams, membership in each of which is acquired by virtue of the fact that one's father was a member. For our present purposes it is enough to consider one of these streams in isolation, and from the point of view of a single stream the rules can be rephrased as follows: the inauguration interval is 40 years and sons join $F - 1$.

There is only one way in which a system can meet all the constraints of the UPL model, and that is by severely regulating the demographic structure of the society in which it exists. I shall refer to the period during which a member of age-group is allowed to beget, and bring up, sons as the **progenitive period** of that individual;[68] and to the period during which all the members of the age-group are allowed to do this as the progenitive period of that

---

[68] Where necessary, the term will also be extended to the period during which a man is allowed to beget, and bring up, daughters. In order to simplify the exposition, I am at present assuming that only sons join age-groups. This is true of most UPL systems, but probably not of all (the Takadi Konso, for instance, seem to offer an exception: see p. 105). But to introduce daughters would make matters a good deal more complicated, without any corresponding gain in insight.

The fact that the notion of a father has not been defined cross-culturally

group. The length of the progenitive period of an age-group S will be symbolized as p_S.

Now, let us symbolize the minimum enrolment age as E and imagine a strict UPL system in which $E = 0$ (i.e., in which sons may enrol at birth). We take it that sons join $F - i$, $i \geqslant 1$. From what was said in Section 1.2.3, it follows that the only people who can join $F - i$ are those born during the cessation interval of $F - i$. For this reason $p_F \leqslant c_{F-i}$.

We can illustrate this from Figure 1.13. Imagine that the Konso decide to introduce whatever demographic restrictions are necessary in order to make their system conform exactly to the UPL model. It will be necessary for them to restrict the recruitment period of each age-group, so as to eliminate overlapping. Let us take it that they decide that the recruitment period of each set is to coincide with its inauguration interval, so that $c_S = v_S$ for all S. Set $F - 2$ in Figure 1.13 recruits its members between the years 36 and 54. Since $E = 0$, the progenitive period of F must fall between the same years.

What happens if E has some other value? A glance at Figure 1.13 makes the answer obvious. If, say, the Konso then decide that the enrolment age is to be 9 years, this means merely that the progenitive period of F, instead of running from 36 to 54, will have to run from 27 to 45. (I assume that they want the progenitive period to be as long as possible; it could be shorter, but it would still have to fall between these years.) A boy born in the year 27 reaches the enrolment age in the year 36, just when the new set, $F - 2$, begins recruiting. On the other hand, a boy born in the year 46 would only reach the enrolment age in 55, by which time $F - 2$ would have ceased recruiting.

Let us now state this in more general terms. Whatever the value of E, it is still true that $p_F \leqslant c_{F-i}$ in a strict UPL system. All that E affects is the period of time within which the progenitive period of F falls: taking it that $E \geqslant 0$, we can say that the progenitive period of F must begin not more than E years before the beginning of the

---

makes the application of the notion of a progenitive period uncertain in at least one case, that of the Karimojong (cf. p. 96 n. 72).

The progenitive period is a period of time defined by the rules of the system, and it may be open-ended. It should not be confused with two other demographic concepts: the individual's period of fecundity (i.e., the period during which he is physically capable of producing children) and his period of fertility (i.e., the period during which he actually does produce children). For a given individual these three periods may well be different.

cessation interval of $F - i$, and must end not less than E years before the end of the cessation interval of $F - i$. In the simplest case, where $E = 0$, and $p_F = c_{F-i}$, the progenitive period of F and the cessation interval of $F - i$ fall at exactly the same time.

Restrictions on the progenitive period exist in many Gada systems, but as far as I know there are no recorded instances where they are so severe that the system meets all the constraints of the UPL model. In the well-attested instances of systems with demographic restrictions, at least some overlapping and waiting occur. This, as we saw, is the case among the Konso, though we also noted that with Jensen's additional rule the system would not have suffered from overlapping.

On the other hand, it appears that the restrictions on the father's progenitive period are usually such that generational spread is kept in check. Let us consider how this can be done. We know that over- and underaging arise when the age-range of each generation is greater than the age-range of the preceding generation. To obviate these problems, then, we must eliminate this growth in the age-range of successive generations. How does the growth occur? A glance at Figure 1.6 or Figure 1.7 supplies the answer. The intervals between the oldest members of successive generations are shorter than are the intervals between the youngest members of successive generations. If these intervals are made the same, then the growth stops, as may be seen from Figure 1.16. In that diagram, the interval has been stabilized at 30 years, and as a result each generation has the same age-range. (The age-range happens to be 20 years, but it could be any other quantity, since it is quite independent of the interval between generations.) In order to achieve this, one needs only two rules: a man gains the right to beget sons 30 years after his father gains that right, and he loses the right 30 years after his father loses it.[69]

Even with rules of this type, however, we have not obviated the possibilities of under- and overaging. In Figure 1.17 the same demographic structure is assumed as in Figure 1.16; but now a UPL system has been introduced. Sons are supposed to join $F - 1$, and the inauguration interval is 50 years. The horizontal broken lines mark

---

[69] It follows, then, that when I speak of the interval between successive generations as being stabilized or fixed at n years, what I mean is that given any two adjacent generations, the oldest member of the junior generation will be at least n years younger than the oldest member of the senior generation, and that the youngest member of the junior generation will be not more than n years younger than the youngest member of the senior generation.

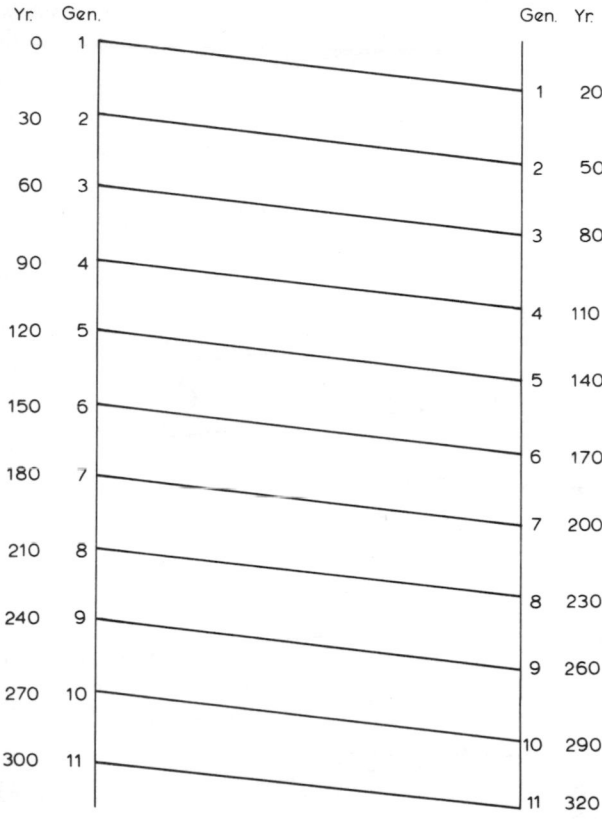

Figure 1.16

the points in time at which the successive groups are inaugurated, and the numbers in the columns headed A.G. (for age-group) stand for the names of the groups. As the diagram shows, the system suffers from overaging; the symptoms may be first waiting and then shrinking. If an attempt were made to remedy the situation by reducing the inauguration interval to something less than 30 years, then the system would suffer from underaging. Note, however, that whatever the inauguration interval, a system operating in this kind of demographic environment cannot suffer *simultaneously* from over- and underaging. Obviously, in order to have neither of these problems the inauguration interval and the interval between successive generations must be the same, and this is the situation represented on Figure 1.18.

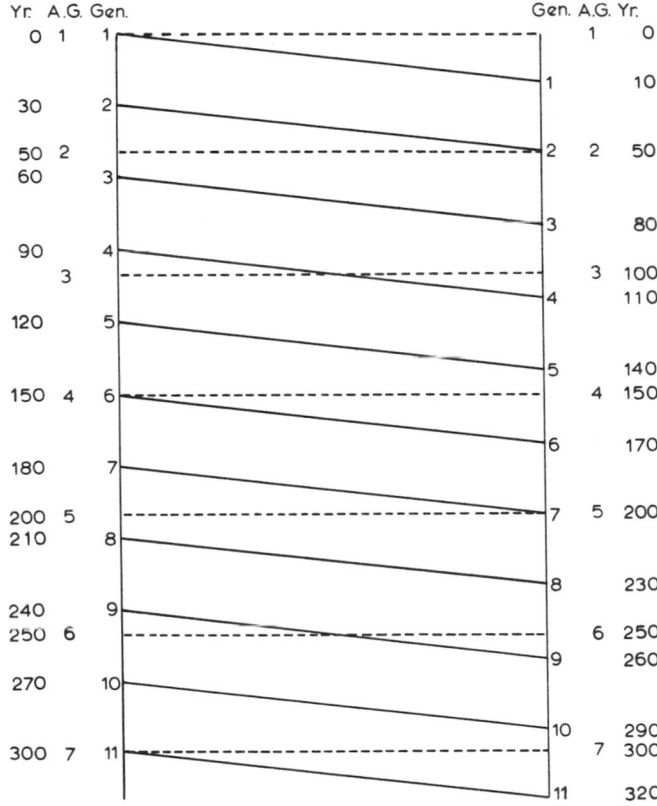

Figure 1.17

It appears, then, that a system can eliminate over- and under-aging by doing two things: by preventing the growth in the age-range of successive generations, and by fixing the interval between generations at the same figure as the f–s (inauguration) interval, that is, the interval between the inauguration of the father's group and the inauguration of the son's group. There remains, however, one other parameter which the system must take into account, and that is the age-range of the generation.

We can best approach this question by considering two extreme possibilities. One is the age-range which is so small that the system conforms exactly to the UPL model, that is, an age-range which in every case equals (or is less than) the cessation interval of the age-set which that generation is to join. Just how small this age-range must

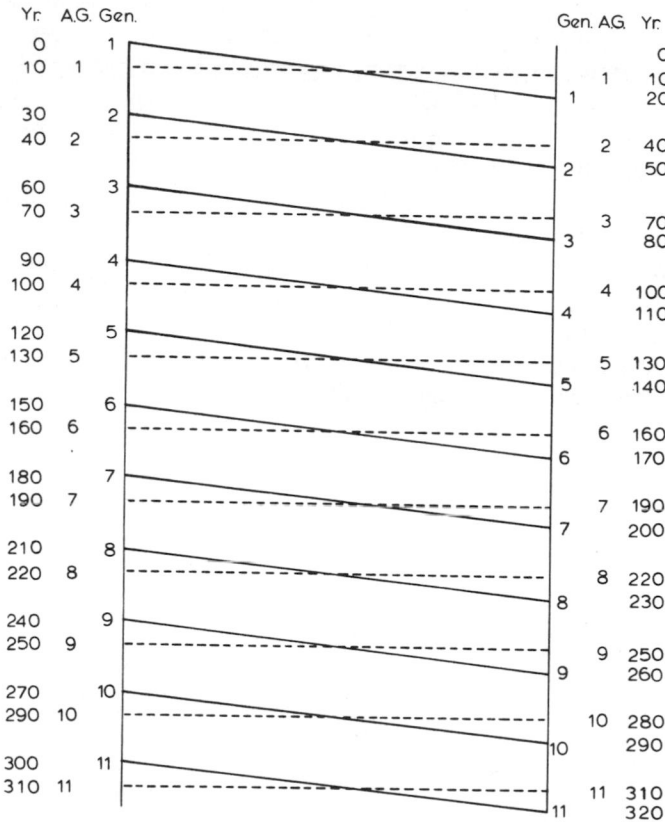

Yr. A.G. Gen.   Gen. AG. Yr.

Figure 1.18

be depends largely on the value of i. Roughly speaking, the greater the value of i, the smaller the maximum possible age-range. To illustrate this, imagine that we were to introduce demographic restrictions which made the known UPL systems conform strictly to the UPL model. In the g-set systems (i.e., the ones in which $i = 1$), the age-range of a generation could be a matter of decades; among the Konso, where $i = 2$, the age-range of each generation would be at most 18 years; in the standard Galla systems,[70] where $i = 5$, the

---

[70] By a standard Galla system I mean any Gada system in which $i = 5$ and in which the inauguration interval is fixed at 8 years. Systems that have these two characteristics are very widespread among the Galla, though the systems differ considerably from one another in other respects.

age-range of each generation would be no more than 8 years (see further Appendix 4).

The other extreme possibility is a very large age-range, say 100 years. Let us take it that the interval between successive generations and the f—s inauguration interval are both 30 years. There are now various possibilities, depending on the phasing of these two intervals. Assume, at one extreme, that each age-group is inaugurated at just that point in time at which the first member of the corresponding generation is born (Figure 1.19). If the system is to retain the UPL characteristic and the no-shrinking characteristic, then in all likelihood there will be overlapping on a considerable scale. Assume, at the other extreme, that each age-group is inaugurated at just that point in time when the last member of the corresponding generation

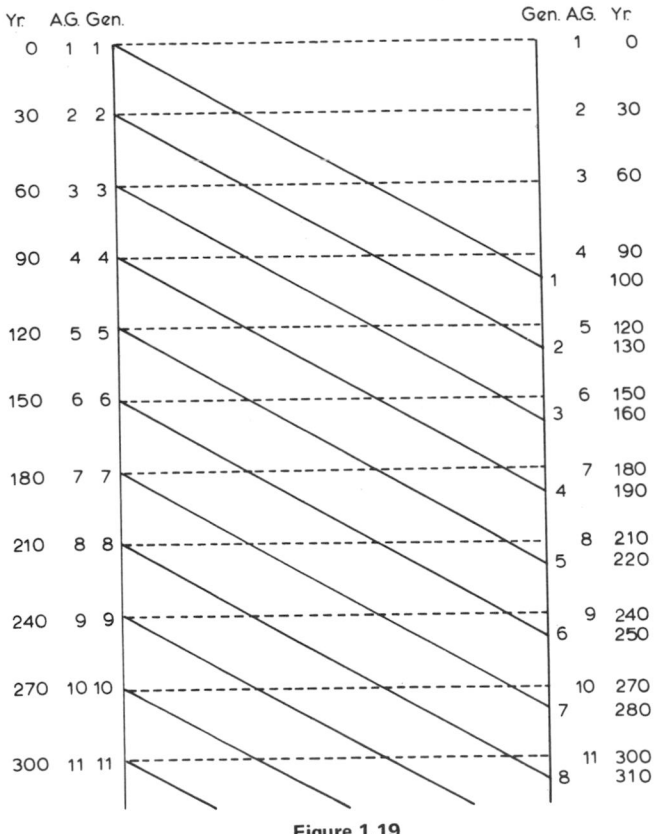

Figure 1.19

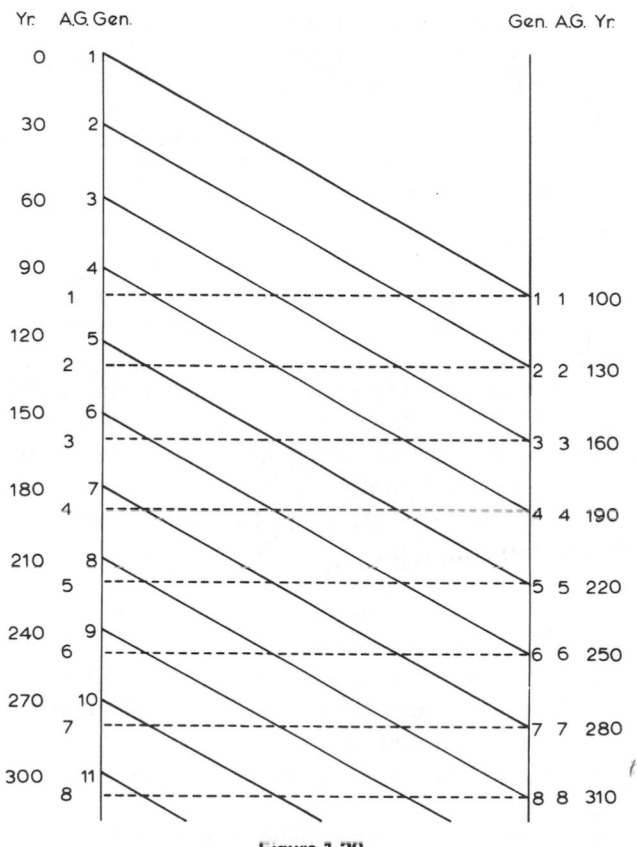

Figure 1.20

is born (Figure 1.20). Now there is waiting to the point where the system suffers from shrinking. Intermediate cases, as we know, will be characterized by both overlapping and waiting. The systems suffer from what one might call **arrested over-** and/or **underaging**, for these problems are not growing more severe generation by generation.

In sum, then, the position is roughly as follows. If a UPL system is to keep generational spread in check, then it must have rules which, given the demographic environment in which it operates, produce generations with the following characteristics:

(i) The age-range of any given generation is fairly small (and from this it follows that the age-range of successive generations cannot be growing).

(ii) The interval between any two generations is about the
      same as the interval between the inauguration of the
      groups that these generations must join.[71]

We know that a great many Gada systems deal (or dealt) with
the problems inherent in UPL systems by means of demographic
restrictions, even though the only such systems for which there is
fairly detailed evidence are those of the Konso and of the Borana
Galla (on which see Chapter II, Section 4.3.1). But, fragmentary
though the data on other systems may be, they are sufficient to give
a general idea of how the demographic restrictions are (or were)
implemented.

Two main methods are used in regulating the individual's pro-
gentive period. One—which can only be used to counter overaging—is
to prevent him from marrying until a certain point in time. We have
already encountered this method among the Konso and among the
Karimojong,[72] and we shall meet it again more than once.[73] Nowadays it is probably the most commonly used method of preventing
overaging, but at one time a second procedure was also widespread,
at least among the Galla: the exposure of children. This practice
naturally attracted the attention of observers, and Michels (1941:
169 ff.) has collected references to it going back as far as the
sixteenth century. In recent times this custom has tended to die out,
though it still exists among the Borana Galla. We can group abortion—employed, for instance, by some Konso (p. 82)—under the
same heading as exposure.

The exposure of children can be used to obviate both over- and
underaging. The sources, however, seem to refer to it only in the
context of overaging, that is to say, they mention only the exposure

---

[71] The notion of the interval between two adjacent generations presents no
particular problems as long as all generations have much the same age-range (see
p. 90 n. 69).

[72] The case of the Karimojong, of course, is not so simple; in the absence of
a generally accepted cross-cultural definition of marriage there are no compelling
grounds for refusing the title of "marriage" to the relationship that Farina and
Dyson-Hudson call "concubinage."

[73] It is worth mentioning that paternal linking systems are not the only
age-group systems in which the point in time at which a man may marry is
related to his age-group or age-grade. See, for example, Mercier (1971: 99) on
the Somba and the various sources on the Masai (e.g., Fosbrooke 1948: 30,
quoted on p. 154). (It should perhaps be added that among the Masai there is
some preference for enrolling sons in F − 2, though in practice most sons join a
more junior group. See Jacobs 1965a: 292 f.).

of children born *before* a certain time, and not the exposure of those born *after* a certain time. No doubt the reason for this is that in the standard Galla system the f—s inauguration interval is 40 years. As one might expect, the demographic structure of the Galla appears to be such that, under these circumstances, overaging is much more of a problem than underaging (cf. Haberland 1963: 308, 452, 536). It may be that there was—at least in some systems—a rule which demanded the exposure of children born after a certain time, but that in practice this rule was rarely called into operation and therefore failed to strike the observers; or it may be that it was possible, as among the Konso, to dispense altogether with a rule to prevent underaging without serious consequences following (cf. Section 3.1.2.6 of this chapter).

Restricting the progenitive period may perhaps be the most common way of coming to terms with generational spread, but it is by no means the only one. Another possibility is simply to accept its effects. How frequently this course was adopted, it is impossible to say. Many of the clearest accounts of Gada systems come from the pen of Enrico Cerulli, who in his various writings must have described at least a score of different systems. Unfortunately, however, he was not conscious of the problem of generational spread (as may be seen, for instance, from Cerulli 1968). As a result, he made no special inquiries about how it was dealt with. Sometimes (as will appear in a moment) he reports rules that clearly do counteract over- or underaging, but without himself fully realizing their significance. Very often he reports no such rules, yet we cannot safely infer from this that in all these instances the effects of generational spread went unchecked. The same considerations apply also to other, less important, ethnographers, and this is one reason why we lack detailed descriptions of systems with demographic restrictions.

There are, however, scholars who are well aware of over- and underaging, and who report systems concerning which they explicitly state that there are no rules to counteract these processes. Let me give two examples. The Darassa system, as described by Jensen (1936: 315 ff.),[74] has a 10-year inauguration interval and places sons in $F - 2$. It suffers not only from underaging (which one would

[74] A rather different account is given by Guidi (1939: 378 f.). It seems mostly likely, however, that Jensen's is the correct version. For one thing, it is much more circumstantial, for another, it is—as Jensen himself pointed out (1941: 86)—confirmed by two other observers, Giaccardi (1937: 1558) and Moreno (1938: 456).

expect) but also from overaging. Indeed, Jensen's impression was that overaging was the more marked of the two processes, and he speculates that at some earlier stage the f—s inauguration interval may have been not 20, but 40 years (1936: 318, 320). A second example comes from Haberland (1963: 452). The lowland Arussi have a standard Galla system, but without any rules to counteract over- and underaging. As a result, both processes are at work. Overaging, however, is the predominant one, and its effects are so marked that the number of participants in the system is continually falling (because of shrinking).

In both these instances it is said that the people feel that something has gone wrong with their system, but have no memory of a time when there were checks on generational spread. Jensen and Haberland assume that originally these systems must have had rules regulating marriage or the birth of children or both. There is some support for this assumption. Certain Galla tribes in which the absence of such rules and the 40-year f—s inauguration interval have combined to produce overaging still preserve the memory of a time when marriage was regulated or when children born at the wrong time were exposed, even though such practices have been abandoned for many decades (Haberland 1963: 312, 316, 390). The fact that demographic restrictions have often fallen into desuetude during (at least) the last 100 years or so[75] is another reason why we lack detailed information about them.

It seems that all systems which do not check generational

---

[75] The assumption that any system which is suffering the effects of overaging, underaging, or both of these must at one time have had demographic regulations is shared, I think, by virtually everyone who has studied these questions. If this assumption is correct, then the demographic regulations certainly began to disappear well over a century ago. The clearest evidence on this comes from Cecchi (1886), who gives an account of the Gada system of the Shoa Galla—it is not possible to localize his data any more precisely—as he found it around 1880. He describes a standard Galla system in which men are all circumcised simultaneously while their group is at the fourth level. (Cecchi's account is rather confused with regard to the exact point in time at which this ceremony takes place, but this need not concern us here. See further the useful analysis in Michels 1941: 85 ff.) At the end of his description Cecchi writes:

> All this is arranged in such a fashion, that between the circumcision of the father and the circumcision of the son there is always a period of 40 years; that is, of 5 *gada*. As a result of this regulation it generally happens that both very small infants are circumcised and old men of 80 [1886: 530].

spread differ from the UPL model in that they permit waiting (as a result of overaging) and overlapping (as a result of underaging). Systems that restrict the progenitive period also, as far as we know, all differ from the model in at least these respects; but in the systems that take no measures against over- and underaging the degree of deviation is evidently much greater; furthermore, it must be increasing generation by generation. As we know, standard Galla systems suffer above all from overaging; and this, in its extreme form, leads to shrinking. We have just encountered one instance of this among the lowland Arussi; of another such system (among the Alabdu Galla, a subgroup of the Guji) Haberland writes that "there are many old men whose parents—if they were still alive—would not yet belong to the system! [1963: 309]"

So far we have considered two types of reaction to the problem of generational spread: one is to deal with it by means of demographic restrictions, the other is simply to accept its effects. A third type of reaction is to deal with the problem—insofar as it is dealt with—either by other means than demographic restrictions or by a combination of demographic restrictions and other means. These other means all involve violating one or other of the constraints of the UPL model.

An instance of this third type of reaction is perhaps found among the Borana, who have a standard Galla system. They are said to hold over- and underaging in check by rules that, in effect, ensure that the interval between successive generations is 40 years and that the age-range of each generation is no more than 53 years. I say "in effect" because it is only overaging that is dealt with by a demographic restriction (a rule forbidding a man to produce sons until 40 years after his father has gained that right); underaging is dealt with, not by forbidding a man to have children after a certain point in time, but (according to some sources) simply by excluding any children born after the proper time (and their descendants) from the system. The system therefore violates the no-shrinking constraint, but in a quite different way from any of the systems so far examined; for in the other systems, shrinking, insofar as it was related to generational spread, was the outcome of overaging. (For further details on the Borana, see Chapter II, Section 4.3.1.)

A stratagem adopted in several UPL systems is to permit what I shall refer to as (vertical) shifting, that is, resignation from one age-group and enrolment in another in the same sequence. The systems that allow this violate the no-resigning characteristic, and also, perhaps, the no-overlapping characteristic.[76] Shifting occurs (as far as one can tell) in the following circumstances. In accordance with the UPL rule, an individual joins $F - i$; but if the system suffers from underaging and if the individual is one of the younger members of his generation, then he may be below what is considered to be the proper age for members of that group (above all if the group is in an age-grade suitable for older people). He therefore shifts to a more junior group. Presumably shifting could also be used to some extent in dealing with overaging, but its use here seems rather paradoxical: why wait till $F - i$ is inaugurated, enrol in it, and then shift upward to some group that was inaugurated before $F - i$?

As far as the Galla are concerned, shifting, both upward and downward, is mentioned as occurring among certain Shoa subtribes (Knutsson 1967: 176). It is also one of the expedients adopted in the Kuria g-group system (see Section 6 of this chapter for another expedient). Here again, it can occur in both directions, but, as one would expect, it is usually downward (Ruel 1962: 27).[77] In both

---

[76] A word on the relationship between shifting and overlapping may be useful. Obviously, shifting necessarily involves a violation of the no-resigning constraint, but it does not necessarily involve overlapping. The possibilities are represented in Table 1.2, which shows that there are two possible kinds of shifting, with and without overlapping. For instances of systems that permit only shifting without overlapping, see the analyses of the Zanaki (Section 2.3 of this chapter) and of the Garbichcho Sidama (Section 3.3 of this chapter). In general, however, it is not necessary to distinguish between the two types of shifting, and they are noted here mainly to make their relationship to overlapping clear. To obviate possible misunderstanding of Table 1.2, I should add that it does not *define* shifting: it would be possible, for instance, to allow both resignation and overlapping and yet not allow shifting.

TABLE 1.2

		RESIGNATION	
		Permitted	Forbidden
	Permitted	Shifting with overlapping	Overlapping
OVERLAPPING			
	Forbidden	Shifting without overlapping	Corresponds to model

[77] Ruel himself relates the predominance of downward shifting to the fact that the inauguration interval of the g-group system tends to be rather long. But, as we know, a long interval is associated with overaging, which, if it were to be remedied by shifting at all, would lead to upward shifting.

these cases, incidentally, shifting can also occur for reasons other than those mentioned here. The Kuria's neighbors, the Zanaki, also counteract underaging by downward shifting; their system is unusual in this context in that the minimum enrolment age is not zero but somewhere in the teens (see further Section 2.3 of this chapter). Finally, it is possible that the Kikuyu g-group system used this method, though the evidence here is thin (see p. 178).[78]

To conclude this section, let me mention some standard Galla systems which deal with the problems of UPL systems by abandoning strict conformity to the UPL constraint. One Shoa Galla subtribe (the Gombichchu) copes with the overaging that is typical of these systems by the following rule: if a man fathers a son before joining his age-group, then that son joins the same age-group as his father. In other words, he joins F rather than F − 5 (Cerulli 1929: 50).[79] An even more remarkable rule is reported from some other Shoa Galla subtribes: if, at a time when he joins an age-group (call it F + 5), a man already has a grandson (presumably a son's son), then the grandson may (must?) enrol in the same group as his grandfather, that is, the grandson joins F + 5 rather than F − 5 (Haberland 1963: 537; Knutsson 1967: 175).[80]

It is also possible to have a rule of this type to deal with underaging: Cerulli (1922: 169) mentions one in the Gada system of

---

[78] On p. 73 we noted the existence of upward shifting among the Karimojong. It arose, however, not in relation to the effects on the system of generational spread but in relation to the fact that the inauguration of a new g-group had been unduly postponed. One's impression in this case is that the shifting was merely an emergency measure and not an activity considered by the participants in the system to be strictly in accordance with the rules.

[79] Cerulli himself appears not to have realized the significance of this rule, and nor, I think, did Michels, who quotes Cerulli verbatim (1941: 92). Michels was aware of the processes that he calls *overjaring* and *verjonging*—they had been brought to light by Jensen some years before—but he did not pay them sufficient attention. Jensen, of course, did appreciate the effects of this rule (1936: 563; 1941: 85; 1942: 221 f.).

[80] I have given this rule in the form in which it is reported by Haberland. Knutsson's version is slightly different—"a man who was already very old when he was initiated . . . could be allowed to bring his grandson with him." Haberland says nothing about having to be very old. I do not know whether Knutsson learnt of the F + 5 rule at first hand or whether he derived it from Haberland.

Both Haberland and Knutsson give accounts of a Shoa Galla Gada system that include material from several different subtribes. Haberland's data seem to refer primarily to the Gulalle and Galan, perhaps also to the Metta (1963: 544, 536). Knutsson says he collected his information "particularly from the Galan, Meta, and Ada tribal areas [1967: 170]."

the Leqa subtribe of the Machcha Galla. His account is not completely clear,[81] but the position seems to be essentially as follows.
When an age-group is at the fourth level, it is assigned a certain grade
(Qondala), and as a result it has to perform four ceremonies in
succession, one each year, beginning the year after it reaches the
fourth level. The ceremonies are thus (ideally) completed 28 years
after the inauguration of the age-group. Now, if a man in group F has
a son before group F − 5 has performed the fourth of these ceremonies, then that son joins F − 5; but if the son is born later, then he
joins F − 10. (It is not known whether there is any rule to deal with
overaging in the system, though we have a hint suggesting that
exposure may once have been the method employed—see Cerulli
1922: 127.)[82]

3.3 * Other Types of Paternal Linking

Up to now the discussion has been largely concerned with UPL
systems, but there are in fact many other types of paternal linking.
In this section I shall consider all those for which there is adequate
evidence.

One of the most easily distinguished types is the **negative
paternal linking system**. In a system of this kind, sons may join F − i,
i ⩾ 1, or any more junior group, but may not join any age-group
senior to F − i. We have in fact already encountered a system of this
sort among the Karimojong, whose rule is that sons must join F − 1
or a more junior group. In this particular case an additional factor is
involved, the strong preference for enrolling sons in F − 1. It is not

---

[81] What Cerulli, in effect, says is as follows: if F − 5 is in the first year of
the Qondala grade, then the son of a man in F joins it; if F − 5 is in the fifth year
of the Qondala grade and has completed the four ceremonies, then the son of a
man in F joins F − 10. Strictly speaking, then, we do not know what happens to
the son of a man in F if F − 5 is in the second, third, or fourth year of
Qondala; but I do not think that there can be any real doubt about the matter.
Note, incidentally, that there is a misprint on p. 169 of Cerulli (1922), ten lines
from the top: for "*Gada B*" read "*Gada A*." Note also that footnote 1 on the
same page, and the text it relates to, are misleading: the child will enter power
(i.e., the Luba grades) 84 years after his birth, and leave it 92 years after his
birth.

[82] Perhaps I may add a query here. Adoption is a common practice among
the Galla. Haberland suggests, for instance, that among the Shoa every third or
fourth individual is adopted (1963: 544). It would be interesting to know how
this practice relates to the Gada system and in particular to the problems of
generational spread.

clear to what extent analogous preferences exist in other negative PL systems.

Most of the other instances of negative PL systems are also East African. There is a whole cluster of systems that are closely related to each other in various ways—its recorded members are the Tugen, Nandi, Kipsigis, Keyo, Pokot, Dorobo, and Tiriki, but no doubt there are more—in which sons must join F − 2 or a more junior group; [83] and it also seems to be considered desirable that at least the eldest son should, if at all possible, join F − 2. The Samburu, in contrast, place all sons in F − 3 or a more junior group (Spencer 1965: 83, 149 f.). I know of a single instance of a system of this type in West Africa, among the Bainouk of Senegal. It is of special interest because reports of paternal linking from West Africa are so rare.[84] In

[83] The sources on the Tugen, the Nandi, the Dorobo, and the Tiriki are clear as regards this rule (Kettel 1972; Huntingford 1953: 60 ff.; 1951: 31; Sangree 1966: 76). Peristiany (1939: 30) is equally unambiguous about its existence among the Kipsigis, and I have no hesitation in accepting his statement, even though Orchardson nowhere reports this rule, and nor, for that matter, do Barton (1923), Dobbs (1921), or Manners (1967). As for the Keyo, negative paternal linking is referred to obscurely by Massam (1927: 53 f., 68) and much more clearly in Welbourn (1968: 214). Serge Torday, who did 3 months' fieldwork among the Keyo in 1966 and has subsequently paid them a brief visit, confirms in a private communication that such a rule does indeed exist. On the Pokot, see the slightly obscure remarks in Peristiany (1975: 180 f.; 1951: 292).

[84] I have only encountered one other account of paternal linking from that region. Paulme (1971b) describes UPL systems among some of the Lagoon tribes of the Ivory Coast: the Atié, the Mbato, certain Ebrié groups (1971b: 223 n. 12), and the Abouré (1971b: 208, 252). For the moment, however, this report should be treated with reserve. Paulme seems to describe systems that meet all the constraints of the UPL model (except, no doubt, that they lack the enrolment characteristic); but there is no mention either of any demographic restrictions or of under- or overaging. We can say with confidence, therefore, that *something* is wrong with her account. Furthermore, there are other recent descriptions of the age organization of two of these tribes, and these make no mention either of paternal linking or of demographic restrictions. These other descriptions are as follows. On the Abouré, see Clignet (1970: 70) and, much more important, Niangoran-Bouah (1960, 1964, 1965; the section dealing with age-groups in the 1965 publication is a virtually verbatim copy of the corresponding section in the 1960 publication, and there are some interesting differences between this description and the one in the 1964 publication). On the Ebrié, Bouscayrol (1949), Person (1963), and Niangoran-Bouah (1969). Certain data given by Person (1963: 74 at top) suggest how Paulme may have come to believe that the system was characterized by unique paternal linking. (There is also information on the Ebrié age-groups in Yegnan 1968, but it does not relate to any of the regions for which Paulme claims paternal linking.)

this system the rules are such that sons must join $F - 2$ or a more junior group (Girard 1965: 53).

We know from our discussion of the Karimojong that a negative PL system will not suffer from the problem of underaging. What is more, such a system might in principle also be exempt from the problem of overaging. Roughly speaking, this would be the case if the f⌐s inauguration interval[85] were less than the minimum age at which men produced sons. If, for example, the f⌐s interval were 10 years, then there would be no problem of overaging and therefore no need for special rules to deal with it. Furthermore, in this case the existence of a negative PL rule[86] would not prevent the system from conforming exactly to the age-set model (assuming the proper initial state for the system).

A priori, however, we would not expect to find a system like this. If it were in any case impossible for a man to join a group senior to $F - i$, then it would be surprising if there were a rule forbidding him to do so. What we would expect is a situation in which some men, at least, reach the minimum enrolment age before $F - i$ is inaugurated—in terms of our model, a system that is characterized by waiting. And this is indeed what we find. From the point of view of the topics under consideration, the simplest of our systems is that of the Bainouk. It appears that they have a rule that successive groups should be inaugurated at intervals of 20 years. Since sons must join $F - 2$ or a more junior group, this means that in this case the f⌐s inauguration interval is 40 years. We also have good evidence on the Nandi: here the f⌐s interval is about 30 years, evidently with little variation (Huntingford 1953: 64 ff.). The Kipsigis and Keyo data are much less satisfactory, but the probability is that the f⌐s interval in these systems was also about 30 years. In the Samburu system, on the other hand, the interval is approximately 40 years.

Given f⌐s intervals of this kind, overaging is clearly a problem. In all these systems the solution adopted is the same: a man is not allowed to marry until he is enrolled in his age-group (among the Samburu, indeed, marriage is not allowed until some time after the individual has enrolled; see Chapter II, Section 4.2.3). Girard (1965:

[85] In the case of a negative PL system, the f⌐s inauguration interval is defined as the interval between the inauguration of the father's group and the inauguration of the most senior group that the son may join, i.e., $F - i$.

[86] I shall use the term PL rule—and its derivatives and analogues—in a loose way to refer to the rule (or rules) by virtue of which a system is categorized as a PL system (or whatever it may be).

58) and Spencer (1965: 95 ff.)—especially the latter—have some interesting comments on how the marriage rule gives the old men the possibility of extensive polygyny (see also Dorjahn 1959: 108 f., van de Walle 1968: 217 ff.). It may be that also among the Keyo the old men have many wives, though perhaps not as a result of this particular rule (Massam 1927: 160 f.). On the other hand, there is evidence that this kind of situation does not obtain among the Dorobo, and it may be that it does not obtain among the Nandi and the Kipsigis either.[87] Since it does not appear that the girls in these tribes marry markedly later in life than Samburu or Bainouk girls, it is probable that the f–s interval is considerably shorter in these systems than in those of the Samburu and Bainouk.

In addition to the fairly clear-cut categories of PL system that we have so far encountered—UPL systems and negative PL systems—there exist a number of other types less amenable to sharp categorization.

One is what may be called the **complex paternal linking** system. In a system of this kind, those of a man's offspring who are eligible to join the system are divided into two or more classes according to some particular criteria; and the age-group affiliation of each of these classes is determined by a PL rule which is different from that determining the age-group affiliation of any other class.

One criterion which can be used in a system of this kind is sex. The Konso of the Takadi area inaugurate new age-groups at intervals of 9 years,[88] and assign all sons to F − 3. Daughters, however, are

[87] On the Dorobo, see Huntingford (1969: 64). The same author says of the Nandi that "the incidence of polygyny is not large: not more than about 10% of marriages seem to be polygynous, and then a man seldom has more than two or at most three wives [1969: 28]." But Snell writes "Polygyny was, of course, widely practised by the tribe, but while it was very common for a man to have two wives, and fairly common to find men with three, more than this number was rare [1954: 21]." The evidence on the Kipsigis is equally hard to make sense of: see Barton (1923: 69), Orchardson (1930–1931: 104), Manners (1967: 254), and Peristiany (1939: 56, where the low age of marriage for men implies only a limited amount of polygyny, and 74). For accurate methods of reporting on the prevalence of polygyny, see Dorjahn (1959) and van de Walle (1968: 194 ff).

[88] The figure of 9 years, like all the other data on the Takadi Konso system, is derived from Hallpike (1972: 194 ff). As mentioned in Section 3.1.2.2 of this chapter, Jensen's account of this system is very different from Hallpike's. So, for example, he states that the inauguration interval is 10 years (1954: 8). Hallpike, however, presents information which suggests very strongly that Jensen was mistaken on this point (1972: 199).

TABLE 1.3

Father	Son	Son's group	f⁻s interval
Eldest	Eldest	F − 6	30 years
Eldest	Youngest	F − 7	35 years
Younger	Eldest	F − 5	25 years
Younger	Younger	F − 6	30 years

assigned to F − 2. In this system—as in the Garati Konso system—members of a group are not allowed to marry until the group reaches level 2. (There seems to be no rule to prevent underaging, which is unexpected in a system where the f⁻s interval is only 27 years.) The PL rule thus allows girls to marry earlier than their brothers. We can call a system like this a **sexual PL system**.

Another type of complex PL system is what may be called a **birth order PL system**, that is, one in which the criterion used is birth order. The Zanaki g-groups, discussed in Section 2.3 of this chapter, constitute one system of this kind. Another, rather elaborate, one exists among the Konso of the Turo area and has recently been described by Hallpike (1972: 200 ff.). His account is brief and leaves some questions open, but the outlines come over clearly enough. He describes what are in effect four UPL rules, based on categorizing male offspring as "eldest sons" (i.e., first-born sons) and "younger sons" (all other sons). The system assigns age-groups in the fashion indicated in Table 1.3.

The equation of the eldest sons of eldest sons with the younger sons of younger sons is very curious. The system prevents overaging by the rule that a man may only marry when his age-group reaches level 3, that is, 10 years after its inauguration. (We are not told what the minimum enrolment age is, but presumably it is zero.) There is no mention of any rule that would obviate the possibility of underaging, but Hallpike's observations in the field suggest that given the demographic structure of the people it does not in fact occur to any considerable extent (1972: 202).[89] Considered in relation to our model, this system must, no doubt, be characterized by some overlapping and waiting.

A birth order PL system that differs rather more widely from the age-set model has been described by Stanley and Karsten (1968).

[89] Hallpike's computer simulation also suggests that this is the case (1972: 214), but no weight can be attached to it as evidence (see Section 3.1.2.7 of this chapter).

It exists among the Garbichcho subtribe of the Sidama.[90] In this system the inauguration interval is 7 years. First-born sons are subject to a UPL rule: they must all join $F - 4$. This evidently leads to both waiting and overlapping. All other sons are subject to a modified negative PL rule. It seems that if they are born before the ceremony at which $F - 4$ is inaugurated, then they join $F - 4$, whatever their age. If they are born later, then they may join any junior group except $F - 5$ (which always has the same name as F, since the groups are named from a cycle of five names). In the case of younger sons, then, there is no overlapping, but some waiting. Just how much is not clear: if they join a group at birth even if they are born after the inauguration of $F - 4$, then only as much as is involved in waiting for the inauguration of $F - 6$; if—as seems more likely from the vague indications in the source—they join in their teens if they are born after the inauguration of $F - 4$, then there is more.

The system contains no special rules to deal with over- and underaging,[91] and as a result the age-range of each group is very great (Stanley and Karsten 1968: 96). The birth order PL rules, however, are such that the absence of checks on generational spread does not affect the system as much as it would a UPL system. Furthermore, there is a rule to deal with one of the problems that arises from overaging. If a youth is "old enough for initiation" (1968: 95)—this may be in the early teens (1968: 97)—when $F - 2$ is inaugurated, then he may join $F - 2$ (though presumably he would not be allowed to join $F - 3$ in this way). When $F - 4$ is finally inaugurated, he ceases to be a member of $F - 2$ and becomes a member of $F - 4$, having been initiated a second time.[92] It appears that all of this man's sons are treated as the offspring of a member of $F - 4$, so this rule can only mitigate the effects of overaging in the short run. I take it that the rule applies to all sons alike, whether first-born or not.

Considered in relation to the age-set model, then, the system has three deviant features: overlapping, waiting, and resigning. The rules that produce these features are complicated and provide a good indication of the difficulties that would face an attempt to build a

---

[90] An extensive account has been published of the age organization of another Sidama subtribe, the Aleta (Hamer 1970); I was unable to understand how this system works, but it is evidently different from that of the Garbichcho.

[91] Underaging, of course, can only be a problem for first-born sons, since it is only they who are subject to a UPL rule.

[92] This is an instance of shifting without overlapping (cf. p. 100 n. 76).

model sufficiently flexible for us not to have to describe a system like this in ad hoc terms.

To conclude this section I shall describe a system that shows up clearly the inadequacy of the notion of paternal linking. This system exists among the Rendille, and like that of their neighbors, the Samburu, it has been described by Paul Spencer.[93]

Fundamentally, the Rendille operate a negative PL system. The rule is that sons join $F - 3$ or a more junior group, with something of a preference for $F - 3$. As in other systems of this type, overaging is prevented by forbidding a man to marry before he has joined his group (among the Rendille, in fact, he does not generally gain this right until perhaps 11 years after the inauguration of his group). The inauguration interval averages out at the same as the Samburu inter-val—that is, 13 or 14 years or so—though in the case of the Rendille there are certain complications surrounding the inauguration interval which are absent in the Samburu system. For present purposes, however, these can be ignored.

So far, then, the Rendille system is very similar to that of the Samburu. But the Rendille also have some rules that are entirely their own. Our information on the peculiar rules is not complete, since Dr. Spencer was only able to spend a limited amount of time with the Rendille; but he is confident of the accuracy of the data that follow, and these data are enough to give us a fair general idea of this aspect of their system.

We begin with the simplest case. Assume that the father is a member of group F, and that the time has arrived when $F - 3$ is inaugurated. We take it that the father has begotten—or will eventually beget—a son. Now there are three main possibilities to consider. First, the son may have attained (or passed) the minimum enrolment age.[94] In this case he simply enrols in $F - 3$. Second, the

---

[93] In addition to the data given in Spencer (1973) I have been able to use a great deal of additional information supplied by Spencer in personal communications. In particular, he very kindly made available to me the results of his survey of the age-group affiliations of all the elders in one subclan (68 men).

[94] It is probably at puberty, or even slightly before. P. T. W. Baxter, who attended a Rendille circumcision ceremony in 1951, says (in a personal communication) that the youngest of the twenty or so who were initiated on that occasion was about 12; while the oldest, three tribal policemen on leave, were pretty certainly over 20. Adamson writes of the Rendille: "From the Chief I learned that in the old days the age for circumcision was between twenty and twenty-five years, after which the initiated men immediately became warriors and had to take on the responsibilities of mature men. Now, as tribal warfare is

son may not yet have been born or may still be an infant. In this case he enrols in a group junior to F − 3. These two possibilities are common to all negative PL systems. The peculiarity of the Rendille lies in the way in which they deal with cases intermediate between these two extremes. If the son is no longer an infant, but has not yet reached the minimum enrolment age, then he cannot, like most of its members, enrol in F − 3 when it is inaugurated. He is, however, allowed to take part when F − 3 perform the Galgulumi ceremony, a rite performed once by every age-group, ideally the year after it is inaugurated, in practice sometimes rather later. After having participated in the Galgulumi, the boy does not act as a member of an age-group until the time comes when F − 4 is inaugurated. By then he has passed the minimum enrolment age, and he is initiated—a process involving circumcision—together with those for whom initiation is simply the means by which they enrol in F − 4.

The son's position is now a peculiar one. He is primarily a member of F − 3—which he is said to have "climbed" into—but he is also subject to a number of the rules to which a member of F − 4 is subject. Those of the rules that we know about fall into three groups. First there are certain rules to which he is subject as if he were both a member of F − 3 and a member of F − 4.

(i) There is a rule that a member of an age-group cannot marry the daughters of other members of that group. More generally, there is a relationship of respect and avoidance between him and them, and the reciprocal term of address *àbà* is used between them. A man who has climbed into F − 3 has this relationship with the daughters both of men in F − 3 and of men in F − 4.

(ii) Members of an age-group have obligations of hospitality to each other. The man who has climbed owes these obligations to members of both the groups with which he is associated.

Second, there are certain rules to which he is subject as if he were only a member of F − 3.

(i) If a man has climbed into F − 3, then this is regarded as his group as far as his children are concerned. In the case of

---

forbidden, the operation is done between the ages of fifteen and twenty [1967: 151 f.]." (Adamson's book contains information—mostly of a minor kind—that is of some relevance to the age-group systems of almost all the Kenyan tribes mentioned in the present work.)

sons, this means that they must join F − 6 or a more junior group. Concerning daughters, see Spencer (1973: 35).

(ii)   As has been mentioned, the members of an age-group are not allowed to marry until something like 11 years after its inauguration. This means, however, that by the time F − 4 is inaugurated, F − 3 will have gained the right to marry. The climber is in this respect treated as a member of F − 3—he can marry "more or less immediately" (Spencer 1973: 34). This makes sense in two respects. First, giving him this right in no way encourages overaging; and second, since he is above the average age of members of F − 4, it is personally convenient for him to be allowed to marry before they are.

Finally, there is a rule that does not fall into either of the preceding categories. The normal reciprocal term of address among members of the same age-group is *maráàt*. If a man climbs from F − 4 to F − 3, then he uses the term *maráàt* reciprocally with members of F − 4. Spencer remarks that "this is consistent with the fact that they were circumcised together (cf. Spencer 1965: 256, on the term *murata*) [personal communication]." With the members of F − 3, the man will use the reciprocal term of address *eídù*, and Spencer says that "this term is not used in any other context as far as I know [personal communication]."

From these data it is evident that a climber has quite strong ties with both the age-groups with which he is associated. It appears, nevertheless, that one can properly speak of his primary affiliation as being with F − 3: in particular, if asked what age-group he belongs to, he will reply that he belongs to F − 3 (Spencer, personal communication).

The inadequacies of our model are shown up quite sharply by this system. We can reasonably say that the system possesses the unique membership characteristic (though not in quite the same way as any other system). But what of the no-overlapping characteristic? Did the son join F − 3 when he performed the Galgulumi with them? If so, then there is no overlapping. Or did he join it only when he was initiated at the inauguration of F − 4? If so, then there is overlapping. For that matter, one might even argue that the son resigns from F − 4, violating the no-resigning characteristic. I can offer no solution to these conundrums; they are presented simply as an indication of how difficult it would be to produce a really satisfactory model.

The Rendille system has so far been presented as if it were simply a PL system. But the truth is rather more complicated. Whether a man can climb into a given age-group is not determined merely by his father's age-group affiliation (and his age at its inauguration). In order to state the true rule, let us adopt the following convention. We shall number Ego's generation 0, his father's 1, his father's father's 2, and so on. Now, the rule is that if Ego had an agnatic ancestor (i.e., a father, father's father, father's father's father, etc.) in generation n who belonged[95] to age-group F, then Ego has the right to join age-group $F - 3n$, irrespective of the age-group affiliation of any of the intervening ancestors. If it is Ego's own father who was in F, then Ego can either enrol in $F - 3$ in the normal fashion, or else climb into it; if it is some more senior ancestor, then Ego can only join $F - 3n$ by climbing into it from $F - (3n + 1)$. Furthermore, in either case he can only climb into $F - 3n$ if he performs the Galgulumi with that group, and in order to do this he must be beyond infancy at the relevant point in time.[96]

In Spencer's case material, the most remote ancestor whose age-group affiliation is taken into account for the purposes of this rule is merely the father's father. In such instances, the father's father belongs to F; the father is a member of $F - 4$; and the son performs the Galgulumi with $F - 6$, is initiated with $F - 7$, and thereby climbs into $F - 6$. It is not known whether cases arise in practice where more remote ancestors are taken into account, but the Rendille certainly do not view the rule as being limited in its application simply to the two generations above Ego's own.

It will be evident from these remarks that the Rendille system is not, in fact, a PL system, since a man's age-group affiliation may be determined not in relation to his father's but in relation (at least) to his grandfather's. It will also be evident, however, that to set up a special category for the Rendille system would be artificial. The system obviously demands to be treated in close relationship with PL systems. The solution seems to be to treat PL systems as a particular type of system within some larger categorical framework. I return to this point in Chapter III, Section 5.

[95] As will be evident from what has gone before, an individual who has climbed into age-group S from age-group $S - 1$ is counted as belonging to S.

[96] The various comments already made about the extent to which a climber belongs to $F - 3$ and the extent to which he belongs to $F - 4$ should, of course, be modified in the light of this paragraph: for $F - 3$, one should read $F - 3n$; and for $F - 4$, $F - (3n + 1)$.

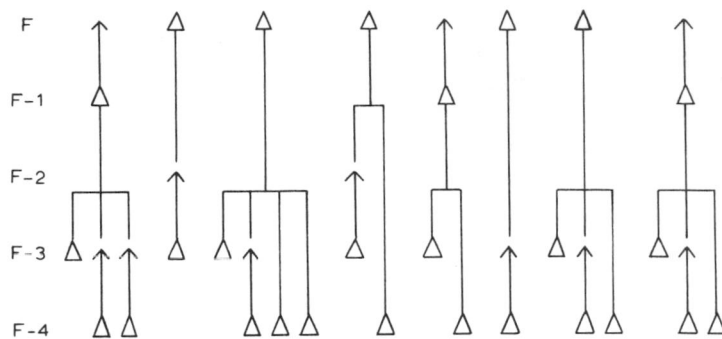

Figure 1.21

Spencer is almost the only ethnographer to provide any quantitative data on the operation of something like a paternal linking rule; his information is therefore of special interest, and since it is not available elsewhere I reproduce some of it here.

Spencer surveyed the age-group affiliations of 68 men. In the case of 65 of them, he was also able to discover the age-group affiliation of the man's father, and it is to these 65 that I confine my attention. In discussing these data I shall use the term *pair* to refer to a father and his son. We have 65 pairs, made up of 65 sons and 29 fathers. Note, therefore, that though each son only appears in one pair, most fathers appear in more than one pair.

In the case of 52 pairs neither the father nor the son had climbed; of the 52 sons, 28 were in $F - 3$, 22 were in $F - 4$, and 2 were in $F - 5$.

In the case of 13 pairs, the father or the son or both had climbed. These 13 pairs are represented in Figure 1.21, the conventions of which are of a type invented by Spencer. Each man is represented by a triangle, and the row in which the triangle is placed indicates the man's age-group. Since all the fathers belong to the same age-group (either originally or by virtue of having climbed into it) I have labeled that group F. When a man has climbed from some group $S - 1$ into S, the triangle that represents him is placed in the row corresponding to $S - 1$ but with an arrow above it that terminates in row S. As may be seen, there are 11 individuals in the diagram who have climbed. Three of them are fathers, and 8 are sons.[97] For the sake of completeness, I have also included in the

_____

[97] Spencer mentions that 8 of the sons climbed and adds that "the fathers of three of these eight had previously climbed age-sets in their own youths

diagram all the recorded brothers of these 8 sons, so that there are also in the diagram 6 pairs in which neither father nor son has climbed. These 6 pairs are, of course, included among the 52 mentioned earlier.

Note that in two instances the son has climbed into $F - 2$. "According to the rules, therefore, these fathers should have been in a position to climb if only they had been a bit older at Galgulumi [Spencer, personal communication]."

4   HOMOLOGY AND HOMOGENEITY

4.1   Homology

In every age-group system there is a tendency for all the groups in the system to resemble one another with respect to certain features. I shall call this the tendency toward **homology**, and the features in question will be referred to as **homologous features**.

Some homologous features are already entailed by the model, notably by the enrolment characteristic. In fact, in all age-group systems that I know of, the rules governing the enrolment of an individual in a group are precisely the same for all groups.

Another widespread, though not universal, homologous feature is the internal organization of the groups. Usually all the groups in a system have exactly the same internal organization; and even when, as in some West African systems, their organizations are not identical, the limits within which variation occurs are narrow.

A related feature is the size of the age-group. One way or another, virtually all age-group systems ensure that roughly the same number of people join each group. The nearest thing to an exception that I know of is provided by the Banapas Bedik system.

> An age-set may include any number of boys; it has happened that a dozen have been initiated at once (1955), and it has happened that only a single one has been initiated (1959) [Smith 1971: 192].

As will appear later, however, a Bedik age-set is a decidedly tenuous entity (Chapter II, Section 4.4.2).

[1973: 34]." As will be evident from Figure 1.21, there are indeed 3 pairs in which both father and son climbed. Note that these 3 pairs include only 2 fathers; the third father who climbed did not have a son who climbed.

The tendency to homology with respect to size makes its appearance in different contexts in different systems (cf. Section 8 of this chapter). In some, for instance, it is to a large extent guaranteed by the existence of a rule establishing a fixed interval between the inauguration of successive groups. In others, there actually seems to be a conscious effort to foster it. This seems to be the case in some systems found among the Gambia Mandinka, and here the desire for homology in this respect can lead to shifting. The ethnographer writes

> It is possible, though it rarely happens, for a person to move from one age set to another. At Keneba, for instance, the set of girls aged about twenty had only ten members while the set below (aged 14–18) had thirty-four, and one of the senior girls in the latter group moved up to join the older set [Gamble 1955: 4].

It is likely that there are other systems in which shifting occurs for this reason, though the evidence is unclear: for example among the Somba (see p. 212) and among the Ngoni. The evidence on the last-mentioned tribe is worth quoting.

> a well favoured warrior might gain promotion from one regiment [age-set] to the next above, either because of his own prowess in war or because the senior regiment was short of men [Barnes 1967: 37].

The second motive for shifting mentioned by Barnes may relate to a desire to make sets about the same size; on the other hand, it may merely be that a regiment had to be a certain size simply in order to be an efficient unit. (On the first motive mentioned by Barnes, see p. 100.)

It sometimes happens that a society wishes a system to possess two homologous features that are irreconcilable. There is an interesting example of this from Pukapuka in the Cook Islands. In their ethnography the Beagleholes write

> The age of a person is reckoned from birth. The first women to give birth to a first-born child in each season of six months [the year is divided into two six-month seasons] announces that her child is the *tai tangata* for that six months period, which is then called *te takalonga o Mea* (the year—six months—of So-and-so). All other children born in the same period are classed in the age group of this *tai tangata* and are known colelctively as a *tai tangata* group. . . . If, as occasionally happens, no first-born child is born in the [six months May to October], then the eldest first-born child of the suc-

> ceeding [six months of November to April] becomes the *tai tangata*
> of the preceding [six months May to October], and all children born
> during the twelve month period are classed with this *tai tangata*.
> There is thus a slight variability in *tai tangata* periods [1938: 233].

In principle, then, the age-sets in this system are homologous, in that
they contain all those born in a 6-month period and in that they
contain at least one first-born child. When it becomes necessary to
sacrifice homology in one respect or the other, they choose to
sacrifice the 6-month period.

4.2 Homogeneity

In addition to the tendency to homology, there seems also to be
a tendency to **homogeneity** in many (perhaps all) systems. By this I
mean a tendency for all members of an age-group to share certain
characteristics.

One way in which homogeneity is achieved is through the
enrolment rules. These may ensure, for instance, that all members of
the set are men, and that all members are past the age of puberty.
But these features can also be interpreted as examples of homology:
it could be said that it is being ensured that all the sets resemble each
other in consisting entirely of men over the age of puberty. Homogeneity would simply be entailed by homology. Sometimes, however,
this interpretation will seem artificial: if we have a system in which
all those enrolled in a set fall within a narrow age-range, the people
who are operating the system will no doubt be thinking in terms of
ensuring that all members of the set are about the same age, rather
than in terms of ensuring that the age-range of each of the sets in the
system is the same. But this alone would hardly justify our postulating a tendency to homogeneity.

There are, however, two other pieces of evidence to support this
hypothesis. One relates to age-grades. When an age-set system and an
age-grade system are integrated with each other, this is almost invariably done in such a fashion that all members of a single set are
assigned the same age-grade (see Chapter II, Section 2). In this case,
homogeneity is clearly a force independent of homology. The other
relates to shifting: there are several instances where it seems to take
place in order to ensure that members of a single set resemble each
other with respect to some characteristic.

Among the Bartle Bay peoples of New Guinea there were
groups that seem to have resembled age-sets in all respects but one:

"if a child did not develop physically as rapidly as his mates he was passed into a lower *kimta* [age-group] [Seligman 1910: 475]." Clearly, shifting occurs here because of a desire to ensure that all members of the group be at about the same stage of physical development, that is, homogeneous in this respect.

Something that seems to be similar is found among the Douala:

> It also sometimes happens that members of the set who are bigger and stronger than their age-mates[98] and oppress them attempt to move into the immediately senior set. Some people demonstrate their superiority over their own group in this fashion and thus gain particular prestige in their village and tribe [Ittmann 1955: 86].

I also have at hand two examples of shifting for this kind of reason from the graded systems of East Africa. Among the Tira Nuba, each age-set of youths is assigned a series of grades; when a set S leaves the most junior grade its place is taken by set S − 1. Now, sometimes a member of S will remain in the most junior grade and become permanently a member of S − 1. This happens to "deformed or backward boys, or boys who in any other way prove themselves unequal to the age-grade tasks, especially to the vigorous standards of the Tira sports and games [Nadel 1947: 229 f.]." Here the idea seems to be that all the members of the set should ideally reach the same minimum standard of achievement. This same idea may perhaps also be involved in some cases of shifting among the Ngoni (see the passage quoted on p. 114). Among the Ngoni, a man might be shifted to the immediately senior set if he showed particular prowess in war. Our source does not tell us why this was felt to be the proper reaction to outstanding ability, and the Ngoni may have had any of a number of motives (e.g., rewarding a good man, ensuring that ability is concentrated in the senior echelons of the organization); but it is possible that the more senior set was assumed to have a higher standard of martial achievement and that the shift was made in order to achieve homogeneity. Even if this was not the motive for the move, it may have been its effect.

My second East African example comes from the Masai, of whom Merker writes as follows.

> If a warrior feels that he is still too young to join his age-mates in leaving the warrior grade he joins the immediately junior age-set. . . .

---

[98] Here, as throughout the present work, the term age-mates refers to members of a single age-group.

The other instance is when a young man inherits large herds of cattle and there is no one else who can look after them. He must then take possession himself, and he marries soon after circumcision. He is then enrolled in the most junior age-set of married men [1910: 75].

In both the cases mentioned by Merker the same motive is involved: an individual is joining the age-set whose style of life accords with his own; if he did not, then age-set homogeneity would be destroyed. In Merker's second instance, it seems that we are sometimes dealing not with shifting but with enrolment in a set that is no longer at the first level, that is, with overlapping.

5 SECONDARY DEVIATIONS FROM THE MODEL

5.1 Secondary Rules

Shifting has now appeared in three different contexts: as a result of paternal linking, as a result of the tendency to homology, and a result of the tendency to homogeneity. In the next section I shall cite some examples of it occurring when a man is expelled from his age-group, and there is not much doubt that it also takes place in yet other contexts.

Now, a system that permits shifting lacks at least one, and often two, of the characteristics of our model (see p. 100 n.). And yet it is clear that most such systems do not, in fact, differ very strikingly from systems that exactly correspond to our model. How can we deal with this situation? In essence this problem was discussed earlier (p. 41), when we pointed out that an improved model would have to be more flexible than the one we have. There are two numerical features of shifting that we might seize on for use in such a model. One is the proportion of participants who shift. Though there are no quantitative data,[99] it is clear that in most of our examples such persons form a small minority. The other is the number of sets away from their own that individuals are allowed to shift. In almost all instances the shifter can only move into an immediately adjacent set, and the direction in which he can move may also be limited.

For the moment, however, the improved model is simply a speculation. We need something that will help us now, and for this

---

[99] Except on the Rendille; but it is doubtful whether this should be counted as an instance of shifting.

purpose I suggest that we might introduce the concept of a **second-ary rule**. This term will be used in a rather loose way to refer to those rules that seem to be of secondary importance.[100] Such rules have a number of characteristics in common. One is that they directly affect only a small proportion of those who are subject to them. Another is that they are generally concessive in form—"such-and-such may be done," rather than "such-and-such must be done." They also have the appearance of extraneousness, in the sense that they look as if they could be abolished without producing any significant repercussions elsewhere in the system. Using these rather vague criteria, it can be said that all the instances of shifting mentioned in this book, excepting some (or even all) of those associated with paternal linking, are the product of secondary rules. In the sections that follow, I shall consider certain other minor deviations from the model, some at least of which can be categorized in the same fashion.

5.2 * Expulsion

In some systems it is possible to expel an individual from his group, a feature not in accordance with the no-resigning characteristic of our model. Rules that permit expulsion invariably have all the hallmarks of secondary rules. Most examples of such rules come from West Africa, [101] but they are also found elsewhere.[102]

Sometimes expulsion is associated with shifting: perhaps among the Yoruba (Fajana 1968: 237); certainly among the Dassanetch, who have a Gada system (U. Almagor, personal communication); and among the Lele of Zaïre, about whom Brausch writes as follows:

> An individual does not have to spend the whole of his life as a member of the same age-set; he may ask to join a more junior set, and he will do so under certain circumstances: if, for instance, after discussions among its members, he is expelled from the age-set into which he was initiated, or if of his own free will he repudiates his set because of disagreements. . . . It must be noted that an individual is never allowed to shift from a junior set to a senior set [1951: 91].

[100] The term "secondary rule" is also used by Hart (1961), but in a quite different sense. In his work it refers to rules about rules, which I shall call "second-order rules." See especially Hart (1961: 92).

[101] They have been reported, for instance, among the Fulani of Fouta-Djallon (Baldé 1939: 93, 103), among the Ika Ibibio (Jeffreys 1950: 163), among the Mbembe (Harris 1965: 41), and among the Yoruba (Fajana 1968: 237).

[102] In Albania, for example (see Appendix 1).

5.3 * Enrolment of Strangers

Another deviation that is quite clearly of a secondary nature is perhaps rather more common than expulsion. In a number of systems it is possible to enrol a newcomer to the society in the age-group that seems most in keeping with his age, thus usually violating the no-overlapping characteristic. Examples are found among the Lele (Douglas 1963: 77), the Afikpo Ibo (Ottenberg 1971: 57, 104), the Garati Konso (Jensen 1936: 367), the Alladian (Augé 1969: 232), and the Akwe-Shavante (Maybury-Lewis 1967: 129).

5.4 * Multiple Membership

Only a very few systems can even be suspected of lacking the single membership characteristic. The ones I have come across are: the Blackfoot, the Hidatsa, and possibly the Mandan systems, in which multiple membership is clearly the product of secondary rules (see Part Two); the Rendille system (pp. 108 ff.); and, the clearest example, the system operated by one of the ethnic groups living in Timbuctoo, the Bela. "Some Bela join additional age-sets, either older or younger than their own, if they have many fields to cultivate. The reason for this is that Bela age-mates work a day a year in each other's fields [Miner 1965: 185]."

6 * PARALLEL SEQUENCES

In some societies there is more than one age-group sequence. In this section I shall be concerned with those cases where the different sequences have the same rules, that is, with what will be called **parallel sequences**. Imagine an age-set sequence, with all the necessary rules governing such matters as the inauguration interval, the recruitment period, the obligations of age-mates to each other, and the relationships between sets (cf. Section 9 of this chapter). Now, imagine that in the same society another age-set sequence is established, having just the same rules; [103] the society then has two parallel sequences.

---

[103] To be more precise, at the expense of mentioning notions that are introduced only much later (Chapter IV, Section 1), I consider that two sequences are parallel if they have the same systemic rules; the sequences may be such as to allow individual age-sets considerable discretion in fixing local rules.

The rules that regulate which of several parallel sequences an individual may join will be referred to as **sequence assignment rules.** These rules are always, or almost always, such that an individual can only belong to one sequence; and when this is the case they always in practice specify which sequence the individual must join. One criterion they can use is sex: women join this sequence, men that. In such cases, however, the sequences are usually (perhaps always) at least slightly different from each other in their rules, and they are therefore not strictly speaking parallel.

Another criterion is locality: an individual belongs to the sequence in the place where he lives. Local sequences of this kind are common and found all over the world. The difficulty is that it is often not clear how to view them: whether as constituting a single system made up of several parallel sequences or as a number of separate systems each with the same rules.

In East Africa there are a number of instances of parallel sequences on some basis other than locality.[104] The best described is in the Turkana tribe. The males of this society are divided into two groups, membership of which is acquired at birth, such that if a man is in one group, then his sons are in the other. Gulliver calls these groups **alternations,** a term that seems to be gaining general acceptance.[105] Each of the Turkana alternations has associated with it an

---

[104] Because my ignorance of the relevant languages makes full access to the sources impossible, I can do no more than mention the parallel sequences that evidently existed among the Puyuma of Taiwan. The population of each Puyuma village was divided into moieties, North and South, each of which had its own clearly demarcated half of the village. (It is not clear to me how the moiety affiliation of an individual was determined.) It appears that each moiety had a distinct age-set sequence, with its own men's and boys' houses and its own quite highly organized structure of authority (Sung 1964, 1965; Chen 1965: 98 ff.).

[105] Gulliver (1958: 919 ff.) suggested that the Turkana alternations may have originated as g-groups, and Lamphear (1972: 496 ff.) appears to have found evidence that supports this hypothesis. It is certainly tempting to postulate some kind of relationship between alternations and g-groups, for, as far as I know, alternations, like g-groups, are found only in East Africa. The other instances of alternations that I know of—and the list is surely not exhaustive—are as follows. They certainly exist among the Samburu and Rendille (Spencer 1965, 1973). It looks as if they exist among the Longarim (Kronenberg 1961a: 262 f.; 1972: 92). Probably they exist among the Topotha, though there is a possibility that in this instance the entities in question are g-groups (Kronenberg 1961b; cf. p. 70 of this volume). The information given by an aged informant to Haberland (1963: 187) suggests that the Borana Galla once had named alternations or something like them. The closest analogue to the alternation that I know of outside East Africa is a type of group that existed among certain Australian aborigines (Bates 1925).

age-set sequence. Gulliver describes the enrolment of youths as follows:

> At initiation the youths of each alternation are dealt with separately, usually on different days but sometimes on the same days at separate but adjacent groves. . . . The two new age-groups which are established in any one initiation season, and which together comprise a total collection of coevals, do not find an especial common interest and mutuality, nor do they coalesce as a single age-class [1958: 903].

Parallel sequences associated with descent groups have been noted among the Borana Galla and Samburu, though the data on the latter are a little obscure (Haberland 1963: 187 etc.; Spencer 1965: 74 etc.). More interesting than these are two instances of parallel sequences of g-groups, one among the Kuria (Ruel 1962), the other among certain Kikuyu tribes (Lambert 1947, 1956). In both cases the individual generally belongs to the same sequence as his father, but both also permit children to indulge in what we may call **horizontal shifting**, that is, shifting from one sequence to a parallel one (Lambert 1947: 4; 1956: 42; Ruel 1962: 27). The sources do not relate this kind of shifting to under- or overaging, but I suspect that there may be a connection (although no doubt it also occurs for other reasons). The grounds for this suspicion are that in both these systems the g-groups in the parallel sequences are not inaugurated simultaneously (contrast the situation among the Turkana). By shifting into a different sequence, a child is therefore joining a g-group with a rather higher or lower average age, and presumably (in some cases at least) one more in keeping with its own age.

I have mentioned that sequence assignment rules are always, or almost always, such that an individual cannot join more than one sequence. The only instances that I know of in which an individual can join more than one of several putative parallel sequences are cases where there are local sequences that may or may not constitute a single system. [106] Even in these instances, it is apparently exceptional for a man to belong to more than one sequence. Evidently there is not much point in having two sequences of the same type if they are going to have a great many members in common; but there is nothing logically incoherent about parallel sequences with many, even all, of their members in common.

---

[106] See Ruel (1969: 207) on the Banyang and Ottenberg (1971: 135) on the Afikpo Ibo.

7 * AGE-GROUP NAMES

The various systems for naming age-groups have been well
described by ethnographers, who have, indeed, shown an almost
obsessive interest in the subject (see Philippe 1965 for an extreme
case). Nor have the theorists been any less enthusiastic. More than
one definition of what an age-set is demands that it have a
name [107] —even though age-sets (as specified by our model) without
names certainly exist, even in systems without age-grades.[108]

Far more misleading than this, however, is the popular distinction between "cyclical" and "linear" age-group systems. The idea
that in certain cases age-groups are "organized into cycles" already
appears in Radcliffe-Brown's letter of 1929 (and is developed in
Radcliffe-Brown 1950: 28 f.). Since then it has turned up in a
number of different forms, with recent elaborations by Paulme
(introduction to 1971a) and Bischofberger (1972: 75 ff.). This
classification of age-group systems has no real basis. It generally
arises from a confusion between age-groups and their names. A rough
distinction can be made between systems in which age-groups are
named from a cycle of names and those in which they are named
according to some other principles or not at all (though there are
cases that do not fall clearly into one category or the other). But no
general correlations have been discovered between the methods by
which age-groups are named and any other features of age-group
systems. [109] In particular, it is wrong to suppose (as does, for

[107] For example, Prins (1953: 10), Huntingford (1963: 76), Ottenberg and
Ottenberg (1965: 35), Lienhardt (1966: 53).

[108] For instance, among the Tiv (Bohannan and Bohannan 1953: 47),
among the Konkomba (Tait 1961: 86), and among the Dida (Terray 1969: 254).
Terray, incidentally, after an admirably explicit statement of the fact that Dida
age-sets—which are known as *zokpa*—have no names, adds "On voit que le
système des *zokpa* ne saurait être assimilé à un système de classes d'âge ou
d' 'age-grades' [1969:254]."

[109] This applies *a fortiori* to systems of naming age-groups and other
features of cultures. Contrast the following view, advanced in a recent textbook:

> A distinction has been made between *cyclical* age-set systems, where
> the same age-set appears again every several generations like a duck
> in a shooting gallery; and *progressive* age-set systems, where a named
> age-set appears only once. The distinction is particularly interesting
> because cyclical and progressive age-set systems tend to be mirrored
> in corresponding contrasts in time reckoning, and in the cosmology
> and world view of people [Keesing and Keesing 1971: 218 f.].

Apart from the observation about time reckoning (which insofar as it is correct
is trivial), the theories expressed here are, to my knowledge, without evidential
foundation.

instance, Radcliffe-Brown) that "In East Africa, where age-sets are arranged in cycles, the cycles are such that a son's son may frequently belong to the same one as his father's father [1950: 28 f.]." In the East African systems that I know of, there is nothing that could be called a cycle of age-groups, but merely a cycle of age-group names. [110] It can happen in some systems that two groups with the same name are simultaneously in existence, but in such cases they appear always to be organizationally distinct. In principle it would be possible to imagine two such groups merging to form a single group, but I do not know of any good evidence that this bizarre possibility is ever realized (cf. Maybury-Lewis 1967: 136, five lines from the bottom of the page; Paulme 1971b: 237; Peristiany 1975: 180).

Although, as has been said, no general connections have been established between the names of age-sets and any of their other features, in a few particular cases ethnographers have fairly convincingly postulated some link. Wagner, for example, in his study of the Abaluyia, noted a case of a cyclical naming system where "the name of the oldest age-grade [i.e., age-set] could not be used again as long as any of its members were still alive [1949: 375]" (cf. Sangree 1966: 70 n., 74 ff.). This may well be a device that helps to maintain the proper inauguration interval. Another connection is to be found in a number of Gada systems which are such that unique paternal linking will lead grandfather and grandson to be placed in groups with the same name. But these are exceptional instances, and, for the moment at least, no evidence exists to support the view that the method by which age-groups are named is an important feature of most age-group systems.

8 * FUSION

Very often, the oldest age-groups in a system, even if they have not formally been dissolved, have virtually ceased to function. But sometimes even old men take an active part in age-group activities. In such cases it is quite often felt that age-groups should have a certain minimum size, and the oldest in the system may drop below that size. The practice exists, therefore, of joining some of the oldest age-groups together to form a single, enlarged group. I shall refer to this practice as **fusion**. The number of groups fused may be two or

---

[110] Age-group name cycles are not restricted to East Africa: they exist, for instance, among the Mandinka of West Africa (Person 1968: 58) and among the Akwe-Shavante of Brazil (Maybury-Lewis 1967: 154).

more, but they always (in fact, and, let us stipulate, by definition) have successive level numbers. Fusion occurred in the Bartle Bay system of New Guinea (Seligman 1910: 475); most other instances that I know of are in West Africa. [111] Occasionally quite young groups may be fused, again because they are considered too small individually. [112]

I am not sure what should be done in order to bring fusion into some clear relationship with the age-set model. One possibility would be to modify the model so that it explicitly allows fusion (within reasonable limits). Another would be to use the model as it stands. Imagine, say, a system in which the three most senior age-groups—call them S, S − 1, and S − 2—fuse. One way of looking at this would be to say that S and S − 1 dissolve and that the ex-members of these groups join S − 2. Under this description there is overlapping and rejoining; but of course there may well be instances of fusion for which a different kind of analysis would be necessary.

9 * INTER-GROUP RELATIONS

Relations between age-groups in a single sequence fall into two main patterns. The first of these is a simple one in which the members of a group owe respect or obedience to all senior groups and are granted respect or obedience by all junior ones. This pattern is often mentioned in the sources, but it is not usually possible to determine—at least from the data given—whether the respect is specific to the age-group system or whether it is simply the usual respect of the young for the old. There are two cases, however, where it can be shown pretty definitely that it is a feature of the age-group system.

One is where the age-ranges of age-groups overlap, as, for instance, among the Jie, where adolescent boys who are members of g-group S + 1 are treated with great respect by older men who are members of S, and are addressed as "father" (Lamphear 1976: 36 n. 35). So also, among the Darassa "true age is irrelevant" in this context (Jensen 1936: 318). A person in a lower group must ap-

[111] Among the Tiv (Bohannan and Bohannan 1953: 48 f.), the Yakö (Forde 1964: 146), the Songhoi of Timbuctoo (Miner 1965: 176), the Somba (Mercier 1971: 109); and, elsewhere, the Lele (Douglas 1963: 77).

[112] Examples among the Tswana (Schapera 1955: 104 f.) and the Dida (Terray 1969: 254).

proach someone in a higher one with deference. An old man whose group is at the first level may have to behave respectfully towards a 10-year-old boy whose group is at the second level. (But see further Chapter II, Section 1.2.6.)

The other is where there are two (or more) age-group sequences in a single society (see Section 6 of this chapter). Among the Turkana

> Young men tend to seek the advice and help and to accept the orders and restraints of the senior men of their own alternation, but they can ignore both counsel and control coming from the other group. . . . An elderly Stone [one alternation] at a ceremony or dance would not give orders to a young Leopard [the other alternation], but he would expect and would normally obtain compliance and respect from a young Stone [Gulliver 1958: 903].

These cases can be contrasted with the Kuria g-group system. Like the Turkana system, it comprises two sequences, though among the Kuria a man belongs to the same sequence as his father. In theory, inter-group rules [113] apply only within a single sequence, but in practice each age-group is equated with a roughly coeval group in the other sequence, and in this way inter-group rules are normally extended in their application to the other sequence (Ruel 1962: 20, 27). The Kuria system also has overlap between the age-ranges of age-groups within a single sequence; but there, when there is conflict between the respect (or familiarity) due to a person by virtue of his age-group affiliation and the respect (or familiarity) due to him by virtue of his age, then he is treated (outside a limited number of situations) as if he belonged to an age-group commensurate with his age (Ruel 1962: 30 f.).

The second common type of inter-group relationship is what I shall call **alternate linking**. In these cases there is some particularly close and (usually) friendly relationship between group S and groups S + 2 and S − 2 (for short, groups S ± 2). This may be associated with hostility between S and S ± 1, though it has been reported without such hostility, and, equally, hostility between adjacent groups has been reported without alternate linking, e.g., among the Alabdu Galla (Haberland 1963: 310). Alternate linking seems to me rather a mysterious phenomenon, and I can do little more here than say why some of the explanations for it that might come to mind are wrong.

---

[113] I use this term to refer to any rules which regulate the kinds of relationships between age-groups that are dealt with in this section.

First, alternate linking cannot be explained as a local phenomenon that diffused to certain neighboring societies. It is found in many parts of Africa; it is well attested in South America (Maybury-Lewis 1967); it is equally well documented in several of the Plains Indian systems, and probably existed in all of them (see Part Two); and in Oceania it was noted among the Iatmül (Bateson 1932: 433; 1958: 244 ff.), although these people, it is true, may well not have had an age-group system of the type discussed in this book.

Second, although alternate linking is often expressed in the idiom of kinship ("father" and "son," "elder brother" and "younger brother"), it is not correlated with any type of paternal or fraternal linking. [114] In the North and South American systems where it exists, there are no rules or conventions of any kind about the relative age-groups of father and son, or brother and brother. In Africa also we find alternate linking in systems that lack the other types of linking, and equally in systems with the most diverse sorts of paternal linking: for instance, among the Garbichcho Sidama, where the ideal age-group for sons is $F - 4$ (Stanley and Karsten 1968: 96); among the Samburu, where sons should join $F - 3$ or a more junior group (Spencer 1965: 83); among the Konso, where sons join $F - 2$ (Jensen 1936: 366 ff.; Hallpike 1972: 185 f.); and in various g-group systems, where the ideal group for sons is $F - 1$ (see, for instance, Berger 1938: 190 on the Tatoga; Dyson-Hudson 1966: 157 on the Karimojong).

A third explanation that comes to mind is a good deal more convincing than the other two and may well have some truth in it. Alternate linking offers a method of dividing the age-sets in a sequence into two groupings: on the one hand $S - 2, S, S + 2, S + 4$, and so on, and on the other $S - 1, S + 1, S + 3$, and so on. Gulliver (1963: 30f.) refers to groupings of this kind as streams. I shall adopt this usage and also—as will appear in a moment—slightly extend it.

One argument that could be advanced to support the view that the prevalence of alternate linking is related to the fact that it allows the creation of streams is that it is very frequently (or even always) associated with streams. In order to advance this argument in an effective form, it would be necessary to develop proper criteria by which to distinguish between alternate linking with streams and alternate linking without streams, and this would by no means be easy. But we can talk loosely about the subject by using rough-and-ready criteria: if each of the two groupings of alternately linked

[114] See p. 211 for the definition of this term.

groups has a name, or if each functions as a unit in certain activities, or if there is anything else that makes us suspect that they constitute identity classes, [115] then the two groupings can be identified as streams. On this basis, it appears that two-stream systems are widespread: they are found not only in East Africa, [116] but also in West Africa, [117] in South America, [118] and perhaps in North America, among the Gros Ventres (see Part Two, Chapter IV, Section 2).

A second possible argument, this time a negative one, would be the rarity of **adjacent linking**, that is, specially close and friendly relationships between adjacent sets. There are one or two instances of it, [119] but it is decidedly uncommon. It might be suggested that this rarity is related to the fact that it is, of course, impossible to form groupings of age-groups on the basis of adjacent linking.

There is something to be said for these arguments, though they are a bit vague and leave a good deal unexplained. One of the unexplained things is this. Let us extend the term stream to cover not only cases where every second age-group is linked (**two-stream systems**) but also cases where there are groupings consisting of every third, fourth, fifth, etc. age-group (**three-stream systems, and so on**). Now, as far as I know, only deviant age-group systems have more than two streams. It may be, then, that a theory that accounted for the prevalence of alternate linking by pointing to the possibility of creating two streams would also have to explain why the possibility of having three or more streams is never (or hardly ever) exploited in age-set systems.

Inter-group relationships are by no means limited to the three types so far considered (the simple seniority pattern, alternate linking, and adjacent linking). There may be quite elaborate rules (and special terminology) concerning relations with all groups as far as $S \pm 4$. [120] In paternal linking systems groups as far apart as S and $S \pm 5$

---

[115] For this notion, see Chapter IV, Section 1.

[116] Gulliver (1963) on the Arusha and Lambert (1956: 28, 47) and Mahner (1970: 2 f.) on the Meru.

[117] Jones (1962: 201) mentions named streams among the Ibo.

[118] Maybury-Lewis (1967: 161) mentions Akwe-Shavante streams that run "log-races."

[119] It has been observed, for instance, among the Bambara (Monteil 1924: 249), the Chagga (Gutmann 1926: 321, 358 f.), the Turkana (Gulliver 1958: 903), and the Murle (Lewis 1972: 90). The notion of adjacent linking, like the notion of alternate linking, covers a great variety of relationships.

[120] See Mercier (1971: 105) on the Somba. Maybury-Lewis (1967: 339) gives terms used by the Akwe-Shavante for all sets as far as $S \pm 3$.

are linked, as in standard Galla systems. I suggested above that in the case of UPL systems we could speak of descent streams. A more refined definition of the notion of a stream might exclude some of these putative descent streams on the grounds that they are not identity classes; but others would no doubt survive, for instance the three named streams among the Takadi Konso (Hallpike 1972: 194).

The various types of linking that have been considered are not mutually exclusive. Among the Rendille there is a special tie between alternate groups (of the type widespread among systems of the Masai group), and also a special linking between every third group, related to the paternal linking rule (Spencer 1973).

Age-Grade Systems

1 AGE-GRADES

When age-groups are a prominent feature of the social organization of a society, they almost always operate in conjunction with
age-grades. If a society is going to give its age-groups important
tasks—religious, political, economic, judicial, or whatever—then by
and large it is going to need some means of changing the allocation of
duties of age-groups. This is partly because age-groups die out and
partly because their average age changes so much: one can hardly
expect old men to do hard work in the fields or young ones to act as
the supreme authority of the tribe. An age-grade system is the most
common mechanism for changing the roles of age-groups.

1.1 A Working Definition

Radcliffe-Brown's definition of an age-grade (quoted in the
introduction) is a useful one and has certainly never been improved
on. But it is not explicit enough: there are plenty of things of which

one could not say with assurance whether or not they are age-grades in Radcliffe-Brown's usage. I shall give a rather fuller explication of the concept then he does, but still a very inadequate one. Age-grades seem to be harder to analyze than age-groups. On the whole, I shall merely mention the problems they pose, not attempt to solve them.

In order to provide a working definition of an age-grade system, we may introduce the notion of a **rule-set**, that is to say, the notion of a collection of rules all of which apply to a given person at a given time. From the person's own point of view we can look on the rule-set as being a set of rights and/or duties.[1]

An age-grade system, roughly speaking, is a collection of different rule-sets, G_1, G_2, . . . , G_n, such that a person who enters the system is successively assigned each set once in this fixed order. For the purpose of analyzing the various systems that actually exist, we can break down this basic idea into a number of components, as follows:

An **age-grade** is one of a finite collection of not less than two rule-sets. The rule-sets are all different from each other, and the collection is totally ordered, say G_1, G_2, . . . , G_n. The rule-sets are assigned and disassigned to persons by rules that meet the following constraints:

(i) No set is assigned to a person before G_1 (the **first-grade constraint**).

(ii) No set is assigned to a person after G_n (the **last-grade constraint**).

(iii) If the highest set a person has been assigned is G_i ($i = 1$, $2, . . . , n - 1$), and that person is assigned another set, then the set assigned is G_{i+1} (the **sequential-assignment constraint**).

(iv) An individual who has been assigned some G_i ($i = 1$, $2, . . . , n - 1$) will eventually be assigned G_n if (but not only if) he survives to the maximum life span[2] (the **whole-sequence constraint**).

(v) No person is at any time assigned more than one set (the **unique-assignment constraint**).

---

[1] For the purposes of the present work I shall say that a person has certain rights and/or duties if and only if he is subject to certain rules. In some contexts it is convenient to look at the rules, in others to look at the rights and duties.

[2] I am assuming that the individual remains a member of the society (see p. 28 n. 7).

(vi) If a person who is disassigned a set is assigned another, then the two events occur simultaneously (the **no-interval constraint**).

I shall refer to the collection of age-grades as an **age-grade sequence**. The rules that assign and disassign age-grades are **transition rules**. Two of the transition rules have special names: the one that assigns the first grade in the sequence (G_1), the **entry rule**, and the one that disassigns the last grade (G_n), the **exit rule**.

From what has been said, it can be seen that an **age-grade system** consists of three elements: an age-grade sequence, transition rules, and persons. By a **person** I mean either an individual or a corporation.[3] This distinction is by no means trivial. It could happen, for instance, that an age-grade is best described as assigning some right to an age-group as a whole, and not to any of its individual members. This would be the case if the age-group, on reaching a certain grade, became the collective owner of some item of property.

Certain features of the definition deserve comment. A negative one is that it sets no limit on the size of an age-grade sequence. It includes everything from sequences that cover the whole of an individual's life to those that cover only quite a small period. This book is mainly concerned with age-grade systems that cover at least a considerable portion of the individual's life, but attenuated systems are quite common. They are always, as far as I know, designed for young people. In our own society we find them in schools. In some traditional Indian societies there were special boys' huts whose inhabitants were divided among a number of grades (see, for instance, Roy 1915: 213 ff.). Among the Nuba, Nadel (1947) recorded a number of age-grade systems limited to youths in their teens and twenties (see p. 116).

Another negative feature is that there is nothing in the definition that limits it to cases where an age-grade system is linked to an

---

[3] I shall not attempt to define the notion of a corporation. For a useful introduction to the jurisprudential literature on the subject (or at least, to such of it as is written in English) see Dias's annotated bibliography (1970a: 191 ff.). In the age-grade definition as it has just been presented, the whole-sequence constraint is phrased in terms of individuals. It is necessary, therefore, to add something to it to deal with corporations, perhaps along the following lines: a corporation that has been assigned some G_i ($i = 1, 2, \ldots, n - 1$) at time t will eventually be assigned G_n if (but not only if) it continues to exist until time $t + M$ (M being, it will be remembered, the maximum life span).

age-group system. In the present work, however, we shall ignore all issues peculiar to age-grade systems not associated with age-groups.

An implicit feature of the definition is that the transition from one grade to the next is clearly marked. Our own society, then, does not have an extended age-grade system. Certainly we may feel that the rules of behavior that apply to a middle-aged man are rather different from those that apply to a youth (cf. Neugarten *et al.* 1965); but we cannot say just when the transition from one set of rules to the other takes place or how many intermediate stages there may be.

I turn now to the constraints on the transition rules. One that immediately catches our attention is the first-grade constraint, for in the preceding chapter the term "age-grade system" was applied to a number of systems that in fact fail to meet this constraint. In paternal linking systems affected by underaging, an individual is often enrolled in his age-group after that group has passed the first grade of the "age-grade sequence." The first-grade constraint is certainly a necessary part of any proper definition of age-grades, but in this book I ignore its existence in the case of paternal linking systems.

The whole-sequence constraint is already in Radcliffe-Brown's definition. It sometimes happens that the most senior "grade" of a sequence is only assigned to individuals who attain special prominence;[4] this constraint excludes such putative grades from the sequence. Furthermore, there are probably sequences that meet all the other constraints in which, however, advancement from one "grade" to the next does not follow automatically, but depends, for instance, on whether the individual has made certain payments or has acquired certain esoteric knowledge. Such sequences are, by this definition, not age-grade sequences.

None of the other constraints concern us much in this part of the book, but they will all appear fairly prominently in Part Two.

1.2 * Limitations of the Definition

In this section I shall briefly mention some of the weaknesses of the definition just given. Most of the points made here are presented at greater length in Stewart (1972: 130–135).

[4] See, for instance, Mills (1926: 178) on the "priests" (*patir*) among the Changki Ao Nagas.

1. To characterize an age-grade simply as a set of rules is, in quite a few cases, to miss the most important aspects of it (cf. p. 6 on the Samburu).

2. In some systems, to say that a set is assigned a certain "grade" is only to say (roughly) that the set has performed some ceremony C of a sequence of ceremonies but has not yet performed ceremony $C + 1$ (see, for instance, the discussion of the Gros Ventre system in Part Two). This kind of case needs to be distinguished from fully developed grades of the sort the Samburu have, but the definition does not help to do so. See also Part Two, Chapter II, Section 5.5.

3. The definition offers no criteria for deciding where a given age-grade sequence begins and where it ends. An improved version would probably contain the characteristic that all grades in a sequence are homologous with respect to certain features. If this characteristic were formulated with sufficient precision, it would no doubt solve the problem of beginnings and ends.

In some systems it looks as if individuals pass through several grades as individuals before being enrolled in their age-groups and then passing through further grades with their groups. Purely for the purposes of exposition, and without any other justification, I shall make the assumption that age-group membership is a homologous feature of the age-grade system whenever the age-grade and the age-group system are integrated (see the next section for this term). In other words, I assume that entry into the first age-grade does not precede enrolment in the age-group.

There are a number of "age-grade" systems where there seems to be only one real "grade," the other putative grades being defined by reference to it (e.g., as junior, or retired). This seems to be the case in the systems of the Nandi and the Kipsigis and related ones; and also perhaps among the Kikuyu (p. 177). Some g-group systems should probably also be looked at in this way.

4. The definition offers no criteria for determining the boundaries between grades in a sequence; and occasionally this is a real problem (see Section 4.2 of this chapter). Furthermore, in some systems it looks as if there are sub-grades grouped into grades (see Yuan 1967 on the Makutaai Ami of Taiwan for an example). The definition ought to provide criteria for deciding what are grades and what sub-grades.

5. If we could build a model of age-grade systems, it would, ideally, be a flexible one, like the improved age-set model (p. 41). Such a model would, for example, accommodate the systems that violate the sequential-assignment constraint. It is uncommon to find a system which combines "age-grades" with age-groups and which violates this constraint, but it does happen. Almost always the constraint is violated in a particular way: the system permits skipping, that is, a person, on being disassigned some grade G_j ($j = 1$, $2, \ldots, n - 2$) may be assigned G_{j+k}, $k > 1$, rather than G_{j+1}.

In general, skipping is associated with shifting, but it can also exist without it, for example, when a whole age-group skips a grade, as may perhaps occur among the Kédougou Mandinka (Stewart 1972: 168 on Charest 1971), or when, as among the Banapas Bedik, individuals skip grades while retaining their original age-set affiliation (Section 4.4.2 of this chapter). Shifting can also occur without skipping, even when the age-groups are assigned age-grades (e.g., among the Tira Nuba and the Masai; see Chapter I, Section 4.2).

6. We have no criteria for distinguishing between rules of age-grades and inter-group rules, and this also is sometimes a real problem. For instance, at the beginning of Section 9, Chapter I, I assumed that the relations between groups in the Darassa and Jie systems are governed by inter-group rules (or whatever). But the Darassa, at least, have age-grades, so how do we know that these relations are not governed by age-grade rules? I suggest a tentative answer on p. 234. For another example of this problem, see the analysis of the Samburu system in Section 4.2.3 of this chapter.

2 THE MAIN TYPES OF TRANSITION RULE

The impression that a casual reader will derive from the ethnographic literature is that there is virtually no limit to the number of different ways in which age-group systems are combined with age-grade systems. Nor will this impression be dispelled by looking at the theoretical literature, whether in textbooks or elsewhere. As far as I know, the general question of how age-groups are combined with age-grades has never even been discussed, and certainly each ethnographer has had to describe the method used in the society he is concerned with in entirely ad hoc terms.

Yet, for all this apparent diversity, it can be shown that the number of different ways in which age-grades and age-groups are combined is in fact severely limited. Of an indefinitely large number of logically possible methods, only a very few are actually used; and of these few one is overwhelmingly the most popular. In this section I shall try to specify both those methods that are used and those that are not. This will be done by isolating the general features characteristic of existing systems, as opposed to those characteristic of nonexistent (or very rare) systems.

Systems that combine age-groups with age-grades can be categorized in a general way according to their relationship to three **combination constraints**.

The most important of these is the **integration constraint**. An age-grade system is **integrated** with an age-group system if the transition rules of the age-grade system are such that it can never happen that a member of some group S is assigned a higher grade than a member of a group $S + i$, $i \geqslant 1$. In other words, an individual can never be assigned a higher grade than someone who belongs to a senior age-group. I shall refer to an age-group system that is integrated with an age-grade system as a **graded (age-group) system**.

The second constraint is the **group-unity constraint**. A system meets this constraint if its transition rules are such that all members of a group are at all times assigned the same grade.

Finally, there is the **grade-filling constraint**. A system meets this constraint if its transition rules are such that each grade in the sequence is always occupied (unless some demographic disaster hits the society). (This constraint differs from the other two in that it is—in principle, at least—also relevant to age-grade systems that are not combined with age-group systems.)

In what follows, I shall begin by considering systems that meet the integration constraint and then go on to examine those that (probably) do not.

An instance of the most common type of transition rule is represented on Figure 2.1. The conventions of this diagram are much the same as those of Figure 1.13, though I have labeled the age-groups differently, since we are not dealing with a UPL system. The roman numerals in each column stand for age-grades, the most junior grade (G_1 in our definition) being I. I shall use roman numerals in this way throughout the book.

The system represented in Figure 2.1 is that of the Changki Ao Nagas (Mills 1926: 177 ff.). As can be seen, the Changki villagers inaugurate a new set every 3 years. The enrolment age is about 12. There are altogether nine named grades; those in grade VII (the

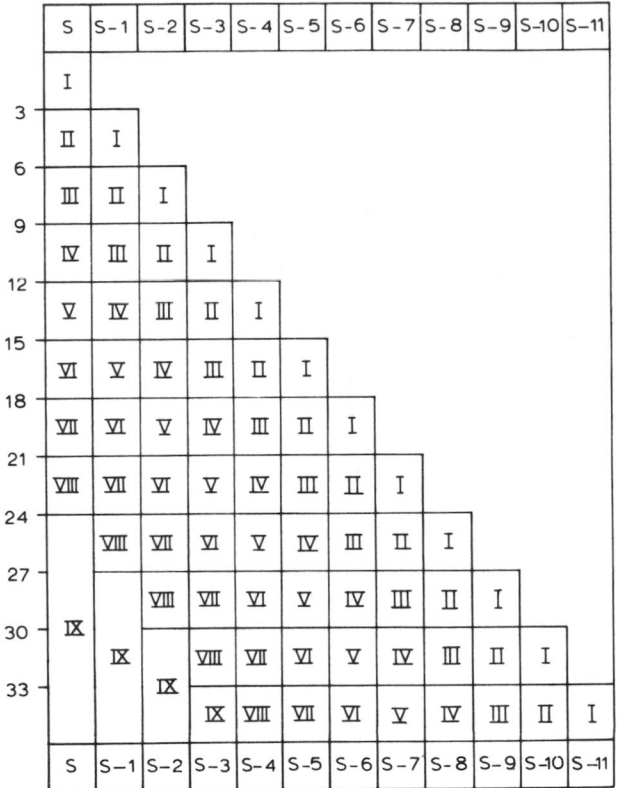

Figure 2.1

councillors, *tatari*), men in their early thirties, "with the advice of yet older groups, run the village."

The transition rules of the Changki system can also be represented as in Table 2.1.

We now need some terminology. A **level rule** is a transition rule that assigns a grade to an age-group, or disassigns one from it, according to the level number of that age-group. A level rule that assigns a grade is necessarily accompanied by one that disassigns the preceding grade (except in the case of the entry rule); and a level rule that disassigns a grade is necessarily accompanied by one that assigns the next grade (except in the case of the exit rule).

Level rules can be represented by a mapping from grades to levels like the one on Table 2.1. But such a table can also be used in a different way: it can represent simply the relationship between

TABLE 2.1

Grade	Level
I	1
II	2
III	3
IV	4
V	5
VI	6
VII	7
VIII	8
IX	9 +

grades and levels that exists at a particular point in time, irrespective of whether that relationship came about as a result of level rules or as a result of transition rules of some other kind. Now, imagine an age-grade system in which some or all transitions are governed by level rules; and imagine further that at a certain point in time we record the relationships between age-grades and level numbers in that system, say by means of a table like Table 2.1; then all the level rules that govern the assignment of grades recorded on that table constitute a single **sequence level rule**. If an age-grade system has only one sequence of level rules, then that system uses **simple level rules**.

Table 2.1 represents a system in which *all* the age-grades are assigned by level rules, but this is not a necessary condition for the existence of a single sequence of level rules. In other words, even if some of the transitions were governed by rules other than level rules—even if, say, the relationship between the sets at levels 3, 4, 5, and 6 and grades III, IV, V, and VI could not be represented by a mapping as on Table 2.1—the remaining level rules would constitute a single sequence. The limiting case of a sequence is where just the entry rule, or just the exit rule, is a level rule.

In the system represented in Table 2.1, where a grade is both assigned and disassigned by a level rule, the relevant levels are consecutive. For instance, grade III is assigned on reaching level 3 and disassigned on reaching level 4. But this is not necessarily the case: grade III in a system could perfectly well be assigned on reaching level 5 and disassigned on reaching level 8.

If all the transitions in a system are governed by simple level rules, then it is necessarily the case that all three combination

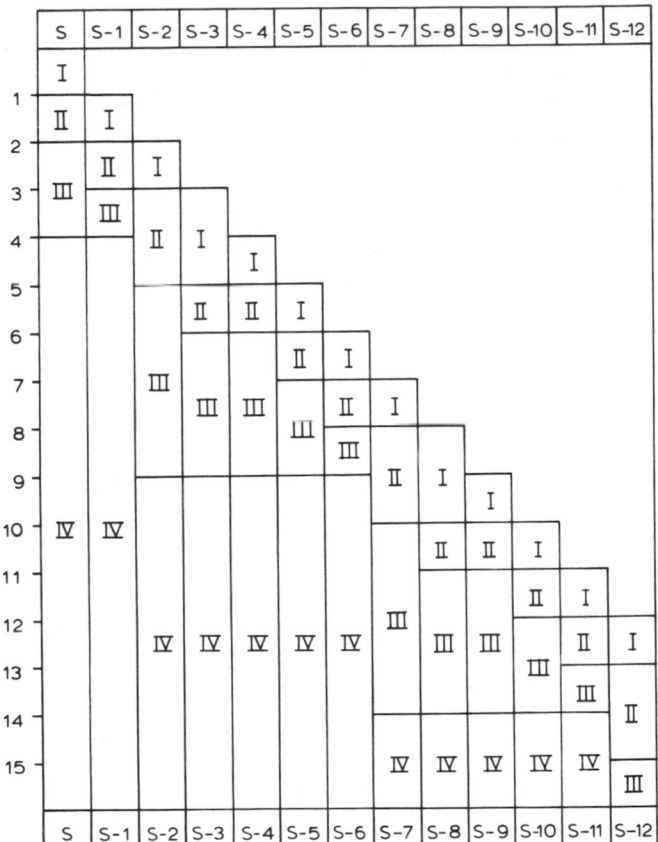

Figure 2.2

constraints are met.[5] (This is also true if, as in the Changki system, the exit rule is not a level rule.) It may be in part for this reason that simple level rules are overwhelmingly the most common type of transition rule. All the Taiwanese systems for which I have information, and indeed almost all the non-African systems that I know of, operate solely with simple level rules (except that some have exit rules that are not level rules, e.g., where the last grade is disassigned only at death).

[5] Assuming that entry into the first age-grade does not precede enrolment in the age-group (Section 1.2.3 of this chapter). Otherwise the grade-filling constraint might not be met.

TABLE 2.2

Grade	L_1 Level	L_2 Level	L_3 Level	L_4 Level	L_5 Level
I	1	1	1	1	1,2
II	2,3	2	2	2	3
III	4	3,4,5	3,4,5,6	3,4,5,6,7	—
IV	5+	6+	7+	8+	4+

From West Africa, but nowhere else, there are reports of what I shall call complex level rules. One such system—a relatively simple one—is represented in Figure 2.2. It is found among the Nawdeba of Togo and has been described by Pascal Wassungu (1971).[6] Age-sets are formed annually, and boys join their sets in their mid-teens. Each set passes through four named grades.[7] These grades are of an attenuated kind, that is, the members of an age-set are little affected by the fact that they belong to one grade rather than another.

Most of the information in Figure 2.2 is set out in a different form in Table 2.2. The table shows that the Nawdeba system can be described in terms of five sequences of level rules (L_1 to L_5), applying at different times. They apply in a cycle, L_1 in the first year, L_2 in the second, and so on, until in the sixth year L_1 applies again. In each year, the new sequence of rules comes into operation at the same time as the inauguration of a new set.

Let us now attempt a definition. A system operates with **complex level rules** if it has more than one sequence of level rules (call them L_1, L_2, . . . , L_n) and if these sequences of rules apply in a cycle. This means that it must also be determined when L_1 ceases to apply and L_2 begins to apply, when L_2 ceases to apply and L_3 begins to apply, and so on until L_n ceases to apply and L_1 applies again. In the (putative) instances that I know of, this is done by rules, which I shall call the **L-cycle rules**.

An examination of Table 2.2 will reveal a significant difference between simple and complex level rules. An age-grade system that

[6] The other sources on the Nawdeba, which are listed in Wassungu's article, do not cast any light on the transition rules. Even Wassungu's article is not wholly clear and self-consistent on this subject, and the analysis of his data that is presented in the text is offered mainly for the sake of illustration. I am by no means confident that it is a correct account of the Nawdeba transition rules.

[7] It is not certain, actually, whether there are four grades in the system or five (Wassungu 1971: 84). I have arbitrarily assumed that there are only four.

operates exclusively with simple level rules necessarily assigns a given grade to a number of age-groups that remains constant (I ignore the possibility of an age-group becoming extinct before it is assigned the last grade). In contrast, if a system has complex level rules it is necessarily the case that the number of groups in at least one grade is not constant, provided that age-groups are not inaugurated before being assigned the first grade. If they are,[8] then there can in principle be a system with complex level rules in which the number of groups in each grade is constant—but this case is hardly likely to arise in the real world.

As the Nawdeba example demonstrates, complex level rules do not necessarily meet the grade-filling constraint; but they do necessarily meet the group-unity constraint and the integration constraint.[9]

Complex level rules have been discussed here as though their existence were an established fact; but this is not really the case. There are relatively full descriptions of three other systems that *seem* to have such rules: among the Asaba Ibo (Jones 1962: 198 f.), the Kédougou Mandinka (Charest 1971), and the Afikpo Ibo (Ottenberg 1971). The first two of these are analyzed in Stewart (1972: 163–169, 252); the trouble is that the data are rather skimpy. In the case of the Afikpo, the ethnography is much better but still not quite full enough from our point of view, given the conceptual problems the system presents. There are several areas in West Africa where one might expect to find complex level rules (if they exist), for example, among the Edo speakers (Bradbury 1957). Future investigations will certainly cast some light on the matter.

In graded systems, transition rules that are clearly not level rules are rare. All the examples for which I discovered adequate documentation are discussed in this book. Some of them can only be described in ad hoc terms (see Section 4.5 of this chapter and Part Two, Chapters II and III). But two further categories of transition rule can be distinguished among such systems, even though each category only has one or two exemplars at the moment.

The first is the **grade-level rule**. The notion can best be made clear with an imaginary example. Take it that there is a graded age-group system with ten grades. Grades I to IV are assigned by transition rules of a type that can only be described in ad hoc terms.

[8] Possible examples are the systems of the Kuria (Baker 1927: 224), the Afikpo Ibo (Ottenberg 1971), and the Bobo (le Moal 1971: 116).

[9] Subject to the reservation mentioned in n. 5 p. 138 above.

TABLE 2.3

Grade	Grade-level
IV	1
V	2
VI	3
VII	4
VIII	5
IX	6
X	7 +

But thereafter the transition rules are relatively simple. As soon as any group S is assigned grade IV, group S + 1 is assigned grade V, group S + 2 is assigned grade VI, group S + 3 is assigned grade VII, and so on. We can deal with this kind of system by using the notion of a grade-level number. The level number of a group S indicates how many groups have been inaugurated since S was inaugurated: when S has the level number 1, no groups have been inaugurated since S was inaugurated; when it has the level number 2, one group has been inaugurated since S was inaugurated; and so on. The **grade-level number** of a group S (with reference to a **basic grade** G) indicates how many groups have been assigned grade G since S was assigned that grade: when group S has the grade-level number 1, this means that no groups have been assigned grade G since S was assigned it, and so on. In our imaginary system the basic grade is IV, that is to say, on being assigned this grade an age-group is given the grade-level number 1. The transition rules of the imaginary system can be set out as in Table 2.3.

There is one other kind of system where the notion of grade-levels is useful. Imagine a society in which age-sets are inaugurated before they are assigned the first grade of the age-grade sequence and in which the point in time at which a set is assigned grade I bears no relationship to its level number. But imagine further that as soon as any set S is assigned grade I, set S + 1 is assigned grade II, set S + 2 is assigned grade III, and so on.[10] Here again it would be convenient to use the notion of a grade-level, the basic grade being grade I.

In general terms, then, in a system of grade-level rules the assignment of some or all grades senior to some grade G is deter-

---

[10] In these examples I have assumed, for the sake of simplicity, that in each case there is only a single age-set in each grade, except for the most senior. But of course this is not necessarily the case.

mined by the grade-levels of the groups, whereas the assignment of grades junior to G—if there are any—and of G itself is determined in some other fashion. The best attested instance of a system of grade-level rules is at the moment the Masai system, which is of the first type mentioned (see further Section 4.2.1 of this chapter). Grade-level systems of the second type (those in which the age-group is inaugurated before the assignment of the first grade) may well exist, but the possible cases present both evidential and conceptual problems (see the references given on p. 140 n. 8). In principle, both simple and complex grade-level rules are possible, though only the former are recorded.

The second additional category of transition rules is the time rule, which after a specified period of time disassigns a grade from a group and assigns it a new one, irrespective of when the group changes level. Time rules exist among the Galla (Section 4.3 of this chapter) and the Banapas Bedik (Section 4.4.2 of this chapter).

I know of no systems that operate exclusively with either of these kinds of rules (even allowing for the fact that an entry rule can never be either a grade-level rule or a time rule).

Grade-level rules stand in the same relationship to the three combination constraints as do level rules (provided that the basic grade is assigned to the groups in the order in which they were inaugurated). A system operating with time rules does not necessarily meet the grade-filling constraint, but only the other two.

So far, the grade-filling constraint is the only one we have seen violated. Graded systems with transition rules that violate the group-unity constraint are not common, but there are some well-attested examples. They fall into two main classes. First, there are systems in which the age-groups are divided into sub-groups. In such cases the transition rules sometimes assign different grades to sub-groups of a single group (though the sub-groups are always in adjacent grades, and always in separate grades only for a limited period of time). The Masai offer perhaps the clearest instance of this (Section 4.2.1 of this chapter). Second, there are systems in which the individual members of a group make a given transition at different times, for example among the Borana Galla (p. 164). The same phenomenon is found among some tribes of the Masai group (Section 4.2.2 of this chapter), but they, in contrast to the Borana, only have individual transitions de facto, not as part of the rules of their system.

The integration constraint is hardly ever violated. I have only come across two possible instances. The clearest is the system of the Banapas Bedik (Section 4.4.2 of this chapter), which has unusual transition rules that also violate the group-unity constraint. It must be said, however, that the Banapas age-sets are exceedingly tenuous entities: their existence seems to be marked mainly by the fact that members of a set use a special term of address to each other.

A less clear instance of a nonintegrated system existed among the Kikuyu. I have tried to reconstruct its outlines in Section 4.4.1 of this chapter, but the facts remain rather uncertain. Very probably the transition rules of the age-grade system were such that a member of some set S might find himself in a higher grade than a member of some set S + i, $i \geqslant 1$. But it also looks as if the transition rules of the age-grade system took no account whatsoever of the age-sets; they operated entirely on individuals, without reference to their age-set affiliation. If this is so, then it seems reasonable to say that there were two separate systems, rather than a single nonintegrated system (cf. Chapter IV, Section 1). Of course the two systems would have to be integrated with each other in a nontechnical sense: since the same people belonged to both systems, the rules to which the systems made people subject had to be fairly consistent with each other.

In both these cases the group-unity constraint is violated, and it is interesting that there are no nonintegrated systems in which it is not (though logically there could be). We never find, for example, systems in which groups can move up a grade by their own decision alone and without affecting the grade assignment of other groups in the system;[11] or systems in which groups can move into a higher grade simply by virtue of some kind of achievement; or systems in which a central authority determines freely the rate at which each group is to pass through the grades; and so on.[12] In all these hypothetical systems, group-unity is maintained, but there is no obstacle to violations of the integration constraint or the grade-filling constraint. It seems that this particular combination of properties is

[11] It might appear that such a system has been claimed for the Arapaho (Kroeber 1904: 158 f.; Curtis 1911: 145; Lowie 1916: 932), but the implication of all the sources is that the integration constraint was not violated. See also Part Two, Chapter IV, Section 3, on the Gros Ventres.

[12] In any of these hypothetical systems it would be possible, at any given point in time, to describe which grades were assigned to which age-groups by means of a table mapping grades to levels. This is true of any system that combines age-groups (with the ordering characteristic) with age-grades and meets the group-unity constraint. But such a table would not represent a *set of rules* mapping grades to levels; and a series of different tables of this kind, drawn up over a period of time for a given system, would not form a cycle. So systems of this kind are quite different from complex level rule systems.

most unattractive; whereas systems that meet all three combination constraints are found all over the world.

3 ALTERNATIVES TO AGE-GRADES

Age-grades are not the only means by which the roles of age-groups can be changed. Another possibility is what may be called a task allocation system. This is a method of assigning duties to age-groups such that a group may be assigned a duty, disassigned it, and then assigned it again. One possibility is for groups to perform tasks in turn: among the Yakö, for instance, the men's age-sets each spend a day in turn in guarding houses from fire during the dry season (Forde 1964: 146). Another is for the tasks to be assigned by some central authority, as for instance in the South African systems where the ruler orders his "regiments" to do what he wants. Task allocation systems are common, especially in West Africa (see, for instance, Gamble 1955: 4 f. on the Gambia Mandinka; Harris 1965: 36 on the Mbembe).

Task allocation should be distinguished from the kind of case where the age-group itself decides to undertake a certain task, either for the benefit of the group as a whole, or to help one of its members (see, for instance, Jensen 1936: 342 on the Konso; Fajana 1968: 238 on the Yoruba).

Task allocation systems are quite obviously different from age-grade systems, and any reasonable typology must distinguish them. The same cannot be said for the second type of mechanism that I suggest exists: the handing down system. In such a system a senior age-group transfers a series of rights to a junior one, not simultaneously, but over a period of time. The rights involved are, for instance, permission to wear certain clothes or ornaments, or rights to certain portions of a sacrificial animal. It seems that in some cases the senior group relinquishes the rights that it grants to the junior one, while in other cases it retains them.

The evidence on handing down systems is rather slight, but they have been noted among the Masai (see the references in Bernardi 1955: 287 f.), the Kuria (Ruel 1962), and the Karimojong (Dyson-Hudson 1966: 177 ff.); the Blackfoot, Mandan, and Hidatsa operate systems that can perhaps be assimilated to this type; and compare Kronenberg (1972: 97) on the Didinga. I do not know just how sharply handing down systems could be distinguished from age-grade systems, and I propose this category only in a tentative fashion.

TABLE 2.4

Grade	Level
I. Bachelors	1
II. Young Men	2
III. Mature Men	3 +

4 *SELECTED SYSTEMS

4.1 Simple Level Rules: The Akwe-Shavante

Our definition of level rules implies that a change in the level numbers of the groups in the system is accompanied simultaneously by any necessary change in their grades. In concrete terms, a single ceremony, or a set of simultaneous ceremonies, marks both the inauguration of a new group and any shifts in grade that this necessitates. This is indeed what happens in the great majority of systems with level rules. There is, however, at least one system—that of the Akwe-Shavante of Brazil, as described by Maybury-Lewis (1967)—which uses what look like level rules, but in which the transitions are not simultaneous with changes of level.

The Shavante inaugurate a new age-set every 5 years, and with a certain amount of simplification their age-grade system can be represented as operating with simple level rules, as set out in Table 2.4.

Table 2.4 is a simplification because the transitions actually take place in two stages. The first of these is what Maybury-Lewis calls "initiation." At this stage the set in grade I (call it S + 1) moves to grade II (it is they who are said to be "initiated"), and a new set (S) is inaugurated. But set S is not, as in an ideal level rule system, automatically assigned grade I on being inaugurated; nor is S + 2 assigned a new grade. So after this first stage there is no set in grade I, sets S + 1 and S + 2 are both in grade II, and all other sets are in grade III.

Some time later—the interval may be up to 6 months—the second stage follows: set S is now assigned grade I in what Maybury-Lewis calls the "induction ceremony" (1967: 104, 157),[13] and set

---

[13] There is a minor inconsistency in Maybury-Lewis's account at this point. His description of the initiation ceremony (i.e., the first stage) ends with a section describing the inauguration of the new age-set, which was called

S + 2 moves up into grade III (1967: 138). Only after this second stage, then, does the distribution of sets correspond to Table 2.4.

Given the ethnographic evidence and the conceptual framework at present available, it seems best to look on the Shavante system merely as a slightly deviant type of simple level rule system. If it turns out that there are other systems that resemble it, then the whole matter can be reconsidered. As far as I know, the only system reported to have the same general features is that of the Keyo, as described by Massam (1927). But I think there is good reason to be sceptical about Massam's data.[14]

4.2 The Masai Group

4.2.1 The Masai

The Masai have perhaps the most famous of all age-group systems, and it is described in innumerable writings. Yet until recently there was much about it that remained obscure. A good modern study has now been produced—though not published—by A. H. Jacobs, and the analysis given here is based almost entirely on his works (1958, 1963, 1965a) and on a personal communication from him (1969). Where these accounts differ from one another, I have chosen the version in the most recent one.

For the older sources, see Schurtz 1902: 129–133, Bernardi 1955, Huppertz 1959: 965–969, and Jacobs 1965b. Each of these four works contains references not found in any of the other

---

Nodzę'ú. He writes "The Nodzę'ú were now formally in existence as an age-set [1967: 136, cf. 338]." Elsewhere, however, he writes as if the set only came into being at the time of the induction ceremony (i.e., stage two) (1967: 105, 154). I have little doubt, however, that the set was indeed inaugurated at the initiation ceremony, of which Maybury-Lewis gives a full description. It would be difficult to make sense of the events of the last day of that ceremony on any other assumption.

[14] He is almost certainly wrong, for example, in stating that the members of an age-group are only circumcised about a year after they have performed the Sakobei ceremony (1927: 67). According to Kiprono (quoted in Welbourn 1968: 214), circumcision precedes the Sakobei, and this is in accordance with what we know of the closely related systems of the Nandi and the Kipsigis. (Torday's field work among the Keyo—mentioned on p. 103 n. 83—was mainly linguistic, rather than ethnographic; a proper modern description of the Keyo age-group system therefore remains a desideratum, particularly since, to judge from what Kiprono says, it is on the verge of rapid decline.)

TABLE 2.5

	Grade	Grade level	
	Grade	(i)	(ii)
I.	Junior Warriors (IlMurran)	—	—
II.	Senior Warriors (IlMurran)	—	1
III.	Junior Elders (IlMoruak)	1	2
IV.	Senior Elders (IlMoruak)	2	3
V.	Retired Elders (IlMoruak)	3	4
VI.	Ancient Elders (IlDasati)	4+	5+

three,[15] and there are various primary sources not mentioned in any of them, among which I consulted Julien (n.d.)—where the data on age organization stem entirely from Fosbrooke (1948)—and Lewis (1930–1946).

An attempt to describe the transition rules of the Masai faces unusual difficulties. The system is remarkably flexible: the order of the various ceremonies related to transitions is not immutable but can vary from one set to another. There seem to be altogether four possible modes, which I shall consider in turn. I shall say nothing here of the factors that determine which mode a particular set adopts, but this is a point on which Jacobs (1965a) supplies a good deal of information.

The first of these four—and the one Jacobs seems to consider the most important—is represented in Table 2.5 (based on Jacobs 1965a: 243). Columns (i) and (ii) in that table represent different analyses of this mode; I shall explain them in a moment. The English names of the grades are those given by Jacobs; the Masai's own terms are given in parentheses. I have followed Jacobs in assuming that there are six grades, though the Masai terminology suggests that a

[15] Admirable though the Huppertz' and Jacobs' bibliographies are, they suffer—like most tribal bibliographies—from an important deficiency: they do not distinguish between primary and secondary sources. (By a primary source I mean any work which contains any data on the tribe that are not derived from some other available work; by a secondary source, I mean any other work that refers to the tribe in question.) The compiler of a tribal bibliography should aim at listing all the primary sources; as for secondary sources, a list of the most important ones is all that is necessary—and often, as in the case of the Masai, all that is practicable. It should always be made clear whether a given work is a primary or a secondary source.

description in terms of three grades would also be possible.[16] Even given all the relevant data, there are no satisfactory means of deciding between such alternatives (Section 1.2.4 of this chapter). In this book I shall, unless otherwise indicated, always follow the division into grades given by the sources, but without the implication that I know of good grounds for preferring that description to any other.

The first of the four modes is also represented in Figure 2.3 (which assumes a system in which none of the other three modes exist). The time intervals indicated by the diagram should not be taken too seriously; they are idealizations based on Gulliver (1963: 27 f.). These figures are not very different from the various ones given by Jacobs, though Jacobs now sets the inauguration interval at 15 years (1968: 16). What matters, for us, is not the length of time between ceremonies, but the order in which they take place. The significance of the shaded areas in the diagram will be explained later. Jacobs found two sets in the Ancient Elders (VI) grade, the oldest of which had very few members. Obviously, by the time set $S - 6$ become Junior Elders (III), all members of S will be dead.

In Figure 2.3 the period that an age-set spends in the Junior Warrior (I) grade is divided into two unequal parts by a broken line. This line indicates the point in time at which the Endungore ceremony takes place. The Endungore ceremony marks the end of the

---

16 Here, as elsewhere, I am concerned only with grades assigned after enrolment in an age-group (Section 1.2.3 of this chapter). It may even be that the Masai distinguish only two grades, since Jacobs says that "the grade of 'ancient' elders (referred to as *Ildasati*, or sometimes as *Lenwaki*, 'of our ancestors') is only a sub-grade of 'elderhood' (*Ilmoruak*) [1965a: 242]." Jacobs does not, however, make it clear why he believes that the Masai view *Ildasati* as a sub-grade, rather than as a grade. The other tribes of the Masai group are all reported to have terms only for two grades, Warriors (or *moran*) and Elders. See Spencer (1965: 81 ff.) on the Samburu, together with the comments in Section 4.2.3 of this chapter. In a personal communication, Spencer states that the Samburu have terms for two age-grades: *lmurani* (pl. *lmuran*), the *moran*, and *lpaiyeni* (pl. *lpaiyen*), or, less commonly, *lmoruo* (pl. *lmoruak*), the Elders. He adds "The Samburu may distinguish really old men from others by using such terms as *ltasati* and *lmoruo*. However, as you point out, this does not refer to a separate grade of retired elderhood. Indeed, the notion of retirement is not as explicit as for instance in Gulliver (1963: 38)." See also Gulliver (1963: 26) on the Arusha; Beidelman (1960: 262) on the Baraguyu; and Gray (1963) on the Sonjo, who do, however, have a special term for each of the two sets in the Warrior grade. (I follow Gray in taking it that the Sonjo age-set is inaugurated at the time of the initiation ceremony, and not at the time when the first prospective member of the set is circumcised. On this assumption they have simple level rules.)

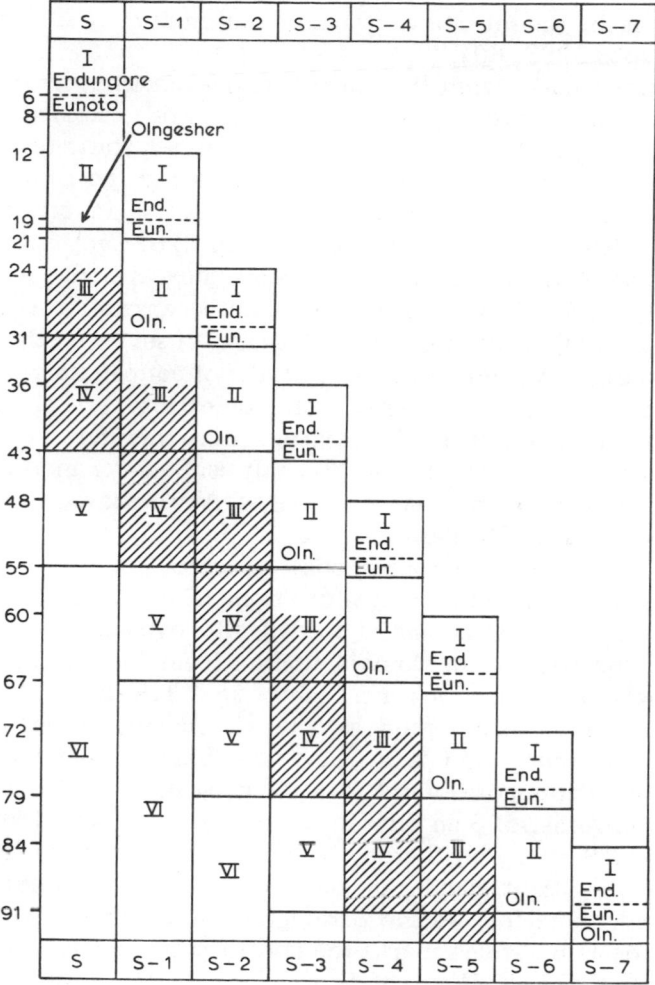

Figure 2.3

recruitment period of the set.[17] It is followed not long after by the
Eunoto ceremony, which promotes the set to the Senior Warrior (II)
grade. The Olngesher ceremony (11 years later according to the
diagram)[18] promotes the set to Junior Elders (III); "as senior warriors are graduated to elderhood by performing the *olngesher* cere-

---

[17]Actually there are secondary rules that allow certain persons to enrol
even after the end of the recruitment period, but these can be ignored here.
Compare p. 117 and Jacobs (1958: 9).

[18]Except that for S it is 12 years later, and for S − 1 it is 10 years later
(due to a slip which at any rate increases the realism of the diagram).

mony . . . each age-set above them is automatically advanced in status [Jacobs 1963: 60]."

Now, it is clear from the diagram and from what has been said that the transition rules of the system cannot be described in terms of levels. The point in time at which a new set starts recruiting is about halfway between one set of transitions and the next. Equally clearly, a description in terms of grade-levels is in order. Which should be chosen as the basic grade? Column (i) of Table 2.5 assumes that the answer is grade III, and this seems unexceptionable. Column (ii) of Table 2.5 represents a more speculative answer; it would only be correct, strictly speaking, if the Olngesher of set S and the Eunoto of S − 1 took place simultaneously—which, of course, is not the case. But if, to the Masai, these two ceremonies are very closely connected—and it seems from the evidence that this may be so—then there is something to be said for this analysis. Such an analysis would be rather similar to one that treated the Akwe-Shavante as having essentially simple level rules.

The second of the four modes is represented in Figure 2.4 (which also assumes a system in which none of the other three modes exist). In this case the age-set is divided into two sub-sets, the Right Hand and the Left Hand. Combining data from Jacobs (1965a: 269 f.; personal communication) and Fosbrooke (1948: 25 f.), the course of events can be represented as follows. Age-set S performs the Olngesher ceremony and is assigned the Junior Elder (III) grade, without the Endungore of set S − 1 having been performed. Soon after the Olngesher of S an Eunoto ceremony is performed for certain members of S − 1, who thereby become Senior Warriors (II). They constitute the Right Hand. At some point after the Eunoto of the Right Hand, there follows the Endungore (indicated on the diagram by a broken line), which marks the end of recruitment to set S − 1. After that, the Left Hand of S − 1 have their Eunoto. The two sections of set S − 1 are now joined in the grade of Senior Warriors (II), and make all later transitions as a single unit.

It emerges clearly from the sources that the members of the Right Hand are all enrolled before any members of the Left Hand are enrolled. It also appears, however, that some members of the Left Hand are enrolled before the Eunoto of the Right Hand, though not long before (Jacobs 1965a: 268). Fosbrooke indicates that a special ceremony (Embolosat) marks the inauguration of recruitment to the Left Hand (as also, earlier, to the Right); but this special ceremony is not mentioned by Jacobs in this context.

Jacobs considers this mode less important than the first one, but it is not clear why. In his paper of 1958 (p. 14) he remarked that

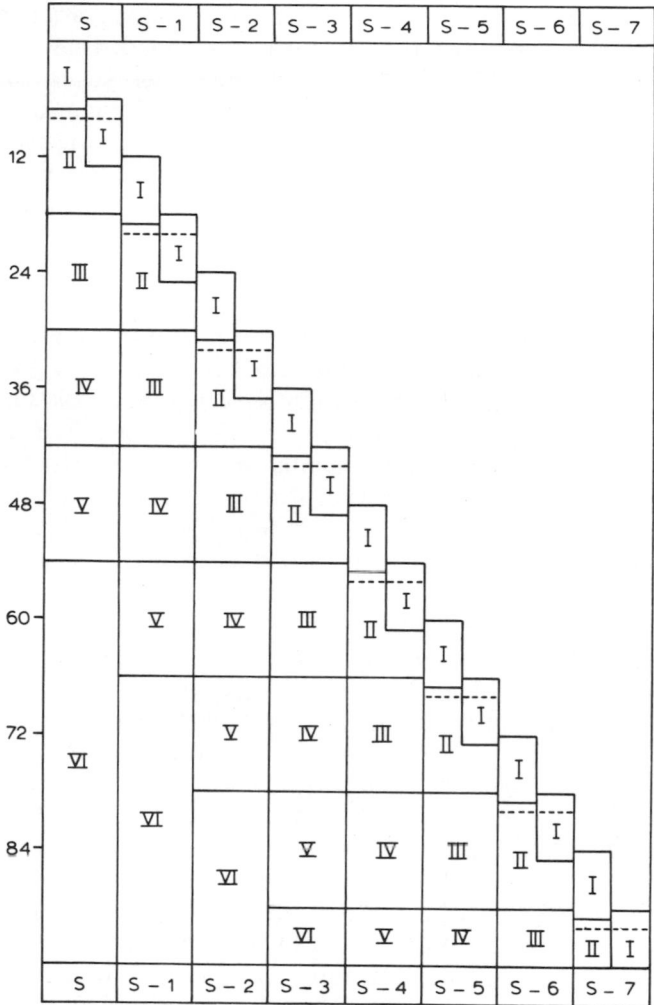

Figure 2.4

four of the preceding seven sets were divided into Right Hand and Left Hand, and that the next set was expected to be divided in the same way. So this mode seems to be the most common one; certainly Fosbrooke and other writers on the Masai seem to look on it as the standard one.

By assigning the Left Hand and Right Hand, for a time, to different grades, the system violates the group-unity constraint. Much the same sort of thing seems to happen among the Izi Ibo (Section 4.5.2 of this chapter).

The remaining two modes of transition both appear to be considered less proper than the two just mentioned. One of them is to perform first the Olngesher of set S, and then successively the Endungore and Eunoto of S − 1 (Jacobs, personal communication). The other, very similar, one is to perform first the Olngesher of S, and then to combine the Endungore and Eunoto of S − 1 in a single ceremony (Jacobs 1965a: 268 f., and personal communication).

4.2.2 The Arusha

The age-set system of the Arusha (described in Gulliver 1963)[19] is very closely linked to that of the Kisongo subtribe of the Masai. Gulliver analyzes the Arusha age-grade sequence as consisting of five grades, and he gives these grades essentially the same names as the first five grades distinguished by Jacobs for the Masai. The transition rules given by Gulliver are, allowing for the absence of a sixth grade, identical with those represented in Figure 2.3 and Table 2.5. Furthermore, the Arusha system "is geared to that of the adjacent Kisongo Masai by Arusha participation in the Kisongo-controlled ceremonies of promotion of junior murran [i.e., Junior Warriors (I)] to senior murran [i.e., Senior Warriors (II)] (eunoto), and transfer of senior murran to elderhood (olngesher) [Gulliver 1963: 28 f.]."

Gulliver's description of the Arusha makes a new and important distinction. The implication of our representation of the Masai system was that the age-sets pass through the grades "in a series of jerks" (to use the expressive phrase that Spencer (1965: 165) applies to the Samburu). And this is also how the Arusha themselves describe their system (Gulliver 1963: 36). But the reality, as Gulliver makes clear, is different. The sets, in effect, flow smoothly through the grades. Consider, for instance, a set that has for some time been assigned the grade of Senior Murran (II). Many of its members will, in fact, already be behaving as if they were Junior Elders (III). "As the system operates in actual practice the ceremonial events (the presumptive rites de passage) mainly give public recognition of an already established change for the majority of men in an age-set; they largely serve to bring formal categories into line with actual roles [1963: 39]."

[19] The other sources on Arusha age organization that I know of (Meek 1950; A. Thomas 1966) do not contain any information relevant to the topics discussed here.

We should distinguish here between two phenomena that could, in principle, exist independently of each other, though they are found together in the Arusha system and also to some extent in related systems. One is that the members of a single group make a given transition at different times, thus violating the group-unity constraint. The other is that any given individual makes a given transition fairly gradually, so that the system lacks the characteristic implicit in our definition that a person is quite clearly assigned either one age-grade or another. I shall consider in a moment why it is that the native model differs from the reality on these points, but first let us look at some evidence from other tribes of the Masai group.

The Samburu transition rules (which are analyzed in the next section) are somewhat different from those of the Masai and Arusha, but the age-grade sequence contains the same basic division between Warriors (or *moran*) and Elders (cf. p. 148 n. 16). Now, there is a ceremony (the *ilmugit* of the milk and leaves) "when in effect the whole age-set become elders [Spencer 1965: 165, cf. 89]." But in practice "there is no precise point at which moran retire to elderhood [1965: 89]." Instead, there is a considerable period of time during which "different moran behave differently according to the extent to which they are prepared to settle down: those who wish to become elders as soon as possible generally try to marry early and start to acquire the dignity of elders; and those who prefer still to remain as moran retain the accoutrements and behaviour of moranhood [1965: 90]." It is clear that both the phenomena mentioned in the preceding paragraph are to be found in this system.

Very similar observations have been made in relation to the Masai. Jacobs writes as follows.

> Although age-grades and the relative position of the age-sets which occupy them tend to establish rigid categories of ideal behaviour, there are numerous discrepancies between what members of any one age-set actually do at any one time and what persons in other age-sets think ought to be done, just as there are inconsistencies between complete age-set conformity as an ideal and other social values which tend to run counter to it. In 1957, for example, senior warriors consisted of some persons who acted like many junior elders and others who behaved as junior warriors. Diagrammatically their age-set might be pictured as part in the warrior-grade and part in the elder-grade. Masai are acutely aware of these discrepancies and see them as the inevitable consequence of their particular form of group socialization. But they also attempt to deal systematically with these inconsistencies by ceremonially promoting regular changes in age-set status [1965a: 251].

Other passages in Jacobs's work make the same point in other contexts and, in particular, indicate that this kind of discrepancy also exists in the transitions between the sub-grades of the Elders grade (Jacobs 1965a: 341 ff.). The same kind of thing is reported by Fosbrooke

> That a moran [i.e., an individual assigned grade I or grade II] may not marry is a rule so frequently repeated that one is almost compelled to believe that in pre-European times they did not marry. But there are many indications to the contrary. Aged informants will sometimes admit that they were married whilst still moran [taking this in conjunction with other evidence] one . . . feels justified in concluding that towards the end of the period of senior warriorhood the moran were beginning to marry and settle down [1948: 30].[20]

This passage brings out clearly the difference between ideal and reality.

These data show that the phenomena we are concerned with are not unique to the Arusha system. Very likely they are even to be found in systems outside the Masai group.[21] *Prima facie*, however, it seems that they assume a more marked character in the Arusha system than in the other two that have been mentioned. Yet this is not something we can be at all sure of. It may be that the differences between the emphases that the sources place on this point reflect no more than the different interests of the ethnographers. In this lies an illustration of the inadequacy of our descriptive techniques. Here are three good ethnographers—Gulliver, Jacobs, and Spencer—trained in the same tradition, writing at the same time, in contact with each other, and describing closely related age-set systems; and yet as soon as we try to specify any except the most general differences between these systems, we find that their data are simply not comparable. This will emerge even more clearly from the next section.

How can we account for this discrepancy between the native models and the reality? The fact that members of a single group in practice make transitions at different times must be related to the

---

[20] According to Jacobs (1965a: 246, 267) the rule is that Senior Warriors (II) may marry and settle down, but that they may not beget children.

[21] Cf. Gulliver (1963: 39 n.). It looks as if something of the sort is also found in the Nandi system (Huntingford 1953: 59, 65), and it may be presumed also to have existed in that of the Kipsigis. This presumption solves a problem raised by Peristiany (1939: 37 f.).

great age-range within each group.[22] Probably in all three systems it is usually of the order of 15 years. Not surprisingly, a way of life that suits a youth in his early twenties will have lost some of its attraction for a man in his mid-thirties. The fact that transitions are relatively gradual for each individual is no doubt connected with the marked difference between the life style of different grades. This seems to be true especially of the Masai and the Samburu. Even if an individual is ready to accept that the time has come for him to make the transition, it involves such a radical alteration in his existence that he would find it hard to accomplish overnight.

4.2.3 The Samburu

The Samburu age-grade sequence, as described by Spencer, differs rather markedly from the age-grade sequences of the Masai and the Arusha, as described by Jacobs and Gulliver. In this section I shall try to show that the Samburu sequence is not actually as divergent as it appears. The apparent difference arises from the fact that the concept of an age-grade used by Spencer is not the same as the one used by Gulliver and Jacobs.

Spencer (1965: 84) represents the age-grade sequence as consisting of two grades, Moran and Elders.[23] These in turn are divided into sub-grades, as follows:

    I. Junior Moran
   II. Senior Moran
 III. Junior Elders
 IV. Firestick Elders
  V. Senior Elders

Figure 2.5 is a representation of this system. As in the Masai diagrams, the intervals given are idealizations (based especially on Spencer 1965: 86), but the relationships of the transitions to each other are realistic. The meanings of the symbols in the diagram are as

[22] As must also the division of some Masai sets into Left Hand and Right Hand.

[23] I ignore a minor complication here by assuming that an age-group is assigned the Moran grade as soon as it is inaugurated. In reality there is a period of a month or two between the inauguration of an age-group and its being assigned the Moran grade (Spencer 1973: 86, 90).

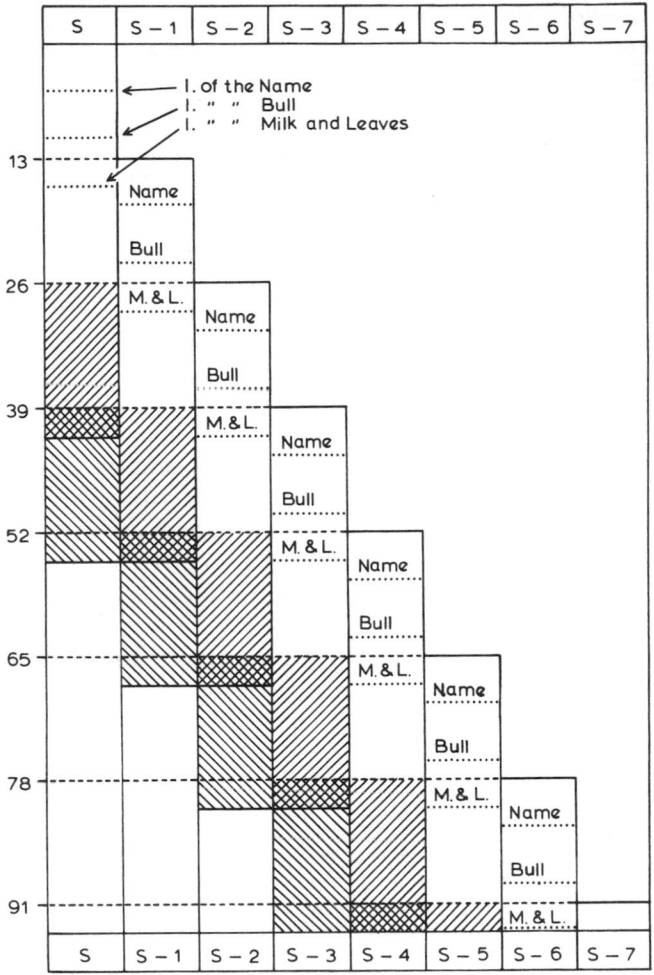

Figure 2.5

follows. The broken lines in a column indicate the points at which the level number of a group rises by one. The dotted lines indicate *ilmugit* ceremonies. The *ilmugit* of the name marks the transition from Junior Moran (I) to Senior Moran (II). The *ilmugit* of the bull marks the point after which no further members may be enrolled in the group. The *ilmugit* of the milk and leaves marks, as we know, the point at which theoretically the whole group makes the transition from Moran to Elder. In practice, individuals start to assume the characteristics of Elders soon after the *ilmugit* of the bull.

The *ilmugits*, it will be observed, have their analogues in the Masai system. The *ilmugit* of the name corresponds to the Eunoto, the *ilmugit* of the bull to the Endungore, and the *ilmugit* of the milk and leaves to the Olngesher. Among the Samburu, the order of the "Eunoto" and the "Endungore" has been reversed, but in fact this difference is less striking than it appears, since in practice enrolments usually cease "a number of years" before the *ilmugit* of the bull (Spencer: 1965: 89).

Let us now follow the history of group S in Figure 2.5. Having performed the *ilmugit* of the milk and leaves in the year 16, it is assigned the Junior Elder (III) grade. Here it remains until the year 26, when S − 2 is inaugurated. Now, in the Samburu system, as in many others, there is a special relationship between alternate age-groups (cf. Chapter I, Section 9). The Samburu call this the firestick relationship, because the act by which a new age-group S − 2 is inaugurated is the symbolic kindling of fire by members of S (Spencer 1965:82). When S − 2 is inaugurated, then, S becomes for the first time the senior partner in such a relationship; and "so far as the junior age-set is concerned during its period in the moran age grade, the elders of the senior age-set are known as *firestick elders* [Spencer 1965: 82]." So group S are in the Firestick Elders (IV) grade as long as group S − 2 are Moran (grades I and II). I have indicated this period by drawing lines sloping from right to left in column S.

We come now to the fifth and last grade. The Samburu have, as we know, a negative PL rule: the sons of men in S must join S − 3 or a more junior group. Many of them join S − 3; about one-half of the men in S − 3 have fathers in S (Spencer 1965: 83). Because of this, when S − 3 is in the Moran grade, group S are known as the fathers of the Moran. I have indicated this period by drawing lines sloping from left to right. The group known as the fathers of the Moran, and all groups senior to it, are, in Spencer's usage, Senior Elders (V) (Spencer 1965: 84).

As Spencer (1965: 84) notes, and as the diagram makes clear, it is possible at one and the same time for a group S to be the Firestick Elders of S − 2 and the fathers of the Moran of S − 3. In other words, in Spencer's usage a group can be assigned two grades at once. Gulliver and Jacobs, on the other hand, evidently have a concept of an age-grade that incorporates the unique-assignment constraint. Now I shall try to show that the Samburu and Masai—Arusha systems are so similar with respect to certain of their features, that there is some reason to believe that had Gulliver or Jacobs been describing the Samburu, then we would have received a quite different account of this age-grade sequence; and, by the same token, that Spencer would have given us a different account of the Masai and Arusha sequences.

The main piece of evidence to support this assertion is the fact that alternate linking exists among the Masai and the Arusha as well as among the Samburu. Jacobs makes it clear that among the Masai, at least, it is, by any criteria we can apply, not a whit less important than among the Samburu. He writes, for instance, as follows: "At the very heart of Pastoral Masai political behaviour is a reciprocal bond of socio-ritual solidarity between members of alternate . . . age-sets. . . . This bond is called *olpiron* ('firestick') [1963: 59]." Gulliver (1963: 29 ff.) describes the analogous link among the Arusha. It seems reasonable to assume that had Spencer been describing these tribes, then there too he would have distinguished a Firestick Elders grade or its equivalent. The shaded areas of Figure 2.3 indicate the period that this putative grade would cover. We may assume that the period between the Olngesher and the transition to the Firestick Elders would have been distinguished as the Junior Elders grade, and that the period after leaving the Firestick Elders grade would have constituted one or two further grades. Since the Masai and the Arusha have no analogue of the fathers of the Moran, it may be assumed that there would not have been any overlapping of "grades" of the kind postulated for the Samburu. (Jacobs and Gulliver, it should be mentioned, treat the relationship between alternate sets separately from the age-grade system, and this is also the procedure adopted in the present work; cf. Section 1.2.6 of this chapter.)

What would the Samburu system look like, as described by Gulliver or Jacobs? Let us hazard a guess. These two ethnographers subdivide the Elders grade in such a fashion that each of the three most junior groups in that grade is assigned a separate sub-grade. It is, of course, impossible to say with certainty whether they would have followed the same procedure with the Samburu. All one can say is that the sources are sufficiently inexplicit, and sufficiently taciturn about justifying the boundaries they place between grades, for us at least to be able to entertain the possibility. Under such an analysis, group S would become Junior Elders on leaving the moran grade. Their subsequent history would be as follows:

> Group S are Junior Elders as long as $S - 1$ are moran
> Group S are Senior Elders as long as $S - 2$ are moran
> Group S are Retired Elders thereafter.

Let me now summarize this discussion. It has not been my intention to assert that any of the three ethnographers misrepresented the system he described. (Contrast the discussion of unique paternal linking systems, which, I believe, often have been misrepresented.) What I have tried to show, rather, is that none of them operated with an explicit and well-developed concept of an age-grade, and that this has had two effects. First, it is hard to compare their data on these systems in detail. Second, many relevant data—the data that would show why one analysis of the age-grade system is better than another—are not reported. Weaknesses of this kind are, of course, characteristic of almost all age-group system ethnographies, most of which are much inferior to the ones we have been discussing. It just happens that these three provide a particularly good illustration of how the absence of a satisfactory conceptual framework can hamper even the best ethnographer.

4.3 Time Rules

4.3.1 The Borana Galla

The Borana operate a Gada system that is usually regarded as being—or at least, as having been in the recent past—the central institution of their society. The early literature on the system, which is not of much importance, is reviewed by Michels (1941: 131–138, 170 ff.). As far as I know, the only pre-1941 source that he fails to mention is Giaccardi (1937). Since 1941 there have become available eight further accounts, which include material collected at first hand: Pecci (1941),[24] Wingfield (1948), Baxter (1954), Haberland (1963), Adamson (1967), Knutsson (1967), Klausberger (1972), and Legesse (1973). Yet despite this substantial body of literature, there remains much that is not known about Borana society, and about the Gada system in particular. Further research on this remarkable tribe would be well worth undertaking.

The account given here is based mainly on Pecci, Haberland, and Legesse (all relevant disagreements between them are noted). Pecci's article is short, coherent, and accurate (Haberland 1963: 185); but it has never attracted the attention it deserves, partly no

---

[24] Pecci's data are also available, virtually verbatim, in Zavattari (1940: 348–361; 1942: 20–33). (For an account of the circumstances that led to their being reproduced thus, see Zavattari 1942: 20 n. 1.)

doubt because it is written in rather a complicated way (Jensen 1941: 87 confessed himself unable to make sense of it). Haberland's ethnography is notable for its wealth of detail,[25] while Legesse's work stands out above all because he carried out a census of age-group members and reported the results in full.

Knutsson did most of his fieldwork among the Machcha Galla, but he also gives an account of the Borana Gada system (1967: 161–169). I have not attached much weight to his information. He does not generally give the sources of his data; the length of time he spent with the Borana seems to have been very limited (1967: 5); he relies heavily on Haberland; and he makes no mention of Pecci (or of Zavattari).

Baxter, in contrast to the authors so far mentioned, studied the Kenyan, and not the Ethiopian, Borana. The fact that he was unable to visit the Ethiopian Borana meant that he was cut off from the main body of the tribe, from the most important tribal functionaries,[26] and also, no doubt, from many of the best potential informants. Furthermore, the Kenyan Borana, though participating in the same Gada system as their Ethiopian brethren, had—and were aware of having—an impoverished ceremonial life compared with the rest of the tribe (Baxter, personal communication). For these reasons Baxter was unable to produce a satisfactory overall account of the system,[27] but, even so, his study contains much useful information.[28] A little of it is available in print in Baxter (1965).

Wingfield (1948: 352) offers a brief account of the Borana Gada system, which is largely a garbled and unacknowledged paraphrase of Plowman (1919). It does, however, contain a few data on one ritual (what I shall call the Retirement Ceremony), which seem

[25] Note that Haberland's diagram of the Borana system (1963: 194 f.) contains misprints in the alignment of the lines that make it highly misleading. It can be corrected by reference to his diagram of the Alabdu Galla Gada system (1963: 314 f.), which has the same transition rules.

[26] Baxter (1954: 357) points out that none of the officers of the Gada system lived in Kenya.

[27] He was not familiar with Pecci's work.

[28] Legesse's work suggests, for instance, that Baxter was the first to provide the correct explanations of the important terms *gogessa* (descent stream) and *luba* (age-group), both of which seem to have been misunderstood by Pecci and Haberland. Although Legesse wrote his book without ever having consulted Baxter's thesis (Legesse 1973: 14 n.), there are a number of points on which Baxter and Legesse agree with each other and disagree with the descriptions by Pecci and Haberland (which diverge scarcely at all).

to be the result of independent observation. Klausberger (1972) is also very short, but generally accurate.

Another brief account of the system—but one based on first-hand investigations—is to be found in Adamson (1967: 351 ff.). This report—which diverges in a number of respects from those in other sources—need not be taken too seriously.. What is useful in Adamson's book is the first-hand description of the Retirement Ceremony held in Marsabit (Kenya) in 1955. It is accompanied by excellent photographs. This description was made available to Haberland before it was published, and he used it in his book (1963: 220 ff.).

The Borana system is represented in Figure 2.6. This diagram has several new features, of which, for the moment, we need note

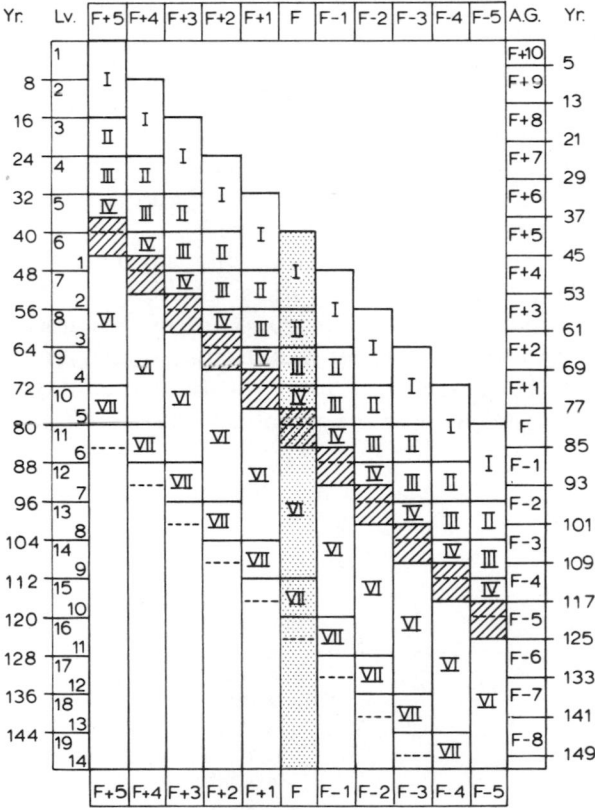

Figure 2.6

only the following. The numbers in the columns headed Yr. represent years. The numbers in the top left-hand corners of the boxes in the column headed Lv. represent the level numbers of group F + 5. The numbers in the bottom right-hand corners of the same boxes represent the level numbers of group F. The inauguration interval is 8 years. As we know from earlier references, the system has a UPL rule: sons join F − 5. In Figure 2.6 the central age-group, F, has been stippled for the sake of distinctness. All men in F have fathers in F + 5, and all men in F − 5 are sons of men in F.

The names of the grades, and the numbers I have given them, are set out in Table 2.6. There is a possible grade, known as Daballe, which comes before Gamme (I). Pecci (1941: 308, 318) lists it among the grades; Haberland (1963: 193) considers that it is not really a grade; and Legesse, while categorizing it as a grade, says that it "would be quite legitimate to think of the *daballe* as a pre-grade [1973: 125]." It makes no real difference to the account given here which of these alternatives is chosen.

The most important grade is Gada (V). Haberland says that the group to which it is assigned exercises "the highest political power over the whole Borana tribe and performs the most significant religious functions [1963: 203]." I am not sure that this is true nowadays, but it certainly was once. In Figure 2.6 this period in the history of each age-group has been shaded in.

A glance at the diagram shows that the first three grades are assigned and disassigned by level rules. Grade IV (Raba Dori) is also assigned by a level rule, since a group enters this grade on reaching level 5, but it is disassigned by a time rule: after a group has spent 5 years in grade IV, there takes place the Bali ceremony, at which the transfer of an ostrich feather symbolizes the transfer of the grade of

TABLE 2.6

I.	Gamme
II.	Cusa
III.	Raba Didica
IV.	Raba Dori
V.	Gada
VI.	Yuba
VII.	Gada Moji

Gada (V) from one age-group (say F) to its immediate junior (F − 1).[29]

The Gada grade is disassigned, ideally, after 8 years,[30] when the Bali ceremony again takes place and the senior group become Yuba (VI). The transition from Gada (V) to Yuba (VI) is therefore certainly governed by a time rule; and if Haberland and Legesse are right, so also is the transition from Raba Dori (IV) to Gada (V).

Pecci and Legesse describe the next transition, from Yuba (VI) to Gada Moji (VII), as occurring simply by a level rule (when the group reaches level 10). It has been represented thus in Figure 2.6. Haberland gives a slightly different, and probably more accurate, account. According to his version a man can make the transition from Yuba (VI) to Gada Moji (VII) at any time he wants during the 4 years after his group reaches the tenth level.[31] Since the position

[29] At this point, Pecci diverges in one respect from Haberland and Legesse. In his view, even though group F is in the Gada grade after the Bali ceremony, it also remains in grade IV until it reaches level 6. (The point at which it reaches level 6 is indicated on the diagram by the dotted line which divides into two parts the period that each group spends in the Gada grade.) Ideally, level 6 is reached 8 years after reaching level 5, so there will be a period of 3 years during which the group is assigned two "grades" (Pecci 1941: 309). If this is indeed how the Borana view their system, then we are dealing with a rare and interesting phenomenon; but since Pecci's statement is not confirmed by either Haberland or Legesse, we must maintain a certain amount of reserve in our attitude toward it.

[30] Knutsson (1967: 163) says 11 years, but he gives no source for this datum, and it is certainly incorrect. It contradicts other, much better, sources (Pecci, Haberland, and Legesse in particular), as well as being inconsistent with the deep rooted 8-year tradition (on which see p. 165). Perhaps Knutsson erroneously added the 3 years of Raba Dori (IV), which Pecci describes as overlapping the Gada grade, to the 8 years of the Gada grade.

[31] The difference between Haberland and Legesse on this point is not, in fact, great. Haberland (1963: 217 ff.) distinguishes two ceremonies. One is the transition from Gada Moji (VII) to Jarsa (retired), which I call the Retirement Ceremony, and which he calls the Jara (or Gadamoji) ceremony. Baxter refers to it as the "culmination ceremony," the "completion of the head" (1954: 247), or the "Gadamoji ceremony" (1954: 233, 328). He gives the native term as *jila gafa gadamoji*, "the festival [*jila*] at the time of the Gadamoji [1954: 209, 385]." Pecci and Legesse give no native name for this ceremony. It takes place when an age-group—let us take one at random and call it F—reaches level 11. This ceremony has been described more than once (p. 161), and most recently by Legesse (1973: 99 ff.), who saw it in person.

The other ceremony Haberland notes is the transition from Yuba (VI) to Gada Moji (VII). Of this he says that at any time during the 4 years after the

of a Gada Moji (VII) is rather onerous, most men, according to Haberland, make the transition as late as possible.[32] This is a phenomenon of the kind remarked among the Arusha and other Masai group tribes: members of a single age-group make transitions at different times, violating the group-unity constraint. In this instance, however, the transition for a given individual is not gradual but sharp.

The last transition of the system is once more by a level rule: on reaching level 11 the group perform the Retirement Ceremony, at which their heads are shorn, and then leave the system. A retired man is a *jarsa mata bufate*, an "old man with a shaven head," or *jarsa*, "old man," for short (Haberland 1963: 224).[33]

The account that has just been given of this system is quite different in form from the ones given by the ethnographers. The concept of a level rule was unknown to them; instead, their whole account is in terms of time rules: 16 years as Gamme (I), 8 years as Cusa (II), and so on, including 27 (or 31) years as Yuba (VI). Figure 2.6 reproduces exactly the figures given by Pecci,[34] Haberland, and

---

Retirement Ceremony by which F became Jarsa (retired), individual members of F − 1 (now at level 10) who are still in the Yuba (VI) grade may receive from individual members of F some of a substance called *kumbi*. By this ceremony the member of F − 1 becomes a Gada Moji (VII). At the end of 4 years all members of F − 1 should have carried out this ceremony.

Legesse (1973: 100, 105) also mentions the *kumbi* transfer ceremony, but his account differs from Haberland's in that (*a*) Haberland implies that only one member of F and one member of F − 1 are directly involved in the ceremony each time it is performed, whereas Legesse describes many members of F transferring *kumbi* to many members of F − 1 on a single occasion, and (*b*) Legesse describes the transfer as occurring immediately after the Retirement Ceremony by which F became Jarsa. Pecci's account (1941: 321) resembles Legesse's, while Baxter's (1954: 365 ff.) is perhaps closer to Haberland's. I think the fact must be that some men become Gada Moji (VII) in the way Legesse describes, immediately after the Retirement Ceremony, and thus spend 8 years as Gada Moji (VII), while others prefer to wait a while, make the transition as individuals, and spend less than the maximum period as Gada Moji (VII).

[32] This accounts for what looks like an inconsistency between Haberland and Pecci. The former states that a man spends 31 years in the Yuba (VI) grade (Haberland 1963: 217), whereas according to Pecci only 27 years are spent as a Yuba. Haberland's figure is given on the assumption that an individual remains a Yuba as long as possible and then spends (ideally) only 4 years as a Gada Moji (VII).

[33] Baxter (1954: 327, 365, 377) writes as if one who has performed the Retirement Ceremony is still a Gada Moji, but this seems to be an error.

[34] A puzzling feature of Pecci's account may be mentioned here. When first presenting his figures on the length of time each group spends in each grade (1941: 308 f.), he represents all the durations, except the 8 years in the Gada

Legesse, but I have described the resulting configuration in different terms. I think the sources had in mind the interpretation given here, but that lacking the concept of a level rule they expressed it, instead, in terms of a carefully integrated set of time rules.

Irrespective of what the sources had in mind when they described the system, a real question arises here. Two different accounts of the system have been put forward, ours (call it the level rule hypothesis) and the ethnographers' (the time rule hypothesis). Are these merely alternative, but equally accurate, descriptions of the system? Or is there some way of deciding that one is correct and the other incorrect?

To answer this we must consider what happens when the system becomes slightly out of joint. The rule is that a new age-group should be inaugurated every 8 years. Now, there are no grounds for doubting the existence either of this rule or of the related one, that a group should spend 8 years in the Gada (V) grade. The 8-year interval appears again and again in the literature on Gada systems and is first mentioned as early as the sixteenth century (Bahrey 1907: 198, 200). But at the same time it is likely that in practice the inauguration interval is on occasion greater than 8 years.[35]

---

grade, as maxima, the minimum in each case being 1 year. So, for instance, he writes of the Yuba (VI) grade as "della durata da 1 a 27 anni." In his diagrams and elsewhere throughout his account he uses only the maxima. The minimum figures may be related to the UPL rules discussed below, but this is by no means certain: we should then expect to find zero rather than 1 as the minimum for all grades up to Gada, something slightly over zero as the minimum for Gada, and no such entry for grades VI (Yuba) and VII (Gada Moji).

[35] Haberland (1963: 579) explains that, although for each ceremony there is a fixed day on which it is supposed to be performed, in practice "the time at which a ceremony takes place depends on a thousand incidental circumstances. . . . This is especially so in the Gada system, in which the eight year cycle of classes and feasts is often not adhered to, and instead frequently stretches out to ten or more years; and yet under these circumstances, people do not think of shortening the duration of the following class [1963: 579; cf. 1963: 211]." Baxter (in personal communications) has also indicated that the Borana tend to delay ceremonies. Legesse (1973: 280) probably believes that it is extremely unusual for an age-group not to be inaugurated in the proper year, though he concedes that "rituals usually take place several weeks after the set date [1973: 189]." If, however, one consults Legesse's own table of ideal and actual dates for various ceremonies in the early 1960s (1973: 89), one finds disparities of up to 2 years (1973: 94); so it is hard to believe that the ceremonies inaugurating age-groups are always held on time. Legesse (1973: 280) also probably believes that delays in inaugurating an age-group would be compensated for later, but this seems to me unlikely. The existence of disparities between the ideal and actual dates of ceremonies does not, of course, reflect on the intellectual abilities of the Borana (as Legesse appears to believe).

In order to see whether there is any difference between our hypotheses, let us imagine the case where some group F starts recruiting 10 years after F + 1. Before the inauguration of F, group F + 3 was at level 3, and after its inauguration it is at level 4. Now, according to the level rule hypothesis, F + 3 would only be assigned grade III on reaching level 4. In other words, if there is an interval of 10 years between the inaugurations of F + 1 and F, then F + 3 will (all else being equal) spend 10 years in grade II. The time rule hypothesis, on the other hand, leads to a quite different prediction: it says that the interval between the inaugurations of F and F + 1 is irrelevant to the question of how long F + 3 spends in grade II. Even if the interval between F and F + 1 is 10 years, F + 3 may be expected (all else being equal) to spend 8 years in grade II.

Similar considerations apply to all the other transitions, except those to and from the Gada (V) grade. It is clear, therefore, that there is a real difference between the hypotheses: they lead to mutually incompatible predictions as to what would happen under the kind of circumstances we have just outlined. If we had some information about an occasion when the inauguration of a new group was delayed, then we might well be able to say that one hypothesis is correct and the other incorrect. Unfortunately we have no such information (though since the system is still in operation it might well be possible to obtain it). However, now that we know that the two hypotheses really are different, there is another line of approach we can adopt in an attempt to decide which of them is correct.

Let us look again at Figure 2.6. It will be observed that in the year 80 a number of transitions occur. Table 2.7 gives a list of the groups which are assigned new grades in that year and, opposite each one, the number of its new grade. (The same set of transitions takes place every 8 years, but the conventions of Figure 2.6 are such that it is only in the year 80 that they all appear on it. Note that in the case

TABLE 2.7

Age-group	Grade
F − 5	Gamme (I)
F − 3	Cusa (II)
F − 2	Raba Didica (III)
F − 1	Raba Dori (IV)
F + 4	Gada Moji (VI)
F + 5	Retire

of F + 4 the year 80, if we follow Haberland, only marks the point in time after which individual members may make the transition to VII. They will not all be in that grade until 4 years later.)

Now, if it were the case that all these transitions were effected by means of a single ceremony, then this would be decisive evidence in favor of the level rule hypothesis, for it would indicate that the transitions were all intimately tied to the inauguration of a new group. In fact, however, it appears that all the transitions are effected by separate ceremonies; but it also appears that these various ceremonies are all supposed to take place at virtually the same time.[36] This suggests strongly that if the inauguration of a new group were delayed, then all the transition ceremonies we have mentioned would suffer a corresponding delay; and hence that the level rule hypothesis is correct.

Like many other tribes, the Borana date past events by reference to age-groups. The period during which a group is assigned the Gada (V) grade is named after the leader of that group, and this unit (the Gada period) is used in reckoning any fairly long period of time. In the column headed A.G. in Figure 2.6, I have marked off the periods during which particular groups were in the Gada grade: so, for instance, group F was assigned it from the year 77 to the year 85. Haberland (1963: 189, 577) remarks that no one was able to give his age in years, but that everyone knew in which Gada period he was born, and often in which year of that period (cf. Legesse 1973: 280). As may be seen from the diagram, the Gada periods do not coincide with the inauguration intervals, even though both are, in principle, 8 years long. This is one of the things that makes descriptions of the system rather complex.

---

[36] Explicit statements to this effect are made only by Legesse (1973: 13, 57, 88 f., 130); and, as was mentioned on p. 164 n. 31, he considers the transition of F + 4 to Gada Moji (VII) and the retirement of F + 5 to be intimately linked. In Marsabit in 1955 the transition of F − 5 to Gamme (I) took place the day before the retirement of F + 5 (Adamson 1967: 365). Haberland's informants told him that in Ethiopia the transition of F − 5 to Gamme (I) takes place a month after the retirement of F + 5 (1963: 220, cf. 193, 196, 204). Haberland generally looks on these two transitions as constituting a single ceremony, the Jara. See in contrast Legesse (1973: 54 ff., 99 ff.), according to which these were distinct ceremonies, though performed in the same place and at about the same time (unfortunately Legesse does not give precise dates). In both ceremonies, group F (which is in the Gada grade) plays a prominent part.

I turn now to the rule that makes all the men in $F - 5$ sons of men in F. How do the Borana deal with generational spread?

The solution to the problem of the older members of each generation (overaging) is of a familiar kind: men are not allowed to father sons until their age-group become Raba Dori (IV) (though oddly enough they are allowed to marry as soon as it is assigned grade III, Raba Didica). This means that no boy is more than about 8 years old when he joins his age-group.

The rule to prevent overaging is reported in all the main sources, and they agree also that the rule is still strictly observed.[37] On the question of whether there is a rule to prevent underaging, the sources diverge considerably. Broadly speaking, Haberland gives one account, and Legesse gives another, with Pecci's data favoring Haberland, and Baxter's on the whole favoring Legesse. I shall begin by analyzing the Pecci—Haberland account, and then consider how it should be modified in the light of what Legesse has to say.

According to Haberland and Pecci, then, the problem of the younger members of each generation (underaging) is dealt with as follows. If a child is born to a member of some group F at a time when $F - 5$ has already been assigned the Yuba (VI) grade, then that child and all its descendants are excluded from participation in the Gada system (except in a marginal way, on which see later). These nonparticipants are known as *ilma jarsa*.[38] Thus, in Figure 2.6, all children of members of group $F + 5$ are *ilma jarsa* if they are born after the year 85. That year is marked by a broken line in the column representing the history of $F + 5$, and there is a corresponding broken line in all the other columns that represent the history of age-groups. The earliest date at which a member of $F + 5$ may father a son is the year 32. The maximum possible age-range of group F (and of any group in the system) is therefore 53 years. Overlapping is

---

[37] Klausberger (1972: 137) says that the rule has been abrogated, and that men now marry between the ages of 18 and 20. I am not convinced of the correctness of this report.

[38] I am here following especially Pecci (1941: 309 f.). I have once more expressed Pecci's data in a form quite different from his own: for instance, his statement of the rule just mentioned in the text is that the *ilma jarsa* are those born after the father has spent 5 years in retirement (i.e., as a *jarsa*). The correct form of the rule is again a matter that can in principle be decided by empirical evidence, even though at the moment we lack the relevant facts.

Haberland was told that the *ilma jarsa* rule comes into force immediately after a man leaves the Gada Moji (VII) grade, but he states that in spite of this he prefers to give credence to Pecci's account of the rule (Haberland 1963: 185).

not eliminated, but it is held within bounds: at any given point in time, the number of age-groups recruiting members will not exceed six.

The effect of these rules is to divide the Borana population into two portions, those who participate in the Gada system, who are known as the *ilma korma*, and those who do not, the *ilma jarsa*. In a personal communication, Haberland summarized his findings on these groups as follows:

> *Ilma jarsa* marry only *ilma jarsa*, and *ilma korma* marry only *ilma korma*. Mixed marriages are said not to occur. As far as I could ascertain, each village consisted exclusively of members of one or other of these groups. There was a substantial separation between the two groups.[39]

According to Haberland (1963: 185), though there exists this method of excluding individuals (and their descendants) from the system, there is no way of returning them to it. So it looks as if the proportion of nonparticipants will continually increase, and indeed Haberland states that at present more than half the Borana population are *ilma jarsa* (1963: 32, 185, 233).

How has it come about that the *ilma jarsa* are so numerous? The only process Haberland mentions is the birth of *ilma jarsa* to *ilma korma*, i.e., underaging. But a system in which a man does not gain permission to rear his sons until 40 years after his father has gained the same right does not sound like one in which underaging will occur at a fast rate, and it is possible to point to another force that may lead to a growth in the proportion of *ilma jarsa* in the population as a whole. That force is the demographic structure of the group itself.

Consider the demographic structure of the *ilma korma*. Here, there are two potent factors that restrict the growth of the population. One is the rule, already mentioned, that limits the right of men to produce sons; the other, and even more significant factor, is a rule that limits the right of men to produce daughters. The ethnographers (apart from Baxter 1954: 320) agree that this latter right is only acquired something between 8 and 13 years after the right to

---

[39] "*Ilma djarsa* heiraten nur *ilma djarsa*, und *ilma korma* nur *ilma korma*. Mischheiraten sollen nicht vorgekommen sein. Soweit ich es überblicken konnte, wohnten jeweils nur Mitglieder der einen oder anderen Gruppe in einem Dorf. Es bestand eine weitgehende Trennung zwischen beiden Gruppen."

produce sons;[40] until then, girls born will be killed. The *ilma jarsa*, in contrast, are not subject to rules of this kind, and so we would expect them to have a different demographic structure and in particular a higher rate of population growth. This may in part explain why they are so numerous.

If we now turn to Legesse's account of the system, we get a quite different perspective on the question of *ilma jarsa* and *ilma korma*. Legesse recognizes the existence of these two categories but obviously attaches little importance to them. His data on the subject are few, vague, and inconsistent. He does not explain at exactly what point the offspring of *ilma korma* come to be categorized as *ilma jarsa*. He says of the *ilma jarsa* that "Such a man, his sons and all his descendants are perpetually retired [Legesse 1973: 133]," but on the same page and elsewhere (1973: 134, 168) he implies that if a line of *ilma jarsa* produce sons at sufficiently short intervals for some generations, then they can reenter the system. It is also far from clear what meaning Legesse attaches to the term *ilma korma* (1973: 160, 203, 335). It may be that Legesse would agree with Haberland that all Borana are either *ilma korma* or *ilma jarsa* (cf. Legesse 1973: 203, 335), but he says nothing of the two groups being endogamous, and indeed intermarriage between them is recorded in his census data (see, for example, numbers 427 and 428, 1973: 308, and 531 and 532, 1973: 311).[41]

---

[40] The *exact* point in time after which men are allowed to keep their daughters is not known. Pecci says this right is gained on entering the Yuba (VI) grade (1941: 309, 321), i.e., 13 years after having gained the right to keep sons. Haberland (1963: 193, 212) says daughters may be kept after the Oda ceremony has been performed; according to him this ceremony takes place in the seventh year in the Gada (V) grade (1963: 210 f.), while according to Legesse it takes place in the fifth year in that grade (1973: 85, 88 f.). Legesse (1973: 128, 131) says daughters may be kept after the circumcision ceremony has been performed; this ceremony takes place at the end of the third year in the Gada (V) grade (Pecci 1941: 320; Haberland 1963: 204). (Legesse's data on the time of the circumcision ceremony are contradictory; on pp. 89 f. he places it in the second year of the Gada grade; on p. 128 he places it in the fifth year of the Gada grade; but on that same page he says that the ceremony takes place in "the 48th year of the cycle," which means, in fact, according to his usage, the third year of the Gada grade.)

[41] To speak of intermarriage between *ilma korma* and *ilma jarsa* is to imply that the age-group affiliation of a girl is, like that of a boy, F − 5. This seems to be Haberland's view (see especially 1963: 173 f.) and is also implied by some remarks of Baxter's (1954: 284) and Legesse's (1973: 65). Furthermore, in his census data Legesse (1973: 297 ff.) evidently gives the age-group affiliation of

The fundamental difference between the accounts given by Haberland and Legesse—of which the question of whether *ilma jarsa* can ever beget *ilma korma* is one aspect—is that for Haberland the *ilma jarsa* are "completely excluded from the system" (1963: 179), while for Legesse *ilma jarsa* are not significantly different from such *ilma korma* as those in the Yuba (VI) grade or the Jarsa (i.e., those who have left grade VII).[42] Both Haberland and Legesse are, broadly speaking, aware of the problem of underaging,[42] but whereas for Haberland the creation of *ilma jarsa* is a solution to that problem (1963: 179), Legesse, when he discusses the question of whether there are any factors that retard underaging, never even refers to the *ilma jarsa* (1973: 168 ff.).

Legesse's view of the *ilma jarsa* is by no means an arbitrary one. He backs it up with some hard evidence, the most striking of which relates to the age-groups. If the *ilma jarsa* are not members of age-groups, then the maximum possible age-range of an age-group is, as we have seen, 53 years, and at a given point in time one would not expect to find more than, at most, about fifteen age-groups with living members.[44] Legesse, however, in his census of age-group members, discovered, first, that some of the more senior age-groups had age-ranges of well over 53 years, and, second, that there were at least twenty age-groups that still had living members (1973: 141 ff.). The second of these data is confirmed by Baxter, who was also able to draw up a list of over twenty extant age-groups (1954: 294).

---

females as F − 5, even in the case of married women. Nevertheless, Legesse also writes that "Only males are involved in the Gada System. Females have peripheral membership in the gada class of their husbands [1973: 146]," and this accords well with what Pecci (1941: 309) has to say on the subject. Obviously these data are not wholly irreconcilable; but equally obviously the place of women in the system remains to be properly described.

[42] Legesse uses the term "retired" to refer sometimes just to the Yuba (VI) (1973: 91, 220), sometimes to the Yuba (VI) and Jarsa jointly (1973: 92, 168), sometimes just to the Jarsa (1973: 196, where the term *jarsa* seems in fact to refer to the *ilma jarsa*), and sometimes to the *ilma jarsa* (1973: 133, 203, 335). It is clear, nevertheless, that Legesse was aware of the fact that Yuba, Jarsa, and *ilma jarsa* are distinct notions (1973: 203).

[43] Haberland follows the terminology first proposed by Jensen and adopted in the present work; Legesse refers to (roughly) underaging as "the gada process."

[44] The very youngest members of an age-group—the youngest *ilma korma*, that is,—will be those born at the end of the period that the age-group spends in the Gada (V) grade. Such a boy might live, let us say, to the age of 80, at which point his age-group will be at level 15.

Although neither Baxter nor Legesse explicitly deals with the question of whether *ilma jarsa* are members of age-groups,[45] these facts leave little doubt that in some sense they are. In this respect, then, Haberland and Pecci must be corrected (or at least supplemented). But does this correction entail any other modifications in the Haberland—Pecci description of the system? Two possibilities present themselves. The first is that in certain cases *ilma jarsa* may pass through certain age-grades *at the same time as the other members of their age-group.*

According to the Haberland—Pecci account, no *ilma jarsa* pass through the age-grades *with* (what would be) *their own age-groups.* However, they do perform as individuals, at any suitable time, certain ceremonies that *ilma korma* perform collectively at times which are a function of the point at which their age-group stands in its passage through the age-grades. The most notable of these is circumcision: for the *ilma korma* this occurs when their group is at the end of its third year in the Gada (V) grade (cf. p. 170 n. 40); whereas the *ilma jarsa* are circumcised in private when they are still children or immediately before marriage (Haberland 1963: 205; Legesse 1973: 122).[46]

Furthermore (still according to Haberland and Pecci) an *ilma jarsa* takes part in certain ceremonies of the Gada system together with whatever age-group happens to be performing those ceremonies when he is of the appropriate age. In particular, when he has married he joins in the Oda and Muda ceremonies, two of the many that are incumbent on the group in the Gada (V) grade (Haberland 1963: 185 f., 203; cf. Pecci 1941: 318); and when he is old he passes through the Gada Moji (VII) grade and into retirement with whatever age-group happens to be doing so at the appropriate time.[47]

[45] Baxter does, however, say that "Every free born Boran is a member of a descent set, luba, . . . and all the children of a man, irrespective of their age, are members of the same descent set [1954: 284]."

[46] In Legesse 1973: 122 I take the "special class of people who are outside the gada grade system" to be the *ilma jarsa.*

[47] Haberland 1963: 186; Pecci 1941: 310; cf. Legesse 1973: 106. Baxter does not mention the terms *ilma jarsa* or *ilma korma,* but he does recognize a distinction between those who perform the Retirement Ceremony with their own age-group, and those who perform it with some other group. He says that people of the latter kind are called *gultu,* and that if a man cannot perform the ceremony with his own age-group (call it F), then he likes if possible to perform it with his son's group (F − 5), in which case the son must perform it with a still more junior group (Baxter 1954: 303, 395; cf. Haberland 1963: 537).

Legesse's account, though exceedingly vague, is consistent with the one given in the preceding paragraphs, at least as concerns those *ilma jarsa* born after their age-group has been disassigned the last grade (VII). What of the *ilma jarsa* born earlier—to take the extreme case, the *ilma jarsa* born when his age-group is at the very beginning of the Yuba (VI) grade?[48] Legesse's account leaves open the possibility that such an *ilma jarsa* passes through the Yuba (VI) and Gada Moji (VII) grades together with his group. Yet this possibility—the first of the two I shall mention—is unlikely. For, though Yuba (VI) is a decidedly colorless grade, with few special rights and duties, and one that a child might conceivably be assigned, Gada Moji (VII) is quite different. In this grade, as we have seen, a man is subject to all sorts of special rules, and the Borana consider it proper only for a person fairly well on in years. Now the very oldest *ilma jarsa* in an age-group would be around 30 when the time came for his age-group to become Gada Moji, and this is much too young. I am therefore convinced that *ilma jarsa* never pass through grade VI at all (Pecci 1941: 310), and that when they do become Gada Moji (VII), they always do so long after their age-group.

But if the age-group affiliation of an *ilma jarsa* does not determine his age-grade, why, then, do the Borana bother to keep trace of it? Are there any rules to which it is relevant? The sources provide no answer that is obviously correct, but there is the possibility—the second of the two that I want to mention—that Legesse is correct in asserting that *ilma jarsa* can beget *ilma korma*. If this is so, it is a fact that has consequences, perhaps significant consequences, for the demographic structure of the Borana; and it would be a reason for keeping track of the age-group affiliations of *ilma jarsa*.

To sum up: the Haberland–Pecci description of the *ilma jarsa* is open to question on the following counts:

(i)   The *ilma jarsa* evidently do, in some sense, belong to age-groups.

(ii) It may be that *ilma jarsa* can beget *ilma korma*.

(iii) It looks as if *ilma jarsa* do sometimes marry *ilma korma*.

Lastly, we must mention that all the main sources agree that in each age-group there are certain official positions which are filled,

---

[48] Cf. p. 168 n. 38. If, by chance, Haberland is wrong in rejecting what his informants told him, then *ilma jarsa* can already be born in the middle of the Gada grade. Even if this were so, it would not significantly affect the argument here.

not by members of that age-group, but by *ilma jarsa.* The system of age-group officers is exceedingly complex, and the sources are often vague or inconsistent in dealing with it. For those who wish to pursue the matter, my own conclusion is that some or all of the Hayyu Garba in the *ya'as* of the two Abba Gada Kontoma are *ilma jarsa,* but that the Hayyu Garba in the *ya'a* of the Abba Gada Arbore are probably all Yuba; and that some of the Hayyu Meddicha are *ilma jarsa,* and some Yuba. (Quite likely officers of group F who are in the Yuba grade when F is in the Gada grade are members of F + 1; cf. Haberland 1963: 193.)

4.3.2 Other Galla Tribes

A simple kind of time rule is said to exist in a number of Galla tribes (Cerulli 1922: 167 ff.; 1929: 31 ff.). The systems in question have six grades and an 8-year inauguration interval. Most of the transitions are by level rules (Table 2.8), but transition from IV to V is governed by a time rule: it takes place after 4 years in grade IV. (Perhaps IV and V are sub-grades, rather than grades.)

4.4 Nonintegrated Systems

4.4.1 The Kikuyu

The term "Kikuyu" can be employed in a number of different ways, some more and some less inclusive. In what follows I shall adopt the usage of Middleton and Kershaw and take it to refer only to the Kikuyu proper, that is to say, "the inhabitants of Kiambu, Fort Hall and Nyeri Districts [1965: 11]." I shall also follow these authors in using the term "Kikuyu tribes" to refer to a larger grouping, which comprises, as its main constituents, the Kikuyu proper, the Embu, and the Meru.

TABLE 2.8

Grade	Level
I	1
II	2
III	3
IV, V	4
VI	5 +

All the Kikuyu tribes had (or have) age-group systems, but they differed considerably from each other. I shall limit myself here to the Kikuyu proper. Even within this grouping there was a good deal of variety (Lambert 1956; though cf. Muriuki 1974: 17). I shall concentrate on the system that existed among the southern Kikuyu, those of Kiambu and Fort Hall, since it is to them that most of the data refer. Unfortunately Lambert is almost alone in his painstaking attempt to specify exactly which areas his information relates to; other sources offer data that cannot be precisely localized and that may even represent a synthesis of practice in several different places.

The extensive literature on the Kikuyu is surveyed in the annotated bibliography in Middleton and Kershaw (1965). Nothing significant has been published subsequently that deals with the age organization of the Kikuyu proper, but there have appeared works on the Embu (Saberwal 1970) and the Tharaka (Lowenthal 1972). The Tharaka are generally counted as a Meru subtribe, and, like the other Meru subtribes, their age organization is a good deal less complex than that of the Kikuyu proper. The Embu system, on the other hand, is quite similar to that of the Kikuyu proper. The origins of Kikuyu age organization are examined by Lawren (1968), and the history of the tribe by Muriuki (1974). There remains a good deal of material collected in the field, and even written up, but as yet unpublished (see, for instance, Middleton and Kershaw 1965: ix and Bernardi 1971: 432).[49]

Kikuyu age organization seems to have been made up of three principal elements:

(i)   What I shall call for the sake of convenience *the age-set system* (though it may actually have been deviant). It was perhaps graded, and is fairly well described.

(ii) A *generation-group system*, less well described, but comprehensible in general terms.

(iii) An age-grade system which was not, I think, integrated with the age-set system, and which in spite of a mass of information about its minutiae, remains quite obscure with regard to its underlying principles. I shall call this third element the *main age-grade system*.

---

[49] The most important of these unpublished studies is no doubt the late L.S.B. Leakey's book on the southern Kikuyu. Leakey refused me permission to see this manuscript, but he informed me that it was in the course of publication.

The most difficult problem of Kikuyu age organization is to work out how these elements fitted together. I do not think that a satisfactory solution can be derived from the published sources. Certainly I have not produced one, and, as a result, I have not produced a description that gives much insight into Kikuyu society. All I have done is to order some of the available data and to point out the main problems. I hope this section will be useful to those who carry out fieldwork among the Kikuyu; it has too many gaps to be of much interest to anyone else.

The various components of Kikuyu age organization operated over different areas, and in this fact lies something of the explanation of how they were related to each other. Unfortunately the sources are at their most unhelpful on this matter, and as a result I have largely neglected it. Investigators in the field will have to take it into account.

In what follows I shall examine the three main elements of Kikuyu age organization in the order indicated above. I begin, therefore, with the age-set system.

The smallest unit in the Kikuyu age-set system consisted of those circumcised in a single year. They formed a named group, which we may call a sub-set. A number of sub-sets formed an age-set, also a named group. Sub-sets and age-sets of this kind were found throughout the Kikuyu area, but there was great local variation with regard to certain of their features: circumcisions did not take place every year, and methods of choosing the years in which to hold circumcisions differed; in addition, the number of sub-sets in a set varied from one area to another. Lambert (1956: 8–22) describes some half dozen types. A feature common to a number of areas was that an age-set consisted of all those circumcised within a period of 13 years, and that 9 sub-sets were formed in those 13 years.

There is a fair amount of information about the organization of the sub-sets or age-sets and about the mutual obligations of age-mates. (Much of it is summarized in Middleton and Kershaw 1965: 36.) The main problem with this material is that if often leaves unanswered the question of which features were characteristic of the sub-set and which of the age-set (see Lambert 1956: 67). But we do know that the sub-set was a highly cohesive group (Kenyatta 1938: 115 f.) and that the age-set had an organization of councils and leaders (Lambert 1956: 70; Kenyatta 1938: 200, 205 f.).

I referred earlier to this age-set system as being perhaps graded. The reason for this lies in some facts reported by Lambert, though

TABLE 2.9

Grade	Level
I. Junior	1
II. Commanding	2
III. Retired	3 +

by no other source. He says that one age-set was known as "the age-set having command," and as such "acted as a police force to the ruling generation [and] had the duty of providing the main defence force and the front line troops in aggressive raids [1956: 69 ff.]." It looks as if an age-set took over this position soon after its most junior sub-set was formed. The age-set that was taking over had to pay certain fees. In Kiambu, these fees were apparently independent of those that—as we shall see—were paid in the main age-grade system; further north, they were not. I shall say a little more about these data in discussing the main age-grade system. Here, I just want to raise the question of whether what Lambert describes is an age-grade system. If it is, then its transition rules would apparently be those set out in Table 2.9 (the names given to the putative grades are my own invention). But perhaps this sort of system deserves a separate category or at least subcategory (see Section 1.2.3 of this chapter).

The second element of Kikuyu age organization is the system of g-groups, generally referred to in the literature as "generations." The sources have this to say about them:

(i)   They were named groups, which successively became the "ruling generation" (in Lambert's phrase). One group took over from the next at the great *ituika* ceremony, which occurred at intervals of perhaps about 35 years (Lambert 1956: 42; Benson 1964: 467;[50] Muriuki 1974: 23; Prins 1953: 43).

(ii) They were groups such that, if a father joined one, then his son joined the one that succeeded it as the "ruling group" (Hobley 1938: 91 f.; Lambert 1956: 40 ff., 61).

[50] Following the practice of the ethnographers, I have written Kikuyu words without the proper diacritical marks. The references to Benson's dictionary are intended solely to help the reader who wants to know the proper spelling of a word. I have not used Benson as a source of ethnographic information.

(iii) "Although there are many instances in which the disparity
        of age is remarkable, still the majority of persons of one
        generation are of approximately one age or period of life
        [Dundas 1915: 247]." In other words, though there was a
        very wide age-range within a given g-group, each had a
        distinct average age; and at the *ituika* an older group
        would be handing over power to a younger one. (See also
        Routledge and Routledge 1910: 9; Hobley 1938: 94,
        187.)

These data leave no doubt that we are indeed dealing with
g-groups, and this view—which differs from the one advanced by
Prins—now seems to be generally accepted (see especially Middleton
and Kershaw 1965). How these g-groups dealt with generational
spread remains obscure. It is possible that an individual did not
become a member of his g-group until circumcision; since uncircum-
cised men were not allowed to marry, this would have prevented
overaging. Underaging may have been dealt with by shifting (cf. p.
100), though the evidence for the existence of shifting consists of a
single unclear hint given by Lambert.[51] He refers to "those elders
who had 'stepped down' or 'stepped up' by special payments," a
statement that may or may not relate to the g-group system. If this
statement does indeed relate to shifting, then it is interesting that it
mentions it as occurring in both directions: this means that shifting
cannot *only* have occurred as a result of underaging. (See further p.
189.)

We are not told how the g-groups were formed, so a problem
which immediately presents itself is that of the relationship between
the g-groups and the age-sets. Among the Karimojong and the Jie, the
g-groups are divided into age-groups that approximate quite closely
to age-sets; among the Zanaki and the Kuria, on the other hand, the
g-groups are not subdivided in any way, though in both these tribes
there exist age-set systems that operate as independent institutions
(Bischofberger 1972: 19, 29, 32; Ruel n.d., 1962: 14). What is the
situation among the Kikuyu? Both Ruel (1962: 34) and Middleton
and Kershaw (1965: 37) have addressed themselves to this problem,
and both are inclined to believe that among the Kikuyu, as among
the Zanaki and Kuria, the age-sets and the g-groups were separate

---

[51] I understand from Professor Middleton (personal communication) that
the statement in Middleton and Kershaw (1965: 37) that begins "Men could
move up and down in the system . . ." represents only a hypothesis.

institutions. In this they may well be correct; most of our sources describe the two separately, and furthermore the age-set system appears to possess the enrolment characteristic, which it almost certainly would not if the age-sets were subdivisions of the g-groups.

On the other hand, to adopt this position is to fly in the face of fairly explicit statements in some of the best sources: Lambert says that the age-sets were "grouped in generations" (1956: 2, cf. also 47), and so does Hobley (1938: 92 f.; see also Muriuki 1974: 22). It may also be significant that among the Kikuyu the same word (*rika*) was used for g-group, age-set, and sub-set (Lambert 1956: 8, 40; Hobley 1938: 92; Benson 1964: 387; Muriuki 1974: 117 f.). Perhaps the question is best left open, especially since there may even have been local differences in this respect.

The passages quoted show that the g-groups, like the age-sets, may perhaps have been integrated with an age-grade system. If so, its transition rules would have been those set out in Table 2.10 (where again the names given to the putative grades are my own). It looks as if there would usually be three or four g-groups in existence at a given point in time (Routledge and Routledge 1910: 9; cf. Saberwal 1970: 68). The duties of the ruling g-group are described at the end of this section.

Let us summarize our results so far. The Kikuyu had three different kinds of named age-group, which I have referred to as the g-group, the age-set, and the sub-set. Each age-set consisted of a certain number of sub-sets. The relationship between the age-sets and the g-groups is unknown: the age-sets may have constituted a separate system, or they may have been subdivisions of the g-groups. If the latter was the case, then they were almost certainly not age-sets as defined by our age-set model.

We know how the age-sets and sub-sets were formed, but we do not know what determined the inauguration intervals and recruitment periods of the g-groups. It may be that the *ituika* ceremony

TABLE 2.10

Grade	Level
I. Junior Group	1
II. Ruling Group	2
III. Retired Groups	3 +

marked the end of recruitment to one g-group and the beginning of recruitment to the next.

One age-set was known as the "age-set having command," and one g-group was (in some sense) "the ruling generation." All we know about the relationship between these two facts is that the "commanding" age-set "acted as a police force to the ruling generation [Lambert 1956: 69]." This seems to indicate that individuals in this set were either members of the junior g-group or had not yet enrolled in any g-group.

I now want to look at the third and most problematic part of Kikuyu age organization, what I have called the main age-grade sequence. I shall begin by summarizing its main features, without attempting to relate them to the other two elements of the age organization. The evidence is so incomplete and inconsistent that even to do this is quite difficult.

It appears that the main age-grade sequence is best described in terms of two kinds of component. The first is a series of what are often called councils (*njama* or *kiama*; Benson 1964: 331, 6); the individual joins each of these councils in succession, at the same time relinquishing membership of the preceding one. The councils were the most important source of authority outside the household in traditional Kikuyu society. In general terms, they performed military, political, judicial, and religious functions. Among at least some of the Kikuyu there seem to have been five such councils. I shall refer to them as follows:

(i) The Junior Warriors' Council, *njama ya aanake a muumo* (Kenyatta 1938: 198; Lambert 1956: 78; Benson 1964: 330)

(ii) The Senior Warriors' Council, *njama ya aanake* (Lambert 1956: 78; Benson 1964: 330) or *njama ya ita* (Kenyatta 1938: 199, cf. Dundas 1915: 243; Benson 1964: 330)

(iii) The Junior Elders' Council, *kiama gia kamatimu* (Kenyatta 1938: 200; Lambert 1956: 82; Hobley 1938: 211, cf. Dundas 1915: 243; Benson 1964: 6) or *kiama kia ituura* (Lambert 1956: 84, but cf. Kenyatta 1938: 35, 194; Benson 1964: 7)

(iv) The Full Elders' Council, *kiama kia matathi* (Kenyatta 1938: 201; Lambert 1956: 83, cf. Dundas 1915: 243; Benson 1964: 6) or *kiama gia athamaki* (Hobley 1938:

211, cf. the comment by Dundas, 1915: 244, on the term *muthamaki*; Benson 1964: 6)

(v) The Senior Elders' Council, *kiama kia maturanguru* (Kenyatta 1938: 204; cf. Dundas 1915: 243, Lambert 1956: 89, and Hobley 1938: 211, 215; Benson 1964: 7), *kiama (kiria) kinene*, or *kiama kia bururi* (Lambert 1956: 84, but cf. Leakey 1952: 35; Benson 1964: 6). This clearly corresponds to what Hobley (1938: 213 and *passim*) calls the *ukuru* (or *ukuu*) grade (Benson 1964: 247). (Cf. also Lambert 1956: 7 for the term *athuuri akuru*; Benson 1964: 533).

These councils fall into two groups—the Warriors' and the Elders'. Let us consider them in turn.

The sources establish beyond question that every ordinary Kikuyu man went through the stage of being a Warrior (*mwanake*, pl. *aanake*; Benson 1964: 10). (On this, see further p. 183) What is not clear is whether every man also became a member of the Warriors' councils. The statements in the sources are hard to reconcile with one another. On the one hand, it is implied that every man became a member successively of these two councils (Kenyatta 1938: 198 f.; and, less directly, Lambert 1956: 79 f.—"It was the club of the married men"). On the other hand, there are quite clear statements to the effect that the *njama ya ita* was a select body consisting only of certain leading men (*athamaki*, Benson 1964: 490), not all of them Warriors, and that this body directed military operations (Lambert 1956: 71, 78; Kenyatta 1938: 205 f.; cf. also Saberwal 1970: 39 f., 69).

It may be that this confusion arises because of local variations. But I think another explanation is also possible. I would tentatively suggest that there were indeed two Warriors councils through which all men passed, and that these were known as the *njama ya aanake a muumo* and the *njama ya aanake*; but that there also existed a body known as the *njama ya ita*, which was constituted in time of war and was composed of leading men from the various grades. Perhaps the reason Kenyatta also refers to the Senior Warriors' Council by this name is that many of the members of the *njama ya ita* were Senior Warriors, with the result that the term was also sometimes used to refer to the Senior Warriors' Council.

All this, of course, is rather speculative; one should perhaps not press these sources so hard. What is certain, however, is that in some areas there was only one Warriors' council (as we shall see in a moment); and even where there were two, it seems that the division between Warriors and Elders (*muthuuri*, pl. *athuuri*, Benson 1964: 533) went deeper than the division between one type of Warrior and another, or between one type of Elder and another.

If we turn now to the Elders' councils, we find that the sources are a good deal more satisfactory. It emerges from them that only the first two of these councils constitute age-grades, since only these two were open to all men who lived long enough. Some of the other respects in which the Senior Elders' Council was different are noted below. On the other hand, there were times when the Full Elders and Senior Elders would hold a joint meeting to the exclusion of the Junior Elders; this certainly happened on ritual occasions (cf. Hobley 1938: 213; Kenyatta 1938: 201). The sources, however, are mainly interested in the councils' judicial activities and generally represent all three meeting together, even though each maintained its distinctness, with the most senior at the front of a semicircle and the most junior at the rear (Kenyatta 1938: 220; Hobley 1938: 211, 217).

With this we come to the end of the sequence of councils. But as was mentioned earlier, the main age-grade sequence also had a second component. In addition to the councils, it comprised a series of rights, attainment of which was dependent on the payment of fees. These fees were paid at varying intervals throughout a man's life, the first of them soon after circumcision.[52] "The fees are regularly spoken of as goats, each fee having its special name—the goat of (*mburi ya*) something or other. Generally, however, they are paid in rams, sometimes in he-goats, and occasionally in beer or bulls [Lambert 1956: 85]." The sources are generally rather vague about whom the fees were paid to (Lambert 1956: 70 is an exception), but we know that they went to some group of senior persons, which varied according to which fee in the series was being paid, and that they were usually consumed forthwith.

Paying the proper fee was one of the major qualifications for entering each of the first four councils, and as a member of a council one continued to acquire certain rights by paying successive fees. Because of this last feature, we can provisionally view the councils as

[52] It will be remembered that a man joined his age-set at the circumcision ceremony. Membership of the first of the series of councils was also only attained after circumcision (though not by virtue of circumcision alone). More generally, it is clear that the main age-grade sequence was only entered on after circumcision.

constituting grades, and the fees (other than those for entry into a council) as demarcating sub-grades. This interpretation follows very directly from Hobley's account (1938: 211) and is also implied by the other sources; nevertheless, it presents certain difficulties (which cannot be profitably discussed on the basis of the available evidence), and in the long run new data or an improved conceptual framework may well render it untenable.

Let us now consider an individual's progress through the grades in more detail. In this account I give the age of a typical man at each transition; but, as we shall see later, some individuals rose through the grades much faster than others, so that occasionally a quite young man would already be an Elder.

A boy who had just been circumcised was known as a *kiumiri* (Lambert 1956: 5, 32, 34; Benson 1964: 542). This stage lasted until the *guthiga* ceremony, which took place some months after circumcision (Kenyatta 1938: 152; Lambert 1956: 53 f.). This ceremony made him a *mundu wa muumo* (Benson 1964: 543), and he continued to be known by this term until he had paid the fee or fees that made him a Warrior (Lambert 1956: 5, 34, 78). We have a list of the fees that had to be paid in northern Kiambu before a *mundu wa muumo* was accounted a Warrior; they include, for instance, the "goat of the gruel," which is "paid for permission to eat with the warriors"; the "goat of the song," which is "paid for permission to join in the dances of warriors and girls" (cf. Hobley 1938: 266); and others of a similar kind (Lambert 1956: 85 f.). In other parts of Kikuyu, the fees were given different names and were different in number, but the principle of paying fees in order to join the Warriors is evidently characteristic of the whole tribe.

Although explicit evidence is lacking, it seems possible to infer that in some areas of Kikuyu the *mundu wa muumo* was a member of a council, while in others he was not. When we listed the councils above, we noted a Junior Warriors' Council and a Senior Warriors' Council. Kenyatta (1938: 198) tells us that a boy became a member of the Junior Warriors' Council as soon as his circumcision wounds had healed: his father gave him arms, and a fee was paid to the Senior Warriors. The title of the council seems to indicate that a member did not by virtue of membership cease to be a *mundu wa muumo*. Now, in other areas there was only one Warriors' council, corresponding in name to what has been called the Senior Warriors' Council (Lambert 1956: 78). It appears also that in some parts of the country there was a prolonged *muumo* stage, during which the *mundu wa muumo* did not belong to any council. I think we may assume that where this was the case, there was only a single Warriors' council.

A man remained a Warrior until about the time of his marriage; he then paid a further series of fees, at the end of which he became a member of the Junior Elders' Council. The members of this council were evidently not really regarded as Elders: they carried out various minor duties on behalf of the true Elders (Lambert 1956: 81, 84; Kenyatta 1938: 201). About the time when a man's first son was being circumcised he paid three fees successively and became an "elder of three goats" and, as such, a member of the Full Elders' Council (Lambert 1956: 88).[53] Hobley writes that an individual could only join this council if the members agreed to accept him; he notes that "As a rule his entry is not refused [1938: 210]."[54] It certainly does not appear that there was any considerable number of men who failed to enter the Full Elders' Council, provided only that they lived long enough; perhaps the Elders' discretion as to who joined was, rather, a power of delaying membership. This council was clearly the most powerful and active of the Elders' councils.

What I have called the Senior Elders' Council was a group markedly different from the other councils. Hobley indeed does not recognize it as a separate council (1938: 211; cf. also Kenyatta 1938: 108 f.). Three features in particular differentiate it. First, it was selective. "Some . . . never become members of the *ukuru* grade; the consent of the other members of the grade is necessary and they do not approve of a candidate who is not well endowed with wordly goods, or, again, prospective candidates may be considered unlucky [Hobley 1938: 213]." (See also Dundas 1915: 244.) Second, in Kiambu and Fort Hall at least, membership was not dependent on payment of a fee in the ordinary series of fees. Lambert writes that membership "merely implies an *ad hoc* function; its members are not necessarily of any grade of eldership above [an elder of three goats] [1956: 84]." Third, "It is particularly this grade . . . whose jurisdiction is regarded as extending beyond the boundaries of the individual's own locality [Lambert 1956: 83 f.]." The council dealt with certain particularly weighty or difficult secular matters (Hobley

---

[53] Hobley (1938: 210) says that a man joined the Full Elders' Council when he was an "elder of four goats." Kenyatta (1938: 108) only mentions two.

[54] The need for the members of a council to assent to the initiation of a new member is also hinted at by Lambert (1956: 89 "The man who pays and is accepted by his predecessors. . . .").

1938: 150, 212; Lambert 1956: 83 f.) and was of great importance
in religious affairs (Kenyatta 1938: 204; Hobley 1938: 151, 211).

We may now turn to the relationship between the main age-
grade sequence and the other elements of Kikuyu age organization. I
begin with the relationship between the main age-grade sequence and
the age-set system. None of the primary sources on the Kikuyu
discusses this question (unless Middleton and Kershaw, 1965, counts
as a primary source). I shall present evidence, however, which makes
it appear likely that there were no rules that related a man's progress
through the main age-grade sequence to his age-set affiliation. Even if
there were such rules, there is little doubt that they were such that
both the group-unity constraint and the integration constraint were
violated. Though not expressed in quite these terms, this is also the
view adopted by Middleton and Kershaw (1965: 35); furthermore, it
accords well with what Saberwal says about the Embu: "the members of an age-set would not move as a corporate group through later
warriorhood, let alone elderhood [1970: 31]."
Concerning the violation of the group-unity constraint there can
be no doubt at all, although in the early stages of the sequence
especially there would naturally be a tendency for members of the
same sub-set (those circumcised at the same time) to pass through
grades more or less simultaneously. We have some fairly explicit data
on the assignment of the Warrior grade. In order to become a Warrior
the *mundu wa muumo* had to pay certain fees. "Each fee is normally
a ram, payable by the individual or, in certain cases, by groups of
two or more individuals together [Lambert 1956: 85]." This statement seems very decidedly to carry the implication that transition to
the grade of Warrior was a matter for the individual and not for the
whole sub-set. There is also a passage in Cagnolo (1933: 97 f.) which
may indicate that some individuals dragged their heels about entering
the Warrior grade; if this was so it would certainly entail a violation
of the group-unity constraint.
As regards the Elders' grades, the evidence is almost as full as we
could wish. We know that they were generally assigned in connection
with events in the life of the individual—his marriage and the circumcision of his first child (though Lambert 1956: 80 makes it clear that
the connection with the time of marriage was only a very loose one).
We also know that some individuals went through the grades much
faster than others. Lambert writes of entry to the Full Elders'
Council that "In general a young man will start to pay fees soon after
marriage, and in practice the ambitious or the wealthy may enter the

kiama [Full Elders' Council] at a comparatively early age [1956: 80 f., cf. 101, 104]." Hobley deals with this point at some length:

> As a general rule the *athamaki* [Full Elders] are men advanced in years, but there is no fixed rule as to this; many are middle-aged or younger. Occasionally one may see quite a young man, practically a youth, among the elders. The elders explained this as follows: the election to the *muthamaki* [Full Elders'] grade lies entirely with the *athamaki*; if they see a young man whose prudence and knowledge has impressed them favourably, they may elect him into their grade; further, the family of a *muthamaki* should always be represented in this grade, and therefore if one dies and leaves no near relation other than a young man, they will elect his son or brother in his place even if he is quite a youth. Such elections are, of course, rare and are only mentioned in case these exceptions should be noticed [1938: 212].

This passage clearly implies that not only the group-unity constraint but also the integration constraint was violated.

If the age-sets (and sub-sets) were not integrated with the main age-grade system, what then was their function? As was mentioned earlier, there were very close ties between members of a set; [55] age-mates helped each other in many ways. These ties probably continued to exist as long as members of the set survived, though no doubt they diminished in intensity in the course of time. In addition to this, the younger sets acted as military units (Kenyatta 1938: 205 ff.). This fact poses a new problem, for it means that there were altogether four different kinds of institution somehow connected with Warriors or military affairs: the Warrior council(s), the *njama ya ita*, the age-sets, and the system of the "age-set having command." How did they all fit together?

Let us say at once that this question cannot be answered in a fashion that is consistent with all the evidence. Lambert, who provides the most information, also provides the most inconsistencies. He ascribes to the "age-set having command" police functions and "the duty of providing the main defence force and the front line troops in aggressive raids [Lambert 1956: 70]." He also says that "The functions of the warriors' council were largely concerned with raiding expeditions and with defence. . . . The . . . *njama ya aanake* . . . supplied the active police force for the preservation of internal order and good government [1956: 79]." On top of all this,

[55] Or at least between the members of a sub-set. I shall not attempt to sort out the distribution of functions between the two.

Kenyatta (1938: 205 ff.) gives a very full description of how each age-set "had its regimental songs and war-cry" and acted as a unit in battle. When one adds to this our uncertainties about the nature of the *njama ya ita*, it becomes evident that the only sensible course at the moment is to hope that new evidence will clarify the situation.

Lastly, the relationship between the g-group system and the main age-grade system. The way into this problem is through the question: what did it mean for a g-group to be the Ruling Group? The sources have this to say:

(i) "The ruling set or generation had certain privileges from which the other sets or generations were excluded. . . . In Kikuyu, for instance, the right to hold a circumcision at one's homestead is a privilege of the ruling generation [Lambert 1956: 135]."

(ii) "When the younger generation has . . . taken over the ruler-ship of the community [at the *ituika* ceremony], the retiring genera-tion withdraw from their religious functions, both in connection with the offering of sacrifices and the curing of *thuhu* [a disease caused by infringements of custom] . . . and in fact from all public functions [Dundas 1915: 246]." Similarly, Lambert speaks of the "tribal sacrifices appropriate to the ruling generation [1956: 136]."

(iii) The ruling g-group can issue orders dealing with various matters of public interest. It does so on various occasions and in particular at the time of the *ituika* ceremony (Lambert 1956: 137; cf. Saberwal 1970: 64). Lambert (1956: 136 ff.) discusses this aspect of the Ruling Group's activities at some length and provides a good deal of illustrative material. Among one Kikuyu subtribe, for in-stance, the Ruling Group issued a proclamation forbidding witchcraft and specifying the kind of punishment to be used against witches. It also issued proclamations dealing with a number of other matters of public interest, for example, "for the conservation of certain kinds of foodstuffs during a threat of famine" and "to prevent destruction of forest areas required as protective belts against outside aggression," and so on (Lambert 1956: 142).

These facts suggest two problems, both of which arise because the age-range of a g-group is so wide. On the one hand, there must be some rather young men (perhaps even boys or infants) who belong to the Ruling Group. On the other hand, there must be some senior but still active men who do not belong to the Ruling Group, either because they are members of the immediately junior group or because they are members of the immediately senior group. How do the Kikuyu deal with these two difficulties?

The sources say very little about the young men. The only useful information is supplied by Dundas, who writes:

> If a young man belongs to a senior generation which retires before he has attained an age at which he could take part in the common sacrifices, he will forever be excluded from the exercise of such priestly functions [1915: 247].

This is very clear, but it still leaves open the question of the rights mentioned earlier under (i) and (iii). One can make guesses about these, but no information is at present available.

The question of the old men is more problematic, but fortunately the sources are also more helpful here. Essentially the problem is that of the relationship between the Elders' councils and the Ruling Group. Concerning this, we know, beyond any doubt, that a man could become a member of the various Elders' councils without being a member of the Ruling Group (see, in particular, Hobley 1938: 92, 94; Lambert 1956: 136). We also have data which make it seem likely that for much of the time the members of the Ruling Group constituted the majority of those in the Elders' councils (Routledge and Routledge 1910: 198; Dundas 1915: 247). But this leaves a certain number of Elders who were not in the Ruling Group. Does this mean that these were, so to speak, second-class Elders, with much more limited prerogatives than the true Elders, those in the Ruling Group? Such a system would certainly be remarkable, for the second-class Elders might be men of great distinction who simply had the misfortune to fall at one extreme or the other of the age-range of their g-group.

In fact, the Kikuyu system does not have this arbitrary character. Consider first the case of those men who are senior enough to take an active part in the Elders councils but who belong to the g-group junior to the Ruling Group. Lambert indicates that these men could, by paying certain fees, acquire most of the privileges of a member of the Ruling Group (1956: 135 f.). They could acquire the right to hold circumcisions in their homesteads, and Lambert seems to imply that there were other individual ritual privileges of a similar sort that could also be acquired in the same way. They could also acquire the right to issue orders dealing with matters of public interest. What they could not acquire was "the right to take part in the tribal sacrifices appropriate to the ruling generation [1956: 136]."

Now, what of the men who might, all else being equal, be expected to take an active part in the Elders' councils but who belong to a retired g-group? Except for one rather obscure statement—to which I turn in a moment—Lambert has nothing to say on this point. Dundas, however, provides some interesting data that deserve to be quoted in full. After explaining that the retired g-group ceases to take part in tribal sacrifices and so forth (see (ii) above), he goes on to say this:

> The judicial *kiama* seems to form somewhat of an exception to the public duties from which a generation completely withdraws. Some elders continue actively on the Council, but others take no part in it; mostly they seem to be guided by considerations of health and vigour, and those members of Maiina [the g-group which most recently retired] who to-day attend the Councils certainly enjoy considerable respect. Nevertheless the responsible body of the *kiama* is taken from the ruling generation. Thus at the present day, if the Government has any demands to make upon the *kiama*, or important dealings with them, the elders of Maiina will not consider themselves responsible. So also when Administrative officers travel in a district the elders of Maiina do not appear, or if they do, are regarded only as spectators. At the present day Mwangi [the Ruling Group] form not only the responsible body of the *kiama*, but they are undoubtedly also numerically in the majority, so much so that I have heard the *kiama* referred to simply as Mwangi [Dundas 1915: 247].

The only passage in Lambert that may perhaps refer to the active Elders who are members of a Retired Group is the one quoted on p. 178. When he speaks of payments for "stepping down," he may be referring to actual changes in g-group affiliation (that is, changes that would affect the g-group affiliation of a man's sons) or he may merely be referring to the acquisition of certain rights that belong to a junior group.

4.4.2 The Banapas Bedik

The Banapas Bedik provide, as has been noted, the only clear example of a nonintegrated system. Pierre Smith (1971) gives an excellent short account of Banapas age organization, so there is no need to do more here than to mention a few of the most relevant points.[56]

---

[56] Gomila (1971), though primarily a work of physical anthropology, gives a general introduction to the Bedik tribe, together with a bibliography.

TABLE 2.11

I.	Les Petits
II.	Les Derniers
III.	Les Quatrièmes
IV.	Les Troisièmes
V.	Les Successeurs
VI.	Les Pressureurs
VII.	Les Hippotragues
VIII.	Les Blanchis

The Banapas Bedik have eight age-grades, which between them cover a man's life from the time he is initiated in his early teens to the day he dies. Smith lists them as in Table 2.11.

Initiation ceremonies take place at rather irregular intervals, generally of about 3 or 4 years. Those who are initiated together—their number varies from one to a dozen (see p. 113)—constitute an age-set. The age-set is evidently a group of very little importance; it is not mentioned anywhere as acting as a unit, and the only link between its members that Smith notes is that they use a special term of address (key) to each other (1971: 194 n.). Another source states that they are "united by a relationship of comradeship which expresses itself in the term of address kèy [Gomila and Ferry 1966: 245]." Should we take this to mean that members of the same set have special obligations to each other? If so, the probability is that they are not very significant ones. The age-sets are not named, but there is a term meaning "our age-set" (Smith 1971: 194 n.).

The Banapas transition rules are decidedly complex. Those who have been initiated are assigned grade I. Transition from I to II is governed by a time rule: each set must spend "five years in this grade [i.e., grade I]; this is the only strict rule in the progression through the grades [Smith 1971: 192]." In fact, because of certain additional features, which need not concern us here, the period spent in grade I may be considered to be 6 years rather than 5 (Smith 1971: 192). Since this is roughly twice the interval between the formation of successive sets "there will generally be, after an initiation, at least two sets in the first grade [Smith 1971: 192]."

As all sets spend the same, fixed period of time in grade I, the intervals at which they are disassigned this grade are the same as the intervals between the successive initiation ceremonies at which they were formed. Each time a set is disassigned grade I, transitions occur in all senior grades up to and including transitions from Les Successeurs (V) to Les Pressureurs (VI). If in these transitions group-unity were maintained, then we might be dealing with grade-level rules, grade II being the basic grade. In fact, however, group-unity is not maintained; that is to say, when one set moves from I to II, certain individuals belonging to other sets at the same time move from II to III, while others move from III to IV, or IV to V, or V to VI. But in none of these transitions (except from I to II) is it normally the case that all members of a set make the transition together, nor is it normally (or perhaps ever) the case that all members of a grade make the transition together.[57] The decision as to who will be assigned a new grade when the proper time arrives is made by a council consisting of the members of the three most senior grades (Smith 1971: 194 f.). Smith does not describe in full the principles on which they operate in making their decisions, but their main objective appears to be to ensure that all the lineages of the village are more or less equally represented in the more senior grades and particularly in grade VI, which Smith describes as "the only institution in the society which, within the limits of its competence, has authoritative power [1971: 194]." Now, the lineages in the village that Smith describes (Banata) are of very unequal size: half the inhabitants belong to three of them, the other half to the remaining eight (1971: 194). If, in spite of this, they are to be more or less equally represented in grade VI, it follows that members of the smaller lineages must pass through the grades much faster than members of the larger ones. (They may indeed even skip grades: see p. 134.) As a result the system violates both the group-unity and the integration constraints.

Finally, let us consider the last two transitions. An individual decides for himself when he wishes to be disassigned VI and assigned VII; he usually makes this transition at around the age of 50 (Smith 1971: 191, 193). After the age of about 60 an individual is assigned grade VIII. Smith does not explicitly state what the transition rule from VII to VIII is, but presumably it is the same as for the preceding transition. Clearly these transitions also permit violations of the group-unity and integration constraints; in practice the grade-filling constraint is evidently met.

[57] Transitions from II to III are a little different from the other ones referred to here, but to simplify the exposition I have ignored this difference. For details see Smith (1971: 192 f.).

4.5 Other Systems

The two systems discussed in this section have transition rules that do not fit into any of the categories mentioned in Section 2. A third system which might have been described here is that of the Chagga, but the sources on it are rather weak (see the analysis in Stewart 1972: 201–204, based on Gutmann 1926 and Raum 1940). There must be systems apart from these three that have eccentric transition rules, but as far as I know none of them have left clear traces in the literature.

4.5.1 The Bobo

The account that follows is based entirely on le Moal (1971).

Bobo age-sets are well organized groups, each with its eponymous leader (p. 115), its deputy leader, and its treasurer. It seems that the sets are fairly small, since each village operates its own system (p. 116). The age-set meets frequently when its members are young (p. 116), and no doubt later as well. New sets are formed at irregular intervals, evidently of the order of 5 or 6 years, and children may be as little as 3 or 4 years old when they join. There is no ceremony at which individuals are enrolled in a set; instead, the children spontaneously organize themselves as an age-set (p. 116).

In spite of a good deal of detail, the nature of the Bobo age-grade system does not emerge with complete clarity from le Moal's paper. It would seem, however, that, from the time that he joins an age-set, a man's life can be divided into three main stages: before initiation (*sinkyefuru*); initiation (no single native term); and after initiation (*zyanekuma*) (p. 115 f.). The preinitiation stage may begin, as we have seen, when a child is as young as 3 or 4 years; it is not stated at what age it usually ends. The ideal duration of the initiation stage is about 15 years, though in practice it usually lasts longer (pp. 117 n., 121). Thereafter a man is in the postinitiation stage until he dies.

Le Moal groups together the initiation and postinitiation stages as the age-grade sequence. Within this sequence he distinguishes six grades: five of them make up the initiation stage, and one of them is identical with the postinitiation stage. There is a native term for each of these grades, but for convenience le Moal refers to them as A, B, C, D, E, and F (F being *zyanekuma*, i.e., the postinitiation stage). To facilitate comparison with le Moal's paper, I shall follow his practice (rather than use roman numerals as hitherto).

In what follows, I shall assume that the Bobo do indeed have an age-grade sequence, though le Moal's data are sufficiently incomplete to leave open the possibility that they have only a series of ceremonies of the kind mentioned in Section 1.2.2 of this chapter. I shall also assume that le Moal has delimited the age-grades correctly, though again this is something that is not obvious from his account (cf. Stewart 1972: 205 f.). These assumptions give one particular set of transition rules; slightly different assumptions about the delimitation of the grades produce, as will appear, transition rules of a different kind.

The transition rules entailed by the above assumptions are represented in Figure 2.7. The numbers in the left-hand margin of the diagram are based on those used by le Moal; it seems that they represent the intervals that the Bobo consider ideal, though the

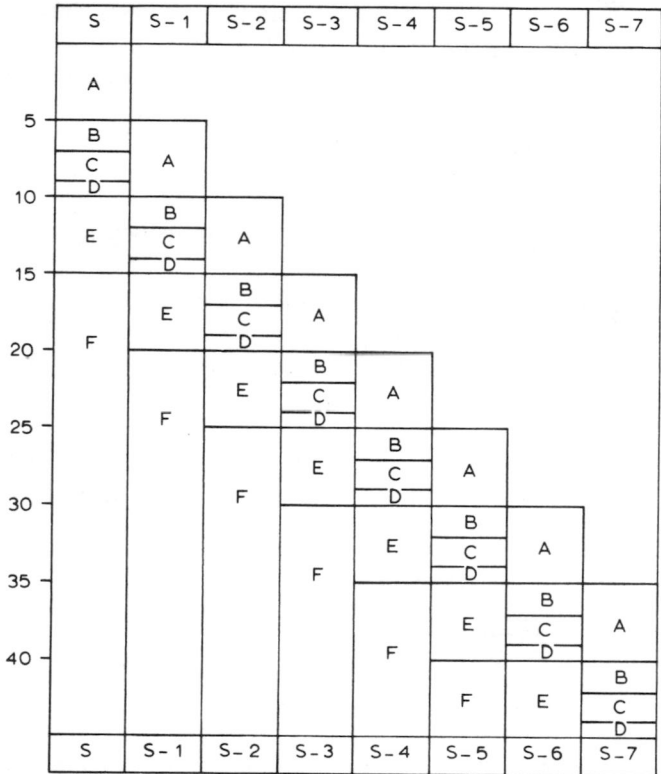

Figure 2.7

actual intervals are evidently irregular and generally rather longer. The relationship between the grades of successive sets as indicated by the diagram is, in contrast, entirely realistic.

The diagram shows that the Bobo system (in le Moal's account) operates to a considerable extent with simple level rules. The ceremony by which set S − 3 is assigned grade A (the *sinkye sawa daga* ceremony), the ceremony by which S − 2 is assigned B (the *yele nwone ko kari daga*), the ceremony by which S − 1 is assigned E (the *yele zo daga*), and the transition of set S to grade F (which occurs without ceremony) are all linked. It appears that the first three of these transitions take place in quick succession and in the order indicated; the fourth (from E to F) occurs simultaneously with the third (from D to E) (le Moal 1971: 117). The rather complex forces which, at irregular intervals, set the whole mechanism in motion, need not concern us here. We can best describe the system in two steps. The first of these can be represented as in Table 2.12.

The reader will notice the resemblance between Table 2.12 and Table 2.8. It can be seen from Table 2.12 that grade B is assigned when a set reaches level 2 and that grade D is disassigned when a set reaches level 3. The second step of our description, then, is to describe the transitions from B to C and from C to D.

The point in time at which a set S − 1 can make the B to C transition depends on set S (in grade E). Set S − 1 are allowed (cf. le Moal 1971: 119) to make the transition only after S have performed for the second time a ceremony known as the *yelebire daga* (pp. 118, 122). Le Moal gives an instance of a set falling behind in the performance of the two *yelebire daga* ceremonies, with the result that the immediately junior set spent some 6 years in grade B, instead of the 2 years that is apparently considered proper (pp. 122, 117).

The factors governing the timing of the transition from C to D are not fully described, but it "normally" takes place 2 years after the transition from B to C (p. 118).

TABLE 2.12

Grade	Level
A	1
B, C, D	2
E	3
F	4 +

It seems possible, then, that we are here dealing with two time rules (which makes the system even more similar to the Galla type represented in Table 2.8). But the operation of the time rules—if they are such—is not unimpeded, since there are other rules that can override them, for example, the rule linking the transition of set S − 1 from B to C to the *yelebire daga* of S, or (perhaps) the rule which demands that sets must consider themselves ready for the next stage of initiation before undertaking it (p. 119).

Like the ones represented in Table 2.8, this set of transition rules meets the integration constraint and the group-unity constraint, but not the grade-filling constraint; note, for instance, that no set is assigned grade B during the years 12 to 15. Grades C and D may also sometimes not be assigned to any set, but this never happens to grades A, E, and F.

It was mentioned earlier that alternative accounts of the transition rules are possible. One obvious one is to see the system as consisting entirely of simple level rules; in other words, to assume that grades B, C, and D are in fact a single grade. Another one would derive from considering the preinitiation stage as a grade. We would then say that grades A, E, and F were assigned not by level rules but by grade-level rules, grade-level 1 being assigned at grade A. Furthermore, these two suggestions could both be adopted.

4.5.2 The Izi Ibo

The Izi Ibo system is highly unusual in a number of respects. Jones (1962: 206 f.) gives a brief description of it, based partly on an unpublished account by J. G. C. Allen (which I have not seen)[58] and partly on data collected at first hand.

I shall analyze the system with the aid of Table 2.13. Each letter in that table may be taken to represent an age-group. Each age-group is divided into two sub-groups, indicated by the number immediately to the right of each letter. I shall refer to them as the first sub-group and the second sub-group. The numeral in parenthesis after each sub-group gives the level number of that sub-group (the

---

[58] Allen's account is in one of the Nigerian "Government Reorganization Reports" of the 1930s. I have not seen any of these reports, and Mr. Jones informs me that the copies which he consulted—and of which he made extensive use in his 1962 study—were mostly in Nigeria. It would be a service to scholarship if someone were to unearth these reports and make them generally available.

TABLE 2.13

Grade	t_1 L_1	t_2 L_1	t_3 L_2	t_4 L_1	t_5 L_1	t_6 L_2
I	C2 (2)	D1 (1)	D2 (1)	D2 (2)	E1 (1)	E2 (1)
		C2 (2)	D1 (2)		D2 (2)	E1 (2)
			C2 (3)			D2 (3)
II	C1 (3)	C1 (3)	C1 (4)	D1 (3)	D1 (3)	D1 (4)
III	B2 (4)	B2 (4)	B2 (5)	C2 (4)	C2 (4)	C2 (5)
	B1 (5)	B1 (5)	B1 (6)	C1 (5)	C1 (5)	C1 (6)
	A2 (6)	A2 (6)	A2 (7)	B2 (6)	B2 (6)	B2 (7)
	A1 (7)	A1 (7)	A1 (8)	B1 (7)	B1 (7)	B1 (8)

way in which sub-groups can have level numbers needs no explanation). Each column represents the state of the system at a later time than the column immediately to its left; I have labelled the columns t_1, t_2, and so on. Reading down a column in Table 2.13 is much the same as looking from right to left in a diagram like Figure 2.1. The history of a given group, which can be followed by looking down a column in diagrams like Figure 2.1, can be followed by seeking the position of the group in each of the successive columns in Table 2.13. The system operates with complex level rules, using a cycle of two sequences of level rules, L_1 and L_2.

The grades in the system are as follows (maintaining our convention that the first grade is not assigned before the individual is enrolled in his age-group):

    I. Younger married men
    II. Older married men
    III. Elders (Ogaranya)

A man joins his age-group and is assigned grade I when he marries.

Let me now quote Jones's account of the system. The insertions in square brackets refer to Table 2.13.

> When the senior age-set [A] became extinct in the whole tribe [at t_4] a new age-set was formed. ... The set which was till then the junior set, for example, Igirigidi [C2, D1, and D2] divided on a basis of age into three sections [C2, D1, and D2], the senior of which [C2] was promoted into the set above, namely, Ochumba [C1], and Ochumba [now C1 and C2], reinforced with this addition, moved up to join the set above it, namely, Ibina [B] in the Ogaranya grade

[III]. The middle section [D1] retaining the original name of Igirigidi, replaced Ochumba in the sub-grade of older married men [II], and the junior section [D2] after providing this Igirigidi [D1] with a feast was recognized as a new set and given its own name, in this case Alibarhuo [1962: 207].

Column t_3 shows the position of the groups immediately before the extinction of age-group A, and column t_4 shows their position immediately afterward. Note that in t_4 sub-group D2 is given the level number 2, and not, as one might expect, the level number 1. The reason for this is that we assume that after the death of the last member of group A, all new recruits to the system will, for a time, join sub-group E1. The situation at t_4 is that the members of A are all dead, but that no one has yet joined E1. Because of this, E1 is not marked in column t_4. On the other hand, D2 has the level number 2 because E1 has, by our definition (p. 31), been inaugurated. Column t_5 represents the situation after E1 has recruited its first member.

The L-cycle rule assumed in our representation is that L_1 applies until a second sub-group begins recruiting; at that point L_2 comes into force. L_2 continues to apply until the most senior age-group (in this case A) dies out, when L_1 starts to apply again. (In Table 2.13 I assumed, for the sake of simplicity, that members of A1 continue to survive right up to t_3; in fact, of course, they might be dead by then; but this makes no difference to our account.) The complex level rules can be represented as in Table 2.14.

The system, as we have so far represented it, has two peculiarities. One is that every second sub-group skips "grade" II (cf. Section 1.2.5 of this chapter). The other lies in the system of naming age-groups. The second sub-group of each group will, for a certain period of its existence, be known by a name different from its original name and its final name, these last two being identical. Take the case of D2 in the passage quoted earlier. At t_3, before the

TABLE 2.14

| | Level | |
Grade	L_1	L_2
I	1 − 2	1 − 3
II	3	4
III	4 +	5 +

extinction of group A, it was known, along with C2 and D1, by the name of Igirigidi, and had the level number 1. At t_4, when group A had just become extinct, sub-group D2 received the name Alibarhuo. It continued to be known by this name during t_5 and t_6, sharing it first with E1 and then also with E2. But now look ahead. As soon as group B becomes extinct (at t_7) sub-group D1 will rise to grade III and be joined there by D2. The pair of them will then be known as Igirigidi for the rest of their existence. More generally, then, we can represent the name history of a second sub-group in three stages, as follows:

(i)   At level 1: The sub-group is assigned grade I, it is still recruiting, and it is known as Alpha (along with the other sub-groups in the same grade).

(ii) At levels 2 and 3: The sub-group is still assigned grade I, but it has ceased recruiting and is known as Beta (along with the other sub-groups in the same grade).

(iii) At level 4 and above: When the sub-group moves to grade III (skipping grade II), it will be known again as Alpha (along with the sub-group immediately senior to it).

The first sub-group, of course, retains the same name throughout its existence.

I said earlier that when a man marries he (a) joins his age-group and (b) is assigned grade I. In fact, this is an oversimplification. As the passage quoted from Jones indicates, after the extinction of the senior group, individuals are assigned sub-groups on the basis of their age, not on the basis of the order in which they married. In other words, it seems that there must be, say, some individuals who will be members of sub-group D1 even though they joined the system later than certain others who belong to D2. Equally, the scanty data do not exclude the possibility that there will be members of D2 who joined the system after certain members of E1. This means that our previous analysis, which assumed that the sub-groups recruited their members when the members married, and which assigned level numbers accordingly, was wrong. That it was wrong is also indicated by the fact that the sub-groups do not have any independent organization until they are disassigned grade I. The correct description is that the sub-groups are only inaugurated when they are disassigned grade I.[59] But to say this is to say that the system lacks the ordering

---

[59] Which means that according to our convention (p. 133) we can no longer call "grade I" the first grade; and that we are faced with the question of what the named entity in "grade I" is.

characteristic: if two (or three) sub-groups are inaugurated simultaneously, then it is no longer true that there is a total ordering on the groups given by the order in which they begin recruiting. And if the system lacks the ordering characteristic, then level numbers cannot be assigned to the groups. (What we did was to assign "level numbers" according to the mean age ordering of the sub-groups.)

III

The Formation of Age-Groups

1 A REVISED VERSION OF THE ENROLMENT CHARACTERISTIC

The enrolment characteristic is, as it stands, the least satisfactory of the constraints embodied in our age-set model. In this section I shall consider what is wrong with it and what can be done to improve it.

With the enrolment characteristic in its present form, a particular relationship is established between the maximum possible age-range of an age-set (a_S) and the length of its cessation interval (c_S). We discussed this relationship in Chapter I, Section 1.2.3, and discovered that it must always be the case that $c_S \geqslant a_S \geqslant r_S$. For present purposes it will be best to divide the logically possible relationships between a_S and c_S into three classes: cases where a_S is less than c_S, cases where it equals c_S, and cases where it is greater than c_S.

The first two of these—the only ones that are in conformity with the enrolment characteristic in its present form—can quickly be dismissed. As has been mentioned (p. 36), there are no known systems in which a_S can be smaller than c_S; and it seems most improbable that any exist. Such systems would exclude some people simply because they were born during certain periods of time, and this is evidently not a criterion for exclusion that is at all attractive.

Cases where $a_S = c_S$ (for all S) certainly exist, but they are not common;[1] and rarely, if ever, are systems of this type a major feature of the social organization of the society in which they exist. Some further mention of them will be found in Section 6 of this chapter, but for the moment I shall neglect them in favor of the much larger and more important class of systems in which a_S is greater than c_S (for all S). Those systems that, in the preceding sections of this book, have been referred to as age-set systems are in fact systems that conform to the model in respect of all its other characteristics but mostly deviate from the enrolment characteristic in such a way that a_S is greater than c_S (for all S). The time has now come to justify the categorization of such systems as age-set systems.

An age-set is a collection of individuals who have been organized as a group, but they are not individuals chosen at random. On the contrary: there are criteria for admission which ensure that they all have something in common that they do not share with any other age-sets in the system. Now, according to our model, this something is that they were born between two particular dates. But a person's date of birth is not usually, *in itself*, a fact about him that is of much interest. In general, it is only significant inasmuch as it gives a good indication of certain other, much more important, facts about him, that is, his state of physical and mental development. But clearly, even within a society, and even among individuals of the same sex, this indicator is still subject to a considerable amount of individual variation. In our own society we use age as a criterion only in a limited range of circumstances. We believe, for example, that a person should not be given the right to vote until he has reached a certain degree of maturity. We do not believe, however, that he suddenly achieves this degree of maturity on his eighteenth birthday. We recognize that age is not an exact measure of maturity, but we use it because, in this case, it has many practical advantages: above all, it is a measure of maturity that is generally accepted and that is cheap and simple to apply. In both these respects it has the advantage over some psychological test.

---

[1] It is incorrect, therefore, to say that "The basic rule [of age-set systems] is that all the men born within a certain number of consecutive years are admitted into one set [Beattie 1964: 146]" (cf. Linton 1936: 118).

Now, in most of the societies that operate age-set systems the considerations that lead us sometimes to use age as a measure of maturity do not apply. (The reasons for this are up to a point obvious and need not be discussed here.) Age-set systems, therefore, do not generally have an enrolment age but, rather, an enrolment maturity level.[2] When this is the case, then the age-range of an age-group can be greater than the length of its cessation interval. This follows from the fact that two individuals of the same age may be at different levels of maturity; in such cases it must happen from time to time that they are enrolled in different sets.

The degree to which the use of a maturity level leads to overlap in the age-range of adjacent sets must, of course, vary from system to system. Two factors can exacerbate this kind of overlap.

The first is found in systems where an age-set recruits its members over a large area. In such cases, different people will decide in different places whether or not individuals are sufficiently mature to join a given set. However much they attempt to apply the same criteria, there will inevitably be some inconsistencies of judgment between different areas, and a level of maturity considered just sufficient for enrolment in the set in one locality may be considered not quite sufficient in another. In such cases, then, two individuals of the same age may find themselves in different sets, even if they are also at the same level of maturity.

The second factor relates to the way in which the level of maturity is judged. One of the advantages of using age as a criterion of maturity is that there are no borderline cases to speak of: either an individual is 18 or he is not. We have completely eliminated both freedom of choice and the need for arbitrary decisions. Some other criteria of maturity have the same advantage, for example, the breaking of a boy's voice, the onset of menstruation in a girl, the attainment of a certain height, the ability to carry out a certain task, and so on. If the elimination of freedom of choice or arbitrary

[2] Maturity, of course, is something that has a number of dimensions, and there may very well be cultural differences in the weight given to these dimensions: here, physical maturity may be most important; there, psychological maturity; in a third place, intellectual maturity; and so on. Differences of this kind do not, however, emerge from the ethnographic data on age-set systems: the usual form is to say that individuals are eligible to join an age-set when they attain the degree of maturity normally reached at about such-and-such an age. For the purposes of exposition, then, I shall follow my sources in assuming that maturity (or level of development) is a concept that can be used cross-culturally, even though (to my knowledge) it has never been given any exact cross-cultural content.

decisions were important—as it is to us with respect to voting—then criteria of this sort could be developed; and a combination of several such criteria could be quite a refined measure of maturity. But in practice, as far as I know, criteria of this sort are never used. Most societies seem content to define the maturity level only coarsely. As a result there is either a fair amount of freedom of choice[3] or else a fair number of arbitrary decisions, and this increases the degree of age-range overlapping.

Since the great majority of age-set systems use an enrolment maturity level, rather than an enrolment age, it seems reasonable to modify the enrolment characteristic accordingly. This can be accomplished by a few simple substitutions, along the following lines:

> There is a certain level of maturity (the **enrolment maturity level**) which combines the following features:
> 1. No individual joins a group before reaching this level of maturity: it is the **minimum (enrolment) maturity level.**
> 2. Any individual who has not yet joined a group, but who is going to join one, and who has reached this level of maturity, joins a group as soon as there is one recruiting members: it is the **basic (enrolment) maturity level.**

The original enrolment characteristic nevertheless has certain advantages over the revised one. It is an oversimplification, but not a gross one, and it can usefully be employed in manipulating the model, for example, in deriving the entailment of the age ordering of sets (Chapter I, Section 1.2.4). There is also a good deal to be said for it if we are interested in the model simply as a means of showing how a number of rather similar systems differ from one another.

The great advantage of the revised version is that it is more realistic than the original. Later on (Chapter IV, Section 2) it will be argued that the age-set model represents the structure that in some sense underlies many age-group systems which are not age-set systems. The structure to which this hypothesis refers is represented by the model with the revised version of the enrolment characteristic.

Under these circumstances, the best course is to retain both versions. The revised version, I suggest, should be looked on as the fundamental one, and the original version as a useful approximation. In what follows, I shall continue to make statements of the form

---

[3] The complexity of the factors that can be involved in determining which age-group an individual joins are well brought out in Ottenberg's account of the Afikpo Ibo system (1971: 58 f.).

"The enrolment age in this system is about n years." Such statements should be interpreted as meaning "The enrolment maturity level in this system is the level of maturity that individuals in the society usually attain at around the age of n years."

2 INFORMAL INAUGURATION SYSTEMS

In the kind of system delimited by the model, the recruitment period of a set is clearly demarcated: there is a definite point in time at which it begins and a definite point in time at which it ends (though the two need not necessarily be distinct). We may call a system of this type a **formal inauguration system,** and contrast it with systems in which the age-set gradually emerges in a rather informal fashion.

Such **informal inauguration systems**[4] are especially common in West Africa. Gamble describes the formation of a set among the Gambian Mandinka as follows:

> The lowest generally recognized groups are those aged about 11 in the case of boys, or 13 in the case of girls, but below these ages one finds smaller children forming age sets of their own. At this stage there is often an element of doubt as to who is in a particular age set, for there is a greater consciousness of age differences between eight and eleven, than between seventeen and twenty. Girls of about eleven will say those aged eight are not in their age set, while the *kafo* [age-set] leader, wishing to have as large a group as possible under her, will say that they are [Gamble 1955: 4].

A quite similar process is described among the Mbembe:

> From the age of 7 or 8, children are encouraged to meet on market days with others of the same age and sex. They are expected quite quickly to choose one of their number as their age-set head . . . and to meet regularly in the house of the father of the head, in the case of boys, and in the house of the mother of the age-set head in the case of girls [Harris 1965: 35].

The Anuak of East Africa form their age-sets in much the same fashion, but later in life—certainly after puberty.

---

[4] The term "informal inauguration" has already been used in this context by Jeffreys (1950: 161) and Imoagene (1969: 26).

> When a group of youths of about the same age and in the same
> village are recognized (informally as among ourselves) to have grown
> to manhood, they select from the older and richer men of the village
> one whom they wish to make their leader or, more correctly, spon-
> sor [Lienhardt 1957: 347].

The Anuak system is in many respects an unusual one, and further
information about it would be of great interest.

How do informal inauguration systems relate to the model? In
such systems recruitment certainly begins and ends, but it is hard to
say exactly when these events take place, since they are not, for
instance, marked by any kind of ceremony. I propose that we assume
that in informal inauguration systems all members of the set are
recruited at a single point in time, and that this point in time is when
it is generally agreed who are and who are not members of the set.
Further investigation of such systems in the field may suggest better
conventions than these; but at any rate, I think the matter is best
dealt with by means of conventions of some kind, rather than by
changing the model.

In certain instances one finds, in effect, a combination of
formal and informal inauguration. The Yakö have a well described
system of this kind.

> The principle of age-grouping operates long before the formal recog-
> nition of a set and a man's age-set membership has, in fact, been
> already established in childhood. Gradually during their childhood
> the boys of a ward sort themselves out into a series of groups of
> increasing seniority and as members of each group reach the age of
> marriage it is formally established as an age-set. If, however, a po-
> tential set is too large or too few in number in the opinion of the
> Ward Leaders, it can be split or joined to its next junior group at this
> time [Forde 1964: 145].

It is not difficult to assimilate a system of this type to our model; we
simply assume that the set recruits all its members at the point in
time when it is given "formal recognition."

3 THE INAUGURATION INTERVAL

In a formal inauguration system, there must be some means by
which a point in time is fixed for the inauguration of a new group.
There are two main methods. One is to have rules that determine—
independently of anyone's decision—when a new group is to be

inaugurated. The other is to give one or more members of the society the right to make this decision.

If the first method is employed, the rule used is almost always one that specifies an exact time interval between the inauguration of successive groups (a **fixed interval rule**). This interval varies over a wide range: the shortest I have noted is 6 months (on Pukapuka),[5] the longest 20 years (among the Bainouk: Girard 1965: 53) and 18 years (among the Konso). (The evidence on the Bainouk is rather limited, but about the Konso there can be no doubt.) When rules of this kind are reported, they may occasionally represent no more than rough-and-ready generalizations, produced either by the ethnographer or by his informants. But in many cases those who operate the system have a single, very definite interval in mind. Maybury-Lewis, for instance, reports that among the Akwe-Shavante the inauguration interval is 5 years;[6] when the Shavante are pressed on this point they "count up to five and tick the years off on their fingers to drive the point home." The ethnographer adds that "as far as I was able to check it, this five-year interval is in fact maintained [Maybury-Lewis 1967: 154]."

Where long intervals are reported, the question arises of how people keep track of the passage of time. When Jensen visited the Darassa, who have a 10-year inauguration interval, he found that most tribesmen did not know exactly how long had elapsed since the inauguration of the last age-group; but there was a small group of experts who knew perfectly well (it was 6 years). They used a number of aids: for instance, there was a certain annual ceremony that had to take place at a different location each time (probably in a 10-year cycle). By listing the locations at which this ceremony had been performed since the inauguration of the last age-group, it was possible to compute the number of years that had passed since then (Jensen 1936: 332). The Konso of the Garati area use a rather similar method to keep track of their 18-year inauguration intervals (Hallpike 1972: 47 f., 73 f.). In the Takadi area, where the interval is 9 years, they keep count "by breaking off a head of millet every year at the main harvest and putting it in a gourd kept for the purpose [Hallpike 1972: 199]."

---

[5] See the passage quoted on p. 114. Note that we can only say that the inauguration interval is 6 months if we define the point in time at which a set is inaugurated in the fashion indicated on p. 31.

[6] Anonymous (1962) seems to indicate that among the Akwe-Shavante of Sangradouro the interval is 7 years.

Systems in which the point in time at which a new age-group is inaugurated is determined in advance by some rule other than a fixed interval rule are not common. One possible instance occurs among a Somali tribe, the Cablalla, whose system is analyzed in Stewart (1972: 223–5), using data from Zoli (1927: 189–193). A curious example comes from the Nandi, who are said to inaugurate a new age-group at every second flowering of the *setiot* bush, that is, about every 15 years (Huntingford 1953: 54 etc.).[7] Several West African tribes appear to have rules of a kind that specifies that a new group S is to be inaugurated when all, or almost all, the members of some group S + i, $i \geqslant 1$, are dead (Jones 1962: 207; niangoran-Bouah 1965: 81; Paulme 1971b: 283 etc.).

Turning now to the second of the methods mentioned earlier, it can be observed that in formal inauguration systems the decision as to when a new group is to start recruiting never (to my knowledge) lies with the prospective members. It is the prerogative either of a chief or of a group of elders. But although it is only they who can legitimately inaugurate a new group, their decision is not taken in a vacuum. Most of the important East African ethnographies give some account of the complex and varying factors that affect their decision. They may be subject to considerable pressure from the prospective members, for in many systems there are important rights that an individual gains only when he joins an age-group.

These rather general remarks can perhaps best be illustrated by quoting from a description of one East African tribe, the Bari.

> There is no regular periodicity of initiation . . . Much depends on the size of the village and the number of children who survive to the age of about sixteen. It is usual to think in terms of a four year interval but this is not applicable to any but the larger villages, where natu-

---

[7] Compare the Kikuyu custom, reported by Cagnolo (1933: 198), of initiating only girls in those years in which the *thongoya* plant flowers, an event that takes place at intervals of about 10 years (cf. Benson 1964: 526). Middleton and Kershaw (1965: 56) remark that this custom may obtain only in Nyeri. Orchardson (in the manuscript of his book on the Kipsigis, though not in the published version of 1961) expresses doubt about the Nandi rule. He writes:

> It has been said (though I do not know on what authority) that the Nandi go to the initiation only in the year in which the Setyot flowers. If this were so one could calculate accurately the length of a generation. But the Kipsigis of my acquaintance, whose fathers came from Nandi and most of whose relations are still there, do not appear to know of this custom. When visiting Nandi country I noticed that the Setyot flowers there one year and two months later than in Kipsigis country (1928: 11).

rally the numbers of children will necessitate some interval of about that length. Despite the ceremonial surrounding the forming of an Age-Class, there seems to be no chosen person to decide when this shall be done, and, though Father Spagnolo [1932: 193] ascribes it to the coming of age of the son of a chief,[8] this will not account for the formation of every Age-Class. The decision seems to be made by the fathers of the boys approaching puberty. In their evening talks they may have been long remarking on the growth of Wani or the strength of Lado, while 'Dogale may have mentioned marriage-cows to his family, or Subek may already have speared a young leopard that was after his father's goats. At any rate the time seems ripe for an initiation and a general agreement is reached to send their sons to the tooth-extractor and to form a new Age-Class [Beaton 1936: 131 f.].

This passage indicates clearly the complexity of the factors that may affect the decision to inaugurate a new age-set. It also shows that one of those factors may be the existence of a particularly proper interval between sets. A less careful ethnographer might take this to be a fixed interval rule. Note furthermore how Spagnolo simplified the data and saw a rule where none existed. Beaton's account is confirmed in Nalder (1937: 127).

So far I have only considered formal inauguration systems. About informal inauguration systems there is a good deal less to say. The main point to note is that in such systems the decision to inaugurate an age-group is by and large left to the prospective members, though others may encourage them in that direction (see the passage on the Mbembe quoted on p. 205). In general the ethnographies do not make it clear exactly what factors affect the length of the inauguration intervals in informal inauguration systems.

4. * PREMATURE ENROLMENT

The only kind of deviation from the enrolment characteristic that we have so far encountered is waiting. Though this is by far the most important type of deviation, it is not the only one. There also exists what will be referred to as **premature enrolment**. A system is characterized by premature enrolment if the minimum enrolment age and the basic enrolment age are not identical (the minimum enrol-

---

[8] The Chagga appear to have had a rule of this kind, or at least a very strong tendency in that direction: see Gutmann (1926: 318) and Raum (1940: 309).

ment age must, of course, always be the lower of the two). The Shilluk provide an example of this phenomenon. It appears that in this tribe a boy joins an age-set by participating in a "*Cong Bul*, or dance."

> Participating in his first *Cong* usually occurs when the boy is from fourteen to sixteen, but a youth may undergo the rites at an earlier age, if his father is dead and it is necessary to accelerate his change of status so that he can represent his family—especially if he has no elder brother [Howell 1941: 61].

In this instance, the basic enrolment age is between fourteen and sixteen, but the minimum enrolment age is evidently lower, though we are not told just how low it is. A system characterized by premature enrolment is, of course, no longer an age-set system. In this particular case, however, it seems reasonable to look on the rule that leads to premature enrolment as being no more than a secondary rule.

There are probably other systems that have premature enrolment of much the same kind as do the Shilluk, but I have no examples at hand.

In a speculative vein, we might guess that premature enrolment could occur in a UPL system. Imagine a system of this kind that, for whatever reasons, is only just beginning to suffer somewhat from underaging. Up to now the system has possessed both the no-overlapping characteristic and the enrolment characteristic. But now the situation arises that boys who are supposed to join group S have not yet reached the enrolment age when group $S - 1$ is inaugurated. One method of dealing with this situation is to maintain the basic enrolment age but lower the minimum enrolment age, so that these boys can join S. The advantage of this approach is, in particular, that it makes overlapping unnecessary. Its disadvantage is that it is only a short-term solution. Underaging is cumulative; eventually the minimum enrolment age will reach its lower limit, zero, and some other method of dealing with the situation will have to be found (probably overlapping).

5 * BROAD-RANGE SYSTEMS

In the first section of this chapter we discussed systems in which $a_S > c_S$ (for all S), but which, with the revised version of the enrolment characteristic, fall within the limits of the model. The present section is primarily concerned with systems with $a_S > c_S$ (for all S) that do not possess the enrolment characteristic, even in its revised form, though they do possess all the other characteristics of the age-set model. Such deviant systems will be referred to as **broad-range systems**.

We have already encountered one type of broad-range system: the negative paternal linking system (Chapter I, Section 3.3). Here I want to introduce the **fraternal linking (FL) system**, that is, one in which the age-group(s) that an individual may join is related to the group(s) that his brother(s) join(s).

Probably the commonest type of FL system is what may be called the **negative FL system**, that is, one in which brothers are not allowed to belong to the same age-group. Writing about the Afikpo Ibo, who have a system of this kind, Ottenberg states that "To have male siblings in the same set would bring two contradictory principles into play: the equality of all set members against the authority of an older brother over a younger one [1971: 57 n.]." No doubt this is true of many, or even all, of the societies with negative FL systems. Almost all the instances of such systems that I have noticed are in West Africa.[9]

It seems that in practice a negative FL rule generally produces a broad-range system that deviates only slightly from the model; but this is not necessarily the case. On the one hand, it might not produce a deviant system at all: this would be so if a new age-set (S) were inaugurated as soon as a brother of someone in S + 1 reached the enrolment age.[10] Such, indeed, appears to be the rule among the Dida and the Konkomba, though in both cases we are told that the rule is not strictly obeyed. On the other hand, a negative FL rule might produce a widely deviant system if, say, it were strictly observed, if the interval between brothers were not regulated in any way, and if the inauguration interval were large.

A more complex kind of FL system exists among the Somba. In

---

[9] Other examples come from the Soninké (Pollet and Winter 1971: 263), the Tiv (Bohannan 1965: 535), the Ekiti Yoruba (Lloyd 1965: 563), the Dida (Terray 1969: 254), the Adioukrou (Paulme 1971b: 259), the Atié (Paulme 1971b: 239), the Konkomba (Tait 1961: 86 ff.), and the Kabré (Delord 1948: 27). The Ébrié have some rule of this kind, but the facts are unclear: see Person (1963: 73f.) and Paulme (1971b: 224). Niangoran-Bouah (1969), however, makes no mention of fraternal linking. The only East African example I have noted is among the Abaluyia (Wagner 1949: 378).

[10] It would be necessary, of course, to have special rules for twins.

spite of certain obscurities in the data, Mercier's account of the relevant facts deserves to be quoted.

> An age-class[11] is composed in principle of the males born during a period of three consecutive years.[12] The "Somba"[13] emphasize that three years is also the normal interval between two successive births in a monogamous family:[14] thus a man should belong to the age-class which follows that to which his immediately older brother belongs. For a variety of reasons this cannot normally be the case (see Mercier 1968: 158).[15] But there are ways of making reality conform to the theoretical model: the diviner may discover that it is necessary to bring forward or to delay the enrolment of a boy in the first age-class, or later make him "jump" one. This can also be a means, at the level of the whole grouping,[16] of completing a "hollow" class. From the cases that were studied, however, it does not appear that this kind of adjustment was often resorted to. It is not possible after the third class [i.e., age-grade] among the Bètâmmadibè, whereas it seems to be permissible right up to the seventh among the Bèsorubè (Mercier 1968: 211)[17] [Mercier 1971: 98].

11 The Somba have both age-groups and age-grades, and occasionally Mercier recognizes this by referring to the age-groups as *promotions* (1971: 103). In general, however, he uses the term *classes d'âge* to cover both groups and grades.

12 The age-group is "formed at an early stage among the children's play groups, but it does not formally come into existence until the time of puberty [Mercier 1968: 158]."

13 Mercier places the word "Somba" in quotes because the term is one applied by outsiders to a population divided into groups, each of which has its own name for itself. Mercier describes primarily the age organization of the northern Bètâmmadibè, and secondarily the age organization of the Bèsorubè.

14 "Sexual relations being prohibited during the two years or so until the child is weaned [Mercier's note]."

15 Mercier (1968: 158) points out that the interval between brothers is often greater than 3 years because of the births of girls and because of infant mortality.

16 By "the whole grouping" I take it that Mercier means the area within which a single age-group system operates, that is, a *kubwoti* or a large *difwδ*.

17 "In fact, changes of age-class do not seem to be very frequent: out of a sample of 38 Bètémbè men, only five had celebrated the *difoni* before the usual age [Mercier 1968: 211 n. 58]." The Bètémbè are a grouping (*kubwoti*) of the Bètâmmadibè. The *difoni*, in this context, is the ceremony that marks the transition to the fourth age-grade. A man is normally about 21 when it occurs (1971: 99). This remark of Mercier's remains obscure to me: it implies that a man joins a group with his contemporaries, but then shifts up to a senior group and thus performs the *difoni* at an early age. But why not join the senior group when it was inaugurated?

A number of interesting points arise from this passage. It is evident that the Somba permit upward shifting. One reason, apparently, is to maintain homology with respect to size (cf. p. 114): this seems to be the meaning of the reference to "hollow" age-classes. Another reason, it seems, is to place a boy in an age-group adjacent to the one to which his brother belongs. If this is so, then it is a rather puzzling phenomenon (cf. p. 212, n. 17).

In the present context, the relevant data are those relating to enrolment. It is worth considering just how the desire to place brothers in adjacent age-groups can affect the system. Let us imagine three brothers B_1, B_2, and B_3, B_1 being the oldest, and B_3 the youngest. Let us imagine, furthermore, that B_1 joins age-group $S-1$ at the basic enrolment age, which appears to be about 12 among the northern Bètâm'madibè, and about 9 among the Bèsorubè (Mercier 1971: 99 f.). The inauguration interval among the Somba is 3 years. With this in mind we can construct three possible cases.

First, the three brothers may be born at intervals of exactly 3 years. In this case, B_2 and B_3 will also be able to join their respective groups ($S-2$ and $S-3$) at the basic enrolment age.

Second, the brothers may be born at intervals of more than three years. Let us take it that B_3 is 12 years younger than B_1. He will then be 6 years below the basic enrolment age when $S-3$ is inaugurated. If he is supposed to join it in spite of this, then we have a system characterized by premature enrolment.

Third, the brothers may be born at intervals of less than 3 years. Given the existence of the rule mentioned on p. 212, n. 14, this is presumably an uncommon occurrence; and the discussion that follows, which assumes a case where several brothers are born in close succession, probably has no application to the Somba. It is quite possible, however, that there exist real systems in which analogous situations arise, so it is worthwhile seeing how they can be analyzed with the available concepts.

Let us imagine, then, that B_3 is only 3 years younger than B_1. He is supposed to join $S-3$, but by the time it is inaugurated he will be 4 years older than B_1 was when he joined $S-1$. Clearly, this is a system with no basic enrolment age, that is, a system characterized by waiting.

But is this an adequate characterization of the system? Consider this question: what is it that determines when B_1 is enrolled? It is not the case that B_1 is simply enrolled at some arbitrary point in time after he has passed the minimum enrolment age. He will actually be enrolled at around the age of 9 (among the Bèsorubè) or

12 (among the northern Bètâmmadibè). Because the age-group he joins is not affected by the age-group affiliation of any of his brothers, the point in time at which he joins is determined, in effect, by a basic enrolment age.

The best way of dealing with this kind of situation seems to be to introduce the notion of a **modified basic enrolment age**. This is an age which is such that any individual joins a group as soon as there is one recruiting if and only if (a) he has not yet joined a group, (b) he is going to join one, (c) he has reached this age, and (d) one or more other conditions are met. It is (d) that distinguishes the modified basic enrolment age from the basic enrolment age.[18] In the case of the Somba, the additional condition (d) is that if the individual has an immediately older brother in some group S, then the group that is recruiting is S − 1.

When the modified basic enrolment age is the same as the minimum enrolment age in a system, then the system has a **modified enrolment age**.

The notion of a modified basic enrolment age might be useful in describing some PL systems; the kind of complications involved will become evident to the reader who tries to work out, for instance, just how to analyze the Garbichcho Sidama system described on p. 107.

The FL systems we have so far considered are not in themselves particularly problematic. Difficulties arise, however, if we compare them with birth order PL systems. It then appears that all the various kinds of PL and FL systems should be brought within a single conceptual framework; but I cannot suggest how this could be done. The task looks even more difficult if we consider the rules that regulate enrolment among certain tribes of the Karimojong cluster.

The Jie have probably the most elaborate and—thanks to the work of Gulliver (1953)—certainly the best-described rules of this kind. Each Jie g-group is made up of a number of sub-groups (Gulliver calls them "age-sets"). New sub-groups are inaugurated at irregular intervals, averaging perhaps 3 or 4 years, and there are ten or so sub-groups in a g-group (Gulliver 1953: 150 f.; Lamphear 1976: 38). The sub-group embraces members from all the Jie settlements. It appears that any given settlement initiates (i.e., enrols) all those who

---

[18] Some constraints probably need to be placed on the kind of thing that can appear under (d), but it would not be easy to formulate them.

are going to be members of the sub-group in a single wet season (Gulliver 1953: 154), and that the recruitment period for the sub-group as a whole extends over several wet seasons because different settlements choose different years in which to make their contribution to that sub-group. The number enrolled from a single settlement in one season ranges from two to twenty (1953: 154). There exist rules that regulate the decision as to who is to be enrolled in a particular sub-group, and it is these rules that will concern us here.

In order to describe them, we need to know something about the group that Gulliver calls the *extended family*. Its members—numbering perhaps fifty or a hundred[19] —generally occupy a single homestead (Gulliver 1966: 76; Lamphear 1976: 10). They have a head, who has very little authority, and

> Between the members of the group there is usually continual co-operation in pastoral affairs, residential and day-to-day intercourse and much assistance in all activities. Above all, there is recognition of reciprocal obligations to assist each other in transactions involving stock such as bridewealth, compensation, gifts and the like [Gulliver 1966: 79].

The members of this group will describe themselves as being related in a particular way. There is a certain amount of minor variation about this, but the typical representation is as follows. The male members of the group are distributed over three generations (Gulliver 1966: 106), which we may call generations 1, 2, and 3. The most senior of these is generation 1 (referred to by Gulliver as the "sons" generation). The men in this generation—who, to judge from the scattered data given by Gulliver, may number as few as five or as many as twenty-five—describe themselves as all being the offspring of the sons of a single man. In other words, their fathers (now dead) were brothers (full or half), and they have a single, long-defunct, paternal grandfather. The men in generation 2 are the sons of the men in generation 1, and the boys in generation 3 are the sons of the men in generation 2. The female members of the extended family—who are not of much interest to us, since they do not join age-groups—comprise the mothers, wives, and unmarried daughters and sisters of the male members.

In fact, the interesting thing about the extended family is that

---

[19] Gulliver (1966: 122, 113, 109, 94); Lamphear (1976: 10, cf. 1976: 7 n. 14).

its members are often not related in quite the way they say they are. I shall return to this later. For the moment, let us revert to the age-group system.

It appears that the decision as to whether a particular man is to join a given sub-group is made by the extended family to which he belongs. But this decision is severely constrained by some rather complex rules.[20] I shall begin by setting out these rules as they are described by Gulliver and will then go on to propose certain corrections to Gulliver's account.

Perhaps the easiest way of presenting these rules is to try to imagine a device that will answer the question "Which members of our extended family shall we enrol in this sub-group?" As its input, this device takes a list of the males in the extended family and certain data about each one of them; as its output, it produces a list of those who are to be initiated. At the same time, we can get the device to do something else. For reasons that need not concern us here, the *order* in which those of a particular extended family who join a single sub-group are initiated is of some significance. We can therefore see to it that the output of the device is an ordered list, giving the order in which those on the list are to be initiated.

We can conveniently split the operation of this device into two portions, as follows. There is a total ordering on the male members of an extended family, that is, given any two of them, one is senior in rank to the other. This seniority order determines the order in which they join their respective age-groups. The first portion of our device should therefore take as its input an unordered list of all the males in the extended family, together with certain information about each, and give as its output a totally ordered list giving their seniority order within that extended family. The second portion of the device will take as its input the output of the first portion; its output will be the output of the device as a whole—the ordered list of those who are to join the sub-group at present recruiting.

Let us now describe the device in more detail. Its input is an unordered list of all the males in an extended family, plus the following information about each:

(i) His generation number (given according to the convention mentioned above).

(ii) His maternal birth order number.

---

[20] So complex, in fact, that the reader may feel sceptical about their reality—but unjustifiably (see Gulliver 1953: 156).

(iii) His mother's marriage number. This is most simply defined by an example. Let us imagine that in a single
generation of a certain extended family there are three
men, A, B, and C. They have five wives between them,
whom they married in the following order: first A married his first wife (A'), then B married his first wife (B'),
then C married his wife (C'), then A married his second
wife (A''), and finally B married his second wife (B''). The
order in which these women joined the extended family
gives the mother's marriage numbers of their sons. So, for
example, the second son of A'' will have the birth order
number 2 and the mother's marriage number 4. Note that
the mother's marriage numbers constitute a different
series for each generation: for instance, even if a man of a
different generation in the extended family has taken a
new wife after A married A', but before B married B', the
sons of B' would still have the mother's marriage number
2.

(iv) His age.

Given this input, the first portion of the device will perform the
following operations on it:

(i) The names are divided into groupings according to their
generation numbers (so there will usually be three of these
groupings). The groupings are ordered according to the
generation numbers.

(ii) Within each grouping the names are now ordered according to maternal birth order numbers.

(iii) Within each of these subgroupings, the names are ordered
according to the mother's marriage numbers. Since no two
individuals in a generation can have the same maternal
birth order number *and* the same mother's marriage number, the names in the device are now totally ordered.

(iv) The device now scans the list of names. Whenever it sees
the names of two men, one immediately next to the other
in order, such that the one lower in the order is 5 years or
more older than the one higher in the order, it reverses the
order of the two names. When no such pairs are left, the
device gives the ordered list of names as its output.

Operation (iv) is in fact only an approximation to what occurs.
Essentially, its real-life equivalent ensures that no one is senior to

someone who is considerably older than himself. Gulliver estimates
the relevant interval as being about 5 years, but makes it clear that
this is only an approximation. *Exactly* what criteria the Jie use, and
exactly how much randomness there is in their procedures, is something we do not know and something it would be difficult, though
not, I suppose, impossible, to discover.

We now come to the second portion of the device, which
demands two further kinds of information. First, we must attach to
each name in the list an annotation indicating whether or not the
man has already joined an age-group. Second, we must inform the
device which generation is eligible to join an age-group. On the basis
of these data the device then eliminates from the list all those who
have the wrong generation number and all those who have already
joined an age-group.

We now have an ordered list of all the uninitiated males in the
generation at present being initiated. The last operation of the device
is the one that determines which of them will be initiated into this
particular sub-group. Now, we know that the Jie g-group system as a
whole lacks the enrolment characteristic, since it permits extensive
waiting by individuals whose g-group has not yet been inaugurated;
but it would still be possible for the subsystem constituted by the
sub-groups within a single g-group to possess this characteristic. In
other words, the g-group system as a whole would have a modified
enrolment age, the only condition under (*d*) being that the individual
have a generation number corresponding to the g-group recruiting at
that point in time.

In fact, however, matters are not quite so simple. In the list
produced by our device, "a seventeen-year-old may be . . . above his
twenty-one-year-old cousin [Gulliver 1953: 154]." If there were
simply a modified enrolment age of (say) 18, then the 21-year-old
would be initiated, but not his younger cousin; and this would be
wrong, since the order of the list is supposed to determine the order
in which men are initiated.

But the Jie do have the notion of a proper age at which men
should be initiated—somewhere around 20 years old (see p. 60; cf.
Gulliver 1953: 154). How can they reconcile this with a list of the
kind our device has produced? There are two main possibilities. One
would be to add a second condition to (*d*) so that it would now be
(*d*) (i) if the individual has a generation number corresponding to the
g-group recruiting at that point in time and (ii) if there is no one
higher up on the list who has not yet been initiated. This would be a
modified enrolment age; its effect would be that the 17-year-old

would be initiated only when he passed that age, with the result that the 21-year-old would be initiated rather late.

The second possibility would be to have (in effect) a premature enrolment system. The system would differ from a premature enrolment system of the kind discussed in Section 4 of this chapter only in that instead of having a basic enrolment age it would have a modified basic enrolment age, condition (d) being simply: if the individual has a generation number corresponding to the g-group recruiting at that point in time.[21] When the older cousin was initiated would be determined by the modified basic enrolment age, and the younger cousin would be initiated at some lower age. This is, in fact, the solution that the Jie prefer. "Where possible, what usually happens is that youths in a socially senior position are brought forward rather earlier, and are initiated into sets [i.e., sub-groups] above their coevals [Gulliver 1953: 156]."

This operation could also be reduced to a form in which it could be carried out by our device, although—as with operation (iv) above—only at the expense of introducing a degree of rigidity that is no doubt foreign to the system as it really is. We fix the modified basic enrolment age at, say, 20 years of age. The device is instructed to scan the ordered list of names from the beginning. As soon as it reaches the name of the first man of 20 or more, it stops and gives the remainder of the list (including that man's name) as its output. This is the final output of the device as a whole, the ordered list of all those who are to join the sub-group at present recruiting. Some of those initiated may be under 20—the minimum enrolment age being, of course, 5 years less than the modified basic enrolment age—but there will be no one who is 20 or over who is not initiated.

The rules we have been examining are such that there is some overlap of the age-ranges of adjacent sub-groups within a single g-group. On the other hand, because of operation (iv) (in the first portion of the device) the amount of overlap of this kind is rather slight. Gulliver, in his illustrative material (1953: 155), gives the age-group affiliations, relative ages, and seniority rankings of nineteen men. If we examine the relationship between relative age and ranking, we find numerous cases where the rank ordering does not correspond to the age ordering,[22] that is, where a younger man is

---

[21] We therefore redefine the notion of **premature enrolment** to include also systems with modified basic enrolment ages.

[22] It is difficult to give an adequate measurement of this phenomenon, but by one (conservative) way of counting there are seven cases. Gulliver (1953:

ranked senior to an older one. But only once do we find a case where
sub-groups within a single g-group have overlapping age-ranges: there
is an instance of two members of a sub-group being younger than a
member of the immediately junior sub-group.[23]

These, then, are the rules governing enrolment in an age-group,
as described by Gulliver. They have been examined in this section
because, in his account, the subsystem constituted by the sub-groups
within a single g-group is a broad-range system.

Now, from our earlier analysis of the Jie system, we know that
the description of the rules that has just been given is not entirely
accurate. Lamphear is certainly right in saying that the Jie system
permits overlapping. In the present context, this means primarily
that at a given point in time not one, but two, generations may be
eligible to join age-groups. Furthermore, if a youth is among the
youngest members of his generation, then the rules governing the age
of enrolment are liable to be stretched so as to reduce to a minimum
the amount of overlapping (p. 60).

But this is not all. Toward the end of our earlier analysis it was
suggested that there must exist some factor in the system, not
mentioned in our sources, that keeps the effects of generational
spread within reasonable limits. I now want to present a guess as to
what this factor may be, making use, for this purpose, of Gulliver's
outstanding work on the Jie extended family.

Gulliver shows that the account given by the Jie of the kinship
relations within the extended family is both internally inconsistent
and irreconcilable with certain easily ascertainable facts about these
groups. As with the age-group system, the native model, though clear
and well developed, is incorrect. In particular, the men in generation
1, who describe themselves as the grandsons (through their fathers)
of a single man, cannot in fact always be as closely related as that.
What is actually happening? Gulliver advances his explanation only in
a tentative way, but it is backed up by convincing case material, and
there can be little doubt as to its essential correctness. Quite simply,

---

155) lists the instances in the Lukong family. There is, incidentally, a misprint in
the diagram of the Lukong family: the wife of "father" (1), who is given the
number II, should actually have the number III, as may be seen from Gulliver
(1966: 65). In the diagram of the Kopengamoi family the wife of "father" (3) is
of course to be numbered IV.

[23] In the most junior generation of the Kopengamoi family, man iv belongs
to the Snakes sub-group, whereas two younger men, v and vi, belong to the
immediately senior sub-group, the Grasshoppers.

the kinship relationships are misrepresented. So, for example, we may find two men in generation 1 who are the sons, not of brothers, but of patriparallel cousins (i.e., they do not have a father's father in common, but only a father's father's father). Yet these two men will describe themselves as being the offspring of a single father's father, will behave toward each other as if they were, and will be known to the world at large as such. Only in certain cases, and by means of very careful investigation, is it possible to discover the true relationships between members of an extended family. The process by which genealogies are rewritten is considered at some length by Gulliver, to whose admirable account the reader is referred (Gulliver 1966: 100 ff.).

The relevance of these facts about the extended family to the age-group system is obvious. Although Gulliver's case material does not provide any examples, it seems reasonable to assume that in certain instances the genealogy is rewritten in such a fashion that an individual is shifted from one generation to another. When this happens he will naturally be shifted to a generation in the extended family whose other members are about the same age as he is. As a result of such shifting he will, I suggest, join some other g-group than $F - 1$.

I suspect that a process of this sort is a significant factor in controlling the effects of generational spread.[24] If this is so, then the Jie system differs from a g-set system not only in permitting overlapping, waiting, and shrinking, but also in lacking the UPL characteristic.[25] It should be added, however, that this guess flies in the face of the most explicit and forceful statements in the sources. Lamphear, for instance, writes that

> The basic and irrevocable principle upon which the Jie system is based is that, simply stated, all the sons of a man must be initiated into the generation-set following his own . . . the Jie are adamant that the basic principle of their system can never be broken [Lamphear 1976: 34].

[24] It also seems to me likely that the rules relating to widow inheritance (p. 57f.), which if strictly observed would exacerbate the problems involved in trying to run something like a g-set system, are in fact sometimes broken.

[25] To be exact, if my guess is correct, then the system certainly lacks the UPL characteristic if the notion of father is defined as a purely biological one. By some other definition of the notion, the system might not lack the UPL characteristic (cf. p. 87, n. 66).

Furthermore, even if there is some truth in my guess, it by no means follows that it provides the whole solution to the problem posed on p. 59. For instance, we know little about the history of the Jie g-group system, and it is possible that at some stage generational spread was held in check by demographic restrictions or by other rules that have since fallen into desuetude. More work in the field will be necessary before we really understand what is (or was) going on.

At least two other tribes in the Karimojong cluster also have rules that regulate enrolment according to a ranking system.

The Turkana have an age-group system which, but for these rules, would conform exactly to the age-set model (i.e., it is a broad-range system). Their rules differ from those of the Jie in the following respects (Gulliver 1958: 901 f.; 1966: 131 f.):

   (i)   Rules referring to g-groups do not exist, since there are no g-groups.

  (ii)   The ranking system applies only to males with the same father.

 (iii)   In the Jie system it is quite common for the seniority ordering to differ from the birth ordering, whereas "in the Turkana nuclear family such modifications are not usual amongst the narrower range of sons of one man [Gulliver 1966: 132]." It is evidently uncommon to find a man in an age-group senior to the one to which his older paternal half-brother belongs.

We may take it, therefore, that the system differs only marginally from the age-set model.

The Karimojong also have rules of this type (Dyson-Hudson 1966:206). Their rules differ from those of the Jie in the following ways:

   (i)   The g-group rules are different.

  (ii)   The ranking system applies only to the sons of one man.

 (iii)   "In deciding on initiation priority the head of the household takes into account the absolute ages and capabilities of his sons also [Dyson-Hudson 1966: 206]." In all three cases—Jie, Turkana, and Karimojong—the ordering given by mother's marriage numbers and maternal birth order numbers can be modified so as to accord more closely with the age ordering. Whether or not the roughly 5-year interval that Gulliver mentions among the Jie is also the relevant one among the Turkana and Karimojong, we cannot say. What is not mentioned in the reports on the Turkana and Jie, but is mentioned here, is that the capabilities of a man are taken into account in determining the order in which initiations occur.

As among the Jie, then, the subsystem constituted by the sub-groups of a Karimojong g-group lacks the enrolment characteristic because of these rules. It also lacks it for another reason, to which we shall turn in a moment.

Neither in the case of the Turkana nor in the case of the Karimojong can we say in precisely what fashion the enrolment constraint is violated; it may be that, as among the Jie, the ranking system leads to premature enrolment, but there are also, as we know, other possibilities.

Rules of the sort we have been examining show clearly how difficult it would be to create a single conceptual framework for what I have loosely labeled PL and FL systems; but they also show, I think, how artificial a sharp distinction between paternal linking and fraternal linking would be, and how desirable it would be to have such a framework.

To conclude this section, let us look at two other kinds of broad-range system. The first is the system in which enrolment in an age-group involves a certain amount of expense, with the result that it is sometimes delayed in the case of poorer individuals. The clearest example of this that I have at hand comes from the Masai, of whom Merker writes as follows:

> The persons whose circumcision [i.e., enrolment] is longest delayed are the poor sons of poor parents and orphans who have no property. The reason is that the circumcised youths hold meat feats to which each in turn must contribute a neat; and so each youth must possess either a beast or a father who will give him one. If he lacks both, then the youth tries to accumulate a few head of cattle by working as a herdsman for someone well-to-do. Until he has acquired cattle he remains uncircumcised. Such youths are known as *el oischó u gischu* [1910: 60 f.].

Another instance comes from the Didinga, amongst whom initiation is a necessary precondition for enrolment in an age-group.[26] The initiation ceremony demands the sacrifice of an animal—either an ox (for first- and last-born sons) or a he-goat (for all other sons). Kronenberg writes that initiation

> takes place approximately between the ages of 12 and 22, depending on the candidate's degree of maturity and on the quantity of cattle that his father owns. A rich man will in general arrange for his son to be initiated at an earlier age than a poor man's son would be, since the son will thereby enter the age-set system sooner and thus reach a higher status sooner [1972: 94].

A somewhat similar situation exists among the Karimojong, and this is the other reason why the subsystem constituted by the sub-groups of a single age-group lacks the enrolment characteristic.

> Initiation requires the sacrifice of an ox. . . . A man whose family is poor in stock may thus have to delay his initiation long after he is theoretically able to enter an age-set [i.e., sub-group]. A man who is completely a pauper may never be able to initiate for the same reason [Dyson-Hudson 1966: 205]. (Cf. p. 63, n. 42.)[27]

A rule of a quite different type is reported from the Nanshih Ami of Taiwan.

> Each set had its own *papuro'ai no sral* or monitors. Those who desire to become monitors are allowed to participate in the initiation ceremony [i.e., enrolment] later. For example, the ordinary age for participating in the initiation ceremony is nineteen or twenty, but if a boy wishes to become a monitor, he can wait for seven years to participate in the next initiation ceremony at the age of twenty-six to twenty-seven; by becoming a senior member of his set he can

[26] Initiation does not coincide with enrolment in the age-group, which may only be inaugurated some years after the prospective member has been initiated (Kronenberg 1972: 97 f.). The system is such that in some cases early initiation will simply give a youth a more senior position within his age-group, while in others it will actually lead to his being enrolled in a more senior age-group than would otherwise have been the case. It is only the latter cases that are relevant in the present context.

[27] Note also that according to Lamphear "the actual age at which a Jie young man is initiated depends largely on the number of sons and the number of available livestock of his father [1972: 92 f.]." Gulliver does not mention the availability of livestock as a factor in determining the age at which enrolment takes place.

automatically be one of its monitors.[28] Those who are late in participating in the intiation are called *misatatadai* [Chen 1965: 96].

If the vague concept of a secondary rule has any validity, then this
clearly is an instance of such a rule.

From what has been said, it can be seen that broad-range
systems are by no means rare. Is the enrolment constraint—even in its
revised form—too strict? It may be so; but it would not be easy to
formulate a satisfactory relaxed version. There are also more respectable reasons for being fairly satisfied with it as it stands. First, most
systems that possess all the other characteristics of the model also
possess this one. Second, broad-range systems in fact only deviate
fairly slightly from it. That is to say, it seems that in all such systems
most members of an age-group fall within an age-range equal to its
cessation interval. Those who fall outside this age-range are nevertheless usually quite near it. As far as I know there are no broad-range
systems in which a significant proportion of the members of any
group fall outside an age-range of, say, 10 years more than the
cessation interval of the group.

6 * THE ENROLMENT AGE

Enrolment ages (or enrolment maturity levels) tend to be low.
The only strikingly high one I have noted is in the *Jahrgängerverein*
systems: these groups sometimes had an enrolment age of 50 (see
Appendix 2). The next highest age I have noted is 20 to 22, among
the Tsamako of Ethiopia. Since these people only inaugurate their
sets at intervals of about 8 to 11 years, some men would evidently
not join until the age of about 30 (Jensen 1959: 375).

In the *Jahrgängerverein* systems $a_S = c_S$ (cf. Section 1 of this
chapter). Almost all the other age-set systems of which this is true,

---

[28] The leader of an age-group is often its oldest member. Among the
Abeokuta Yoruba a youth will sometimes shift down one group in order to
belong to a group in which he has more authority than in his original one
(Fajana 1968: 235). The leader of a group sometimes comes from the immediately senior group, as for instance among the Cablalla Somali (Zoli 1927: 191),
the Ngoni (Barnes 1967: 36 f.), and the Zulu (Krige 1936: 36); cf. also
Niangoran-Bouah (1969: 73 f.) on the Ébrié.

however, are ones in which members are enrolled at birth (**natal enrolment systems**)[29] or very soon afterwards. There are a number of systems for which it has been claimed that individuals belong to sets from birth, but such claims are not always convincing (cf. Bernardi 1952: 317 n. 3). Natal enrolment systems actually appear to be rather uncommon. One of the best documented is the one on Pukapuka (p. 114). Other well-attested examples come from West Africa, which is probably the region where such systems are least rare: they have been described, for instance, among the Godie (Degri de Djagnan 1967: 430) and among the Ika Ibibio (Jeffreys 1950: 161 f.). The former inaugurate a new set every year, the latter every other year. It is also possible in this region to find very low basic and minimum enrolment ages: 7 weeks, for example, among the Nnobi Ibo (Daly 1964: 263; cf. Forde and Jones 1950: 30 for the location of this group).

The reason why natal enrolment is so rare is not far to seek: children have to be several years old before they can recognize the existence of rights and duties or undertake any significant joint activities.

---

[29] A natal enrolment system is not merely a system in which the enrolment age is 0; it is a system in which everyone who joins an age-group does so at birth.

IV

Further Developments

In this chapter a number of questions are raised about the nature and significance of the age-set model. The answers given are tentative, sketchy, and programmatic; most of the new concepts introduced remain virtually undefined. What matter are the questions.

1 A REVISED AGE-SET MODEL

Imagine we are faced with what is evidently a graded age-set system and that we want to describe it. We assume that the system can be divided into two components: the age-grade system and the age-set system. Now we know more or less what kind of thing an age-grade is: it is a collection of rules, though it may also have other properties (cf. p. 133). But what kind of thing is an age-set? The model simply says that it is a "group." We might begin by trying to interpret this as meaning that an age-set is merely a collection of individuals. (We would then also have to make some kind of allowance for the fact that the membership of the age-set may change from time to time.) But a moment's thought will convince us that this will not do. Take our imaginary system again. On examining it more closely we find that each age-set has a leader, which it retains throughout its existance, a name, which it retains in the same way, and that each is permanently subject to the rule that no member may marry the daughter of a member. These are characteristics of the age-set as such; they cannot (except perhaps in a very artificial way) be derived from the characteristics of the members of the set—and in this they contrast with a feature such as the average age of members of the set—nor can they (in a natural way) be accounted for as part of the age-grade sequence. Evidently we need a better interpretation of the term "group".

We can approach this task by making use of the notion of a **social identity** (Goodenough 1965). This notion relates to the way in which the rules of a society are properly formulated. When such rules directly regulate people's behavior they do not, on the whole, do so by referring to them by name, for example, "Harry Smith and Tom Brown and . . . have the right to vote." Instead, they use social identities, for example, "All adults have the right to vote, except lunatics, peers, and criminals." A social identity can be looked upon as a kind of label which is tied to a person so that he can be referred to in a social rule; if some concept that categorizes people in a given society is not used in formulating any social rule in that society—for example, among ourselves "eccentric," as opposed to "lunatic"—then it is not a social identity in that society.

The particular rights and duties of a person with a given social identity are determined by its **directional rules.** Most social identities also have rules that determine how they shall be assigned and disassigned (**assignment rules**). I shall stipulate that, in contrast to its assignment rules, the directional rules of an identity are peculiar to that identity. A social identity exists in a particular society if and only if directional rules for it are current; but at a given point in time it may not be assigned to anyone.

The set of all those who have a particular social identity constitutes a **(social) identity class**; from what has just been said it is evident that a social identity can exist in a particular society and yet the corresponding identity class be empty; for example, the (British) identity class "Secretary of State for Foreign Affairs" is empty (though still in existence) if the incumbent has suddenly died and his successor has not yet been appointed.

Age-groups are identity classes, and we can set up cross-culturally applicable criteria for identifying particular identity classes as age-sets by means of a revised version of the age-set model, as follows:

A collection of identity classes in a society constitutes an **age-set sequence** when the corresponding social identities are governed by rules such that in that society they generate an unbounded number of social identities with the following characteristics:

(i) There is a total ordering on the social identities given by the order in which they begin being assigned.[1] This is the **ordering characteristic**.

(ii) Each social identity ceases permanently to be assigned before the next one starts (the **no-overlapping characteristic**).

(iii) There are always at least two identity classes in existence (the **two-group characteristic**).

(iv) No identity class dissolves before one that came into existence before it. This is the **dissolution characteristic**.

(v) There is a certain level of maturity (the **enrolment maturity level**) that has the following properties:

1. No individual is assigned a social identity before reaching this level: it is the **minimum (enrolment) maturity level**.

2. Any individual who has not yet been assigned a social identity, but who is going to be assigned one, and who has reached this level of maturity, is assigned one as soon as there is one being assigned: it is the **basic (enrolment) maturity level**.

This is the **enrolment characteristic**.

(vi) No individual is at any time assigned more than one social identity (the **single membership characteristic**).

(vii) An individual is only disassigned a social identity under one of the following circumstances:

1. When he leaves the society, or

2. When the identity class is dissolving.

This is the **no-resigning characteristic**.

---

[1] Begins being assigned = is inaugurated = comes into existence $\neq$ is actually assigned to someone. Cf. Chapter I, Section 1.2.1.

(viii)   An individual who has been disassigned a social identity
because he has left the society, or because the corresponding identity class is dissolving, is not again assigned
an identity. This is the **no-rejoining characteristic.**

The term **group**—which does not appear in this revised model—
can be reserved for a particular type of identity class.[2] One characteristic of this type is that the class has by definition more than one
member. This is, of course, not true of all identity classes (e.g.,
President of the United States). Another is that the members of the
class constitute an organization or have some special relationship to
each other—and this also is not true of all identity classes (e.g.,
fathers).

It is by no means certain that everything we would want to call
an age-set does in fact have both these properties: for instance, it
may be that the Bedik know of age-sets with only a single member
(p. 113), and it is possible—though I have no clear examples to
hand—that there are age-sets lacking the second characteristic of
groups just mentioned.[3]

Most of the items in the model are constraints on assignment
rules, and the remainder constrain **creation rules,** i.e., rules governing
the creation of new social identities. The model specifies that there
must be creation rules that will generate an unbounded number of
social identities, and then its first three items set further constraints
on these rules (the second and third items can also be seen as
constraints on assignment rules). Age-sets are an extreme case in the
simplicity of their origins; many identity classes have long, complicated histories in which creation rules play little or no part.

The implication of the revised age-set model is that each age-set
has its own rules. This is obviously reasonable in cases where the

---

[2] Not everything we call a group in ordinary usage is an identity class—for
instance, we talk of a group of friends having lunch together—and some things
that are not called groups in ordinary usage—e.g., large business corporations—
would fall under the notion of group that I have in mind. What I call a group
seems to be very similar to what Ehrlich refers to as a "social association"
(1913: 31, 34 = 1936: 39, 42).

[3] If age-sets are not by definition groups, then the notion of an age-group is
no longer much use (assuming, of course, than an age-group is necessarily a
group). Its place can be taken by the analogous notion of an age (identity) class.

rules of sets in a single system differ from each other;[4] but what of the more common situation where all the sets have exactly the same internal organization? Each age-set is a separate identity class, since, for instance, a man with the identity "member of age-set S" has obligations to others with the same identity which he does not have to those with, say, the identity "member of age-set S + 1." But still, we must somehow take into account the fact that the obligations of members to S + 1 to each other are just the same as the obligations of members of S to each other.

The way to do this seems to be to distinguish between two kinds of age-set system rules, systemic and local. The assignment and directional rules of a particular age-set are **local rules**. We stipulate that these local rules are all constrained by the **systemic rules** (in practice the constraints are generally severe). Systemic rules that act in this way are therefore rules about rules (**second order rules**), for what they govern is not the behavior of individuals with particular social identities, but rather the rules governing that behavior. Other systemic rules, however, are **first order**, e.g., the creation rules.

Let us now see how these concepts will fit the system imagined at the beginning of the chapter.

The regulation about marriage is a second order systemic rule that constrains the local directional rules.

The fact that each set has a leader means that one member of each set has this identity in addition to his identity "member of age-set S." Systemic creation rules bring these social identities ("leader of age-set S") into being; and second order systemic rules constrain the relevant local rules, i.e., the assignment rules (if any) and the directional rules.

The case of the age-set name is different. Let us assume that the age-sets are named from a cycle of five names (cf. Chapter I, Section 7). These names are assigned by first level systemic rules, and here something new is happening: reference is made not to the social identity "member of age-set S" but to the identity class "age-set S" as a single entity, i.e., as a **corporation**. Now a corporation is a

---

[4] As, for instance, among the Afikpo Ibo where "Each set has the right to determine its own internal organization, rules, and duties, but most follow the pattern of the senior sets formed before them. The regulations of a set can be altered and new ones established by consensus of the set members [Ottenberg 1971: 61]." Cf. Chapter I, Section 4.

person, and a person can have a social identity. If age-sets, as wholes, have rights and duties peculiar to age-sets, then "age-set" is a **corporate (social) identity;**[5] but if the rights and duties of age-sets as wholes are the same as those of some other kinds of associations as wholes, then these other associations and age-sets are all members of a single identity class. In our imaginary example the cycle of names is peculiar to age-sets, and so "age-set" is a corporate social identity.

Clearly, the age-grade definition can be rewritten in much the same terms as the revised age-set model:

An **age-grade** is one of a finite collection of not less than two identity classes. The collection is totally ordered, say G_1, $G_2, \ldots, G_n$. The social identities corresponding to these classes (say $\gamma_1, \gamma_2, \ldots, \gamma_n$) are assigned and disassigned to persons by rules that meet the following constraints:

(i)   No identity is assigned to a person before γ_1 (the **first grade constraint**).

The way in which the other constraints should be revised is obvious.

The term "identity class" covers both identity classes that are incorporated (i.e., corporations) and those that are not; and the term "person," as we know, includes both individuals and corporations. This means that the age-grade definition allows the possibility of incorporated identity classes whose members are themselves corporations. This is no more strange or problematic than, say, business firms whose shares are owned by other business firms.

Age-grades do not have creation rules; all the constraints are on assignment rules. "Transition rules" is the special term for the assignment rules of age-grade systems.

I suspect that a distinction similar to that between the systemic and local rules of age-set systems could be applied to the rules of age-grade systems, but it is not clear to me just how.

The effect of revising the age-set and age-grade definitions in terms of identity classes is to show that age-grades and age-sets are not, as originally appeared, entities of quite different kinds, but

[5] I use this term to refer to the kind of social identity a corporation has, as opposed to the **individual (social) identity.** An individual can exist outside any society, and hence have no social identity; but a corporation always has at least one social identity. According to the kind of notions I have in mind, a corporation is always, or nearly always, a group; in fact it may well be that it should be one by definition.

TABLE 4.1

Grade	Level
I	1
II	2
III	3
IV	4

rather entities created from much the same elements and differing mainly in the way in which they relate these elements to each other.

This new way of looking at age-sets and age-grades gives criteria for deciding how to describe certain systems whose nature would have been obscure under the earlier definitions. Imagine a society in which there are four age-grades for men. Only those in age-grades are allowed to wear feathers in their hair, and in each grade the feathers are of a different type from those worn in any of the other three grades. There are no other directional rules. Every 5 years there is a ceremony at which all boys who have reached puberty in the time that has passed since the last ceremony of this sort are assigned the first grade. At the same time, all those who were until then in the first grade are assigned the second grade, and so on. If, for a moment, we look on the sets of individuals who pass through the grades together as constituting age-sets, then we can set out the transition rules as in Table 4.1.

The original age-set model offered no way of deciding whether these sets of individuals—let us call them **age-divisions**[6]—constitute age-sets or not. The new model makes the decision depend on whether the age-divisions are identity classes, i.e., whether there are directional rules that refer to social identities corresponding to the putative identity classes. In the system we have imagined, the only possible rules of this kind would be the transition rules. In principle we could postulate age-sets for them to operate on; but imagine that we have a formal language suitable for describing age organization:[7]

---

[6] I shall take this term to cover both age-groups and also things which, if they were groups, would be age-groups. (If we were to adopt the course mentioned on p. 230 n. 3, then the term would be used to cover both age-classes and those things which, if they were identity classes, would be age-classes.)

[7] Cf. Lowenthal (1972) and Kettel (1972).

It seems almost certain that a briefer and equally accurate description could be produced without the postulate. In this sense it can be said that the system has no age-sets.

The new view of age-sets and age-grades suggests yet another deficiency in the age-grade definition (cf. Chapter II, Section 1.2). Imagine a system like the one we have just described, but in which the members of an age-division address one another, and only one another, as "mate." Since there is only one age-division in each grade, it would be possible to treat this as a rule of the age-grade system. Such a treatment might—at least in a formal language—turn out to be simpler than postulating the existence of age-sets in order to formulate the rule. Nevertheless, I suspect that it would be best to postulate age-sets in such a case, and we can ensure that this is done by adding a constraint to the age-grade definition to the effect that there is no rule that all the grades in the system have in common. This would be a constraint on the directional rules, unlike any in the definition as it stands.

The discussion in the preceding pages has been of a rather rarified kind, and it is worth considering just how relevant the issues raised are to the working ethnographer.

It has become apparent that a pretty complicated conceptual structure is needed in order to distinguish clearly between age-groups and age-grades. Is the distinction really necessary?

Two things suggest that it is, at least until something better turns up. One—which was mentioned in the Introduction—is that all the best ethnographies employ a distinction of this kind where it applies. The ethnographies that do not do so leave many questions unanswered as a result. The other is that the distinction is in many cases explicitly recognized by the societies that operate graded systems, not in the sense that they have words for "age-group" and "age-grade"—I know of no reports of that, though it may happen—but in the sense that they often give names to both the groups and the grades.

But even someone who accepts the age-grade/age-group distinction may ask what the point is of trying to formulate it so sharply. The most convincing answer is to point to other parts of this book, where the treatment is substantive rather than programmatic. There the use of concepts more clearly defined than hitherto has enabled us to gain new insight into the workings of a number of systems of age organization of different kinds.

2 THE AGE-SET STRUCTURE

The age-set model is used in this book primarily as an analytic device. It has enabled us to identify certain components of age-group systems and to show how they fit together. Possibly there are models that delimit different structures that would do this job just as well (cf. Chapter I, Section 1.3). But the age-set model has a further merit, which none of these others would share: the structure it circumscribes—the age-set structure—holds a special, central position among all related structures.

This centrality shows itself in various ways. One is that if we could somehow make a census of age-group systems—an enterprise whose difficulties have already been mentioned (p. 30 n. 12)—we would find that far more of them fall within the bounds of the age-set structure than of any related structure of comparable complexity and rigidity. Another is that age-set systems are scattered all over the globe in a way that leaves no doubt that they originated independently in a number of places. This cannot be said of any type of deviant system (again, defined by a model comparable to the age-set model in the complexity and rigidity of the structure it delimits).

I would also suggest that the age-set structure in some sense underlies even deviant systems. This idea was already adumbrated earlier in connection with PL systems. I assumed, more or less tacitly, that each PL system represents the outcome of an attempt to combine a nonshrinking age-set system with a PL rule. I showed that many of these systems had certain features—they could be called **correctional devices**—whose effect is to make a system more like a nonshrinking age-set system than it otherwise would be.

Now, in fact no PL systems are age-set systems, and some of them are very different indeed from age-set systems. Why not take them just as they stand? Could not each one be perfectly well described without invoking age-sets?

Consider first negative PL systems.[8] They differ less from the age-set model than do any other PL systems, for they only violate the enrolment constraint, and that not in any very striking fashion. Even so, waiting produces anomalies: it must sometimes result in a

---

[8] In this section I have unfortunately had to mention one or two concepts introduced only in asterisked sections of the text. The reader who has skipped those sections will find references to the relevant definitions in the index.

man being substantially older than all (or almost all) the rest of his age-group, and hence in his being assigned an age-grade that is not consonant with his age.[9] There is no real doubt that if the PL rules did not exist in these systems, then, all else being equal, they would possess the enrolment characteristic.

Now turn to the other PL systems, those that differ much more widely from age-sets. The anomalies in the age-grade systems are more striking here, and are of various kinds. One thing that happens in many systems is that individuals are assigned age-grades that are clearly only suitable for persons either older or younger than themselves. Another oddity is that old men may find themselves having to behave respectfully to young ones (cf. p. 124). In the Konso system, the situation has arisen where the most senior grades of the sequence are virtually unoccupied (Chapter II, Section 3.1.2.3). The participants in these systems are often—perhaps always—aware that things are not as they should be (cf. p. 98). The Darassa say that everyone naturally wants to be in an age-grade that corresponds as closely as possible to his age; but God has decreed that some will be disappointed in this wish, and they accept his decree with resignation (Jensen 1936: 319 f.). To disregard the anomalous nature of these age-grade systems is to present a misleading picture of them; to view them as anomalous is to imply that they—or their antecedents—were once integrated with age-sets, or something very close to age-sets.

Another peculiarity of many PL systems is that because of overaging the proportion of the population which participates in the system is continually declining. This process points unmistakably back to a time when generational spread had not affected these systems as much as it now does, so that they were closer to the age-set model. Whether, as is generally assumed, all these systems once had demographic restrictions, which have now weakened or vanished (cf. p. 98 n. 75), or whether, as is quite possible, some of them have rather different histories, is not a question that I shall try to answer. I am sure that much could be learned about the development of these systems from investigations in the field.

The relevance of age-sets to PL systems is also demonstrated by the fact that the Jie and the Karimojong (and I imagine other tribes

---

[9] As far as I know, none of the descriptions of negative PL systems mention this as happening; yet if, for instance, Spencer's account is correct, then it must happen among the Samburu. If it does not occur, then these systems are even more like age-set systems than I have assumed, and the relevance of the age-set model to them needs no proving.

also) evidently want their g-groups to be much more like age-sets than they actually are (see Chapter I, end of Section 2.1 and beginning of Section 2.2). The Jie distaste for overlapping is especially interesting, since overlapping is not an obviously unnatural phenomenon, like old men treating young ones with respect.

The notion that the age-set structure underlies deviant systems applies not just to PL systems, but also to others. It can be made a little less vague and a little more general with the help of one or two new concepts.

Let us distinguish between internal and external social identities. An **internal social identity** is one that only exists by virtue of the fact that an age-group system exists, for example, the identities "member of age-group S" or "leader of age-group S." All other social identities, for example, father, son, brother, are **external**.

We shall also need the idea of a **deviant rule**, i.e., a rule that, if it were introduced in an age-set system, would cause that system to become deviant.[10]

If a deviant rule refers to an external social identity, I shall call it an **external deviant rule**. If it refers to an internal social identity but not to an external one, then I shall call it an **internal deviant rule**. For instance, rules that allow members of an age-group to be expelled are generally of the latter kind (see Chapter I, Section 5.2).

By definition, every deviant system contains one or more deviant rules. A system is **externally deviant** if it is deviant by virtue of possessing an external deviant rule, and **internally deviant** if it is deviant by virtue of possessing an internal deviant rule. A system can, of course, be deviant in both ways: the Karimojong system is externally deviant by virtue of its PL rule and internally deviant by virtue of the rule that a man must spear an ox on becoming a member of an age-group; for, given the fact that a few people cannot afford an ox at the proper time, this rule occasionally leads to

---

[10] Assuming rules are formulated cross-culturally, we can say that some would cause any age-set system to become deviant, but others would cause only some to do so; and some rules might cause a system to become deviant in one society, but not in another. For instance, a particular negative fraternal linking rule might cause deviance in a society where sons can be born at short intervals, but not in one in which there is always a difference in age of at least 3 years between siblings (cf. p. 211). What is said here of deviant rules applies, of course, to others as well: rules that would generate an age-set system in one society might not do so in another.

waiting (cf. p. 224). In what follows, however, if I describe a system only as internally deviant, anything said about its deviance will refer to deviance by virtue of internally deviant rules, even if it is also externally deviant; and I shall use the term externally deviant in a parallel way.

Now, if we apply these concepts to the matter at hand, it turns out that internally deviant systems, though not particularly uncommon, never, or hardly ever, deviate much from the age-set structure. This is not a logical necessity. We can easily imagine internally deviant systems in which every individual joins two age-groups, or in which an individual joins an age-group whenever he feels like it, or in which individuals often move from one age-group to another. And we can extend the notion of an internally deviant system to include many other possibilities. Let us bring under this concept all systems in which deviant relationships exist between age-groups, provided only that the rules that establish these relationships do not refer to external social identities. Imagine, for instance, a system such that the recruitment period of group S ends when the recruitment period of S − 2 begins, for all S. Imagine, further, that this occurs because of a rule to that effect (and not, say, because of a combination of a certain UPL rule and certain demographic restrictions). Then here also is an internally deviant system; and we can construct many others on similar lines, for example, a system with a rule that group S only starts recruiting when the last member of S + 1 dies (for all S), or one in which groups dissolve in some other order than the one in which they began recruiting.

It might, of course, simply be a matter of chance that there are, to my knowledge, no clear reports of eccentric[11] internally deviant systems. I may have overlooked such reports; or it may be that the systems exist, but have never been properly described;[12] or it may be that the systems do not exist, but might perfectly well exist (after all, it is not difficult to imagine a world without PL systems). All these are possibilities, but my guess is that none is actually the case. I think it will turn out that only externally deviant systems are eccentric, and that this is a significant fact about age organization. As a hedge, however, I add that if eccentric internally deviant systems

[11] An eccentric (age-group) system is a deviant system whose deviance is not caused by secondary rules.

[12] See Smith and Dale (1920: 310) on the Ila, and Fajana (1968: 235) on the Yoruba, for possible instances (both systems allow shifting).

do turn up, then I suspect that it will only be in situations of rapid change.[13]

Of course, not all externally deviant systems are eccentric. As far as one can tell, neither FL systems nor the age-groups of the Blackfoot, Mandan, and Hidatsa (dealt with in Part Two) differ greatly from the age-set model. The same can be said of some PL systems, though most of them are highly deviant. They constitute the main body of eccentric systems, but there does seem to be at least one other category. In West Africa there are tribes in which the age organization is affected by the idea that each family or descent group should, as far as possible, either be equally represented in each age-group or age-grade, or else equally represented in the most important age-group or age-grade.[14] The only such system which has been described in detail is that of the Banapas Bedik (Chapter II, Section 4.4.2); but in this particular case it is the age-grades, not the age-groups, that are the entities affected.

The purpose of this section has not been to formulate a clear empirical hypothesis—desirable though that would be—but merely to give some reasons for looking at age-group systems in a particular way. The idea I have had in mind is that structures of the kind defined by the age-set model have a certain naturalness about them, that they are in some way independent, self-contained entities; whereas similar structures—above all those which differ only in respect of one or two of the characteristics, but then rather widely— are to be understood as the product of some external force interfering with an age-set structure. Faced with a deviant system, the relevant question is "What is it that has resulted in this system being different from an age-set system?". A good ethnography answers this question, at least at one level. Faced with an age-set system, the question is "What is there about structures of this kind that makes them so widespread?". Here it is the theorist who must reply, but I have no idea what his answer should be.

---

[13] Perhaps one or two other hedges are also needed, e.g., to deal with the possibility of the age-group structure being determined entirely by some external force, say a king.

[14] Systems of this sort seem to exist among the Bende Ibo (Jones 1962: 200), the Abé (Paulme 1971b: 280 ff.), the Gã (Field 1940: 168 ff.), the Kru (Fraenkel 1966: 158), and the Ebrié (Person 1963: 73). Compare also Hallpike (1972: 197, bottom of the page) on the Takadi Konso.

*PART TWO

▌ Introduction

Among the Indians of North America, five tribes—all of them on the Plains—had well-developed systems of age organization: the Mandan, Hidatsa, Blackfoot, Arapaho, and Gros Ventres.[1] These systems had already been described at length before World War I, at a time when little was known about age-groups in other parts of the world, and they were the subject of a general study by Lowie (1916) which, though it has its faults, also has many virtues. In the last 30 years, admirable ethnographies have been published on all of these tribes except the Arapaho. And yet the main body of those who have concerned themselves with age organization—the Africanists—have found it difficult to come to terms with this material. I think Gulliver is expressing a widely held view when he writes of the Plains Indian systems as follows:

[1] Less developed age groupings were found elsewhere in North America; see, for instance, Dorsey (1884: 342), and Drucker (1951, index s.v. age-grade groups). In spite of the evidence set out in Lowie (1915), I doubt whether any of the Arikara ever had a system of age organization.

Unfortunately, despite a considerable literature, the sociological
aspects of these systems are far from clear; the nature of intragroup
and intergroup relations, and their connections with social control
and other activities is vague (e.g., Lowie 1916). Useful comparison
with the graded African systems is not, therefore, possible [1968:
160].

Anyone who has tried to make sense of Plains age organization
will sympathize with Gulliver. The general works that have been
produced since Lowie's paper—Whyte (1944), Eisenstadt (1954), and
Mails (1973)—help very little. The older ethnographies consist largely
of a mass of minutiae about regalia and ceremonies; they scarcely
attempt to answer such simple questions as where and when the
age-groups met, let alone such complicated ones as what the place of
the age organization was in the way of life of the people. Most of the
more recent ethnographies fail to face these problems squarely, and
some make difficult reading because they presuppose a great deal of
background knowledge in their readers. All in all, a rather rebarbative
body of materials.

Nevertheless, the information that Gulliver is looking for is
mostly there, albeit not immediately in sight. The only tribe for
which I felt the evidential problems were unduly severe was the
Arapaho, and for this reason I have not dealt with them here.[2] As for
the other four, I think we can form a better picture of their age
organizations than we can—from the existing literature—of any but a
very few of the African ones.

In this part of the book I have tried to give a general account of
these four systems, in the hope of making them accessible to those
who are interested in age organization but have no background in
Plains Indian studies. I have also tried to show that the conceptual
scheme developed in Part One can help in describing these systems,
even though three of them have many unusual features. Very little
new information is going to come to light about Plains Indian age
organizations, since most of them have been extinct for almost a
hundred years; all that remains is to think about the facts that we
have.

---

[2] Quite a lot is recorded about some aspects of Arapaho age organization,
and it can be determined, for instance, that they had an age-set system. But the
published evidence on how the age organization fitted in with the other institutions of the tribe is meager, obscure, and contradictory. I doubt whether it will
be understood except in the context of a large-scale reconstruction of Arapaho
society in the nineteenth century.

∎∎

The Mandan and the Hidatsa

1 HISTORY

The age organizations of the Mandan and the Hidatsa, as they are reflected in our sources, are systems in a state of flux, and to treat them purely synchronically would be seriously to misrepresent them. The changes that were occurring in the age organizations were the product of certain other—rather drastic—social changes, and it is only in the context of those changes that they can be understood. We therefore begin by sketching in some features of the history of the two tribes in the eighteenth and nineteenth centuries.[1]

[1] There is an invaluable history of the Mandan by Bruner (1961), and, while nothing of quite the same sort exists for the Hidatsa, much historical information on that tribe is to be found in Bowers's ethnography (1965), and Stewart (1977) gives a brief sketch. For the archaeological background, Lehmer (1971) is indispensable and Wood (1967) is useful. Bowers's unpublished *History of the Mandan and Hidatsa* (1948) is also, in spite of its title, primarily an archaeological work; although it makes little use of written sources, it includes important historical data supplied to Bowers by his native informants.

The earliest first-hand description of the Mandan was written by the Canadian explorer La Vérendrye, who visited the tribe in 1738. He found them living in six large fortified villages by the Missouri River, all of them near the point where it is joined by the Heart River, in what is now North Dakota. There were also one or two small Mandan villages further upstream (Stewart 1974). The tribe derived a substantial portion of their subsistence from agriculture and played an important role as traders between various other tribes. The archaeological evidence suggests that the Mandan had lived in villages in the Missouri valley for centuries before La Vérendrye's visit, and they continued to do so throughout the period that concerns us here.

Some of the Hidatsa at this time were sedentary and also lived on the banks of the Missouri. We do not know how many villages they occupied, but their total population was probably less than that of the Mandan. Their villages lay upstream from the Mandan villages as far as the Knife River. Other Hidatsa lived a largely nomadic existence in the territory above the Knife. They had strong ties with the nomadic Crow tribe. At some point in the not too distant past the ancestors of the Hidatsa and of the Crow had formed a single unit, and though the two languages were no longer quite mutually intelligible, the tribes retained the memory of their common descent and were on good terms with each other throughout their known history.

No village tribes lived upstream of the Hidatsa, but there were several that lived in the Missouri valley downstream of the Mandan. Their closest neighbors in that direction, though still separated from them by a considerable distance, were the Arikara, who occupied a number of villages in South Dakota. The treeless plains which border both sides of the Missouri valley trench were the territory of nomadic tribes, almost all of whom were in conflict with the Mandan and Hidatsa at one time or another (as were also the Arikara). From at least the latter part of the eighteenth century the most numerous and hostile of these nomads were the Sioux, or Dakota.

Even before the arrival of La Vérendrye, European goods had reached the villagers of the Missouri, and these goods appear, in various ways, to have brought an era of unique prosperity to the area. Unfortunately, trade goods and horses were not all that the white men introduced; in (probably) 1781 there was a fearful small-pox epidemic, which wiped out most of the Mandan and at least half of the Hidatsa. At the end of the eighteenth century, the remnants of the two tribes together numbered around 3,000, the Hidatsa being in the majority (Thompson 1962: 172 f., which needs to be corrected in the light of his unpublished journals; cf. Stewart 1977).

The epidemic led to a regrouping of the tribes. The Mandan moved upstream to live close to the Hidatsa, where they occupied two villages located within a couple of miles of each other.[2] One of them was called Nuptadi, the other Mitutanka. Their inhabitants spoke slightly different dialects of the Mandan language, but apart from that they were nearly identical in culture. The Hidatsa, at the end of the eighteenth century, were living in three villages at the mouth of the Knife, also separated by only a few miles from one another and from the Mandan. Each of these was inhabited by one of the three Hidatsa subtribes: the Hidatsa-proper,[3] the Awatixa, and the Awaxawi. The cultural differences between the three Hidatsa villages, though not marked, were greater than the differences between the two Mandan ones. Hidatsa, like Mandan, is a Siouan language, but the two are not mutually intelligible. The Awaxawi spoke a dialect which differed slightly from that spoken by the other two subtribes.

The political structures of the two tribes were broadly similar. In each case the village—which was a largely autonomous unit—was ruled by a council of senior men and two main chiefs. In addition, the Hidatsa, from the end of the eighteenth century, had a tribal council consisting of a few representatives from each village in the tribe.[4] Throughout the period that they lived together near the Knife the two tribes were in alliance, though not always without frictions (Stewart 1977). In case of attack they defended each other, and any peace treaty had to be made with both of them (Bowers 1965: 29).

The inhabitants of the allied villages continued to live near the mouth of the Knife until 1837, when they were once again the victims of a devastating smallpox epidemic. The Mandan came close to being completely extinguished, and the proportion of Hidatsa who survived was not large. This epidemic, like the first one, resulted in

---

[2] The Mandan moved up to the Knife River some time between 1781 and 1787. The rather complicated question of exactly where the various Mandan and Hidatsa villages were located in the eighteenth and nineteenth centuries is discussed at length in Stewart (1974).

[3] The Hidatsa-proper are the Hidatsa whom we mentioned as living a largely nomadic existence above the Knife before the 1781 epidemic. After the epidemic most of them became more sedentary, while those who preferred a nomadic way of life joined the River Crow (Bowers 1965: 27).

[4] Bowers (1950: 23; 1965: 29) implies that the Mandan also had a tribal council, but I have not come across any other references to it.

various population movements. The outcome was that in 1845 the remnants of the three Hidatsa subtribes, together with the Mitutanka Mandan, founded a new, joint village, called Like-a-Fishhook. The Nuptadi Mandan continued to live near the Knife until about 1858, when they too moved into Like-a-Fishhook village. The site that had previously been occupied by the Mitutanka Mandans was taken over by the Arikara tribe; they lived there until, in 1862, they also settled in Fishhook.

In the period before the 1837 epidemic, each village had its own system of age-groups. Like most other features of their cultures, the age organizations of the two tribes were very similar in structure but different in detail; furthermore, within both the Hidatsa and the Mandan tribe, villages differed slightly from one another in their age organization. A complicated situation arose when first four and then five villages were united in Like-a-Fishhook; broadly speaking, what occurred was that each of the two tribes established a single, largely independent, system of age-groups.[5] This was in keeping with the overall pattern of life in Fishhook: the Mandan, the Hidatsa, and—when they arrived—the Arikara each maintained their distinct religious and ceremonial organizations, though in the case of the Mandan and Hidatsa there was a good deal of intermarriage and a clear tendency for the two societies to fuse. Long before this could happen, however, the aboriginal social organization had largely vanished.[6]

Fishhook village was abandoned in 1886, the three tribes having been dispersed in a number of small settlements on their reservation. A group consisting mainly of Hidatsa (known after their military leader as the Crow-Flies-High band), who had broken away from Fishhook in about 1870 and had maintained an independent existence outside the reservation, finally settled within its confines in 1894. The 1880s seem to have been in many ways the turning point in the extinction of the traditional culture of the Mandan and the

---

[5] All these points relating to age organization are dealt with at greater length later.

[6] Nowadays the two tribes are no longer really distinguishable; instead there exists a joint Mandan–Hidatsa people who speak only Hidatsa and English, Mandan having died out. These people have a distinct culture whose values have much in common with those of their nineteenth-century ancestors; but their political, ceremonial, and religious organization shows very little continuity. Various aspects of Mandan–Hidatsa culture as it was in the early 1950s are described in several useful articles by E. Bruner, listed in the bibliography of Bruner (1961).

Hidatsa (cf. Bruner 1961: 260 f.). The main Hidatsa religious ceremony (the Naxpike) was held for the last time in 1879 (Bowers
1965: 309), and the main Mandan one (the Okipa) soon after.[7] The
Sioux, whose menacing presence had for so long been an important
factor in determining the way of life of the village tribes, were
pacified. The buffalo were extinct. And it was around this time that
the old age organization of the tribes ceased to function, suppressed,
it is said, by the government (Wilson n.d.: 2, 58).[8]

2 SOURCES

Many white men visited the Mandan and the Hidatsa in the
years after La Vérendrye's pioneering journey, and a number of them
gave some account of the two tribes; but it was almost a century
before a description of their age organization was written. Its author
was the great German traveler Maximilian, Prince of Wied—Neuwied.
He spent the winter of 1833—1834 living in a fur-trading post next to
Mitutanka village and carried out a systematic investigation of the
culture of the two tribes. The outcome was an ethnography that, for
its period, was quite outstanding; it included several pages devoted to
the age organization of the Mandan, and a rather briefer description
of equivalent groups among the Hidatsa.[9]

Apart from Maximilian's work, nothing of much significance
was written about Mandan and Hidatsa age-groups while they were

[7] "The full ceremony was last observed in 1881, but a performance lacking
the features of torture was held in 1889 [Curtis 1909b: 26 n.]" (cf. Curtis
1909b: 23; Bowers 1950: 105).

[8] Lowie, who worked among the Mandan and Hidatsa in 1910 and 1911,
writes as if the age-societies were completely extinct. In contrast, Bowers states
that in 1932 a few Hidatsa societies still survived (1965: 182), and Smith (1972:
64), referring perhaps to the early 1950s, states that the Hidatsa Stone Hammer
society continued to exist. I imagine that these groups are radically different
from their nineteenth-century namesakes.

[9] The description of Hidatsa age organization is one of a number of
passages omitted from the English version of Maximilian's work, and I have
therefore translated it in full in Appendix 5. The English version of Maximilian
also contains many errors. I have given references to the 1843 edition, the text
and pagination of which are reproduced in the 1906 edition. The German text of
Maximilian is a rare book, and I have therefore sometimes quoted, in a footnote,
the original German of a passage whose interpretation is important to my
argument. For further information about editions of Maximilian, and about his
manuscripts (to which I was unfortunately not granted access), see Stewart
(1977).

still in existence. There are very brief references in the diary of
Francis Chardon, a fur trader at the post next to Mitutanka from
1834 to 1839; and there are slightly fuller references in the writings
of Henry Boller, another fur trader, though a far better educated
one, who describes life in the post next to Like-a-Fishhook between
1858 and 1860. Matthews's *Ethnography and Philology of the
Hidatsa Indians*, based on first-hand acquaintance with the tribe
between 1865 and 1872, gives little beyond a list of native terms
(1877: 47 n.).

With the twentieth century we come to descriptions based
entirely on the memories of old men.[10] The first two of these,
written by Curtis (1909a, 1909b), are of no great importance, but
the next, by Lowie (1913), is a major source, not less significant than
Maximilian and a great deal more detailed and extensive. Lowie drew
a few data from the field notes of Gilbert L. Wilson, who worked
among the Hidatsa during the first two decades of the century; these
notes, together with some later ones not used by Lowie, Wilson
collected together into a manuscript (Wilson n.d.), which also contains a little material on the Mandan societies. Further information
was recorded soon afterwards by Densmore as part of her study of
Mandan and Hidatsa music (1923), and there are a couple of references to the age-societies in Beckwith's collection of Mandan and
Hidatsa myths (1938).

The last person to be able to gather important new information
about the age organization of the two tribes was Alfred W. Bowers,
who carried out his fieldwork in the late 1920s and early 1930s.
Bowers's ethnography of the Mandan (1950) contains only incidental
references to the men's age societies, though it does provide a great
deal of indirect help in understanding their place in the life of the
tribe. His remarkable study of the Hidatsa (1965), however, has a
section devoted to their age organization that represents a great
advance over everything written before, including, in particular,
Lowie (1913). Lowie's data (except where he draws on Maximilian)
relate almost exclusively to the period when the Hidatsa lived in
Fishhook, and his account assumes that the tribe was at that time a
homogeneous entity whose age organization could be treated almost

---

[10] The first twentieth-century work on the Mandan, Will and Spinden
(1906), is of interest only for the archaeological information it contains. The
linguistic and ethnographic data are drawn—none too accurately—entirely from
printed sources.

purely synchronically.[11] Bowers, in contrast, deals with the age-groups diachronically; taking as his starting point the period before the 1837 epidemic, he shows that in fact the system which existed among the Hidatsa in Fishhook was not an entirely coherent or stable one and that it can only be understood as an amalgamation of the three slightly different systems which existed before the village was founded.

On the whole, more is known about the Hidatsa than about the Mandan, perhaps because the Hidatsa suffered somewhat less from the second smallpox epidemic (1837). We are certainly better informed about Hidatsa age organization; Maximilian, to be sure, has more to say on the Mandan system, but Lowie was able to gather considerably fuller data on the Hidatsa, and Bowers, as we have seen, has almost nothing on the Mandan. If it happens then, as it sometimes does, that a phenomenon is attested for the Hidatsa but not for the Mandan, one can on occasion reasonably assume that this merely reflects a gap in the sources on the Mandan, rather than a real difference between the two tribes.

3 CULTURE

The history of the Mandan and Hidatsa in the eighteenth and nineteenth centuries falls into three phases: the period before the first epidemic (1781), the period between the first and the second epidemics (1781 to 1837), and the period between the second epidemic and the dispersal on the reservation (1837 to, say, 1894). In what follows, our point of reference will be the middle period, which contrasts with the first period in being fairly well documented, and with the third in being a time of relatively slow change. This section will sketch in the way of life of the Knife River tribes,[12] and

[11] Lowie was aware of the fact that not all the villages in a tribe had the same age organization, but he had almost no evidence on intratribal differences (1916: 944). It was partly for this reason that he underestimated their significance. He was also no doubt misled by Maximilian, who deals with the age organization of each tribe as a single whole, without explicitly stating that each village operated an independent system, let alone that these systems differed somewhat from each other.

[12] Some of the text of this section appears also in Stewart (1977). Unless otherwise stated, the information comes from Bowers (1950, 1965).

the following one will examine the place of the age-groups within that way of life.

Mandan and Hidatsa villages were stable, and in many ways self-sufficient, entities that could maintain their identities over many decades, even when they moved from one site to another. They consisted of the large wooden-framed, earth-covered structures known as earth lodges, each of which probably held an average of around 15 people (Stewart 1977). Marriage was generally matrilocal, and the lodge belonged to the line of mothers and daughters that lived in it.[13] The size of the villages varied considerably; in 1832–1833 the largest of the Mandan and Hidatsa villages (Hidatsa-proper) had over 80 lodges, while the smallest (Awaxawi) had only 18 (Maximilian 1841: 212 f. = Stewart 1974: 295; cf. Bowers 1965: 16 f.).

The five villages near the Knife River were not occupied throughout the year. During the coldest months of the winter—generally between mid-November and late February or early March—these summer villages were abandoned, and the inhabitants of each one established a separate winter village (Maximilian 1841: 121 = 1843: 345). The sites chosen for winter villages changed from year to year, but they were always in heavy timber, and generally only a few miles from the summer ones. The wood provided material to build lodges, fuel, and food (cotton-wood bark) for the horses; it also provided shelter from the weather, not only for humans, but also for buffalo, whom they hunted (Bowers 1965: 56 f.).

The tribes depended for their food supply partly on agriculture, an almost exclusively female activity, and partly on hunting, an almost exclusively male activity. The main animal hunted was the buffalo, and a major feature of the annual round was the great summer buffalo hunt, when virtually the whole population of the village moved away for about a month, often to a considerable distance, in pursuit of the herds.

The political systems of the Mandan and Hidatsa—already briefly mentioned—seem to have worked well. They combined a high degree of personal autonomy with firm leadership and unity against enemies. Each village had a war leader, chosen for his military

---

[13] For the Hidatsa, see Bowers (1965: 138). As regards the Mandan, Bowers writes that "the lodge belonged to the [matrilineal] clan of which the females were members [1950: 26]", but from what follows in the same paragraph it is evident that the clan had only a reversionary right, which came into effect if the matrilineage that owned the lodge died out.

abilities, and a peace leader, chosen partly for his ability in getting the villagers to cooperate with one another, and partly as a result of his having been very active in the religious life of the community. These two men would—all being well—hold office for many years. In addition, leaders were chosen for special activities: each year, for instance, someone was elected by the village council as leader of the summer buffalo hunt, and, among the Hidatsa someone would be chosen each year as leader of the winter village (Bowers 1965: 57 f., 62 f.).[14] It was rare for one man to act as leader in several different activities or to serve more than once or twice as a summer hunt or winter village leader (Bowers 1965: 51); the system gave many men the opportunity to exercise authority.

In the period between the epidemics, each tribe had seven named exogamous matrilineal clans, representatives of each of which were found in each village of the tribe.[15] The clans were important entities. The Mandan ones—though apparently not the Hidatsa—each had a leader. Members had many obligations to one another: for instance, individuals with no immediate family (old people and orphans) were the responsibility of their clan, and if a man was killed, then it was the duty of his clansmen to exact revenge. Among the Hidatsa—and quite possibly among the Mandan also, though the fact is not attested—the clan was held responsible for its members' misdeeds and would exercise social pressure and even physical force against any of its members who were misbehaving.

In both tribes the clans were divided among moieties, one containing three clans, the other four. Among the Mandan these moieties were of considerable ceremonial significance, and they were probably exogamous in this period. The Hidatsa moieties were not exogamous, nor were they of much importance in any other respect.

The religious life of the Mandan and Hidatsa was remarkable for its richness and complexity. Certain aspects of it need to be mentioned here because even though the age organization of the two tribes was essentially secular in nature,[16] some of its most idiosyncratic

[14] It seems that the Mandan did not have special leaders for their winter villages (Bowers 1950: 251).

[15] There was, in addition, one Hidatsa clan, the Xura, which only had representatives in Awatixa village.

[16] "The Hidatsa do not consider the men's societies as sacred, and speak freely of their participation in society activities . . . unlike the sacred ceremonies which are never discussed except under rigidly prescribed conditions [Bowers 1965: 175, 209]." "It is not possible to work very long among the three tribes

features had precise analogues in the ritual organization. This means that the native concepts relating to the age-groups can only be placed in proper perspective through a knowledge of the fundamental religious notions of the tribes.[17] The same is true, indeed, of the other three Plains Indian tribes that had age-group systems, and, since the religions of these tribes shared some basic features with the religions of the Mandan and Hidatsa, the account of the latter given here will also serve as an introduction to the discussions of other tribes.

The Mandan and Hidatsa believed that whatever a man achieved, he achieved not by virtue of personal qualities inherent in him but entirely by virtue of the amount of supernatural power he possessed. Power was viewed as a commodity of which one could have more or less. It was used up by any particularly difficult or dangerous undertaking: being a leader in some enterprise, carrying out a raid on an enemy tribe, fording a river, hunting—all these and many other activities could only be executed successfully at the expense of one's stock of power; furthermore, power could be diminished—as we shall see in a moment—simply by transferring part of it to someone else.

All power derived from supernatural beings, many of which were identified as animals. A man might say, for instance, "My god is the horse" (Bowers 1950: 170). Power could either be acquired directly from a spirit, or indirectly by transfer from someone who already possessed it.

In order to acquire power directly, a man had to suffer, either by fasting for periods of anything up to 7 days, or by self-torture, or by a combination of the two. It is not entirely clear from the sources what the rationale behind these activities was. In some cases, cer-

---

of the Fort Berthold Reservation [i.e., the Mandan, Hidatsa, and Arikara] without stumbling on the profound distinction drawn by the Indians between the performances of the military or age-societies and the rites connected with the sacred bundles. Though the former have some ceremonial features, the most conservative Indian feels not the slightest hesitation in discussing them. On the other hand, there is great difficulty about getting any Pagan Indian to say anything about the bundles and an attempt to see the contents is met by the demand for an exorbitant fee, as already happened in the Prince of Wied's day [Lowie 1919: 415]" (cf. 1913: 236).

[17]Many sources contain information on Mandan and Hidatsa religion, but Bowers is the only author who gives a satisfactory account of the structure of these religions as wholes. Even so, there remain a number of general questions which he does not deal with explicitly and the answers to which cannot be derived from the mass of detailed information he provides.

tainly, the self-torture was in the nature of an offering directed at a particular spirit. "He began to cut off his fingers [a common form of self-torture] and offer them to the Sun, Moon, and big birds of the sky," according to the account that a Mandan informant gave to Bowers (1950: 167) concerning the power quest of another Mandan. In other cases, such activities seem to have been undertaken with no particular spirit in mind, and here the rationale may well have been—as it was in other tribes—that some spirit would take pity on the person suffering.

Self-inflicted suffering of this sort always brought with it an increase in power (Bowers 1965: 285); if the individual was fortunate, he was also vouchsafed a vision. The Mandan informant quoted as saying that his god was a horse went on to say this. "When I was a young man, I led a horse around the sacred cedar standing in the center of Like-a-Fishhook Village by means of thongs in my flesh until I fell down unconscious. As I lay there, a horse came to me and promised me success in hunting and warfare. I killed two enemies a long way from home because of this dream. The horse sang me his sacred songs . . . [Bowers 1950: 170]." When an individual received a vision of this sort, he put together what is known as a *bundle*,[18] that is, a collection of small objects associated with his vision, wrapped up together. Thereafter, his relationship to his supernatural guardian was mediated by this bundle. He would take it with him in war, in order to enjoy the protection of the guardian, and he would perform rituals to it. The sacred songs the horse sang to the Mandan informant were memorized by him, and they would constitute part of the ritual of his bundle.

Not all bundles, however, were acquired directly. The most prominent class of bundles were those whose origins went back to mythical antiquity. In such cases there would exist a myth telling of the circumstances under which some supernatural being (again, usually an animal) had given to a member of the tribe instructions on how to make up the bundle and how to perform the accompanying rites. Bundles of this sort are known as *tribal bundles*, in contrast to the *personal bundles* mentioned previously. The tribal bundle and its rite, like the personal bundle, was essentially a channel by which supernatural power could be tapped. Both tribal and personal bundles could be transferred to other persons, but in the case of

[18] It is nowhere explicitly stated that all visions of this sort led to the production of a bundle, but such, I think, was probably the case.

personal bundles such transfers were rare (the bundle being generally left with its owner's corpse), whereas tribal bundles were handed on from generation to generation (except under quite exceptional circumstances). Broadly speaking, Hidatsa tribal bundles passed from father to son, while Mandan tribal bundles passed from mother's brother to sister's son.

The characteristic of bundles that is of special relevance to the age organization is the method by which they were transferred: they were purchased (see further pp. 271 ff.). Most, perhaps all, tribal bundles could in principle be sold four times. For this purpose duplicate bundles were produced. The question of how the rules of bundle duplication fitted together with the rules of bundle inheritance is too complicated and obscure to be dealt with here; for some discussion, see Stewart (1977). It seems that it was only with the fourth sale that the seller lost all the advantages conferred on him by ownership of the bundle (Bowers 1965: 309), though possibly each sale involved some diminution of power.

The tribal bundles were a source of benefit, not merely to their owners, but also, in varying degrees, to others in the village. The major Mandan and Hidatsa religious ceremonies were all either ones at which bundles were purchased—as was the Naxpike—or else feasts for bundles—as was the Okipa. These ceremonies mostly took place inside a lodge, but before an audience; they were often elaborate and protracted. Each tribal bundle was connected in myth with certain other tribal bundles, and at such ceremonies the owners of these other bundles would also be present. A feast could be given for a bundle either by its owner—as indicated by the informant just quoted—in which case it is what Bowers calls a *bundle renewal feast*—or else by someone else. The person giving the feast would offer a pledge to that effect long in advance, in exchange for supernatural benefits either received or desired. He would then collect an immense amount of property, which would be distributed to various eligible persons at the ceremony. The most prominent recipients would be the other bundle owners who were present, and they would call on their supernatural beings to bless the person who had pledged the feast or who was purchasing the bundle. (Probably this was viewed as diminishing their own power.) Some ceremonies only involved and benefited a limited number of people, helping them, for instance, in warfare; but others—such as the two major ones mentioned above, which were beneficial in a general way, or the ones designed to produce a good crop or to bring buffalo to the village—helped the whole community.

4 THE AGE ORGANIZATION IN THE SOCIETY

Mandan and Hidatsa age organization can be analyzed in terms of two elements, the age-groups and what we shall call the *age-societies*. As an initial approximation the age-groups may be thought of as age-sets (from which, in fact, they differed only slightly), and the age-societies as age-grades (from which they differed quite considerably). There were separate age-society systems for men and women, the women's being less elaborate, and different also in other respects. In what follows I shall deal only with the men's societies. This section will be devoted to outlining the systems and to indicating their significance within the cultures as wholes; the sections that follow will discuss in detail the relationship of these systems to the age-grade definition and the age-set model.

It will be helpful if we have before us the age-society sequence of one of the villages. Let us choose the one inhabited by the Awatixa subtribe of the Hidatsa. According to Bowers (1965: 175), the following age-societies were to be found there:

    I.   Stone Hammers
   II.   Little Dogs
  III.   Crazy Dogs
  IV.   Crow Imitators[19]
   V.   Half-Shaved Heads
  VI.   Black Mouths
 VII.   Dogs
VIII.   Old Dogs
  IX.   Buffalo Bulls

The members of each of these societies had the exclusive right to wear certain regalia, sing certain songs, and perform certain dances. These collections of rights were bought and sold between age-groups. For the moment we may think of each age-group, when it is inaugurated, as buying the first society (the Stone Hammer society in the case of Awatixa) and later selling that society to the immediately junior age-group and simultaneously buying the next one (the Little Dog society, in Awatixa) from the immediately senior age-group; and so on. We have then an age-grade system with simple level rules and one grade assigned to each age-group.

The differences between the age-society repertoires of the villages (p. 248) were almost entirely limited to the lower part of the

[19] The name refers to the Crow tribe.

list. From the Half-Shaved Head society to the Bull society the
sequence was the same for all five villages[20] "and seems to have been
fixed for a considerable time [Bowers 1965: 178]." One or more of
the Hidatsa villages had as its most senior society, immediately above
the Bulls, a Raven society,[21] and one or both of the Mandan villages
had as the most senior society, immediately above the Bulls, a
Black-Tail Deer society.[22] These were evidently no longer active
after the 1837 epidemic (Bowers 1965: 178).[23] In both tribes, men
who had sold their last society were known as Stinking Ears (Lowie
1913: 225, 294; cf. Densmore 1923: 108).[24]

The size of the age-groups that purchased these societies no
doubt varied a good deal from time to time and from village to
village. The kind of magnitudes involved can, however, be indicated
in a rough-and-ready way on the basis of some scattered figures in
the sources.[25] We can think of the youngest age-group, whose

[20] So Bowers (1965: 178), and I am inclined to accept his statement, even
though it does not accord with all the other evidence. Maximilian's list of the
Mandan societies (p. 286) bears it out, but in his Hidatsa list he places the Old
Dogs before the Half-Shaved Heads and leaves out the Dogs entirely (1841: 218
= Appendix 5 of this volume). The lists of Mandan and Hidatsa societies vary a
good deal, and there is not much to be gained in this context from comparing
them (cf. p. 284).

[21] Mentioned by Maximilian (1841: 218 = Appendix 5 of this volume),
Curtis (1909a: 182), and Lowie (1913: 282 ff.). Bowers seems to have had some
evidence that it was only found in one of the Hidatsa villages (1965: 178).

[22] Mentioned by Maximilian (1841: 143 = 1843: 356), Curtis (1909b:
144), Lowie (1913: 320 f.), Densmore (1923: 87 f.), and Beckwith (1938: 239).
Bowers (1965: 178) has some obscure comments which may imply that at the
time of Maximilian only Mitutanka had a Black-Tail Deer society. Culbertson
(1952: 137) records this as a Hidatsa society, but probably erroneously.

[23] Culbertson, in 1850, was told of the Black-Tail Deers (see preceding
note), but this does not prove that they were still active. The Ravens are not
included in a list of Hidatsa societies compiled in 1859 (Boller 1966: 211).

[24] The term "has reference to peculiarities of an aged buffalo bull [Wilson
n.d.: 2]."

[25] I have noted the following figures. *Hidatsa.* In about 1865, 40 boys
bought the Stone Hammer society, and elsewhere the society is mentioned as
having about 40 members (it is not clear whether the same age-group is being
referred to) (Lowie 1913: 244, 247; Wilson n.d.: 1, 4, 37). Bowers (1965: 180)
states that there would be 30 or more members. In about 1876 about 30 men
bought into the Kit-Fox society (Lowie 1913: 257). The Buffalo Bulls are said
to have had 30 or 40 members (Densmore 1923: 138), but this figure seems
rather high. *Mandan.* The Black Mouths had over 25 members in Mitutanka in
1833 (Maximilian 1841: 274 = 1843: 426), and had 20 in Fishhook in about
1884 (Lowie 1913: 314). The As-Chóh-Ochatä (on which see p. 290) had at

members would mostly be in their teens,[26] as having perhaps 40 members; the Black Mouths, by far the most active society in the system, and consisting of men in their thirties and early forties, as having some 20 or 25 members; and the oldest age-societies as having around half that number.

The great majority of those eligible joined in purchasing the most junior society when the opportunity arose, but there were a few who for various reasons did not. For instance, if his family was somewhat cut off from the community as a result of a quarrel, or as a result of one of its members having recently led a war party which had returned with losses, then a boy might stay out. Or again, it might be that the boy's relatives were for one reason or another unwilling or unable to assist him in accumulating the goods necessary for the purchase (Bowers 1950: 62 f.; 1965: 136, 181).[27] At any rate,

---

least 14 members in Nuptadi in 1833 (Maximilian 1841: 281 = 1843: 430). The Mitutanka Half-Shaved Heads had, in 1833, something like 18 to 20 members (Maximilian 1841: 286, 313 = 1843: 433, 448). The Nuptadi Dogs had 27 or 28 members in 1834 (Maximilian 1841: 309 = 1843: 446). A Buffalo Bull society—almost certainly from Mitutanka—had at least 9 members in 1834 (Maximilian 1841: 315 = 1843: 449; note that in Bodmer's picture 12 men are depicted, of whom 2, not 1 as in Maximilian's account, wear the full head-dress). Densmore (1923: 85) was told that the society numbered 90 or 100 men, but this is an obvious exaggeration. In about 1870, the Kit-Fox society was sold; the selling group numbered about 30 members, while the purchasers, as one would expect, seem to have numbered slightly more (Lowie 1913: 297). The approximate date of this occasion can be determined as follows: Lowie's informant, Black Chest, set his age at 62 in 1910 or 1911, when Lowie collected his data (1913: 300); at the time of the Kit-Fox purchase he was about 20 (1913: 297).

[26] Maximilian says that the members of the most junior Mandan society (the Crazy Dogs) were between 10 and 15 years old, while their Hidatsa equivalents (the Stone Hammers) were boys of 10 or 11 (1841: 139, 217 = 1843: 354, and Appendix 5 of this volume). An Awaxawi informant who was born in about 1820 told Lowie that he first joined an age-society at the age of 7 (1913: 237). Wilson got estimates of the ages of all forty of the boys who bought the Stone Hammers in about 1865: the youngest were 11, the oldest 18, and the average was about 14½ (Wilson n.d.: 36). Lowie, incidentally, claims that the Plains Indians "originally never reckoned their age by years [1963: 106, cf. 1947: 293]," but this statement is certainly too sweeping. See, above all, Hilger (1952: 87) and Kroeber (1902: 26) on the Arapaho. (Bass 1966: 8 may be discounted.) Births are sometimes noted in winter counts, as in the Mandan one published by Howard (1960); cf. Smith (1960). Various references to age are found in Hidatsa and Blackfoot autobiographies (Wilson 1914; Hall 1906; Uhlenbeck 1912), and compare McClintock (1910: 444).

[27] Bowers (1950: 62, second and third lines from bottom) should obviously read "Not all boys of the age eligible to buy would organize to join." See Bowers (1950: 88).

the fact that an individual had failed to join the most junior society—
or indeed any other society—did not *ipso facto* exclude him from
joining a more senior one (see p. 294).

For how long did an age-group own a given society? Let us
attempt a calculation. The Awatixa had nine age-societies. An individual might join the first one at around the age of 12, and leave the
last one at, let us say, 66. If his age-group buys and sells the societies
in the fashion assumed above, then on average it will have owned
each society for 6 years. Furthermore, on the same assumptions, 6
years is also the average length of the inauguration interval over the
period during which the hypothetical age-group is passing through
the societies; so the age-range of each age-group inaugurated in this
period is likewise about 6 years. In fact our assumptions are decidedly oversimplified, and furthermore there is every reason to suppose
that there was a good deal of variance, from time to time and from
village to village. However, the calculation does give some idea of the
kind of magnitudes involved. Such evidence as there is on these
matters is examined in Section 5.8 of this chapter; it suggests that 6
years is more likely an underestimate than the opposite, even though
we have perhaps been generous in assuming that our man is as old as
66 when he sells his last society (cf. however Wilson n.d.: 2).

The members of an age-society would meet in somebody's earth
lodge;[28] usually, no doubt, the person who lent the lodge was a

---

[28] Curtis writes of the Mandan that "Each society had its own lodge as a
meeting-place,—to which only members and past members were admitted
[1909b: 13]." This is certainly incorrect. In spite of their frequent and elaborate ceremonies, the only permanent ceremonial lodge found among the two
tribes before about 1870 was the Mandan Okipa lodge, and even this was
probably occupied by a family when not in use for a ceremony (Bowers 1950:
114 f.). References to the use of ordinary residential lodges for ceremonies exist
both for the Mandan (Lowie 1913: 296, 298, 299) and for the Hidatsa (Lowie
1913: 237, 239, 266, 271, 282; Boller 1959: 201, 222; Wilson n.d.: 15, 20, 40).
From about 1860, members of the two tribes came increasingly to live in small
wooden cabins, rather than in the roomy earth lodges. These cabins were too
cramped for ceremonies involving many people, and it was probably for this
reason that the Mandan Okipa lodge in Fishhook village began to be used by the
Hidatsa for various social and ceremonial functions formerly held in any ordinary earth lodge (Bowers 1965: 402 n., 39, 161, 352, 383; cf. also Bowers 1950:
303). It is quite possible that in the 1870s and 1880s this lodge was sometimes
used by Mandan and Hidatsa age-societies. So, also, we find that in the Crow-
Flies-High band village (32 MZ 1) recently described by Malouf (1963) and
occupied mainly in the mid-1880s (1963: 148), there was a single earth lodge
roughly in the center of a village, which otherwise consisted of cabins. The lodge
served as a structure in which dances and ceremonies took place—among them

member, but not invariably (Lowie 1913: 299). In the case of two Hidatsa societies we know that the members always met in the lodge of one of the society's officers (Lowie 1913: 237, 239; Wilson n.d.: 15); in the case of another, "For their lodge they used that of any member which was of convenient size [Lowie 1913: 271]." One of the Mandan societies is known to have met in different lodges on different occasions (Lowie 1913: 299), but it was evidently more usual to meet always in the same residence, which was referred to as "the society's lodge" (Wilson n.d.: 15, 40).

Most age-societies, perhaps all of them, had various kinds of meetings, ranging from the full, formal, public performance of their ceremony, to the informal private gathering where the members simply sat around and talked, perhaps over a meal. I shall first say something about the singing and dancing of the societies, and then describe some of their other activities.

Of the ceremonial elements owned by the age-societies—dances, regalia, and songs—the dances seem to have been the least distinctive. The sources say almost nothing about them, and Maximilian, in his description of the Mandan, remarks that all the age-societies' dances were "essentially identical" (1841: 139 = 1843: 354).

The regalia were another matter. In the first place, each society has its characteristic musical instruments—whistles, rattles, drums— whose functions might be as much decorative as musical. Each member of the Hidatsa Little Dog society, for instance, had hanging from a string round his neck a whistle made from the wing bone of a young eagle, wrapped with colored quillwork,[29] and having suspended from it several buckskin strips terminating in quill-worked loops (Lowie 1913: 268). In addition, each Little Dog had a rattle of an equally distinctive kind (Lowie 1913: 269), and the society had drums, which may or may not have been different in appearance from the drums of other societies. In contrast, another Hidatsa society, the Half-Shaved Heads, had no whistles or rattles, but only drums (Lowie 1913: 273).

The members of each society adorned themselves in a characteristic way, having such things as distinctive clothing, sashes, head-

---

presumably those of the age-societies—and does not seem to have had any ordinary residents. (Cf. Malouf 1963: 154 on Badland Village, the other Crow-Flies-High band site.)

[29] Lowie (1913: 268) calls it "bird-quillwork," by which I take it that he means that the ornamentation was made out of the quills of birds' feathers, rather than (as was more usual) out of porcupine quills.

dresses, hair styles, insignia, masks, and body painting. These accoutrements are extensively described and illustrated in the sources, and specimens are on display in the American Museum of Natural History in New York.[30] Generally speaking, regalia seem to have been worn only for the dances.

In each society there were a few members who were distinguished from the rest by special insignia. Such men are usually referred to as *officers*, and we shall retain this usage; but they did not in general have any authority over their comembers. The number of different types of officer, and the number of officers of each type, varied from one society to another, but the officers were always men of distinction and, in particular, men noted for their bravery (Bowers 1965: 184, 208; Lowie 1913: 257, 267).[31] Each type of officer had a special role in the ceremony of the society—he might, for instance, take some particular position in a parade, or perform on some particular instrument—and might also be subject to some other special rules. The Hidatsa Black Mouths, for instance, had, among others, two officers, each of whom carried a special type of decorated pipe; they had the duty of settling quarrels and keeping peace in the tribe (Lowie 1913: 275; cf. also p. 269 of this volume).

Lastly, each society had

> its own songs, which constituted their most valued possession. These songs were in fact what the new members acquired by purchase: in the Indian way of thinking they were not buying membership—the right to enter the lodge and to participate in its proceedings—so much as they were purchasing the songs, the right to sing which belonged to the society. Once having disposed of its songs, a society would not have dared to make further use of them [Curtis 1909b: 13 f.].

What is said here with reference to the Mandan societies applies equally to the Hidatsa (cf. Wilson n.d.: 6).

> These songs are of three general classes: (1) Dancing songs, (2) war songs, and (3) "serenades", the latter being sung by members of the society when going around the village or sitting on top of the lodges. To these may be added the love songs, which differed

---

[30] Other museums also have holdings, e.g., the Museum für Völkerkunde in Berlin (see Hartmann 1973, Plates IX, 52, 53, 55).

[31] The method by which officers were appointed is discussed on p. 274.

from the serenades, but were sung in a somewhat similar manner.[32]
Songs were always referred to a certain society, the title being given
as a "Fox Society war song", or a "Dog Society serenade" [Dens-
more 1923: 112].

The importance of having a variety of songs appears from the fact
that one of the reasons that led to a certain society becoming
obsolete was reported as being that "there were only two songs, so
that the people soon tired of the dance [Lowie 1913: 253]."

Some of these songs were evidently sung at meetings, while
others were not. The dancing songs were obviously sung (only?) at
meetings, as were the serenades, which were sung when the society
paraded around the village. On the other hand, the war songs, the
love songs, and the serenades sung when sitting on top of the lodges
seem to have been sung (only?) outside meetings (cf. Bowers 1965:
147). It is most unlikely that all the societies had representatives of
each type of song, but it seems that some societies had a number of
songs in a given category.

A society could perform its ceremony either in its lodge, or
out-of-doors;[33] different regalia, less regalia, or no regalia at all were
(at least in some instances) worn at the indoor performances (Lowie
1913: 274, 286, 298). No doubt spectators were absent from indoor
dances of the more informal kind. One society is said to have danced
indoors in the winter and outdoors in the summer (Lowie 1913:
259), but other societies sometimes danced both in- and out-of-doors
on the same occasion (Lowie 1913: 277, 299).

The outdoor performances consisted of two elements, a parade
through the village, in which the officers and ordinary members
marched in a definite order, and the dance itself. It is said of two
Hidatsa societies that they only performed their public dances in the
summer (Lowie 1913: 259, 274), but Maximilian mentions a number
of public dances in the winter of 1833–1834. A typical one occurred
on 28 December 1833, when the fur-trading post (Fort Clark) was

---

[32] This list may not be exhaustive, since Densmore records "[Kit-]Fox
Society Funeral Song" (we do not know whether Mandan or Hidatsa). Her
comments on this song, however, suggest that it may have been just a war song
(1923: 123).

[33] The possibility of both outdoor and indoor performances is only explicitly attested for some of the societies, but I think it probably holds for all,
or at least for the great majority.

visited by the Half-Shaved Head society from the Mitutanka winter village. When they had performed their dance, they were rewarded with a quantity of tobacco, and then "went on to Ruhptare [i.e., Nuptadi, presumably the winter village], where they also danced; they spent the night there, and then showed their arts to the Mönnitarris [Hidatsa] [Maximilian 1841: 287 = 1843: 434]." Similar dances in the fort are mentioned by Chardon.[34] The visit to other Mandan and Hidatsa villages was normal practice,[35] and gifts were given to the dancers both in their native village (Chardon 1932: 46) and in the other villages (Chardon 1932: 47, cf. 50).

In addition to these occasions when a single age-society performed, there were also said to be festivities involving all the villages—or at least, all the villages of one tribe (the facts are not clear)—at which all the societies staged their ceremonies (Maximilian 1841: 267 = 1843: 422).

There do not, in general, seem to have been rules as to how often a society should perform its ceremony, though to this there was at least one exception: the Hidatsa Buffalo Bulls were supposed to dance in public four times a year, once in each season (Bowers 1965: 198; the Mandan and Hidatsa, like some other tribes, including the Blackfoot, attached a special religious significance to the number four). I imagine that other societies performed their ceremonies in public with roughly similar frequency; at any rate, a man who had belonged to the Mandan Kit-Fox society in the 1870s said, "Some time in the spring we went outside in our regalia and danced publicly, whereupon we would return to the lodge, dance again, and then have a feast. This happened about three or four times a year [Lowie 1913: 299]" (cf. also p. 266 of this volume).

Meetings without dancing—or with only informal dancing—were probably a good deal more frequent (Lowie 1913: 274, 299), though they figure less prominently in the literature. What the societies did apart from performing their ceremonies varied from one to another (see pp. 268 ff.), but all of them had feasts, and many had activities related to love and war.

[34] 1932: 28, 36 f., 45, 50 ("Oh! God, but I am tired of dancing"), 65 (this entry is not by Chardon), 69, 96 (in January), 101, 110, 114, 120, 123 f., 156, 161. See also Boller (1959: 287).

[35] See Maximilian (1841: 282 = 1843: 430 f. (cf. p. 290 n. 81 of this volume); 1841: 309 ff. = 1843: 446 f.; 1841: 313, 315 = 1843: 448 f.; 1841: 297 = 1843: 439; 1841: 302 ff. = 1843: 442 f.) and Chardon (1932: 8, 47, 60 f., 168 f.).

The formal performances of a society's ceremonies were commonly preceded or followed by a feast (Lowie 1913: 282, 302; Densmore 1923: 85, 109), but there must also have been feasts at meetings with little or no dancing. Various kinds of outsiders were invited to the feasts: in battle the Hidatsa Dogs would say, "Whoever kills a Sioux or strikes the first coup,[36] shall be feasted by us [Lowie 1913: 290]." Old people were sometimes allowed to participate (Lowie 1913: 259). In some cases there existed a formal "friendship" between a certain men's society and a certain women's society, and this same "friendship" existed also between alternately linked societies in the men's sequence (see further Section 6.1 of this chapter). These "friendly" groups would invite each other to feasts and dances (Lowie 1913: 231, 299).

When they thought of love—which was probably often—the younger societies turned their attention to the unmarried girls. The members of the Mandan Kit-Fox society often went out at night, in their ordinary clothes, and walked from lodge to lodge, singing in front of each one. This was done to please the village girls (some of whom accompanied them and joined in the singing) (Lowie 1913: 299, cf. 306). Daylight did not reduce the young men's ardor. The Hidatsa Little Dogs, for instance, had a special love song which they sang in the daytime, standing in a circle on the roof of their lodge. Its words were directed at their sweethearts, and it was only one of a number of such melodies to which they had rights (Lowie 1913: 272). The Mandan Kit-Foxes occasionally performed their dance simply for the fun of it—and in order to attract the attention of the girls (Lowie 1913: 302).

The older societies, of course, consisted of respectable married men. "On some nights all the members sent for their wives. Then water was poured on the fire, and in the darkness each man seized and hugged someone else's wife [Lowie 1913: 266]." On such occasions the normal incest prohibitions did not apply—at least this was so in the case of the Hidatsa Dog society—and a man might find himself making love to his mother-in-law or even his (classificatory?) sister (Lowie 1913: 290).

The relationship of the societies to warfare was of a considerably less active nature. The Hidatsa Half-Shaved Head society—and in this it was no doubt typical—"frequently met for the discussion of

[36] That is, strikes an enemy (dead or alive) under the circumstances—which were precisely specified—in which the blow would become part of his formal war record.

martial affairs, but dances were not held very often [Lowie 1913: 274]." What Lowie refers to was perhaps not a practical discussion of military matters, but rather a session of formalized boasting about past, and perhaps future (Bowers 1965: 379), achievements.

A military element also entered into meetings where there was dancing. When the Mandan Little Dog society forgathered "many dancing songs were used in the lodge, and after any of them a warrior might rise, go forward, and strike the drum as a signal that he wished to relate one of his deeds of valor [Densmore 1923: 111]." The men of the Mandan Black-Tail Deer society "all wear a ring of grizzly-bear claws on their heads, and show on their persons all the symbols of their acts of heroism, such as feathers on their heads, plaits of hair on the arms and legs, scalps, painting, etc. [Maximilian 1841: 143 = 1843: 356]."[37] When a member particularly distinguished himself in battle, a special meeting was held, no doubt one with dancing (Bowers 1965: 208).

The societies also promoted and rewarded bravery in many other ways. As has been mentioned, it was above all for his courage that a man was honored with the rank of officer. One who held such a position often had to behave in a particularly bold way in battle, commonly, for instance, by planting his officer's emblem in the ground and then not fleeing from the enemy unless the emblem was plucked out by someone else from his own side (cf. Pakes 1968). The members of a society had a special obligation to help one another in battle.[38] When a society was being transferred, the sellers often recited their war deeds, and exhorted the purchasers to emulate them (e.g., Lowie 1913: 346, 270). In combat, the Stone Hammers struck coups with their society emblems (Wilson n.d.: 24; Lowie 1913: 242).

Just as the societies had their serenades and love songs, so too they had their war songs. If an attack was expected the following day, the Mandan Crazy Dogs would go round the village in the late afternoon singing their war songs (Densmore 1923: 111). The Mandan Kit Foxes performed their dance almost exclusively when

[37] Lowie (1913: 293) describes the Hidatsa Buffalo Bulls as following the same practice. For an account of the symbols used by the Mandan and Hidatsa to indicate the military achievements of individuals, see Bowers (1950: 70–74; 1965: 279 f.) and Mallery (1893: 437–440).

[38] Densmore (1923: 110), Lowie (1913: 258), Bowers (1965: 93, 210). As Bowers indicates, this is simply an instance of the many ways in which the members of an age-group helped one another. See further p. 277.

war was imminent—they begin it as soon as news arrived of the enemy's approach (Lowie 1913: 302). A war song could also be sung just before going into battle with a war party (Densmore 1923: 123; Bowers 1950: 171).

There is no indication that these dances or songs were intended to help in the acquisition of supernatural power. What they did was to make the participants ready for battle, defiant, proud, and brave. And the sight of finely dressed and painted groups of warriors, flourishing their battle emblems, boasting of past achievements, singing war songs, and dancing fiercely through the village, must also have had a powerful effect on the mood of all the other inhabitants.

These martial elements have led a number of scholars, including such outstanding experts as Lowie (1913), Wilson (n.d.), and Bowers (1965) to refer to the Mandan and Hidatsa age-societies as "military associations" (or the like). But there is scarcely more justification for this than there would be for calling them "erotic associations." War, like love, was one of the dominating interests of the young Mandan or Hidatsa man, and it is not surprising that this interest finds its reflection in the age organization. But the significance of the age-societies in the actual conduct of warfare was minimal. The age-society did not normally, if ever, act as a military unit,[39] and it is noteworthy that Bowers's extensive accounts of Mandan and Hidatsa military practice (1950: 64–74; 1965: 212–281) make virtually no mention of the age-societies.

One of the most idiosyncratic features of these age-society systems is the heterogeneity of the societies in a single sequence. One aspect of this is that the societies were—quite correctly—viewed as being of varied origins. Of the nine Awatixa societies, for instance, three or four were recognized as imports: the Half-Shaved Head society and the Crow Imitator society were both acquired from the Crow tribe (Bowers 1965: 183, 176; Lowie 1913: 27, 266),[40] while

---

[39] I have come across a few references which suggest that an age-society acted as a unit in warfare, but they are almost all vague or otherwise questionable (Densmore 1923: 123; Bowers 1950: 171, 311; 1965: 193). The only clear example refers to the Hidatsa Raven society. "If anyone [I think this means any member of the Raven society] during a battle began to sing, 'If anyone makes a stand, I, too, will not flee,' all the Ravens stopped and made a stand [Lowie 1913: 284]."

[40] Among the Crow, these societies were not in any way linked to age-divisions, but this was no obstacle to their transfer.

the Black Mouths, and perhaps the Bulls,[41] were originally Mandan. The remaining societies—the Stone Hammer and the four Dog societies—were, in contrast, considered autochthonous; they are frequently mentioned in Hidatsa mythology, and there exist special myths, probably varying somewhat from village to village, that account for their origins (Bowers 1965: 176).

Obviously the tribes did not view the sequence of societies as having been fixed once and for all. The Hidatsa—and surely also the Mandan—believed that their age organization had its origins in the quite distant past, but they also thought that the number of societies it comprised had gradually increased in the course of time (Bowers 1965: 212). The Mandan probably added new societies to their sequence even after Maximilian's visit of 1833–1834 (see p. 288). A new society was acquired by payment to the people who already owned it, but these owners did not thereby lose it.[42]

The activities of the various societies in a sequence were also in many ways different from one another. So far we have sketched in the activities that all, or most, societies had in common. The best way of indicating the idiosyncratic ones is to look down the list of Awatixa societies.

The first of these, the Stone Hammers, had the right to steal food for their meetings. The boys would give the villagers fair warning, and then at night try to slip undetected into the lodges of the village and make off with food for a feast. These raids—which were carried on in accordance with numerous rules—are graphically described in the sources (Lowie 1913: 249 ff.; Bowers 1965: 134 f.).

The next society known to have had special features is the Black Mouths (so called because they painted the lower halves of their faces black). As has been mentioned, Black Mouth societies existed in all the Mandan and Hidatsa villages; if there were any significant differences between their functions, then the sources have failed to record them. These societies were prominent in village life,

---

[41] "No complete origin tradition could be secured," writes Lowie (1913: 291), but his two informants both suggested autochthonous origins (though different ones). Bowers at one point lists the Bulls among those societies which "are of traditional Mandan origin and are not believed to have been of very great antiquity with the Hidatsa [1965: 176]"; but elsewhere he writes that "Both the Mandan and Hidatsa sacred and origin myths make common reference to the buffaloes of the four seasons and directions, so on this basis one would not be able to determine which group first organized the society [1965: 198]."

[42] See further Section 5.2 of this chapter; also Bowers (1965: 211 f.; cf. 91 f.).

and they crop up again and again in the literature. The essence of their position was that it was they who had the duty to use force when it was necessary in order to defend the interests of the village as a whole, either against outsiders or against individual villagers. The decision as to where the interests of the village lay was in general made by the village council, but the Black Mouths probably also had some say in this, since they would meet with the council whenever any important matter was under discussion (Bowers 1965: 186).

More specifically, we can summarize the Black Mouths' duties under a few main heads. First, they ensured that people behaved as they should during communal activities. When the tribes marched away from the village for the great summer buffalo hunt, for instance, it was the Black Mouths who maintained order on the march, kept people from falling behind, and generally looked after the welfare of their fellow tribesmen (Bowers 1965: 52). The hunt itself was a highly organized collective activity, and the Black Mouths could severely punish anyone who tried to hunt alone, since this might scare away the herds. Similar tasks arose in the winter: they supervised the moves to and from the winter villages, and when a buffalo herd was near the winter village they made sure that no one scared it away before it had moved to a position where it could be hunted with maximum success. Equally, when one of the major religious ceremonies was to be performed, the Black Mouths would meet to help in its organization (Bowers 1950: 35, 324; 1965: 185). From time to time—perhaps every two weeks or so in the summer—the people in Fishhook had to clear away the rubbish that accumulated between the lodges. The Black Mouths would pass round the village calling out "You women, go and clean the ground outside your lodges," and if a woman did not obey they would hit her with a stick, or fire a gun (loaded only with powder) beside her (Wilson n.d.: 39–41). Similarly, when fortifications had to be built around Fishhook, it was the women who had to do the work and the Black Mouths who made sure they did it (Lowie 1913: 279).

Second, the Black Mouths had to prevent conflict within the village. Disputes arising from theft, murder, adultery, and the like were generally dealt with by the clans of the individuals concerned. It can be assumed that only clansmen in the disputants' village would interfere, and no doubt clansmen who were close relatives of the disputants would take a particularly active part. In the case of minor disputes, the Black Mouths would not normally intervene at all (Bowers 1965: 185); only if the usual procedures proved for some reason inadequate, and serious trouble threatened, would they step in (Bowers 1965: 72). In the case of murder, the Black Mouths assumed control of the situation immediately, not in order to punish the killer, but to prevent the dispute from escalating and leading to some of the villagers breaking away (Bowers 1965: 74). The clan of the victim would seek (it is said) both to kill the homicide and to exact blood money from his clan (Bowers 1965: 74; cf. Bowers 1950: 100 and p. 277 of this volume).

Third, the Black Mouths had the job of ensuring that the village did not drift more or less accidentally into war with some other group. They prevented unauthorized war parties; they intervened in disputes between individuals from different villages from among the five Knife River villages; and they were active in maintaining the peace when trading parties from other tribes visited the village.

Fourth, "the physical defence of the village was entrusted to the police society which received its instructions from the council [Bowers 1965: 275, 46]." This can hardly mean that able-bodied warriors in other societies stood idly by watching the Black Mouths beating off a Sioux attack. Nor is there any evidence that the Black Mouths acted as a unit in battle. What they did, presumably, was to guard the village—especially at night—and ensure that warning would be given of attacks. Once it was known that the enemy was approaching and battle imminent, then, like other societies, they might go out and perform their ceremony (Lowie 1913: 314; and p. 267 of this volume).

Because of these important duties, the Black Mouths had non-dancing meetings far more frequently than any other society. The Mandan ones met every 2 or 3 days (Bowers 1950: 94), and their Hidatsa counterparts were certainly not less active; even in the winter, in many respects a quieter time of year than the summer, they evidently met several times a week (Bowers 1965: 186).

According to Bowers's account of the Hidatsa—and the same is probably true of the Mandan—the Black Mouths were the pivotal society of the whole system This society was quite different from any of the others in the sequence, and these others can in a number of respects be divided into two groupings, those below the Black Mouths and those above them. As we have seen, one feature that distinguishes these two groupings is that the sequence of societies superior to the Black Mouths was substantially the same for all the villages of the two tribes, whereas there was a good deal of variation from village to village in the list of more junior societies. We shall see later also that the order in which the age-groups in a given system acquired the societies junior to the Black Mouths showed considerable variation—at least during some periods of history—while the order in which the senior societies were acquired was strictly fixed.

Bowers says that among the Hidatsa the Black Mouth "members automatically became members of the [village] council when relinquishing their society to the preceding age-group [1965: 46]." It is not clear, however, that ex-Black Mouths constituted the *whole* membership of the council,[43] and it is possible, indeed, that this statement is an oversimplification.[44] Certainly, there is no evidence that the Mandan had a rigid rule of this sort.[45] But at any rate, there seems no doubt that those in societies senior to the Black Mouths were thought of as being in one category, while those in junior societies were thought of as being in another (Bowers 1965: 181, 184 f.).

The last of the Awatixa societies with idiosyncratic features was the Buffalo Bull society. Membership was restricted to the owners of major tribal bundles, that is, to men with a great deal of supernatural power. In contrast to the other societies, its dances probably had a definite purpose: either to bring buffalo to the village, or to assure their continued supply (Bowers 1965: 198; Densmore 1923: 84 f.). There were a number of such buffalo-calling rituals in the ceremonial repertoires of the Mandan and Hidatsa.

The Bulls obviously constitute an exception to the generally secular character of the men's age-societies, and we may take the opportunity to mention other points at which the age organization touches on religion.[46] The most important of these is in the purchase ceremony.

The initiative for a purchase usually came from the buyers, but it could also come from the sellers (Lowie 1913: 300, though cf. 296). The purchase ceremonies described in the sources fall into three main parts. First, the buyers collectively supply the sellers collectively with a large amount of property, sometimes piling item on item until the sellers say they are satisfied. Next, the buyers

[43] "The village council was of indefinite size, since elevation to membership was based on personal achievements and public acclaim. Although it was composed chiefly of those who had passed the Black Mouths in age, it was essentially a group of mature men [Bowers 1965: 33]."

[44] In Fishhook village, at least, a man had to be in an age-society above the Black Mouths to be on the village council, but he also had to have "distinguished himself in warfare or . . . participated in recognized ceremonial and social activities [Bowers 1965: 39]."

[45] See, for instance, Curtis (1909b: 13) and Bowers (1950: 33).

[46] On this, see, in general, Lowie (1913: 236) and Bowers (1965: 208 f.).

provide feasts for the sellers on successive evenings over a period of time whose length is determined by the sellers. In the case of the more junior societies, this might be as little as 4 days (Lowie 1913: 238, 257), but in the case of more senior ones it was greater, frequently 20 days, and sometimes 40. At the end of this period there was often a second collective payment, after which the sellers ceremonially transferred their regalia, and all their rights in the society, to the buyers, who then almost always paraded through the village and performed their new dance in public (Lowie 1913: 248).

In all this there is nothing religious, and the resemblance between these aspects of age-society purchase and a bundle transfer is only of a general kind. There is, however, another side to the transaction. Ideally, each member of the buyers' group entered into a special relationship with a particular member of the sellers' group, if possible a clan father.[47] I shall refer to the individuals in this relationship as the *age-group father* and the *age-group son*, or simply as the Father and Son (with capital letters, to contrast with the words in other senses).[48]

Now, in addition to the collective payment and transfer of rights between the two age-groups, there were also individual payments and transfers of rights between those who stood in this relationship. These occurred mainly on the last day of the ceremony. The Son presented his Father with food, and also with something more substantial, often a horse. In exchange, the Father instructed him in the songs of the society, gave him his age-society regalia, and transferred to him some of his power. In part the power was transferred by a kind of blessing. One of Lowie's Hidatsa informants described such an occasion as follows:

> On the last morning [of the purchase ceremony] a buyer went
> to his [age-group] father, bringing him a horse, and saying, 'Father,

[47]The kin terminology of the Mandan and Hidatsa is such that a male refers to all male members of his father's clan by the same term that he uses in referring to his father, and they, in turn, refer to him by the same term as they use in referring to a son (Bowers 1950: 42 f.; 1965: 78, 90). In the literature, all those whom a male refers to as "father" (*tate* in both Mandan and Hidatsa), apart from his actual father, are called *clan fathers*, a usage that will be adopted here.

[48]Note, also, that among the Mandan, "The sellers addressed the buyers collectively as 'sons,' who in turn addressed the sellers as 'fathers' [Bowers 1950: 84]." The same was evidently true of the Hidatsa (Bowers 1965: 93; Lowie 1913: 225, 237). It should be borne in mind that when—as was usually the case—an age-group was buying from the immediately senior group, then the Fathers would only be, say, 8 or so years older on average than their Sons.

I wish to take your place now.' Then the father replied, 'Very well, bring your wife here.' When the wife had arrived, the father prayed in behalf of both husband and wife. Then he opened up his medicine bundle, took out some object seen in a vision by himself, and burnt incense. He raised the image over the smoke and sometimes he sang. Addressing the sacred object, he requested it to preserve his [age-group] son from danger. Besides, he furnished both his son and his son's wife with complete suits of clothing [Lowis 1913: 264].

Power was also transferred to the Son by another method, known as "walking." On each of the evenings on which there was a feast[49] the wife of each Son would ceremonially approach her husband's Father in the lodge, and then go outside with him to have intercourse. Power was transferred in this way from the Father, who in turn derived it from the buffalo (Bowers 1950: 336; 1965: 455). In practice the Father did not always want to have intercourse—if only to preserve his power—and there were various ways in which he could avoid it (Lowie 1913: 228 f., 304; cf. Bowers 1950: 319). Presumably power acquired in this way passed from the Son's wife to her husband by intercourse and by virtue of frequent proximity (Bowers 1950: 336 f.).[50]

Bowers remarks of the Hidatsa that "some men preferred to have the same 'father' for each successive society purchase while others thought more supernatural powers would be obtained if different 'fathers' were selected for successive purchases [1965: 209]," and the same was evidently true of the Mandan (Lowie 1913: 226, 304). A Hidatsa informant said that the relationship came completely to an end after the ceremony was over (1913: 226), but a Mandan told Bowers that from time to time he invited his various Fathers to a meal and gave them little gifts (1950: 84). It is clear, in any case, that the relationship was of no real importance outside the ceremony.

Before trying to place this exchange between Father and Son in its larger context, we may mention a few minor points, most of them relating to certain practical questions.

Because of attrition, the Fathers' age-group must generally have been smaller than the Sons', and of course it might easily happen that the number of Sons who needed Fathers from a given clan was

[49] Maximilian (1841: 275 = 1843: 427); Lowie (1913: 304).
[50] Walking did not occur in the transfer ceremonies of some of the more junior societies, since all or most members would still be bachelors (Bowers 1965: 181 ff.). If a man had no wife at a time when he was supposed to participate in a walking ceremony he could, in effect, borrow one (Maximilian 1841: 143 = 1843: 356; Lowie 1913: 228; Bowers 1965: 113, 124).

greater than the number of men of that clan in the Fathers' group. This difficulty was met by allowing a single Father to have up to four Sons (Bowers 1950: 84; 1965: 93; cf. Lowie 1913: 297). The parallel with tribal bundle purchases needs no emphasis.

Sometimes a buyer did not have a clan father in the sellers' group. In one instance, among the Mandan, it is said that the purchaser could in this case select anyone he liked among the sellers (Lowie 1913: 297). In another instance, among the Hidatsa, it is said that a buyer who was in this position—or who could not afford to feast a clan father—simply had to do without an age-group father and make his own regalia (Lowie 1913: 243 f., cf. 281).

In general, Sons probably chose their Fathers, rather than the converse (Lowie 1913: 237, 243, 296 f.; contrast Bowers 1950: 84). But there must have been some restrictions on their freedom of choice, since it appears that someone who had an officer as a Father would receive the regalia of that office and himself become an officer (Lowie 1913: 292, 298, 305, but cf. 280); and, as we have seen (p. 262), only particularly distinguished men became officers. One of Lowie's Hidatsa informants[51] said on one occasion that "the fathers decided which of the sons were to become officers, for they knew which were the bravest warriors and also the best singers," but he stated a year later that the *buyers* "appointed officers according to their bravery [1913: 257 f.]." Another informant from the same tribe described a particular purchase ceremony at which the latter practice was followed (1913: 244). If an officer was killed, then the members of his society elected a replacement from among themselves (Lowie 1913: 257 f., 275).

The resemblance between the Father—Son transaction and a bundle purchase is marked, and it even extends to a certain degree to the nature of the object transferred, since the age-society regalia were at times treated as if they were bundles. Individuals, or whole age-groups, would on occasion make offerings to their regalia,[52] an action about whose rationale we know nothing, but which precisely parallels the offerings a man made to his personal bundle (the feasts given to tribal bundles being merely a grander version of the same thing). More striking still is the case of one of Lowie's informants who, as an officer of the Hidatsa Little Dog society wore a special sash; on several occasions, after extensive fasting and mutilation of his fingers (a typical form of self-torture), he received visions from

---

[51] The informant is first named as Poor Wolf (Lowie 1913: top of 257), but subsequent references and p. 225 n. show that this is an error, and that the informant was actually Wolf Chief (a man some 30 years younger).

[52] Lowie (1913: 254 f., 274); Densmore (1923: 85).

this sash (1913: 267 f., cf. 260). The sash presumably gave him power, and in one vision it even revealed a song to him. It seems, in fact, to play exactly the part that an animal does in the more usual type of vision, the actual sash he wore being, apparently, the bundle for the spiritual sash that he saw.[53] Wilson (n.d.: 22) refers to something similar.

Despite these instances, however, the distinction between bundles and age-society regalia is clear enough, and it constitutes one of the major differences between an age-society purchase and a bundle purchase. There are two other important differences that must be noted.

One is that the persons involved in the transactions were different. This was especially so in the case of the Mandan, where, as has been mentioned, bundles were generally handed down within the matriclan. The clan father played no special part in Mandan bundle transfers, though he was a significant figure in certain other respects (e.g., it was a man's clan fathers who supervised him when he undertook self-torture to increase his power, Bowers 1950: 94, 135, 167 f.). Only in one respect did the clan father have a role in religious life parallel to his role in the age-group system: when, in bundle rituals, the walking ceremony took place, the "rule was for a young man always to select an old man of his father's clan" to "walk" with his wife (Bowers 1950: 318).[54]

The Hidatsa, it will be remembered, usually bought their tribal bundles from their actual fathers. That, at least, was the theory of the transaction. In practice, the father was often dead by the time a son reached the stage where he could purchase the bundle; and even if the father was still alive, his role in the transfer was only a minor one (Bowers 1965: 308, 362, 415). The person who played an important part was the clan father. Here there is a contrast with the Mandan. In both tribes, someone had to give instruction to the purchaser in the (often very extensive) myths and rituals relating to the bundle, and, if necessary, make up a new bundle. Now, among the Mandan it was the seller (i.e., a member of the purchaser's own clan) who did these things (Bowers 1950: 182 etc.), whereas among the Hidatsa they were the responsibility, not of the seller, but of some other member of the purchaser's father's clan (Bowers 1965: 362 etc.). Correspondingly, the clan father had an important role in the

[53] Note, however, that on one occasion "In commemoration of the vision my informant made a backrest cover of buffalo skin with the horns [Lowie 1913: 268]."

[54] The remark is made in the context of the description of a particular ceremony, but I think it is of general reference.

bundle transfer ceremony itself. Hidatsa bundle sales and age-society sales are therefore quite similar in this respect.

The third important difference between a bundle purchase and an age-society purchase is that the latter was collective (Bowers 1965: 209, contrast 1965: 93). In transferring regalia, Father and Son could not simply carry out the transaction when the two of them were ready for it; they had to act in conjunction with all the other members of their respective groups. If even a single member of an age-group did not want to sell, then he could veto the transaction (Maximilian 1841: 141 = 1843: 355; Wilson n.d.: 3; cf. Lowie 1913: 292).

Apart from the purchase ceremony, religious elements in the age-society system are not prominent. Certain societies shared origin myths with particular bundles, and indeed had some collective supernatural power (Bowers 1965: 208, 181). For instance, the Lumpwood society, found among the Awaxawi and Hidatsa-proper, had buffalo-calling powers, and its drum was believed to bring rain when beaten (Bowers 1965: 183; Lowie 1913: 260). Occasionally the age-societies as such took part in a religious ceremony; the most striking example is the Mandan Red Stick ceremony, a buffalo-calling rite that could be pledged either by an individual or by an age-group (Bowers 1950: 316).[55]

All in all, the links between the age-societies and religion are not negligible; but they are no more important than the links between religion and any other aspect of Mandan and Hidatsa life. These were people who paid a great deal of attention to the supernatural, and the features we have just described should not blind us to the sharp distinction that the two tribes drew between their age-society systems and their bundle systems (p. 253 n. 16).

The bonds between members of a single age-group were quite strong. Among the Hidatsa, at least, age-mates behaved to each other rather like brothers (Bowers 1965: 93). In this tribe, certain relatives, known by a term that Bowers translates as "joking relatives," had the right to criticize or tease a man whenever he misbehaved in any way (1965: 124 ff.). This right extended also to all the members of that man's age-group (1965: 211). Naturally enough, among the Hidatsa—and no doubt the Mandan also—brothers could belong to the same age-group (Bowers 1965: 112).

A man's age-society often contributed toward the cost of some

---

[55] For other instances see Bowers (1965: 180 f., 443 f., 457 ff.). Bowers (1950: 116) describes a religious observance that was part of all Mandan age-society meetings.

expensive ritual undertaking.[56] If, in the course of acquiring power, a man undertook excessively severe self-torture, his fellow clansmen or his age-mates stepped in to restrain him (Bowers 1965: 59, 237). In case of misfortune he could turn to his age-mates for aid; they would help, for instance, in the recovery of stolen horses (1965: 210). When a middle-aged man married a young wife, he often called in his clansmen and his age-mates to help him to keep an eye on her (1965: 155). When a man died his age-society gave his relatives food and gifts for his funeral ceremonies (1965: 210, 172). If one man killed another, then it seems that the killer's age-society often presented the victim's relatives with gifts, in order to prevent their taking revenge on the killer (Wilson 1933: 265).

How did the age-societies fit into the villagers' way of life? With the exception of the Black Mouths, the societies were essentially social clubs that from time to time staged secular ceremonies. Mandan and Hidatsa men had plenty of free time for such things: hunting, religion, and warfare, the largely male activities, were intermittant and not markedly time-consuming.[57]

With rare exceptions (p. 271), the dances and songs of the age-societies were performed entirely for their own sake. A good part of their appeal lay in the opportunity they afforded for wearing intricate and beautiful costumes: Mandan and Hidatsa men were always exceedingly concerned about their appearance.[58] More generally, as the extreme elaboration of their religious rituals shows, the Mandan and Hidatsa liked performing ceremonies. A feature which distinguished those of the age-societies was that almost all men participated in them. Religious ceremonies in contrast, were generally confined to bundle holders and certain associates; others could only be present as spectators. In both tribes the important bundles—

[56] See, for instance, Bowers (1950: 67 f., 77, 132 n., 284; 1965: 48, 401, 403, 417, 427). Bowers (1965: 398) seems to provide an instance of *all* the age-societies contributing to the cost to an individual of a particular ceremony, but the details are unclear.

[57] Nineteenth-century accounts make it clear just how much leisure the men had. "Among these Indian tribes one of the main occupations of the young men is trying their luck with the girls and women, and this takes up most of their time, excluding what they devote to adorning themselves [Maximilian 1841: 131 = 1843: 350]" cf. Henry 1897: 327; Boller 1959: *passim.*

[58] For instance, each young Mandan carried, attached to his wrist, a small mirror. "The Indian dandy glances frequently in this mirror (*tout comme chez nous*), and if he has traveled some distance, especially when it is windy, as is so often the case here, he immediately takes the mirror in hand, and in the most careful manner puts his dress in order again [Maximilian 1841: 108 = 1843: 338]."

the ones with elaborate rituals—seem to have been confined to a limited section of the population;[59] so, for many, the age-societies must have offered welcome opportunities to satisfy their taste for ceremonial by participation rather than by mere observation.

One way to see what part the age-societies played in village life is to imagine what the effect would have been if they had vanished overnight. The only really marked change would have been in the political system, which would have been seriously disrupted by the disappearance of the Black Mouths. Apart from that, things would have gone on very much as before. The social life of the men would have been somewhat impoverished, but age-society meetings were only one among many activities that brought them together; council meetings, bundle feasts, hunts, many kinds of sports, war parties, informal gatherings—all these ensured that no Mandan or Hidatsa man would be too cut off from his fellows. Some colorful ceremonies would have been lost, but they were not—in contrast to some of the religious ceremonies—considered of any particular significance for the well-being of the village as a whole. The absence of the mutual aid that age-mates provided would have been felt on certain occasions, but the effect would not have been severe, since on all—or virtually all—such occasions help was also provided by clansmen. Still, it is possible that, at least for some men, this would have been the greatest loss.

In sum, the age-society system as such was not a central feature of the social structure. The tasks carried out by the Black Mouths could just as well have been carried out by a group that was not part of an age-group system; and if this had been done, then the disappearance of the rest of the age organization would not have changed Mandan or Hidatsa society in a radical fashion.

5 AGE-SOCIETIES AND AGE-GRADES

From what was said in the preceding section, it will already be evident that the age-societies differed in a number of respects from what are usually thought of as age-grades. In what follows these differences are examined in more detail.

---

[59] See especially Bowers (1950: 75). (In view of what the author says on the last line of that page, and in view of our general knowledge of the religion of the tribe, it seems that the word "large" on line 13 of p. 75 is a slip of the pen, and that we should read "small.") Bowers adds that after the 1837 epidemic "there was probably a much higher percentage of the population owning these

5.1 Owning Several Societies or None

For purposes of exposition, we have assumed so far that all purchases of societies occurred simultaneously. In fact, this was far from being the case. Within broad limits, an age-group was free to decide for itself when it would buy a new society or sell its old one, and there was no obligation on it to do these things at the same time.

It follows from this, first, that at certain times an age-group would buy a new society before having sold its old one, and thus find itself in possession of two societies at once.[60] The system therefore violated the unique-assignment constraint of the age-grade definition. The violation, however, was not as striking as it might have been, for when a group owned more than one society, it acted as if it owned only the senior of the societies it possessed (except, of course, that it eventually sold the junior one).[61]

A second consequence is that a group sometimes found itself owning no age-society at all.[62] The system therefore also violated the no-interval constraint.

For reasons which will appear later, I suspect that at least from the time of the first smallpox epidemic (1781) there were generally—perhaps always—more age-groups than there were age-societies in the Mandan and Hidatsa villages. It was therefore probably common to find a group owning more than one society, and this multiple ownership may have continued for considerable periods of time. One of Lowie's Hidatsa informants, referring to a period soon after the foundation of Fishhook village in 1845, mentions that his age-group owned two societies simultaneously for 8 years (Lowie 1913: 273). By the same token, groups probably did not often find themselves without any age-society, and certainly not for such a length of time. Maximilian tells us that such a state of affairs could last "for half a year or more" (1841: 140 = 1843: 354).

Owning no society is a much clearer and more striking deviation from the age-grade definition than multiple ownership. It is worth bearing in mind that it was probably less common, and less protracted, than its counterpart.

---

hereditary bundles [1950: 182]." Even so, "not many lodges had notable shrines [i.e., bundles] [Wilson n.d.: 30]."

[60] For the Mandan, see Curtis (1909b: 14) and Section 5.7 of this chapter; for the Hidatsa, Bowers (1965: 183, 211 etc.) and Lowie (1913: 233, 273).

[61] For the Mandan, see Curtis (1909b: 14); for the Hidatsa, Bowers (1965: 211).

[62] For the Mandan, see Maximilian (1841: 140 = 1843: 354) and Curtis (1909b: 14). The same thing must sometimes have happened among the Hidatsa, though I have not recorded any references to it.

5.2 Intersystem Transfers

It was mentioned earlier (p. 268) that an age-group could buy an age-society even from an alien system, whether graded or not. There is no account in the sources of just how a new society was added to the existing sequence, but it will be evident from what has just been said that the operation presented no special difficulties. An age-group might simply own its new society in addition to any it already possessed. It would presumably count the new one as the senior of the societies it owned, and the new society would thus take its place in the sequence directly above the most senior society already owned by the age-group that purchased the new society. Obviously, the acquisition of an alien society would in general mean that, for a time at least, there would be more age-societies than age-groups.[63]

5.3 Out-of-age Members

Among the Hidatsa—and also, probably, among the Mandan—the age-groups in a sequence were alternately linked (Section 6.1 of this chapter). One way in which the linking expressed itself among the Hidatsa was this. The members of some age-group S who were about to buy a new age-society G could ask a member of S − 2 to join them in the purchase, and he would then become a full member of the G age-society (Lowie 1913: 231 f.).[64] Thus the sequential-assignment constraint was violated. If—as I suspect—he also remained a member of the age-society owned by S − 2, then the unique-assignment constraint was also violated. If society G was the last in the sequence, then the last-grade constraint might be infringed.

Something rather similar existed in the Hidatsa Bull society. It appears, from the scanty data, that this society included one or more young boys as members (Lowie 1913: 291; Bowers 1965: 199). The boy (or boys) did not, apparently, belong to any other age-society, being too young. The constraints violated, then, were the first-grade

---

[63] This would not be the case if an age-group bought the alien society before having bought any of the societies in the existing sequence, or if an age-group bought the alien society after having sold the last society in the existing sequence. Neither of these is likely actually to have occurred.

[64] Bowers makes no mention of this phenomenon (see especially 1965: bottom of p. 207 and top of p. 208), so perhaps Lowie's account should be treated with a certain amount of reserve. Age-group S would evidently have to have reached the third level for this practice to be possible.

constraint, the last-grade constraint (unless the boy never joined any other age-society), and perhaps the no-interval constraint.

It is not known whether the Mandan also had *out-of-age members* of this kind. There is an indication in Maximilian that the Mandan Crazy Dogs at one time had some members from an older age-group than the one that owned the society.[65] This presumably involved violating the sequential-assignment constraint and (perhaps) the unique-assignment constraint.

These phenomena are obviously only marginal features of the Mandan and Hidatsa systems. They affected very few individuals,[66] and they do not differentiate the age-societies from age-grades in any very striking way.

5.4 Incomplete Sequences

For a variety of reasons, even a man who had survived into old age, and who had taken some part in the age organization of his village, might not have joined all the societies in its sequence. I have already mentioned that some boys failed to join the most junior society but participated with their coevals in buying some more senior society (p. 259). In such a case the first-grade constraint is violated.

It is said that among the Hidatsa

> Those who lost status as a result of indifference to ritual responsibilities, evidence of cowardice or laziness, and unwillingness to assist their kinsmen in social and ceremonial activities, were weeded out of the age-grade societies, leaving only those who conformed to the highest traditional standards [Bowers 1965: 455, cf. 181, 184, 192, 194, 209, 211].

No other source mentions selective elimination of this sort among the Hidatsa, and Lowie, indeed, implicitly denies its existence (1913:

---

[65] "Sie [the Crazy Dogs] bestehen aus jungen Leuten von 10 bis 15 Jahren. . . . Ehemals konnten auch alte Leute in dieser Bande seyn, dann durften sie aber nie vor dem Feinde weichen, man hat dieses seitdem zu der jetzt bestehenden Regel abgeändert." "They [the Crazy Dogs] are young people from 10 to 15 years of age. . . . Formerly adults might also belong to this band. Those who did were not allowed to retreat from the enemy [cf. p. 266]. This has since been altered to the present rule [Maximilian 1841: 139 = 1843: 354]."

[66] I have not considered in this section those instances in which a non-member of the age-group that owns a given society is given some special task in relation to that society, but without actually being a member of the society (cf. Bowers 1965: 182, 207 f.).

236); but I think we can trust Bowers. The silence of the other sources does, however, suggest that the number of men who dropped out in this way was fairly small. This phenomenon means that the system violated the whole-sequence constraint.

Something that is probably quite similar has been claimed for the Mandan. "Each step up this ladder of prestige [i.e., the age-society sequence] was more expensive than the previous, and only a select few reached the highest society [Johnson 1965: 347]." In a personal communication (1969) Professor Johnson commented on this passage as follows:

> I am afraid that I cannot give you a specific reference for the idea of increased cost in Mandan age-graded societies. The notion came to me from an older Mandan informant and in discussion with James Howard and others who know something of the society. I feel quite certain that the idea is correct but it is difficult to verify.

The notion that senior societies were more expensive than junior ones is very plausible (cf. p. 272), though I think it would be wrong to assume a regular increase in cost with every successive purchase in the sequence. We know that the Buffalo Bull "society in both the Mandan and Hidatsa villages was limited to those males who had purchased sacred bundles containing buffalo skulls together with the right to instruct younger men in the ceremonial painting of these skulls [Bowers 1965: 198]."[67] This seems to confirm that only a select few reached the top of the sequence. The ones who dropped out on the way up should not, however, be thought of as the victims of poverty. Almost certainly we are dealing with the kind of selective elimination that Bowers mentions for the Hidatsa. If a man had lost status, then one way in which this would manifest itself would be in the refusal of his relatives to help him in accumulating the property needed for an age-society (or bundle) purchase.

Bowers also says of the Hidatsa that "Theoretically, everyone ought to belong to a society—in practice, many did not join in or were in and out through life [1965: 211]." The reasons for not joining, or for only intermittently participating, are not given. At any rate, it looks as if the system allowed skipping,[68] thus violating the

[67] The bundles containing buffalo skulls were the most important ones (Bowers 1965: 95, 332 f., 419, 434).

[68] Bowers's statement is too vague for us to be certain. It may also be that a member of an age-group, having failed to join with his age-mates in purchasing

sequential-assignment constraint and the no-interval constraint. Contrary to the inference that might be drawn from Bowers's statement, I think that the proportion of men who never joined a society was probably very small (cf. Lowie 1916: 919).

5.5   Age

A feature that distinguishes the age-societies from what are normally thought of as age-grades is that in many instances there was no intimate connection between the activities characteristic of a particular society and the usual age of its members.[69] Lowie mentioned this in almost all his writings on the subject, and he often pointed to a rather striking piece of evidence to show that the Mandan and Hidatsa did not view any of the societies as *necessarily* confined to individuals of a certain age. When he was collecting his data there were still a number of old men who, many years before, had, together with their respective age-groups, purchased membership of certain societies. Because of the collapse of the system they had never sold these rights, and the result was that in old age they still considered themselves members of societies that they had joined in boyhood or youth.

Nevertheless, each society was to a greater or lesser degree associated with some stage in the life of the individual. In the case, for instance, of the Stone Hammers or the Bulls, this association was strong—young boys could hardly have much supernatural power, and it would be odd if the most respected elders of the village were to go around the lodges at night pilfering food. Other societies had less clear-cut associations with a particular period of the individual's life, but even so there was a sharp distinction between those that were above the Black Mouths and those that were below (cf. p. 271).

These links between an individual's age and the society he belonged to were important because they were largely responsible for maintaining the period of time it took to pass through the sequence of societies at a fairly constant length. Most graded age-group sys-

---

some society, would later buy that same society with the members of a more junior age-group; in other words, there would be shifting, but no skipping. It seems to me more likely, however, that there was skipping, but no shifting (cf. p. 294).

[69] The definition of age-grades used in this book does not allow us to distinguish between the age-societies and age-grades on this basis; but that is simply a weakness of the definition.

tems use level rules, and so the time it takes to pass through the grades depends solely on the length of the inauguration interval. In the Mandan and Hidatsa systems no such simple mechanism existed; it was therefore crucial that the Black Mouths in particular be men of a certain age—mature, but not old. Among the Hidatsa, and the same is no doubt true of the Mandan,

> Young men who had advanced to the point of buying into the Black Mouth society, were frequently stopped at that point for a number of years [cf. Lowie 1913: 276]. When the Black Mouths were asked to sell by a younger group, they would invariably present the matter to the two older Dog and the Bull societies for their approval. If the older and better-informed men felt that the younger men were moving along too fast and were not ready to assume such important obligations, or if conditions in the village or relations with neighboring tribes were not right, the sale was delayed [Bowers 1965: 184].

5.6 The Hidatsa in Fishhook

A number of lists exist of the Mandan and Hidatsa age-societies,[70] but no two of them are in entire agreement as to the order of the societies. The main reason for the inconsistencies is that the age-groups in a village did not, in fact, always purchase the societies in the same order.

This was first clearly stated by Lowie (see especially 1913: 232 ff.), who connected the variations in sequence with the "agelessness" mentioned in the preceding section. In this he was certainly correct; but he also seems to have assumed that variations in sequence of this sort were a long-standing feature of the system, an assumption that Bowers's investigations among the Hidatsa have rendered uncertain.

Some of the details of Bowers's analysis (1965: 174 ff.) are not entirely clear, but it can be summarized as follows. Before the first

---

[70] In addition to the lists for both tribes compiled by Maximilian and Lowie, I know of the following. *Hidatsa.* In 1850, Culbertson (1952: 137 = Schoolcraft 1853: 630); in 1859, Boller (1966: 211; the Basket Band must be the Lumpwoods, cf. Lowie 1913: 259); in 1862, Morgan (1959: 158 f.); in 1881, Clark (1885: 355; presented as a list of Arikara societies, but identified by Lowie 1915: 652 f. as being in fact a Hidatsa list); Matthews (1877: 47 n.) and Curtis (1909a: 182), both unordered, the former very incomplete; Wilson (n.d.: 1); Densmore (1923: 108); Beckwith (1938: 238 f.); and Bowers (1965: 175; the only one that distinguishes between the different villages). *Mandan.* Curtis (1909b: 144); and Densmore (1923: 108).

smallpox epidemic (1781), and, indeed, to a large extent even after that epidemic but before the second one (1837), there was little or no variation in the order in which the societies were purchased. In Fishhook village, however, a new situation arose, for the three slightly different Hidatsa systems that had existed before its foundation (1845) were now fused into one. Since the sequences were virtually identical from the Black Mouths upward, no problems arose there, but the number of societies in the lower part of the sequence came to be larger than in any of the old villages (1965: 177). For instance, among the Awatixa, the society immediately senior to the Crazy Dogs was the Crow Imitators. This was lacking in the other two Hidatsa villages, where, instead, the next society an age-group bought after the Crazy Dogs was the Lumpwoods, an institution unknown to the Awatixa. The new, joint, system in Fishhook incorporated both the Crow Imitators and the Lumpwoods.

This obviously gave rise to the question of which of the two should be senior and which junior. The result of a number of such problems was

> to introduce inconsistencies into the system and to introduce competition between some societies for position in the system. Since competition is not characteristic of the Hidatsa age-grade system, they temporarily reconciled these conflicts by providing two "routes" to the Black Mouth society until one "route" became more popular than the other, with the resultant cessation of the unpopular societies [Bowers 1965: 175 f.].

Bowers mentions this "competition" between the societies more than once, but he gives no clear indications of how it manifested itself; nor do we know just how the system of two "routes" worked. However, his account does help explain why it is that Lowie was unable to reconstruct a single, firmly fixed sequence of age-societies for the Hidatsa.

In the absence of such a sequence one cannot speak of the age-groups as being, or not being, integrated with the age-societies. But just how different the system was from a graded age-group system may be seen from an account given to Lowie (1913: 233) by a Hidatsa informant, referring to a time when the tribe was in Fishhook village. A certain age-group (call it S), having sold its age-society, turned to S + 1 and offered to buy first one and then the other of two societies owned by S + 1. Both offers were refused, and so the group bought an age-society from S + 2.

There is one crucial question to which Bowers provides no proper answer: was there *ever* a time when the Hidatsa villages had sequences of age-societies in which the order was firmly fixed? The whole tone of Bowers's work implies that there was such a time, but he never says so clearly, and he leaves open the question of when it was (whether before 1845 or before 1781). There can be no doubt that conditions in Fishhook led to the sequential-assignment constraint being violated in a particularly striking way; but we cannot be certain that even before then the systems did not violate it, albeit to a lesser extent.

In about 1858, when the Nuptadi moved into Fishhook, the Mandan must also have faced the problem of amalgamating systems. There is no evidence as to how they coped with it, but certainly they faced fewer difficulties than the Hidatsa. They had to amalgamate only two, rather than three, systems, and the differences between these two systems were almost negligible (see Section 5.7.5 of this chapter).

5.7 The Mandan on the Knife

Among the Hidatsa in Fishhook village there must always have been more age-societies than age-groups, and as a result there must always have been some multiple ownership. Whether the Hidatsa systems were like this before the 1837 epidemic is not known; but the Mandan ones certainly were.

The evidence for this view comes from an analysis of Maximilian's account of these systems as he found them in 1833–1834. This text was discussed at some length by Lowie (1913: 294 ff.), who reconstructed the sequence of societies at the time of the prince's visit as follows:

I.   Foolish Dogs
II.   Crows, or Ravens (Hähderuch-Ochatä)[71]
III. * Half-Shaved Heads
IV.   Soldiers (Káua-Karakáchka)[72]
V.   Dogs
VI.   * Old Dogs
VII. Buffalo Bulls (Beróck-Ochatä)
VIII. Black-Tail Deers

[71] This is a Crow Imitator society, like that of the Hidatsa (Lowie 1913: 309 n.; 1916: 928 f., 944).
[72] Another name for the Black Mouths.

Maximilian's own list (1841: 139–143 = 1843: 354–356) includes only six societies, omitting the two marked with asterisks; but he mentions these two outside the list and provides enough information to indicate where they fitted into the sequence.

Now, if there were (at least) eight societies, why is it that Maximilian begins by listing only six? The answer—as Lowie realized[73]—is surely that there were at that time only six age-groups in Mitutanka.[74] Between them these groups owned a considerable number of societies, as will appear if we examine the evidence on those societies that do not appear in Maximilian's original list of six:

1. *The Half-Shaved Heads.* 2. *The Old Dogs.* 3. *The Unnamed Dance.* Immediately after presenting the list of six societies, Maximilian writes:

> There are also other dances that may be bought and sold, among them a second dance of the Káua-Karakáchka, and also the Half-Shaved Head dance, which the lower class[75] may buy before they are old enough to become Káua-Karakáchka. . . . Another dance is that of the Old Dogs. . . . The band of Dogs can buy it from the Buffalo Bulls before they themselves become Buffalo Bulls or are allowed to buy themselves into the Beróck-Ochatä band [1843: 357].[76]

It is clear from this passage that there were not two "supplementary dances" as Lowie suggested, but at least three; in addition to the two that are mentioned by name, and to which Lowie refers,

---

[73] See especially Lowie (1913: 235 at the bottom and 236 at the top).

[74] Since the fur-trading post where Maximilian spent the winter was right next to Mitutanka, it is no doubt to this village that his data primarily refer.

[75] Maximilian uses the terms "class," "band," and "association" (*Verein*) synonymously to refer to the age-societies. He does not distinguish terminologically between age-societies and age-groups. In this instance, by "the lower class" he evidently means the age-group immediately junior to the age-group that owned the Soldier society, since he later describes in detail the occasion on which the Crows purchased the Half-Shaved Head dance from the Soldiers (1841: 274 = 1843: 426).

[76] "Es gibt auch noch andere Tänze, welche sich kaufen und verkaufen lassen, hierhin gehört ein zweiter der Káua-Karakáchka, ferner der Tanz des halbgeschorenen Kopfes, Ischohä-Kakoschóchatä, welchen die untere Classe kaufen kann; bevor sie noch das Alter hat, Káua-Karakáchka zu werden. . . . Ein anderer Tanz ist der der alten Hunde. . . Die Bande der Hunde kann ihn von der der Stiere kaufen, bevor sie selbst Stiere werden, oder sich in der Bande Beróck-Ochatä einkaufen darf [1841: 144]."

there was a third, unnamed dance, the "second dance" of the Black
Mouths.

4. *The Little Dogs Whose Names Are Unknown.* Lowie (1913:
294 f.) tells us that the most junior society mentioned by Maximilian
is the Foolish Dogs, but that when he (Lowie) visited the Mandan he
was told of the existence of three even more junior societies.[77]
Lowie assumed that these were added to the Mandan sequence in the
period after Maximilian's departure. This may well be true of the two
most junior of these societies, but the third one, the Little Dog
society, which Lowie thought was "adopted from the Hidatsa in
recent times" (1913: 294), is in fact already mentioned by Maximilian, though not in any very explicit fashion.

In his list Maximilian names the first society as "the Meniss-
Ochka-Ochatä . . . , the Foolish Dogs, or the Dogs whose names are
unknown [1843: 354]."[78] Lowie (1913: 306 n.) evidently assumed
that Maximilian was here offering two alternative translations of the
Mandan term *mini s'ō xka ō xat'e*; but it would be surprising if a
term could bear two such different meanings. It is more reasonable
to assume either that these were two alternative names for the same
society or else that these were two societies owned by the same
age-group.

The second of these hypotheses has strong evidence in its favor.
The Hidatsa have two distinct societies called, respectively, the
Foolish (or Crazy) Dogs and the Dogs Whose Names Are Unknown.
This last is an alternative name for the Little Dogs, both terms being
abbreviations of the full name, Little Dogs Whose Names Are Un-
known (Bowers 1965: 194, 197). If, among the Hidatsa, the Foolish
Dogs and the Dogs Whose Names Are Unknown were two distinct

---

[77] They were, beginning with the most junior, the Cheyenne society, the
Kit-Fox society, and the Little Dog society, after which followed the Foolish (or
Crazy) Dog society, the first on Maximilian's list. Densmore begins her list
"White, Fox, Dog (including Young Dog and Foolish Dog) [1923: 108]." I
imagine that what she calls the White society is identical with the Cheyenne
society (she gives the native name as *so'hta o'hate* (1923: XIX), while Lowie
gives the Mandan name of the Cheyenne society as *cō'ta ō'xat'e*; the second
word in each case means "society"). Densmore may well have got her list from
the same informant as Lowie, a man called Wounded Face.

[78] "Die erste Bande oder den ersten Verein bilden die Meniss-Ochka-Ochatä
(*ch* guttural), die thörichten Hunde, oder die Hunde, deren Namen man nicht
kennt (les chiens fols, ou les chiens dont on ne connait pas le nom) [1841:
139]."

societies, then they are likely also to have been distinct among the Mandan.

There is further, and even stronger, support for the second hypothesis in another passage from Maximilian:

> The so-called Hot Dance[79] . . . is now danced in Ruhptare [Nuptadi] and by the Mönnitarris [Hidatsa], who bought it from the Arikkaras. It is performed by the little dogs whose names are unknown [1843: 357].[80]

Now, when Maximilian says that a society called the Little Dogs Whose Names Are Unknown perform the Hot Dance, is he referring to the village of Nuptadi or to the Hidatsa? Clearly he is referring to Nuptadi (as indeed we would expect, since this information comes in a chapter devoted to the Mandan); for he tells us elsewhere (1841: 218 = Appendix 5 of this volume) that among the Hidatsa the Hot Dance was identical with (*einerlei mit*) the Stone society (the most junior of the Hidatsa sequence, otherwise known as the Stone Hammers).

We can be certain, then, that the village of Nuptadi had the Little Dogs Whose Names Are Unknown in its age-society sequence. What we do not know for certain is whether Nuptadi also had the Foolish Dogs and whether the other Mandan village, Mitutanka, had the Little Dogs Whose Names Are Unknown. In other words, when Maximilian writes of the first society as "the Foolish Dogs, or the Dogs Whose Names Are Unknown," he may be indicating that in both villages the most junior age-group owned both of these societies; or he may be indicating that in one village (Nuptadi) the youngest age-group owned the Little Dogs, while in the other (Mitutanka) it owned the Foolish Dogs. (There are also, of course, other possibilities, but these are the two main ones.)

    5. *The Hot Dance.* The passage just quoted from Maximilian indicates that, of the two Mandan villages, only Nuptadi had the Hot Dance. This is the single indisputable piece of evidence that the age-society sequences in the two villages differed from each other. This dance seems to have become obsolete among the Hidatsa after the first epidemic (Lowie 1913: 253), and since Lowie could learn

---

[79] On this dance, see Section 5.7.5 of this chapter.

[80] "Der sogennante heisse Tanz . . . wird jetzt in Ruhptare und bei den Mönnitarris getanzt, welche letztere ihn von den Arikkaras kauften. Die kleinen Hunde, deren Namen man nich kennt, führen ihn auf [1841: 144]." Lowie (1913: 308 n.) noticed this passage but failed to appreciate its significance.

nothing about it among the Mandan (1913: 309), the chances are that it also vanished in Nuptadi well before the inhabitants of that village moved into Fishhook.

6. *The As-Chóh-Ochatä.* In December 1833, fourteen men from the As-Chóh-Ochatä society of Nuptadi came to Fort Clark, where Maximilian was staying, and danced there (Maximilian 1841: 281 f., 144 = 1843: 430 f., 357).[81] There is nothing in the text to indicate how this dance fitted into the sequence;[82] nor do we know whether it was to be found in Mitutanka. When Lowie visited the Mandan nearly 80 years later he was not able to identify it with any certainty (Lowie 1913: 319 f.).

The evidence on these additional societies offers two possible cases of a single age-group owning three age-societies. The age-group in Mitutanka that owned the Black Mouths and the Half-Shaved Heads may well at the same time have owned the unnamed dance; while in Nuptadi the most junior age-group, which owned the Little Dogs and the Hot Dance, may at the same time have owned the Foolish Dogs.

Maximilian's failure to distinguish consistently between the two Mandan villages makes it difficult to reach clear conclusions. The best one can say is that in Mitutanka there were (almost certainly) only six age-groups, but a considerably larger number of age-societies, perhaps almost a dozen.[83] Whether the age-groups all purchased these societies in the same order is something we do not

---

[81] The English translation (1843) arbitrarily substitutes "band of bulls" for "Aschó-Ochatä" on p. 430, and on p. 357 omits the name entirely. (Maximilian spells the name in two different ways.)

[82] It is just possible that the As-Chóh-Ochatä was a dance unconnected with the age-society sequence (see Maximilian 1841: 219 = 1843: 397 on such "independent" dances among the Hidatsa); but this seems most unlikely, since Maximilian discusses it together with the age-societies, and refers to its members as a *Bande.*

[83] An incidental question that may be mentioned here is: what criteria did Maximilian use in dividing the societies into two classes, those on the list of six and the rest? Given that an age-group only performed the most senior dance it owned, the obvious procedure would have been to include in the list of six the six societies which at that time were active. This may well have been what Maximilian did: at the time of his arrival the Half-Shaved Heads belonged to the society that owned the Black Mouths, and it sounds as if the Old Dogs belonged to the group that owned the Buffalo Bulls. The Hot Dance, evidently a late acquisition (Bowers 1965: 176; Maximilian 1841: 144 = 1843: 357), would have been below the Little Dogs/Foolish Dogs in the Nuptadi sequence. The sole stumbling block to this theory is that Maximilian saw the As-Chóh-Ochatä

know; nor do we know whether the Mandan found anything disturbing in the disproportion between the number of groups and the number of societies. Conceivably this kind of disproportion was characteristic of the Mandan systems from the earliest times, but it is possible to point to certain recent factors that could either have given rise to it or at least exacerbated it.

One such factor is the decline in the number of Mandan villages, already mentioned earlier (p. 247). Since Nuptadi and Mitutanka had (at least) slightly different age-society sequences, it is reasonable to assume that the pre-1781 villages also had rather different sequences and that the series of amalgamations that eventuated in the two Knife River villages also involved the amalgamation of these age-society systems, giving rise to rather longer, and perhaps less rigidly ordered, sequences than had previously existed.

Another factor is the decline in the number of men in each village. This decline must have had either or both of two effects on the age-society system: a reduction in the average size of age-groups, which would be of no consequence to us here; and an increase in the length of inauguration intervals, and hence a reduction in the total number of groups. The latter is the effect that interests us, since it would be consistent with the existence of more age-societies than age-groups.

Two processes led to a decline in the average number of men in a village, as compared with the situation before 1781. One of these is simply a decline in the size of the villages' populations. In 1833–1834 there were 38 lodges in Nuptadi and 65 in Mitutanka (Maximilian 1841: 104 f. = 1843: 335). The preepidemic villages were certainly on average considerably larger even than Mitutanka, perhaps as much as twice as large;[84] probably only one or two outlying

---

dance; but this can be explained by pointing out that the list of six refers primarily to Mitutanka (p. 287 n. 74), while the As-Chóh-Ochatä who danced came from Nuptadi.

[84] Bowers writes that "The protohistoric Mandan sites of the Heart River region have ruins of one hundred and twenty-five to one hundred and fifty lodges, while later villages of historic times were much smaller, owing to the smaller population [1950: 28 f.]." Although the largest of the Heart River sites (Double Ditch) did have over 150 lodges, Bowers is probably exaggerating the average size of these villages in this passage (see the table in Bowers 1948: 161, partially reproduced by Wood 1967: 154). New estimates will appear in a paper by Donald J. Lehmer in vol. 13 of the forthcoming Handbook of North American Indians (edited by William C. Sturtevant); but these also are based on surface remains, old maps, and the like, for none of the relevant sites have been the object of modern excavations.

northern settlements were smaller than Mitutanka, the half dozen big villages near the mouth of the Heart all being larger (cf. Stewart 1974).

The evidence for the other process is much weaker: it is generally thought, however, that the Mandan became far more vulnerable to their nomadic enemies—above all the Sioux—after the 1781 epidemic. This may well have led to a decline in the proportion of men in the population as a whole. At any rate, Thompson (1962: 178) says that in 1797–1798 among the Hidatsa "the Men are nearly equal to the women in number," while Catlin (1841: 187) thought in 1832 that women outnumbered men two or three to one. *If* these observations are correct with regard to the Hidatsa, then they would probably be true of the Mandan as well.

The last factor that may have exacerbated the disproportion between the number of age-societies and the number of age-groups is the acquisition of new societies from alien tribes. Several of the twelve societies mentioned by Maximilian may have been bought after the 1781 epidemic (one thinks in particular of the Hot Dance, the Little Dogs, and the Crow Imitators).

5.8 The Age-Groups in the Age-Society System

We are now in a position to say a little more about the three connected matters raised originally on p. 260—the length of time that an age-group owned a society, the inauguration interval, and the age-range of a group.

For the Mandan, the only useful datum on this topic is the inference from Maximilian mentioned earlier—that there were six age-groups in Mitutanka in 1833–1834. The minimum enrolment age was probably a bit under 10 (p. 259 n. 26), and the members of the oldest group were at least in their fifties (Maximilian 1841: 143 = 1843: 356). This suggests an average inauguration interval (and age range) of around 7 or 8 years; though at the same time Maximilian gives the age-range of two of the age-groups as 6 years (1841: 139 f. = 1843: 354). The fact that there are more age-societies than age-groups does not affect the average length of time that age-groups own each age-society; assuming that each group must pass through all the societies in the sequence, this remains the same as the average inauguration interval.

For the Hidatsa, the best evidence is the carefully drawn-up list of members of the group that bought its first society in 1865 (see p. 259 n. 26). According to this, the age-range of the group was 7 years.

A Hidatsa informant who told Lowie (1913: 247) that his group had
an age-range of only about 4 years must surely have been mistaken,
even though Lowie (1913: 228) considered him his best informant.
Poor Wolf, born in about 1820, was a member of a group that owned
the Half-Shaved Heads for 9 years, from about 1847 to 1856; and
from about 1848 his group also owned the Black Mouths, which they
retained for some 14 years (Lowie 1913: 273 f.)[85] These figures
suggest inauguration intervals of rather more than 7 years.

5.9 Conclusions

How different *were* the Mandan and Hidatsa age-societies from
age-grades? In terms of our age-grade definition they failed to satisfy
a single one of the constraints it embodies. And yet, in each case
there is something about the violation of the constraint that makes it
not seem too serious: it affects few people, or it does not continue
for long, or it is almost nominal (in the case of multiple ownership),
or it may well be the product of special circumstances (the Hidatsa in
Fishhook).

I think the age-societies are a good deal more remote from the
anthropologist's ordinary concept of age-grades than from the impoverished age-grades of my definition. This is because, though the
age-societies belonged to age-groups, they nevertheless in many ways
resembled the analogous societies in Plains tribes where the societies
did not belong to age-groups. Just how close the resemblances were is
a question that has not been seriously examined since Lowie's paper
of 60 years ago (1916); it certainly deserves to be looked at again,
and from a rather different point of view.

6 AGE-GROUPS AND AGE-SETS

6.1 The Age-Group as an Identity Class

I mentioned earlier (p. 277) that members of the same age-
group had important obligations to each other. Neither of the
sources that report these obligations (Bowers and Wilson) distinguishes between age-groups and age-societies; but since they do not

[85] See also Lowie (1913: 284), where there is obviously an error, since
Poor Wolf, at the age of 45, had been a Soldier for about 14 years. (Even
allowing for this, the figures given do not fit together particularly well.)

describe these obligations as being specific to any particular age-
society (or societies), it seems reasonable to assume that the obligations held between members of the age-group.

The fact that the age-divisions were identity classes emerges
with particular clarity from the existence of alternate linking.[86]
Among the Hidatsa, the members of S and S ± 2 were $maki'rak\bar{u}\ E$,
"friends," and helped each other when it came to collecting the mass
of property necessary to buy a new society (Lowie 1913: 229 f.; cf.
Bowers 1965: 210). Lowie, who devoted particular attention to
alternate linking, was perfectly conscious of the need to discover
whether it was the age-societies or the age-divisions that were thus
linked; his investigations showed beyond doubt that it was the age-
divisions that were involved, and he correctly inferred from this that
it was necessary to distinguish between the age-society and the
age-group.[87]

The same distinction is forced on us by other data that Lowie
reports. We learn that one Hidatsa age-group—and there is no reason
to think it atypical in this respect—continued to meet for feasts even
after it had sold its last age-society (Lowie 1913: 291). Furthermore,
Lowie found that among the Hidatsa

> the feeling of affiliation with one's age-mates in the buying of mem-
> bership was very strong. Even when, for some reason, a man had
> not joined in the purchase of a society, there seems to have been a
> feeling that he ought to belong to that body, though he might not
> regard himself as fully entitled to membership. Thus, though for
> some obscure reason Poor-wolf had not participated in the collec-
> tive purchase of the Stone Hammer society by his age group, he was
> nevertheless permitted to join them later, make an emblem for him-
> self, and sell it together with his coevals. However, the notion that
> membership was based on purchase was not absent even in this case,
> for Poor-wolf spoke with great reluctance about this society, because
> he felt that both his son-in-law and my interpreter, having acquired
> membership in the approved way, had a superior right to tell about
> the Stone Hammers [Lowie 1913: 232].

Finally, there is some reason to believe that the age-groups as
such had "officers" of a particular kind. Maximilian says that each

---

[86] There is no doubt about the existence of alternate linking among the
Hidatsa (cf. Section 5.3 of this chapter); two of Lowie's informants claimed that
it also existed among the Mandan, but one denied it (Lowie 1913: 294). No
other source mentions its existence among the Mandan, but even so I think the
balance of probabilities is that the Mandan system did have this feature.

[87] See above all the excellent analysis in Lowie (1916: 977f.).

Mandan age-group (for thus we must interpret him in this context) had a single leader (in addition to any officers of the age-society), and that this man was in charge when a sale or purchase was made (1841: 140 = 1843: 354 f.).[88] One of Lowie's informants told him, in an account of a particular purchase among the Hidatsa, that "Two leaders, who, however, were not regarded as officers, decided whether the membership should be sold [1913: 264]." Since there is no evidence that these men had authority in any other context, it is hard to believe that such an important decision lay solely in their hands. All the indications are that the whole age-group had to agree to a sale or purchase (cf. p. 276). In all probability these men were something more in the nature of spokesmen than leaders.

6.2 How the Age-Groups Differed from Age-Sets

The differences between the age-groups and age-sets are closely related to the differences between the age-societies and age-grades, and can be listed in much the same order.

That an age-group owned several societies at once is not a fact that would distinguish it from an age-set; nor, in principle, is the ownership of no society at all such a fact. The latter case, however, does give rise to the question of whether the age-group continued to function when it owned no society. If, at a time when age-group S owned no society, age-group S − 2 decided to buy a new society, could they turn to S for help? And if, at such a time, a member of S died, did the other members contribute to the funeral expenses? There is no direct evidence that allows us to answer these and similar questions, but it seems to me very likely that obligations of this sort did exist even when the group owned no society (cf. p. 294). If they did not, then this would be a feature distinguishing the age-groups from age-sets in a peculiar, but not very marked, fashion—not very marked, since such intervals were probably neither common nor lengthy.

The existence of out-of-age members meant that the system lacked the no-overlapping characteristic and the single-membership characteristic; but the out-of-age members are a marginal feature of the system and can certainly be looked on as the product of secondary rules.

---

[88] "Eine jede dieser Banden hat einen Anführer (Headman der Americaner), der über den Verkauf der Rechte und Attribute derselben verfügt. An diesen wendet man sich vorzüglich bei vorkommenden Gelegenheiten."

Selective elimination meant that the system lacked the no-resigning characteristic. In the unlikely event that there was also shifting (p. 282 n. 68), then the no-overlapping constraint would also be infringed. The probability is that selective elimination also affected only a limited number of men—the fact that of all our sources only Bowers mentions it is certainly significant.

All in all, it looks as if Mandan and Hidatsa age-groups were not very different from age-sets.

6.3 External and Internal Deviance

At the end of Part One of this book, the view was advanced that all eccentric systems are externally deviant. I have just suggested that the Mandan and Hidatsa systems were not, in fact, eccentric; but it is still worth asking whether they were externally or internally deviant.

With one possible exception, the deviant rules mentioned in the preceding section all refer to social identities of the age-society system and are therefore external. The exception is the rule (or rules) about selective elimination, which *may* be internal.

The Blackfoot

1 CULTURE

The Blackfoot were the largest and most powerful of the Indian tribes of the northern Plains. Since at least the late eighteenth century they have lived in the area immediately to the east of the Rockies in northern Montana and southern Alberta.[1] They were divided into three subtribes: the Piegan, the Blood, and the Northern Blackfoot, or Siksika. The subtribes shared the same language and differed from each other culturally only in minor ways; and though they had no unified leadership or other joint institutions, they seem never to have fought each other and to have possessed a sense of identity (Wissler 1911: 7).

The Blackfoot were archetypal Plains Indians, living a nomadic existence, owning many horses, and subsisting largely on buffalo.[2]

---

[1] See especially the map in Ewers (1955: 122).

[2] Unless otherwise stated, the information on social organization that follows is taken from Wissler (1911) and Ewers (1955). It is intended to describe life in the mid-nineteenth century, which I shall refer to as the *traditional* period.

Each subtribe was divided into a number of bands. Roughly speaking, a band was the group of people who traveled together and camped together. Its size was very variable, a small one consisting of less than twenty lodges (tipis), while a large one might have over a hundred. Ewers (1955: 138) considers that a mid-nineteenth century estimate of eight persons per lodge is a reasonable approximation. A Blackfoot was free to move from one band to another when he wished, but at any given point in time he would know just which one he belonged to. A wife usually moved to her husband's band on marriage, though sometimes the husband went to his wife's band. There was no rule against marriage to another member of the same band, but it was considered undesirable.[3] The members of a band "always hang together at all times," in the words of an informant (Wissler 1911: 20). The band as a whole was responsible for the behavior of its individual members; all had to contribute to the payment of penalties, and if necessary risk their lives in defense of a member who had killed someone (Wissler 1911: 20, cf. 24 f.). From time to time new bands came into being and old ones vanished, their survivors becoming members of other bands. Each band had a name given to it by the other bands, one that usually referred (often in no very flattering way) to some peculiarity of its members (Short Necks, Small Robes, Liars, Lone Eaters, etc.).

Within the band, such public authority as was exercised—and it did not amount to much—lay with a group of notables, referred to by Wissler as the *head men*. One of these, as *primus inter pares*, would be the band's spokesman where necessary and was known as its *chief*. The positions of head men and chief were not clearly defined, in the sense that there was no formal appointment to, or retirement from, these positions. There might, indeed, at times be more than one chief. The system was fluid and competitive. An individual with ambitions to be a head man "makes feasts, gives presents, buys medicines, and supports ceremonies; thus making his home the center of social and ceremonial activities, the leadership of which he assumes. His rivals are stirred to activity also and the contest goes on apace [Wissler 1911: 23]." In order to aspire to such a position a man had also to be a successful warrior.

In the winter—say November to March—the band moved scarcely at all. It settled itself in a sheltered valley where there would

---

[3] So Wissler (1911: 19). A more extensive discussion of the question by de Josselin de Jong (1912) suggests that some bands had little or no objection to endogamous marriages, while others were firmly opposed to them.

be grass for the horses, wood for the fires, and protection from the wind. Since supplies of the first two commodities in a given area were limited, the bands generally kept their distance from one another.[4] That the bands moved little if at all during the winter is no doubt to be explained by the hard conditions at that time of year. Bands did not return to the same wintering spot every year.

During the spring (roughly April and May) the band was able to move on to the plains again and to roam in pursuit of the buffalo. Toward the end of the season the women dug for edible roots.

With the advent of summer, the various bands of each subtribe began to move to a single location. Every year the Blackfoot performed a great bundle ceremony called the Sun Dance. Sun Dance bundles—for there were several of them—were distinguished from others in that they belonged to women. The Sun Dance centered around the transfer of such a bundle[5] or else around a feast to such a bundle (Wissler 1918: 233). A woman would vow to carry out the ritual in exchange for some great supernatural benefit, such as the recovery of a sick person in her family. At the beginning of the summer, news of this vow would be passed on to the various bands, and over a period of weeks they would congregate around the band of the woman who had made the vow.[6] When the bands camped together they organized themselves in a circle—the *camp circle*, as it is known—in which each one had a (fairly) fixed place. "Once formed, the circle was not broken until after the sun dance, a period estimated at from two to four months. The whole body may move about and even make a long journeys [Wissler 1918: 268]" (cf. Ewers 1955: 128). While camped together in this way, the subtribe first carried out a joint buffalo hunt, partly in order to obtain the large supply of buffalo tongues needed for the Sun Dance, and then the ceremony itself, which lasted some 10 days and provided an opportunity for the young men to torture themselves in order to acquire power from the sun. "There was a feeling that an annual sun

[4] The bands wintered separately, according to Ewers (1955: 124; 1958: 88) and Wissler (1911: 20). However, Wissler says that "In winter, the tribes scattered out, normally two to five bands in a camp, often many miles apart [1918: 268]." Curtis probably gives the correct account when he says that "occasionally two or three gentes [i.e., bands] camped together" in the winter (1911: 29).

[5] Although a Sun Dance bundle could evidently also be transferred without the accompaniment of the Sun Dance (Wissler 1912: 219).

[6] The sources do not consider the question of what happened when more than one woman vowed the Sun Dance.

dance was, from a religious and ethical point of view, necessary to the general welfare [Wissler 1918: 232]."

After the ceremony, usually toward the end of August, the bands split up once again and engaged in intensive buffalo hunting and berry picking in order to lay up supplies for the winter.

The summer months (say June to August) were thus the only time when all the bands of a subtribe would be in a single place.[7] The number of people present when they had all gathered was substantial: anything from a hundred to up to four hundred or more lodges (e.g., Spry 1968: 410), and so perhaps several thousand souls. A subtribal council maintained order and directed the activities of this multitude. It contained at least one representative of each band, and also, as will appear, representatives of the age-societies. The subtribe had a chief, who was at the same time a band chief. His "main function was to call councils, he having some discretion as to who should be invited. . . . Everything of importance was settled in council [which] was rarely convened except in summer [Wissler 1911: 25]." The chief was elected in an informal fashion. His period of office had no fixed duration but would come to an end as a result of death, old age, or impoverishment—for a Blackfoot chief had to be wealthy and generous (Curtis 1911: 15).

Blackfoot political life, and indeed Blackfoot life in general, had an atmosphere of internal violence quite alien to the Mandan, and fairly alien to the Hidatsa (Goldfrank 1945: 8 ff.). Maximilian remarks that the tribe were said to be more hot-tempered than other peoples (1839: 573 = 1843: 253). The murder of an overbearing chief or of a political rival was not uncommon (Wissler 1911: 23; Curtis 1911: 16). In the camp that Maximilian saw in 1832, he found that for every ten or twelve tipis there would be six or seven women whose noses had been cut off for adultery (1839: 572 = 1843: 110). This violence was greatly exacerbated by heavy drinking, which one way or another led to innumerable deaths (Ewers 1958: 258 f.). The Mandan and Hidatsa, in contrast, had no serious problems in dealing with alcohol.

There is some question as to why it was that the Blackfoot (and other tribes) congregated in the summer as they did. Oliver (1962) has argued that the Indians' movements mirrored those of the buffalo: they, too, seem to have dispersed into bands in the winter and

___

[7] "On occasions when the three [sub-]tribes came together, they usually camped separately, each forming its own circle, and the [age-]societies of the three did not join in their dances and feasts [Curtis 1911: 29]."

concentrated in much larger groupings in the summer. Oliver suggests that these huge summer herds were most efficiently slaughtered by a larger group of hunters than a single band could provide. This attractive hypothesis still needs further investigation, however, and other possibilities—for instance, that defensive factors were significant (cf. Thompson 1962: 252)—need to be critically examined.

The structure of religious ideas among the Blackfoot was fundamentally much the same as among the Mandan and Hidatsa,[8] and it will suffice here if we merely indicate the main differences between the systems.[9]

In describing the Mandan and Hidatsa, we mentioned the distinction between the tribal bundles, whose origins went back to mythical antiquity and which were handed on from generation to generation, and the personal bundles, which were generally not handed on at all. A further distinction between these types of bundle is that the rites relating to the personal bundle are performed by its owner alone, and purely for his benefit, while the rites relating to tribal bundles involve other bundle owners and are often of benefit to the whole community.

To judge from Bowers's account, this distinction is a fairly sharp one among the Mandan and Hidatsa. It can evidently also be applied to the Blackfoot, though with some modifications and possibly allowing for a larger number of bundles that do not clearly fall into one category or the other. At any rate, the accounts collected by Wissler (and Duvall) of the origins of various bundles fall into two distinct groups: those that are retailed in the first person (Wissler 1912: 72 ff.), in which the owner of the bundle explains how he had a dream or vision in which he was given power, and those that are in the third person, where the owner makes no claim to have been given the bundle in person (Wissler and Duvall 1908: 74 ff.). To be sure, the fact that an origin story is told in the first person is no guarantee that the owner did not purchase the bundle, for

[8] Wissler gives an attractive illustration of the notion that human achievements are not the product of inherent abilities. ". . . the writer once remarked that the inventor of the phonograph was a remarkable man. The immediate reply was that he was in no wise different from others but that in a dream he was told to take certain materials and place them in certain relations, with the promise of certain results. The carrying away of the voice was regarded as a great medicine power and the inventor in question as merely a lucky individual, who must have experienced great prosperity and happiness in consequence [1912: 102]."

[9] Except where otherwise stated, information on Blackfoot beliefs is based on Wissler (1912, 1918).

when such a transfer takes place, the original transfer is reproduced
as faithfully as possible. Theoretically, the recipient of a ritual is in
the precise relationship he would be if experiencing the dream himself; hence, it is impossible to tell from the form of a narrative
whether the narrator himself had the initial experience or not. He
feels justified in speaking in the first person. Thus, many of the preceding accounts [of visions in which power was given] are probably
many times removed from the initial recipient [Wissler 1912: 103].

Now, Wissler himself divides his description of Blackfoot bundles into two parts, one headed "Personal Charms and Medicines,"
dealing with what we shall call personal bundles, and the other
"Medicine Bundles," dealing with what we shall call tribal bundles.
He himself says that the only difference between the two groups is
that the tribal bundles have more elaborate rituals (1912: 107), but
the division also corresponds closely to that between bundles with
first-person origin narratives and bundles with third-person origin
narratives.[10] It seems to me therefore that we can make a distinction—though probably not a sharp one—between, on the one hand,
personal bundles, which must often have been used only by one
person, their original creator;[11] and, on the other, tribal bundles,
which were almost always purchased and which, in contrast to
personal bundles, had widely known origin myths and powers.
      Granted this general resemblance between the Blackfoot
bundles and those of the two village tribes, we can now point to a
number of contrasts. The Blackfoot bundles were not in any way
inherited, and there is no mention of any right to sell a bundle more
than once.[12] More strikingly, the mythical structure behind the
bundles is very much less developed. Both the Mandan and the
Hidatsa had elaborate myths about their tribal bundles; within each
tribe these myths were largely integrated with one another, and,
taken together, they constituted in each case a history of the tribe
right back to the creation. The Blackfoot lacked anything of the sort,
and this is no doubt to be connected with the lesser prominence of
the communal element in their tribal bundles. Only a very few of the
Blackfoot tribal bundle rituals (i.e., transfers or pledged feasts) were

      [10] The only clear exception is myth No. 21 (Wissler and Duvall 1908: 103
ff.), which refers to a personal bundle described in Wissler (1912: 95).
      [11] I do not know what happened to a Blackfoot man's personal bundles
when he died.
      [12] In spite of this there were several examples of each type of tribal bundle,
differing from each other (if at all) only in minor respects.

of benefit to someone other than the giver of the ceremony and those closest to him. Among the Mandan and Hidatsa, in contrast, there seems to have been something like an annual round of bundle ceremonies that were of significance for the whole community.[13]

The more individualistic character of Blackfoot bundles had its counterpart in the distribution of wealth. In the two village tribes, there seems not to have been much economic inequality, for there were a variety of mechanisms that ensured both that no one fell below a certain level and that anyone who accumulated a lot of property quickly dispersed it again. Men who were highly thought of were not rich (Bowers 1965: 289). Among the Blackfoot, in contrast, there were great differences of wealth, and, though a man with little property might have high standing because he had once been rich enough to own important bundles and give gifts to followers, many of the leading figures were men who owned large herds of horses (Ewers 1955: 240 ff.).

2 HISTORY

For our purposes there is no need to attempt to trace the history of the Blackfoot further back than the latter part of the eighteenth century.[14] It was about that time that they first came into direct contact with Europeans, and it was also then that what was probably a part of their age organization was first described (by David Thompson). They were already living in much the same area as they occupied in the nineteenth century, having probably moved into it recently from the northeast (Thompson 1962: 254).

Like the Mandan and Hidatsa, the Blackfoot traded first with the Canadians and then, but only much later, from 1831 onward, with the Americans. Also like the village tribes, the Blackfoot were victims of the great smallpox epidemics of 1781 and 1837, but they seem to have lost relatively fewer people and to have recovered more rapidly. They signed their first treaty with the United States as late as 1855, and even for some years thereafter they continued to see only a very few whites in their country. In 1862, however, a gold rush started, and the years 1865 to 1870 were marked by inter-

[13] See, especially, Bowers (1950: 108).
[14] The most useful works on Blackfoot history are Ewers (1958) and Lewis (1942).

mittent conflict between the Blackfoot and the settlers. This fighting was brought to a sudden and permanent end in January 1870, when the U.S. cavalry slaughtered almost two hundred members of the tribe (who actually belonged to a band friendly to the whites). That same winter (1869–1870) the Blackfoot suffered another smallpox epidemic.

Although intertribal warfare also now came to an end—the last major battle was fought in 1870—the Blackfoot continued to die in large numbers, for the years 1870 to 1874 were marked by an unrestricted and deadly trade in alcohol, the outcome of a change in the legal status of Blackfoot territory in Canada. With the formation of the Mounties in 1874, this trade was largely wiped out.

In 1877, Canada signed a treaty with the Blackfoot, as a result of which three reservations were established in Alberta, one for each subtribe. The Canadian Piegan reservation, however, included only a minority of the Piegan, the remainder of them constituting the population of the Blackfoot reservation in Montana, whose area was reduced several times after 1855 and reached its present extent in 1896. It is sometimes implied that the division between the North Piegan (in Canada) and the South Piegan (in the United States) was the result of the creation of these reservations (Wissler 1913: 370; McClintock 1937: 2), but in fact it dates back at least to the middle of the nineteenth century (Ewers 1955: 244; 1958: 212; Schultz and Donaldson 1930: 26). Presumably the northern and southern groups then, as later, had separate Sun Dance camp circles (Schultz and Donaldson 1930: 83), and there is evidence that they had separate age-society systems (McClintock 1910: 449; cf. Curtis 1911: 19, Wissler 1913: 375 n.). However, virtually nothing is known about differences (if any) between the systems, and so they will not be treated separately.

The extinction of the buffalo around 1880—described particularly well by Schultz (1962)—changed the whole economy and settlement pattern of the tribe. Yet even the preceding century had in all probability seen important changes. But nothing much can be said about them, because, though extensive source materials exist, they have not yet been properly analyzed. The only attempt to describe Blackfoot social history in these years is Lewis (1942), a stimulating work, but exceedingly speculative and thinly documented. His views on the development of the age-societies (1942: 40 ff.) are indeed so ill-founded as not to demand detailed refutation. Lewis does, however, make at least a prima facie case for the view that the tribe became substantially richer during the century or so before the end of buffalo hunting—partly as a result of the fur trade, which brought them many new goods, and partly as a result of a postulated increase in the size of their herds of horses. Such an increase in wealth must certainly have had significant consequences, among which may have been (though Lewis does not mention this) an increase in inequalities of wealth, and (as Lewis suggests) an increase in the frequency of bundle transfers.

In contrast to the villagers, the Blackfoot did not see their culture suddenly collapse at the end of the nineteenth century. There were massive changes, but there were also institutions that survived, among them the Sun Dance and, to varying degrees, the age-societies. But of course these institutions did not survive unaltered. In what follows I shall deal with the age organization as it was in the traditional period, except that in Section 6 the discussion of sources will also contain some remarks on the later fate of the age-societies in the four reservations.

3 THE AGE ORGANIZATION IN SOCIETY

The Blackfoot age-societies were in many ways similar to those of the Mandan and Hidatsa. The sketch that follows is therefore brief and concentrates mainly on pointing out differences.

The Piegan and Blood sequences consisted of nine and ten societies respectively, which is to say that they were much the same size as the Mandan and Hidatsa ones. The order in which they were acquired was firmly fixed (Wissler 1913: 368). The Northern Blackfoot probably had rather more societies, at one point perhaps as many as fourteen, and informants disagreed about their order (Wissler 1913: 368; Curtis 1928: 419). Wissler (1913: 419) believed that these differences were merely due to forgetfulness, and that, when the system was functioning, the order of societies was as firmly fixed as in the other subtribes; but he also correctly points out that among the Northern Blackfoot "there are indications of a tendency to readily incorporate new organizations into the series and to drop them again with equal readiness [1913: 420]." The sequences of the three subtribes were similar, both in composition and in order, especially as regards the more senior societies (Wissler 1913: 426). To give an example, six of the nine Piegan societies were represented in both the other sequences, and only one, the most junior, was represented in neither.

The Blackfoot age-societies only functioned in the summer,

when most or all of the subtribe was assembled in the camp circle.
This is in contrast to the village tribes, where even the most elaborate
and protracted of the age-society ceremonies, the transfer of a
society, might take place in the winter villages (Maximilian 1841:
273 ff. = 1843: 426 ff.).[15]

A Blackfoot subtribe was considerably bigger than a nineteenth-
century Mandan or Hidatsa village, and the number of men in a single
age-group correspondingly larger: the younger ones could have from
40 to 60 or even 80 members (Maximilian 1839: 578; Wissler 1913:
422; Curtis 1928: 182 f.).

In all three subtribes it was a rule that an age-society should be
sold in the fourth year after purchase. As will appear later, there are
some unanswered questions about just how this rule applied in
practice, but the evidence as to its existence is overwhelming (Curtis
1911: 19; Uhlenbeck 1912: 43; Wissler 1913: 419, 425, 428; Curtis
1928: 182, 188; Goldfrank 1945: 41; Hanks and Hanks 1950: 163).

Apparently reliable sources differ widely about the enrolment
age. Some suggest that it was around 8 or 10 (Maximilian 1839: 577
= 1843: 255; Wissler 1911: 420—"the little boys"; Uhlenbeck 1912:
44). Others indicate the late teens or early twenties (Curtis 1911: 19
n.; Wissler 1913: 390, 426 f.; Curtis 1928: 182; Ewers 1958: 104).
Curtis (1911: 19) at one point places it at about 15. These inconsistencies cannot be wholly accounted for by any simple hypotheses
concerning differences between the subtribes or changes through
time. Assuming ten societies, and 4 years spent in each, then the
members of the oldest society would, on one view, be men of about
50, on the other, men of about 60.

A major difference between the village systems and the Blackfoot ones is that among the Blackfoot there was no single society like
the Black Mouths that had a monopoly of police duties. Instead, the
subtribal chief, acting as usual in accordance with the council,
decided in the spring that one, two, or three of the societies would
act as police for that year (Curtis 1911: 17; Wissler 1913: 370). The
most senior societies would not be chosen, since their members
would be too old; nor would the most junior ones, if their members
were as young as some sources suggest (Maximilian 1839: 577 =
1843: 255).

The tasks of the Blackfoot police come under the same main
headings as those of the Black Mouths, but the job of maintaining

---

[15] However, even the villagers generally preferred to have these ceremonies
in the summer, since it "was more agreeable for feasting [Wilson n.d.: 9]."

order in the big summer camps was more demanding than that of keeping peace in the village. The Blackfoot, as we have seen, were less restrained than the villagers; the camp circle was a temporary arrangement, and thus made up of people whose links to each other were less close than those of the members of a single village. The camp circle moved from place to place, and it was on a massive scale—in the mid-nineteenth century "the Piegan in camp formed a circle fully a mile in diameter, with the lodges placed close together, many deep, and children as well as horses frequently became lost in the maze of lodges [Curtis 1911: 29]." The policeman's lot was also made unhappy by the well-developed Blackfoot sense of humor and taste for practical jokes (Grinnell 1893: 222 f.; Curtis 1911: 17; cf. Wissler and Duvall 1908: 6).

It was noted earlier (p. 269) that the Hidatsa Black Mouths met with the village council when an important decision was being discussed. Much the same thing occurred among the Blackfoot. The subtribal council included not only the chiefs but also the leaders of the age-societies (Curtis 1911: 15; Wissler 1911: 25). According to Curtis age-societies "were the dominating factor in the [sub-]tribal organization, and indeed the power of the head-chief depended largely on coöperation with them. . . . Theoretically the societies chosen to control the camp were subject to the orders of the [sub-]tribal chief, but their duties were so clearly defined that practically they were their own masters [1911: 16 f.]." A North Piegan relates that when the police society[16] decided that the time had come to move camp, they would invite the subtribal chief to their lodge, give him a feast, and get his consent (McClintock 1910: 464; cf. Wissler 1913: 418). The same informant said that the All Brave Dogs "formerly had great power, because they were composed of chiefs who had earned a reputation for bravery and everyone feared to act in opposition to them [McClintock 1910: 454]." The story is told of how, when the Piegan council debated the question of whether to make peace with the Crows, the leader of the Raven Carrier society came forward, and said that its members were against peace (Schultz 1907: 200). All this suggests that the bonds between age-mates were pretty strong, comparable to those between comembers of a band. The fact that the age-societies were of much greater political significance among the Blackfoot than among the village tribes is obviously related to their sharing the police work.

[16] He actually specifies the Braves, but I think this occurred only because they were acting as police at the time.

Those Blackfoot societies that were entrusted for the summer with police duties were then so active that they needed headquarters. These were provided by tipis pitched in the center of the camp circle (Bradley 1923: 279; cf. McClintock 1937: 19). The tipi used by each society was a double one, consisting of two normal ones attached to each other, or even a treble one (Curtis 1928: 183). Here the members could take council, eat, dance, or simply lounge about when off duty (Grinnell 1893: 224). According to Grinnell (1893: 224), not merely the police but virtually all the societies had headquarters of this sort, and their tipis constituted a small inner circle within the large camp circle (cf. Maximilian 1839: 578 = 1843: 256; Wissler 1913: 386, 418, 421; McClintock 1923: 252; Curtis 1928: 188). If, as seems to be the case, Grinnell is correct, then there must have been frequent informal gatherings in these tents. The tipis used were generally, but not invariably, those of the leaders or officers of the society (Wissler 1913: 386). It fits in with all this that the societies often competed with one another in various games and in racing on horseback and on foot (Wissler 1913: 376; Ewers 1958: 155 ff.).

Obviously, then, among the Blackfoot, as among the Mandan and Hidatsa, there were meetings at which singing and dancing took place and those at which it did not. Furthermore, for some, probably most or all, societies, one can distinguish between the full formal performance of the society's ritual, taking place out-of-doors, often in the morning, and the sociable, informal dancing in the tipis in the evening (Wissler 1913: 373, 380, 387, 389, 395, 412, 421 f.). The notion existed that some societies, at least, should perform their full ritual four times a year (Uhlenbeck 1912: 46, 50; cf. p. 264 of this volume). Like their village counterparts, the Blackfoot dancers expected to be rewarded with gifts, especially from the leading men (Wissler 1913: 387, 395; McClintock 1910: 453, 460; 1937: 23).

The rituals and internal organization of the Blackfoot age-societies were of a kind already familiar to us. Taken as wholes, however, the Blackfoot sequences give the impression of being less heterogeneous than those of the villagers. With rare exceptions[17] the societies were viewed (probably wrongly) as being autochthonous, and the sharing of police duties meant that none of them assumed a pivotal position like that of the Black Mouths among the Mandan

---

[17] The All Brave Dogs in all three subtribes (McClintock 1910: 452; Wissler 1913: 388, 420; Curtis 1928: 182 n. 1); the Soldiers and Bees among the Northern Blackfoot (Wissler 1913: 420).

and Hidatsa. Each sequence had (at least) one society that differed sharply from the rest in possessing great supernatural power (the Kit-Foxes among the Piegan, the Horns among the Blood, and perhaps both among the Northern Blackfoot). For example, members of the Piegan Kit-Fox society had methods of causing a storm to arise if they wanted (Grinnell 1893: 262), and those in the Blood Horn society could kill an enemy by witchcraft (Wissler 1913: 411, 416, 418). These societies, unlike others, maintained secrecy about their activities (Wissler 1913: 399, 411, 416).

Societies were transferred in essentially the same way as bundles (Wissler 1913: 428), and so it is worth quoting what Wissler has to say about the latter kind of transaction:

> This transfer is often spoken of as a purchase or sale, because the individual relinquishing the ritual receives property. The conception of the Indian, however, is that the owner of a ritual is given property not to compensate him for its loss, but as an expression of gratitude on the part of the one about to receive it [1912: 273].

Blackfoot society purchases differed from those of the village Indians in several ways, but above all in being more individualistic. There was no collective payment by one age-group to another, only individual payments between members of the different age-groups. (One man could sell his regalia to several if necessary; cf. Curtis 1928: 183.) Furthermore, though it was usual to buy a society together with one's age-mates, it was also possible for a man to approach a member of some society of which he was not a member, and purchase his place in that society (Wissler 1913: 374, 387 f., 395, 429). I shall call this transaction *individual replacement.* I assume, though there is no evidence to that effect in the sources, that in such cases a man would normally buy into the society immediately senior to the one to which he already belonged, and that he would then cease to be a member both of his previous society and of his previous age-group. Individual replacement apparently took place in circumstances rather like those in which a bundle feast was pledged. A man who wanted some benefit, generally recovery from illness for himself or a relative, would vow to buy into a new society (McClintock 1910: 464; Curtis 1928: 188–191). Presumably this was not a common occurrence. There is no indication of the mechanism by which it was thought that such a vow could bring supernatural aid.

Less importantly, Blackfoot transfers had the peculiarity that, in many cases at least, if group S were buying an age-society from group S + 1, then some men senior to group S + 1 would be called in to manage the ceremony, which generally lasted 4 days (Wissler 1913: 376 f., 402, 413 n., 427; Curtis 1911: 19). In one case we are told that these senior men consisted of all and only the members of S + 2 (Wissler 1913: 427). This suggests the existence of alternate linking (cf. Section 5 of this chapter).

The only instance where buyer and seller are referred to as Son and Father is in the purchase of the Blood Horn society (Wissler 1913: 413). Given the idiosyncratic nature of the Horns, it would be risky to infer that the same terms were used in all other purchases. The Blackfoot knew of something like the Mandan and Hidatsa "walking," but only, it seems, in those societies with a strong religious aura (Wissler 1913: 413 f.; Curtis 1928: 188). In the case of one of these societies (the Bulls), and also in the case of one or two that were not religious, certain of the regalia came to be treated as bundles after the extinction of the society (Wissler 1913: 403, cf. 1912: 159; 1913: 402, 404, cf. 1912: 116). All in all, the relationship between age organization and religion among the Blackfoot was very similar to what it was among the village tribes.

The same can be said of the relationship between age organization and warfare. Since raiding played such an important part in the life of Blackfoot men, there was a martial air about the societies, bravery was encouraged, and war deeds were recounted (e.g., Wissler 1913: 377, 390). But Ewers's account of Blackfoot military practice (1958: 124–144) makes no mention at all of the age-societies. They do, however, seem to have acted as units in defense. A South Piegan chief, expecting a raid on the camp's horses, issues orders. "The various bands of the All Friends society [i.e., the age-societies] were told off into four groups, and ordered to steal quietly out to the north, south, east, and west of the camp and there await the arrival of the enemy [Schultz 1907: 219]." When the fighting started, the Blackfoot "sprang forward with cries of 'Now, Crazy Dogs! Now, Raven Carriers! Take courage . . .' [Schultz 1907: 220]."

There is very little detailed information about the relationships between members of the same age-society, but indirect indications, some referred to earlier, suggest that the ties between them were strong. Wissler (1913: 428) writes of companionship as "one of the fundamental conceptions" of the age organization, and Goldfrank says that the age-societies "developed a solidarity that was in striking contrast to the general brittleness of Blood relationships [1945: 40]." "Each member of a men's society hailed his fellow-member as *taka*, a term of friendship that frequently implied a greater degree of affection and loyalty than was lavished on a close relative [Goldfrank 1945: 19]" (cf. Goldfrank 1945: 40; Wissler 1912: 16). She is able to give a concrete illustration, dating apparently from around the turn of the century, of the fact that "great efforts were made by the wealthier members to be 'brotherly' and back up the poor [Goldfrank 1945: 29]."

If the age-societies had suddenly vanished, the life of the Blackfoot during at least 8 months of the year would have been virtually unchanged. Only, perhaps, the solidarity between members of the same society would have been missed. Yet during the brief summer months the system was of great importance—in politics, defense, and policing, in formal ceremonies and informal dances, in feasts and gatherings, and in games. Even in matters of religion the age-societies were not insignificant. In fact, together with the camp circle and the Sun Dance they were the most important subtribal institutions, and without them the amount of interaction between men from different bands would have been greatly reduced.

Yet, though the societies were important, the fact that it was age-groups that owned them was not. Like the Mandan and Hidatsa societies, they were fairly "ageless." If, overnight, each had become the property of a group of men whose average age was no different from that of any other society-owning group, then certainly some adjustments would have been necessary; but life in the camp circle would have continued much as before.

4 AGE-SOCIETIES AND AGE-GRADES

4.1 Owning Several Societies or None

We have mentioned the existence of a rule that an age-group should sell its society in the fourth year after purchase. Evidently this meant in practice either after 3 years or after 4 years (Wissler 1913: 428). It did not mean that every fourth year all the groups simultaneously sold their old societies and bought new ones, with a new group being inaugurated and an old one retiring (i.e., simple level rules). Indeed, old men told one investigator that they could not recall any summer in which any two societies were sold (Curtis 1911: 19); but their memories must have been at fault.

Having said this, however, we have said almost all that the evidence allows. Much remains unclear, as Curtis (1928: 188) recognized. There is evidence that sometimes a group found itself not owning any society (Grinnell 1893: 222; Curtis 1911: 19), but nowhere is it mentioned that a group sometimes owned two societies simultaneously. Nevertheless, this must have happened and was presumably dealt with as among the Mandan and Hidatsa. On the other hand, the fact that it is not mentioned in the sources probably indicates that it did not occur on a large scale, that is, that the number of age-groups was pretty much the same as the number of age-societies.

4.2 Acquisition of New Societies

The Blackfoot took the view that the order of the societies in a sequence reflected the order in which they had been acquired by the tribe, the most senior being the first acquired (Wissler 1913: 368). There seems to be at least some truth in this, for there is evidence that the most junior Piegan society, the Pigeons, was also the most recently added (McClintock 1910: 449; Curtis 1911: 19; Wissler 1913: 375). Like most of the other societies, it is said to have been founded as a result of a dream, that is, in much the same way as a bundle. If such new societies were first taught to an age-group of youths who had not hitherto owned a society, then their addition would not have led to an age-group owning more than one society.

4.3 Out-of-Age Members

Out-of-age members were a marked characteristic of Blackfoot societies. One type has already been mentioned—the man who moves into a senior society as a result of individual replacement. If he moved into the society immediately above the one to which he already belonged, this would not entail a violation of any of the age-grade constraints. If not, he would be skipping.

In describing their age-society system as a whole, Blackfoot informants would say that each society had four members who were older than the rest and four who were younger (Wissler 1913: 390, 427, 429). This was something of a simplification, but it is near enough correct for our purposes. There is no evidence that these out-of-age members came from any particular age-groups. An age-group evidently tended to retain the same out-of-age members as it moved up through the sequence of societies (Curtis 1911: 18; Wissler 1913: 373, 427).

Various violations of the age-grade constraints occurred as a result of the out-of-age members. An instance is recorded of a youth joining, as his first society, a fairly senior one as one of its young men (Wissler 1913: 427), thus violating the first-grade constraint. He later joined the first society in the sequence together with his coevals, and so violated the sequential-assignment constraint. He was then a member of two societies at once, infringing the unique-assignment constraint. Old men members would, presumably, always entail the violation of the sequential-assignment constraint, and sometimes of the unique-assignment constraint and the last-grade constraint.

4.4 Selective Elimination

The Blackfoot system had nothing like the selective elimination noted among the Hidatsa (Chapter II, Section 5.4): "There were no important restrictions to membership, since even the purchase price was insignificant. Conversely, there are no provisions for dismissing members who fail to live up to ideals, nor were we able to find special ideals of conduct [Wissler 1913: 429]."

These remarks of Wissler's demand just a little modification. Purchase prices may have been insignificant in the traditional period, but they certainly rose later (Wissler 1913: 427). Furthermore, Hanks and Hanks say that the more senior a society, the more it cost to purchase, "so that fewer could afford to join as the series progressed [1950: 163]" (cf. Hanks and Richardson 1945: 13). In a personal communication, the authors write that "the progressive increase in price may well be a reservation phenomenon," and they point out that the cost of bundles rose considerably in the 1890s.

Wissler may be wrong in saying that ideals of conduct were absent. In the 1920s, at least, members of the Northern Blackfoot Horn society were expected to obey a number of precepts, some moral (e.g., not lying, not speaking evil of others, not striking others), some not (e.g., eating no waterfowl—under pain of a sore face—not allowing feathers to be burned in their tipis) (Curtis 1928: 191 f.). It is quite possible that the society had rules of conduct like these even in traditional times. There is nothing to show, however, that infringements could be punished by expulsion.

There are slight indications that the number of members in two of the Piegan societies, the fourth and the seventh in the sequence, was restricted (Wissler 1913: 386 ff., 395). I find it hard to believe that this was so (cf. Curtis 1928: 191 f.), but in any case the evidence is so scanty that it is not worth discussing the various possibilities.

4.5 Conclusions

The differences between the Blackfoot age-societies and age-grades are all of kinds familiar from the Mandan and Hidatsa. Only in the case of the out-of-age members do the Blackfoot societies diverge more from age-grades than do those of the Mandan and Hidatsa. In other respects they are closer, for there was no selective elimination, the number of age-groups was more in accord with the number of societies (so that owning more than one society was less common), and the sequences were firmly fixed (at least among two of the subtribes).

5 AGE-GROUPS AND AGE-SETS

Much of what was said about the Mandan and Hidatsa systems under this heading applies also to the Blackfoot. Here, also, the solidarity between members of the same age-society is, almost certainly, a solidarity between age-mates. Alternate linking is only explicitly mentioned in late sources, but it probably existed in the traditional Blackfoot system, though perhaps it was not of great importance (Goldfrank 1945: 40; Hanks and Hanks 1950: 163; Dempsey 1956: 48; cf. p. 310 of this volume).

Another indication of the existence of age-groups is the practice of retaining the same out-of-age members through the successive societies. Also significant is the way an age-group was inaugurated: "In the early summer those who were of the appropriate age met, elected a chief, and notified the Doves [the most junior age-society among the Piegan, called the Pigeons by Wissler] of their wish [Curtis 1911: 19]."

It is pretty clear that the Blackfoot age-group system was not eccentric and that it was only externally deviant.

6 SOURCES AND LATER DEVELOPMENTS

Since the time of Matthew Cocking—an employee of the Hudson's Bay Company who visited the tribe in 1772 and wrote the earliest indisputably first-hand account of it—the Blackfoot have attracted the attention of a multitude of authors, and the literature on them is far more extensive than on any of the other four Plains tribes that had age-divisions. References to Blackfoot age organization are frequent, and the list of sources that follows is not exhaustive; but nothing important has been left out.

David Thompson visited the Piegan several times from 1787 onward, and though he makes no mention of a series of age-societies, he does describe the activities of the camp police, whom he calls the Soldiers (1962: 261 f.). They were probably one of the age-societies.

Some 50 years after Thompson's first visit comes the next reference to the Blackfoot societies, in the work of Maximilian (1839: 575–579 = 1843: 254–257), who visited them in 1833 and whose data probably relate primarily to the Piegan. He was the first to make it clear that there was a sequence of dances through which a man passed as he grew older (1839: 577 = 1843: 255). The prince lists seven age-societies, but it is not excluded that there were in fact more,[18] for Maximilian's information on this topic was mostly derived at second hand from the interpreter Jacob Berger, and not—as in the case of the village tribes—from Indian informants and from observation (Maximilian 1839: 577 n.; not in English edition).

Maximilian's immediate successor in this field is much less help. He is Lieutenant James H. Bradley, who for 5 or 6 years before his death in 1877 was stationed at Fort Benton and Fort Shaw in the Blackfoot country of Montana (Bradley 1896: 140). His data were presumably gathered at first hand from the South Piegan (Bradley 1923: 279 f., 284 f.).

The year in which Bradley died was also the year in which J. W. Schultz (1859–1947), our most entertaining informant, arrived among the Blackfoot (Schultz 1962: viii).[19] Schultz wrote innumerable books and tales of his life among the Piegan, the most famous being *My Life as an Indian*. None of his works, perhaps, are entirely bereft of fictional elements, but the incidental mentions in them of

[18] Wissler (1913: 382) suggested that the society of Braves must have existed at the time of Maximilian's visit, even though he does not mention them. This may be so; but Wissler's theory, that the functions which Maximilian ascribes to the Soldiers, or Catchers, are actually those of the Braves, has nothing to recommend it: Schultz (1907: 139) confirms Maximilian's statement that the Catchers acted as police.

A minor puzzle in Maximilian's account is his mention of the dance of the "Tollkühnen" (1841: 575 = 1843: 254, dance no. 8). Perhaps it is to be identified with the "Tanz der Tapferen oder Krieger" (1841: 576 = 1843: 255, dance of the braves or warriors). If so, then we may reject Lowie's hypothesis on this subject (1916: 940).

[19] It is worth mentioning in this context that the chronological indications in Schultz (1907) (e.g., 1907: 287) are highly misleading.

Blackfoot institutions, and in particular of the age-societies, are based on a long acquaintance with the tribe and seem to be trustworthy.[20] Together with his wife, Schultz also wrote a general account of the Blackfoot, which contains some information on our subject (Schultz and Donaldson 1930: 82–94, 161–163, 171).

Although both Bradley and Schultz knew the South Piegan when they were still buffalo-hunting nomads, the subtribe's age organization was already in decline. It is probably significant that Bradley only mentions two or three societies, and Schultz (in his tales) only (I think) five. Some of the most senior societies had already long been extinct, perhaps as a result of the 1837 epidemic (cf. Curtis 1911: 27; 1928: 190). Much more important, however, were the many deaths in the years 1869–1874, which produced something like a collapse of the system (Curtis 1911: 19 ff.; 1928: 183; Ewers 1958: 160 n.). Grinnell, who visited the South Piegan several times from 1885 onwards (Schultz 1962: 83), evidently found only the Braves and the All Brave Dogs in existence (1893: 221). He nevertheless gives an account of the system as it was in traditional times, and reports some origin myths (1893: 104–112).

Beginning in 1896, the Piegan were visited by Walter McClintock, who wrote a small pamphlet on their age-societies (1937). All the original data in the pamphlet come from two sources. One is the autobiographical account of an old North Piegan, recorded in 1905 and published in a fuller version in McClintock (1910: 445–465); the other is McClintock's own observation of one of the societies (the All Brave Dogs) in action at the South Piegan Sun Dance of 1905, to be found virtually verbatim in McClintock (1923: 219–222). McClintock is the only author who describes an age-society ceremony in some detail on the basis of first-hand observation. His remarks on the place of the age-societies in the life of the tribe as a whole (1937: 11) are, unfortunately, plagiarized from Curtis (1911: 16 f.) and Wissler (1913: 370).

There is nothing in McClintock's writings to indicate that any other society than the All Brave Dogs was still active among the South Piegan, and this accords with what Curtis (1911: 22) found in

[20] So, for example, in his account of how an adulterous woman has her nose cut off, Schultz mentions the All Brave Dogs society (1907: 114); and this is precisely in accord with McClintock's information on the subject (1937: 29). (Here, and throughout, I refer to the Blackfoot age-societies by the names given to them by Wissler, irrespective of the usage of the original source. In this case, for instance, the society that Wissler calls the All Brave Dogs is called the Crazy Dogs by Schultz.)

1909. Curtis says that the society was last sold in 1877 and that the 25 old men who still had rights in it performed a dance each summer. Beyond this it evidently played no part in the life of the people. Curtis gives an extensive account of the traditional South Piegan system.

Uhlenbeck (1912: 43—50) published two South Piegan texts relating to age organization, one of them autobiographical, both dating from the early years of the century. They do not indicate which societies were active at the time. We know, however, that the All Brave Dogs did not die out, at least not permanently, for a recent work (Lancaster 1966: 6 f.) mentions the dance being performed in 1962. It does seem, though, that this was the only dance that survived into the twentieth century, and we shall see in a moment that more of the old system survived among the other subtribes.

The most important single study of Blackfoot age organization is Wissler (1913), which covers all three subtribes but concentrates on the Piegans. Origin traditions are recorded in Wissler and Duvall (1908: 105—125). Wissler seems only to have been interested in the traditional system; he has almost nothing to say about contemporaneous societies.

The Blood age-societies are first mentioned by Maclean (1895: 225), quoted in full by Wissler (1913: 395). Apart from Wissler, the next important source is Goldfrank (1945). She did not attempt to collect new data on the traditional system but gives a superficial account of the societies as they were in 1939. It seems that several of them were still being bought and sold between age-groups, or at least had been in the recent past. One of the societies, the Horns, had gained particular prominence, and enough evidence survives in other sources to show that it had been important from well back in the nineteenth century and that its existence was at no point interrupted (Grinnell 1893: 221; Maclean 1895: 365; Wissler 1913: 410 ff.; Curtis 1928: 191 f.; Long Lance 1928: 38 ff.). At some stage, however, it ceased to be related to the system of age-groups (Dempsey 1956: 47).

Dempsey, in 1953, found that there were thirteen age-groups among the Blood, each owning a single society; but of these societies only one could be identified with a traditional age-society, and even that had changed its name. The system was in decline, no transfer having been made for over a decade. A few years earlier, however, the age-groups had held almost monthly dances and had been divided into streams, each group trying to outdo the groups in the other stream in the quality of its dances. The Horns, in contrast, were still powerful in 1953. We cannot tell whether the age-groups Dempsey found were revivals or direct heirs of the traditional ones.

Apart from the autobiography recorded by McClintock and mentioned earlier, the only data that explicitly refer to the North Piegan age-societies are those in Curtis (1928: 182 f.). He writes mainly about the traditional system, but mentions that two societies (the All Brave Dogs and the Braves) were still active—no doubt merely putting on dances in the summer—when he visited (presumably 1925; cf. 1928: 192).

Curtis (1928: 188–193) also provides a good deal of information on the traditional Northern Blackfoot system, collected apparently at much the same time. He found six active societies, at least five apparently constituting a sequence owned by age-groups. The most senior of these five had been revived in about 1920 (Curtis 1928: 188). Which, if any, of them were still active in the early years of the century, when Wissler was in the field, we do not know, for all Wissler has to say of the contemporaneous situation is that "the horns still flourish among the Blood. There are many members among the North Blackfoot and the North Piegan and a few among the South Piegan, but so far as we know, the ceremonies are rarely held except on the Blood reserve. . . . It is the custom of the society to give a public ceremony at the sun dance [Wissler 1913: 410]." Curtis (1928: 191 f.) deals with the Horns at length, but separately from the other active societies, since his informants did not class it with them. He was told that it was an ancient institution among the Northern Blackfoot—a claim confirmed by Wissler's data—and that it had recently been revived at the suggestion of the Blood (cf. Hanks and Hanks 1950: 173). As among the Blood, it was a powerful religious institution.

Hanks and Hanks worked among the Northern Blackfoot in the years 1938–1941. They give a few data on the traditional system but concentrate on the contemporaneous one. They found four of the traditional societies in existence, and some vestiges of the age-group system. Two of the four were moribund, one still held an annual dance at the camp circle, and the last, the Horns, continued to be powerful—"its strength is regarded as comparable to that of the Christian churches [Hanks and Hanks 1950: 173]."

IV

The Gros Ventres

1 INTRODUCTION

The Gros Ventres were a small tribe—about the size of a
Blackfoot subtribe—who lived directly to the east of the Blackfoot.
In the nineteenth century their territory lay in northern Montana
and southern Saskatchewan, centering on the Milk River. Like the
Blackfoot, they are first described by Cocking, in 1772; and from
that time on, until the extinction of the buffalo and the radical
cultural changes that accompanied it, their history was closely linked
to that of their larger neighbors. This was so much so, in fact, that a
number of observers took the Gros Ventres to be one of the
Blackfoot subtribes; but their actual affiliations lie with the Arapaho,
who lived far to the south, on the headwaters of the Platte. The
language of the Gros Ventres is "intelligible to the Arapaho for at
least the greater part [Kroeber 1908: 145]," and the two tribes are
conscious of their relationship: for instance, in the late 1820s a
number of Gros Ventres bands traveled south and stayed with the
Arapaho until the early 1830s.

The social organization of the tribe did not differ in major respects from that of the Blackfoot. In the period immediately before the extinction of the buffalo, there were about twelve bands, which in the summer formed themselves into a camp circle (Flannery 1953: 25). In the winter the bands dispersed and camped in groups of two or three (1953: 28 f.). Each band had a leader, and there was a chief of the whole tribe (1953: 31—36; Curtis 1909b: 112). These men had influence rather than power.

Almost nothing is known about the internal history of the Gros Ventres. Presumably their fate in the century before 1880 was rather like that of one of the Blackfoot subtribes; certainly the outside forces that acted on them were very similar, for they lived in much the same fashion in much the same area. Since the extermination of the buffalo, the Gros Ventres have been settled on a reservation in northern Montana. They abandoned many features of their culture, and in particular their age organization, at about the time they began living on the reservation, and therefore substantially earlier than did the Blackfoot.

Many of the fundamental religious concepts of the Blackfoot reappear among the Gros Ventres, but as part of a markedly different structure.[1] In the Gros Ventre view men do possess inherent abilities and they should make use of them. A Gros Ventre could supplement his natural endowments by seeking power in much the same fashion as a Hidatsa, Mandan, or Blackfoot, notably by solitary fasting and self-torture; and power would be given to him in a vision, leading to the manufacture of a bundle, all in the familiar fashion. But—and here the contrast with the other tribes is marked indeed—power of this kind was held to shorten a person's life, and parents, far from encouraging their offspring in the power quest, actively discouraged them. As a result there were many who never sought power. Generally speaking a personal bundle could be transferred by sale or gift, but only once, that is, from the original recipient to a second party. There were one or two exceptions to this—notably doctoring power, which its possessor could always sell up to four times, whether or not he was the original recipient—but "such multiple diffusion by transfer did not, it seems, proceed far in actuality [Cooper 1957: 296]."

The relative insignificance of personal bundles was linked to two other prominent features of Gros Ventre religion: their belief in a Supreme Being, and the importance of their tribal bundles.

[1] The information on Gros Ventre religion that follows is derived from Cooper (1957).

Instead of viewing the universe as populated by a large number of independent supernatural beings, the Gros Ventres saw it as dominated by a single Supreme Being. Other supernatural beings existed, but all of them, in the last analysis, derived their power from the Supreme Being. He was omnipotent and omniscient and took an active interest in mankind. His appearance was unknown.

The Gros Ventres tribal bundles are called *pipes*, by virtue of the most important constituent in each of them. There were two main tribal bundles, about which a good deal is known, and perhaps also some minor ones, on which the available information is very deficient. The two main ones were the Flat Pipe and the Feathered Pipe. In the rituals connected with these pipes, benefits were entreated from the Supreme Being, though in the case of the Feathered Pipe a lesser supernatural, the Thunderbird, was also besought. The Flat Pipe had an annual cycle of three rituals, which were for the good of the whole tribe; a Feathered Pipe ritual was usually held each spring (Cooper 1957: 148 f.). In addition, individuals could undertake to have various kinds of pipe rituals performed for their special purposes; these rituals can be grouped under the general heading of pledged rituals. There were also rituals when these bundles were transferred, an event that was supposed to occur, in each case, at 4-year intervals (Cooper 1957: 34, 133). Although the transfer ceremony involved a number of prestations between the various participants, there is no evidence that it was looked on as a purchase. This is a point of some importance to which we shall return later.

The sources on the Gros Ventres demand little discussion. The most important of them is the excellent joint ethnography of Flannery (1953) and Cooper (1957). To supplement it there are older studies by Kroeber (1908) and Curtis (1909b). As far as I know, these are the only primary sources on Gros Ventre age-groups; nothing was written about them while they were still functioning.

2 THE AGE-SETS AND STREAMS

The Gros Ventres, like their cousins the Arapaho, had a true age-set system. The minimum enrolment age was somewhere in the mid-teens,[2] and at a given point in time there would be between a

---

[2] Flannery (1953: 37); Cooper (1957: 175, 240).

dozen and two dozen of the sets in existence (Kroeber 1908: 232). This suggests an inauguration interval of perhaps 2 to 5 years (cf. Flannery 1953: 39). According to Flannery's informants, inauguration was informal—a group of young men began to meet and came to acquire a name, e.g., Rosebuds, Many-Little-Horses, Potbellies, and the like (Flannery 1953: 232). Kroeber (1908: 232), in contrast, was apparently told that each time an age-set had performed its last age-grade dance (see later), its surviving members inaugurated a new set, and that the new one took the name of the retiring one. All sources agree that the age-set had a name that it retained throughout its existence, but Kroeber is alone, and almost certainly wrong, in implying that there was a cycle of age-set names. It is possible, however, that the young men first organized themselves informally and that the set was then later formally inaugurated by a senior set on its retirement. At the time of its inauguration, an age-set might have some thirty or forty members (Flannery 1953: 38).

A single age-set could draw its members from all the bands of the tribe, and the most prominent age-set activities, the performance of the age-grade dances, took place only in the summer, when all or most of the tribe was gathered in a single place. But age-mates did have obligations to each other which mattered all the year round. They helped and protected one another (Cooper 1957: 175); they went on war and hunting parties together (Kroeber 1908: 233; Flannery 1953: 40); and when a young man was killed by enemies, his age-mates assembled round his bier and danced, sometimes sobbing at the same time (Flannery 1953: 40). It was even said that the ties between age-mates were so intimate that their children were forbidden to marry one another (Flannery 1953: 39).

The age-sets were organized into two larger groupings called the Stars and the Wolf-men. It is not known what criteria were used in determining which of these groupings a given age-set joined, but Flannery (1953: 38 f.) has plausibly hypothesized that the groupings were streams, and it is as such that I shall refer to them here. The age-set only joined its stream some time after it had come into existence (Flannery 1953: 37 f.), and perhaps it was this event that marked its formal inauguration. Each stream had two leaders and certain other officials, a distinctive dance of a purely secular kind, and certain distinctive songs. Singing and dancing presumably took place from time to time when the whole tribe was gathered together in the summer. The members of different streams would also compete with one another in horse-racing, gambling, and boasting contests (Flannery 1953: 42).

There is a curious parallel between the nature of the age-groups in the Indian tribes we have considered, and their religious organization. At one extreme lie the Blackfoot, among whom individual bundles were more important than they were in any of the other four tribes, and whose age-groups were distinguished from age-sets, among other things, by individual replacement. At the other extreme lie the Gros Ventres, among whom individual bundles were of little significance compared with tribal ones, and whose age-groups were true age-sets, possessing a clear corporate nature. In the middle lie the Mandan and Hidatsa, both in respect of their bundles and of their age-groups. The Arapaho are close to the Gros Ventres, though the corporate nature of their age-sets was slightly less marked (they were not named, for instance).

3 THE AGE-GRADE DANCES

The Gros Ventres did not have age-societies like those of the Blackfoot, Mandan, and Hidatsa. Instead they had a sequence of six dances—I shall call them the *age-grade dances*—which were performed in turn by each age-set. These dances, together with two others, were known to the Gros Ventres as the *benaanwu*, a term meaning "all the lodges," or "sacred lodges," or "sacred dances" (Kroeber 1908: 229; Cooper 1957: 173). The lodges referred to are the special structures erected on the occasion of each dance. I shall follow Cooper in referring to the *benaanwu* as the Sacred Dances.

The six dances that constituted—by our definition, though not perhaps in terms of the usual concept—an age-grade sequence were as follows:

    I.   The Fly Dance
   II.   The Crazy Dance
  III.   The Kit-Fox Dance
  IV.   The Dog Dance
   V.   The Drum Dance
 VI.   The Law Enforcers' Dance

It is very likely that this order was firmly fixed, though the data on the system were collected so long after it had ceased to exist that informants were not always quite certain about this point. One particular source of confusion was that while most of the age-grade dances were last performed around 1870 or 1880, the Drum Dance became extinct something like half a century earlier.

The two other ceremonies grouped by the Gros Ventres under the same concept of the Sacred Dances were the Sacrifice Dance and the Old Women's Dance. The age-sets were only marginally involved in the first of these ceremonies, and not at all in the second, but both shared a number of features with the six age-grade dances. Apart from the pipe rituals, which were somewhat more important, the eight Sacred Dances were the only religious ceremonies that were of significance for the whole tribe, rather than merely for particular individuals. The existence of major religious ceremonies unrelated to bundles is something that distinguishes the Gros Ventres from the Blackfoot, Mandan, and Hidatsa, as does also the fact that the main age-group rituals were religious in nature (Curtis 1909b: 113; Cooper 1957: 173).

The Sacred Dances all took place in the summer. One or more were performed every year (Flannery 1953: 39). The whole tribe was probably always present, except in the cases of the Law Enforcers' Dance (VI) and the Old Women's Dance (Cooper 1957: 180). A performance was pledged in advance in much the same way as a bundle feast. The vow would be made by an individual who had received, or wished to receive, some benefit from the Supreme Being (though see Cooper 1957: 174, 200 f., for an exception). The Old Women's Dance was the only one that women could vow, and it could only be vowed by women; a man, therefore, could vow either the Sacrifice Dance or one of the age-grade dances. The Sacrifice Dance was the most solemn of all the Sacred Dances, and inferior in dignity only to the Flat Pipe and Feathered Pipe rituals. It also appears to have been the most demanding for the pledger, for though he did not undergo the self-torture that was characteristic of the ceremony, he had to give away a great deal of property (Cooper 1957: 194). The Sacrifice Dance could be vowed only once in a lifetime, and a man would make the pledge only under dire circum-stances. Otherwise, if he wanted to pledge a ceremony in order to gain supernatural benefits, he would select a tribal bundle rite or an age-grade dance.

If he selected an age-grade dance, then he committed his age-set to organizing and performing the ceremony. Presumably there had to be some consultation with age-mates, and with others in the tribe, before the pledge was made. An age-set could perform the same dance more than once,[3] so a man could choose either to repeat the

[3] "The Gros Ventre companies [i.e. age-sets] could and did repeat the ceremonies, especially the earlier ones, but do not seem to have done so more than once or twice [Kroeber 1908: 232]." (So also Curtis 1909b: 113; cf. Kroeber 1904: 155; Cooper 1957: 205.)

last dance his age-set had performed, or else perform the next one in the sequence. The choice was to all appearances made in such a fashion as to ensure that the integration constraint was not violated and that the set did not pass too quickly through the sequence. Though there was little in the dances that obviously limited them to performers of a certain age, the Gros Ventres evidently had feelings about the right age at which to perform each dance (cf. Curtis 1909b: 113; Cooper 1957: 205, 236).

The dances in the sequence—which are described in considerable detail in the literature—had a lot in common with one another, and in this they correspond more closely to the usual notion of an age-grade system than do the Mandan and Hidatsa age-societies. Each ceremony lasted for 4 days, with the possible exceptions of the first and last in the sequence, which may have taken only a single day each (Kroeber 1908: 239; Cooper 1957: 236, 240 f.). During this period, the pledger's age-set was under the leadership of the pledger and three, or more probably four, advisers, known as "elder brothers" and drawn from the next senior set in the same stream, that is S + 2 (Kroeber 1908: 242, 246, in the light of which Lowie 1916: 933 is to be corrected; Flannery 1953: 38; Cooper 1957: 203).[4] This council of five, supported by the age-set, which acted as the executive of its decisions, took over all authority in the camp for the duration of the dance. Apart from this, however, the age-sets do not seem to have acted as a police force, though such a force, organized independently of the age-set system, probably did exist during the summers (Curtis 1909b: 118; contrast Flannery 1953: 45).

All in all, the age organization was an important factor in the religious life of the tribe. The significance of the age-sets in secular affairs cannot be so accurately assessed, but it was certainly far from negligible.

4 TRANSITION CEREMONIES

In his comparative study of Plains Indian age-groups, Lowie advanced the thesis that "Each and every dance of the five graded series [i.e., Blackfoot, Mandan, Hidatsa, Gros Ventres and Arapaho] was entered upon payments: each complex of prerogatives was a

[4] This kind of alternate linking also existed among the Arapaho (see Lowie 1916: 931 f.; Elkin 1940: 214, 220). (Elkin 1940: 214 is almost certainly mistaken in saying that Grandfathers came from S + 2: contrast Lowie 1916: 932.)

commodity that could be bought and sold [1916: 972, cf. 968]."
Lowie justified this proposition at length, recognizing that the Arapaho and Gros Ventres presented him with special difficulties (1916:
973 f.). He then used it as the basis of an argument that culminated
in a highly speculative theory about the origins of age-groups among
the Plains Indians (1916: 978 f.; the theory is repeated in Lowie's
later writings, e.g., 1963: 106 f.).

The origin theory itself does not merit critical attention, but it
is worth demonstrating, as will be done, that, among the Gros
Ventres, age-grade dances were *not* in fact commodities that could be
bought and sold. The same is true of the Arapaho, but their system
so much resembles that of the Gros Ventres in the relevant respects
that there is no need to lengthen the discussion by examining the
evidence relating to it.

The group whom Lowie identifies as the sellers of the age-grade
dances are the men known as Grandfathers. (I shall capitalize this
and related terms—Grandson, etc.—in a manner analogous to that
indicated on p. 272.) Each member of the age-set that was about to
perform a dance had to become the Grandson of a particular Grandfather. The man who vowed the ceremony had to have a Grandfather
to himself, while the other members of the age-set could form
themselves into groups of up to four—or in the case of the Fly Dance
even more—under a single Grandfather (Cooper 1957: 205, 240 n.
37).[5] The Grandfather had to belong to an age-set senior to that of
the Grandson, so that he would already have performed the dance;
and apparently the Grandfather's age-set had to belong to a different
stream from the Grandson's (Cooper 1957: 205). Beyond this, however, there seem to have been no restrictions on the choice of
Grandfathers,[6] so that though all the Grandsons performing a given
dance would belong to a single set, their Grandfathers would generally belong to several different ones.[7]

---

[5] In some instances there would be a main pledger and some associate
pledgers (Cooper 1957: 186). An associate also had to have a Grandfather all to
himself (Cooper 1957: 176, where Flannery's footnote is based on a misunderstanding of Cooper's usage).

[6] Even men whose set had performed their last age-grade dance could act as
Grandfathers (Flannery 1953: 39; Cooper 1957: 238). If a man's stream affiliation was at this stage still relevant to whether he could act as a Grandfather for a
given Grandson, then to that extent the age-sets continued to exist even after
they had passed through all the age-grade dances.

[7] There is no explicit statement in the sources to this effect, though it was
already presumed by Lowie (1916: 974), who had found it to be the case among

The main functions of the Grandfathers during the age-grade dances were to act as instructors to the Grandsons; to paint the bodies of the Grandsons and their wives (the Granddaughters) each day of the ceremony; and to carry out a rite, referred to by Cooper (1957: 212 ff.) as the sex-test, with the Granddaughters. These tasks seem to have been performed for all dances except the Fly Dance. The relationships between the Grandson and his wife on the one hand, and the Grandfather and his wife (the Grandmother) on the other, that were established by the ceremony were permanent ones, differing from those between grandparents and grandchildren, and of considerable importance. Their main characteristic was that Grandparents could not refuse the requests of Grandchildren, and vice-versa (Cooper 1957: 177 ff.). A man might presumably have several Grandfathers, since there is nothing to indicate that he chose the same Grandfather for successive dances of the sequence.

I turn now to the arguments against Lowie's thesis that the Grandsons purchased the dances—or more precisely, the right to perform them—from the Grandfathers. Although in the passage quoted at the beginning of this section Lowie does make this claim, when it comes to justifying it in detail he says that among the Arapaho and Gros Ventre "What a group acquires by purchase here is not an exclusive possession but a quantity of ceremonial knowledge which they share with all their predecessors [Lowie 1916: 973]." When Lowie says that "exclusive possession" was not purchased, he has it in mind that among both the Arapaho and the Gros Ventres more than one age-set might have the right to perform a given dance. In neither case are the facts entirely clear, but since, as we have seen, a Gros Ventre age-set could perform the same dance more than once, it is highly probable that set S would be allowed to perform a dance for a second time even though it had already been performed once by S − 1. Lowie recognized that the system was in this respect quite different from the Blackfoot, Mandan, and Hidatsa ones. He therefore advanced the view that what the age-set paid for was not the (exclusive) right to perform the dance, but the knowledge necessary in order to perform it. The distinction is a perfectly acceptable one,

---

the Arapaho (1916: 932). Lowie's view can be supported by pointing to the close resemblance between the Arapaho and Gros Ventre systems. Furthermore, there are explicit statements to the effect both that old retired men could act as Grandfathers (see preceding note), and that "The 'grandfathers' would usually be older than the participants but not by any means necesarily very old men [Cooper 1957: 176]."

but even in this refined form Lowie's thesis is false. Among the points to be made against it are the following:

(i) There is nothing in the sources to indicate that either the Gros Ventres or their ethnographers saw the right to perform the age-grade dances or the knowledge of how to perform them as purchasable commodities, let alone that the Grandsons were buying them from the Grandfathers. Compare what was said earlier (p. 321) about the tribal bundles, and contrast the case of the Mandan and Hidatsa, where the relevant notions already appear in Maximilian's account.

(ii) While it is true that the Grandsons made prestations to the Grandfathers, the Grandfathers appear at the same time to have made prestations of equal value to the Grandsons (Cooper 1957: 211 f.; Kroeber 1908: 243, 248). This is in complete contrast to the situation among the Blackfoot, Mandan, and Hidatsa, where goods and food flowed almost exclusively towards the sellers. Furthermore, the prestations between Grandfathers and Grandsons were by no means the only ones that occurred in the course of the age-grade dances.

(iii) Though the sources do not explicitly say so, there can be no doubt that when an age-group performed a given dance more than once, the same prestations were made at later performances as at the first one. One informant suggested suggested that the same Grandfather was retained by an individual for all performances of a given dance (Cooper 1957: 205).

(iv) Just as, in all probability, a Gros Ventre age-set did not gain exclusive rights to a dance by virtue of payments to the Grandfathers, so also there is no evidence that a Grandfather surrendered the right to act in the same role when some later age-set came to perform the same dance. Lowie himself recognized that his inability to demonstrate this latter point weakened his case (1916: 973 f.).

V

Conclusion

It has hitherto been the practice of scholars to treat the age-group systems of the Plains Indians as if they were in all essentials the same as one another. Even Lowie does this, at least at times (e.g., 1963: 106 f.). Yet, as we have seen, there are deep differences. The major division is between the Mandan, Hidatsa, and Blackfoot on one side, and the Gros Ventre and (probably) the Arapaho on the other. The Mandan and Hidatsa systems are indeed very similar to each other in all respects, and they resemble the Blackfoot system in their relationship to the age-set and age-grade constraints. But the place of the age-societies in Blackfoot life was different from their place in the life of the villagers, as one might expect given the contrast between nomads and cultivators.

The preceding chapters have also shown that by using the age-set model and the age-grade definition it is possible to bring the notoriously intractable age organizations of the Plains into the same framework of concepts as we used for analyzing such apparently remote phenomena as, for instance, the Karimojong generation-groups. Investigators have long felt that these things are somehow related, but I think that hitherto little progress had been made in clarifying the nature of the relationship. Needless to say, much still remains to be done.

APPENDICES

Appendix 1
Albania

I give here a full translation of von Hahn's data on what appears to be an age-set system in the city of Elbasan in central Albania (von Hahn 1854: 168). In a footnote to this passage, the author writes

> These interesting data were supplied by my Geg[1] teacher. Unfortunately I neglected to check and complete them on the spot. This task therefore remains for my successors.

I do not know of any other sources that mention age-groups in Albania, though they may exist, since my survey of the literature was superficial and was hampered by my ignorance of Albanian.

In this passage von Hahn gave several native terms, transcribing them in a modified version of the Greek alphabet. In the translation that follows these terms have been transliterated by S. E. Mann, who also supplied those footnotes followed by the initials SEM.

---

[1] Geg is one of the two main dialects of Albanian.

The Agelai[2] of Elbasan

As in all localities of any size, so also in Elbasan every youth belongs to a group of coevals that presents a united front to the world and protects its members against the insults of outsiders.

It appears to us a most curious fact, however, that in Elbasan these associations continue to exist after their members are no longer youths; they then provide the nucleus of a type of group that seems to be without parallel elsewhere.

These associations (*hosak-u[3]* or *taifë[4]*) have on average 25 to 30 members of the same age and following the same occupation, be it as merchants, artisans, retainers, or whatever. They are usually formed when the members (*shokë-t*, i.e., *socii[5]*) enter adolescence. From the beginning they have a definite organization, each member contributing an identical, fixed sum to their treasury, which is entrusted to an elected president. He invests the money where it will bring in interest, renders an annual account, and spends the interest on two or three annual feasts, which normally take place in the open air. Every association has two members who act as servants—a cook and a waiter; they are persons who are too poor to pay their contribution in cash, and who therefore donate their services instead.

Each association has certain statutes, and if someone breaks them, he is fined. The fines (*tafmet*)[6] consist generally of a couple of *okas[7]* of brandy; the person penalized must present this to the association, and if he stubbornly refuses he is expelled.

The bond of association is very strong; the members are firmly united, and consider themselves obligated to mutual help and defense in every area of life.

It often happens that a number of associations visit the same place, for instance a church that is celebrating the name-day of its patron saint; under these circumstances the associations always keep apart from one another, though in the case of two associations that

[2] The Greek term *agelai*, which von Hahn uses here, refers to associations of young men found in Sparta and Crete. It is not impossible that at least in Crete these groups were in fact age-sets (cf. Szanto 1893), but such a view does not seem to be generally accepted (cf. Busolt 1926: 752). For further references, see Meister (1963).

[3] Untraceable: almost certainly misspelt or misheard for something else [SEM].

[4] *Tayfa* (Turkish spelling) or *tajfë* (Albanian spelling if it existed) is a "company," "group," or "club" [SEM].

[5] *Shokë-t* is simply an Albanian plural word of Latin derivation meaning "friend," "companion." The hyphenated fragment is the definite article [SEM].

[6] *Tafmét* might be a local pronunciation of *tahmét*, but again the word is untraceable. The context seems to require "forfeit" or something similar [SEM].

[7] The word *okë* (Albanian spelling) or *oka* (Turkish spelling) is common Balkan for 1¼ kilograms. As it is also a capacity measure its equivalent must vary according to the substance measured, and for brandy (*raki*) this could be over 3 pints [SEM].

are on friendly terms, each sends two or three representatives to the other.

Relations between associations are not, however, always friendly; jealousy provides ample material for quarrels, and these can lead to violence, especially when one association brings with it a youth to which another one considers itself to have a claim.

These associations are usually of long duration; it is said to be not at all uncommon for them to dissolve only when their members reach their fiftieth year. When they are dissolved, each member has his original contribution returned to him.

Appendix 2
Jahrgängervereine

The most accessible reference on the *Jahrgängervereine* is Trümpy (1965), an excellent account of the origins and spread of this institution. Trümpy uses a wide range of sources, including archival materials, provincial newspapers, pamphlets, and personal communications. It was not, however, part of his purpose to describe the functioning of the *Jahrgängervereine*, and one can only hope that someone will turn their attention to the subject soon, while the written material can still be supplemented by information from those who belonged to these groups.

Trümpy gives a survey of the very few secondary sources on the *Jahrgängervereine*, one of the most interesting of which is evidently Berlepsch (1864). (A second edition appeared in 1875. I have not seen a copy, but it does not appear to contain additional material on this subject.) Berlepsch says nothing about the history of the institution, but he gives a useful description of its functioning. Since his book is not widely available, I give here a full translation of his data on *Jahrgängervereine* (Berlepsch 1864: 598 f.). The notes are my own. Berlepsch gives as references Appenzeller (n.d.), and Scheitlin

(1829). Trümpy (1965: 437 n. 3) considers that Berlepsch's data on Zürich were probably based on first-hand knowledge.

The *Jahgängervereine*[1] are a completely original type of association, which exists to date only in Zürich, Winterthur, and St. Gallen.[2] They consist of men who were all born in the same year,[3] and who therefore grew up at the same time, went to school together, entered the army as a group, and are thus united by the bond of common memories. All the barriers that later years erect between youthful friends and playmates, through class, rank, and family connections are pretty well absent. Every "gentleman" sees every other as his "brother age-mate" (*"Bruder Jahrgang"*),[4] whether he be a day laborer or a senior civil servant, whether an artisan, a merchant, an artist, or a scholar. Because of this, such groups can no doubt only exist where there are no strong preexisting class distinctions.[5] The *Jahrgängerverein* is formed when its members reach their twenty-fifth year.[6] They generally meet three or four times a year, particularly in May, in order to go on an outing. At every meeting the members make contributions, which are then invested

---

[1] The term means "association of those born in the same year(s)."

[2] Trümpy shows that even at the time Berlepsch was writing, the *Jahrgängervereine* were more widely distributed than Berlepsch here suggests. Later they spread further still. They appear to have originated in St. Gallen in the early eighteenth century, and to have developed strongly in the nineteenth century. In Switzerland in recent times they are (or were) especially common in Vaud, Valais, and the Bernese Jura, and they are found sporadically in some other areas (Trümpy 1965: 440). They spread to neighboring parts of Austria and Germany, and since 1866 have existed in Sweden, where in 1953 they had 16,000 members (Trümpy 1965: 440 n. 21).

[3] This appears normally to have been the case, but there were exceptions: Trümpy (1965: 439) notes an association in Wädenswil consisting of those born in 1815, 1816, and 1817, and he implies (1965: 440 n. 18) that there was also a group in Zug consisting of those born in 1874, 1875, and 1876. On the same page, Trümpy remarks that, in smaller localities, those born in two or more successive years generally formed a single group, in order that the association should have a reasonable number of members.

[4] Age-mates usually used the term "brother." Trümpy (1965: 443, 446) considers that this usage was taken over from the Freemasons.

[5] The fact that the *Jahrgängervereine* cut across class barriers was noted more than once (Trümpy 1965: 446 n. 53). Scheitlin (1829: 4, quoted in Trümpy 1965: 445 n. 51) mentions the "Mischmasch der Stände und Personen."

[6] This rule was by no means universal. For instance, Scheitlin states that "Normally the age-mates meet for the first time in their thirtieth year [1829: 5]." Trümpy writes that "The older documents permit the conclusion that the original reason for the foundation of *Jahrgängervereine* was the desire to celebrate together the completion of their fiftieth year [1965: 448]." He is referring here, apparently, to early nineteenth-century documents from St. Gallen

where they will collect interest. Anybody who inherits a large estate, makes a wealthy marriage, or is in any other way especially favored by fortune during the period in which he belongs to a *Jahrgänger-verein* makes a special contribution. Every 5 or 10 years—that is, when the group celebrate their thirtieth and their thirty-fifth year and so on—they dip into their funds and arrange a larger excursion; and when the members reach their fiftieth year, certain associations break into their cash-box and make a major pleasure trip *in corpore*. Aside from this, members give help—both in word and deed—to fellow members who are in need or in trouble. When an age-mate dies, all the others attend their deceased brother's funeral.

(Trümpy 1965: 443 f.), which show the following pattern (the first date in each pair is the year of birth, the second the year when the group first met):

$$
\begin{array}{ccc}
1764 & - & 1803 \\
1772 & - & 1810 \\
1774 & - & 1808 \\
1779 & - & 1809 \\
\end{array}
$$

From these and other, less definite, data Trümpy infers that there was a tendency to form the *Jahrgängervereine* increasingly early in life. There is another source, however, which suggests that the emphasis on old age continued into modern times. Elisabeth Liebl, who was not specifically investigating this subject, writes as follows:

> Certain informants . . . mentioned collective celebrations by persons born in the same year. This was done especially at ten-yearly intervals—so, for instance, the fiftieth, sixtieth, and seventieth year, that is to say, above all the later age-grades. Certain accounts show that it was usual to eat together and make excursions [Geiger and Weiss n.d.: 403].

Appendix 3
Central Asia

The first of the passages that follow is a translation of Snesarev (1963: 158 f.), and the second of Snesarev (1960: 140).

The Khorezmian men's association—*ziyafat*—was above all an association of ceovals . . . united from childhood by the common interests of those of the same age. It is in Khorezm that the age principle of such organizations can most clearly be observed. . . . They met during the three summer months, usually once a week. . . . The membership of each group in Khorezm remained the same throughout the season; moreover, because of the strict observance of the age principle in the selection of members, in Khorezm the same membership was retained from year to year, and often coevals who as young men [had been united] in youthful *ziyafats* were also members of the same *ziyafat* in old age, when they were respected elders.

It is noteworthy that these associations were formed strictly on the basis of age; the age of the members of these groups in different places varied only insignificantly. Thus, in the Turtkul region there were four groups . . . :

1. From 17 to 20 years old
2. From 20 to 25–30 years old

3. From 30 to 45 years old
4. From 40 to 50 years old.[1]

Old men of 60 and over did not meet in *ziyafats* in this locality. A more minute system of divisions existed in the Kipchak region:

1. From 10 to 15 years old
2. From 15 to 20 years old
3. From 20 to 30 years old
4. From 30 to 40 years old
5. From 40 to 60 years old.

There were also five age divisions of the members of *ziyafats* in the Khankin region.

[1] This seems to be a misprint for "from 45 to 60 years old."

Appendix 4
The Age-Range of Generations
in Strict UPL Systems

On p. 93 it was mentioned that in strict UPL systems there would, roughly speaking, be a tendency for the age-range of generations to get smaller as i grows larger. I consider here why this should be so.

Let us imagine a strict UPL system in which sons join $F - i$ and in which v_S is the same for all S. We define g_{S-i} as the length of time between the inauguration of S and the inauguration of $S - i$. Given that v_S is constant, $g_S = iv_S$ for all S.

Let us also assume that $v_S = c_S$ for all S, bearing in mind that c_S is the maximum possible age-range of each generation.

If all strict UPL systems had all these characteristics and if g_S were a constant over all systems, then i and the maximum possible age-range of each generation would be inversely proportional.

In fact, however, i and the maximum possible age-range of each generation are not inversely proportional in strict UPL systems. We only made them so by allowing ourselves three assumptions in addition to those embodied in the definition of a strict UPL system.

Let us compare these additional assumptions with what we know about real (i.e., nonstrict) UPL systems.

(i)   There are real UPL systems in which v_S is not the same for all S, and in which, therefore, it is not true that $g_S = iv_S$ for all S. On the other hand, the assumption that v_S is the same for all S in a given system is not notably unrealistic. Among real UPL systems, the only ones in which v_S is not (according to the rules) the same for all S are the g-group systems, and even in these it is likely that v_S does not vary greatly.

(ii)   There are real UPL systems in which v_S does not have the same value as c_S for all S. But here again, the two tend to be close to each other, and of course they average out as the same in the end (see Part One, Chapter I, Section 1.2.5).

(iii)   The most unrealistic additional assumption is that g_S is the same for all systems. In fact it varies considerably in real UPL systems. Among Gada systems for which there is fairly reliable evidence, its value ranges from 20 years (Darassa) to 40 years (standard Galla systems). In some g-group systems, at least, its value seems to be even higher (see Part One, Chapter I, Section 2.5). None of these, of course, is a strict UPL system, but such values are not inconsistent with strict UPL systems. In principle, after all, the value of g_S in a strict UPL system could lie anywhere between, roughly speaking, the age of puberty and the maximum life span (M).

For these reasons, i and the maximum possible age-range of generations are not, in fact, inversely proportional in strict UPL systems. On the other hand, as the examples on p. 93 show, among known UPL systems there is a tendency for v_S to shrink as i grows: as far as I know it is not possible to find two well-attested systems such that both i and v_S are greater in one than in the other. This tendency exists because the three additional assumptions, though not exactly correct, do offer rough approximations.

Appendix 5
The Hidatsa

The following is a passage from Maximilian (1841: 217–219), which was mostly left out of the English translation (it belongs in 1843: 397). The names now used for the age-societies have been added in square brackets where they differ from the ones that Maximilian uses.

Like the Mandans, the Mönnitarris [Hidatsa] have their bands or associations, which are distinguished by songs, dances, and certain insignia.

1. The stone band [Stone Hammers], *la bande de la petite roche*, Wiwa-Óhpage (pronounced shortly and together, *g* guttural, *e* full). It consists of youths of 10 to 11, who wear feathers on their heads.
2. The band of big sabres [Lumpwoods], *la bande des grands sabres*, Wirrachischi (*r* pronounced with tip of tongue, *ch* guttural, the whole shortly and together). They are 14 to 15 years old, and when dancing carry sabres in their hands.[1]

[1] Since sabres are rarely found among the Indians, and can only be obtained from traders, it seems that this band must be of recent origin [Maximilian's note].

3. The raven band [Crow imitators], *la bande des corbeaux*, Haiderohka-Ächke (*ch* guttural, *e* in the second word half). Young people of 17 to 18 years old.

4. The band of little prairie-foxes [Kit-Foxes], *la bande des petits renards de prairie*, Ėhchoch-Kaïchke (*ch* guttural, final *e* half). When they parade they wear otter and wolf pelts.

5. The band of little dogs, *la bande des petits chiens*, Waskúkka-Karischta. They wear feathers on their heads, and red or blue cloth sashes hanging diagonally across their shoulders.

6. The band of old dogs, *la bande des vieux chiens*, Washúkke-Ächke (*äch* guttural).[2] They wear feathers on their heads, the above-mentioned sashes over their shoulders, and a wolf pelt round the waist. They carry a Schischikué [rattle], which consists of a short stick with buffalo calf hooves suspended from it. Round their necks hangs a war whistle, Ih-Akohschi (pronounced shortly).

7. The band of bow lances [Half-shaved Heads], Sohta-Girakschohge (*gi* guttural, *e* full) or Súhta-Wirakschohke (*e* full). They wear feathers on their heads, and carry bow-lances, Bidúcha-Háski (*ch* guttural). This is the same band as the one that the Mandans call Ischohá-Kakoschóchatä [Half-Shaved Heads].

8. The band of enemies [Black Mouths], *la bande des ennemis*, Máh-Ihah-Ächke (*äch* German, *e* half, the whole pronounced shortly). They carry guns and are the same as band whom the Mandans call Kaúa-Karakáchka, the so-called soldiers.

9. The band of bulls, *la bande des boeufs*, Kädap-Ächke (*dap* unclear, *äch* as in German, *ke* half). They wear the pelt of the head of a buffalo, together with its horns, and cloth sashes round the waist with little bells attached to them and to their legs. As weapons they carry lances, guns, and shields (*pare-flèche*).

10. The raven band, *la bande des corbeaux*, Pehrishkäike (*käi* together, *e* half). They are the oldest men. Each of them carries a long lance covered with red cloth, called Biddá-Parachpa (*ach* guttural)[3] from which raven feathers hang down. They have finely decorated clothing, feathers

[2] There seems to be two errors in Maximilian's text at this point. First, according to Bowers (1965: 197) the term Waschúkke-Ächke means Dog Society, not Old Dog Society (these were two distinct societies, cf. the list on p. 257 of this volume). Second, both the Dogs and the Old Dogs were, according to Bowers, senior to the Black Mouths.

[3] The Mandans call them Kähka-Pánpi (*anpi* as in French) [Maximilian's note].

on their heads, headdresses of military eagle feathers,[4] Wah-Aschú-Lakukárahä, and even borrow fine clothes from other bands.

11. The hot water band [Hot Dance], *la bande de l'eau chaude*, Màhsawähs. This is identical with No. 1. — As among the Mandans, they dance around naked between glowing coals, and take meat out of a pot of boiling water. Their hands, part of their forearms, and their feet are painted red.

The women's associations are as follows:

1. The band of wild geese [Goose Society], *la bande des outardes*, Bihda-Ächke (*da* and second word very short). When they dance they carry wormwood (*absinthe*) and a corn cob in their arms, and a feather is fixed diagonally to the front of their heads. This band consists of the oldest women.

2. The band of enemies, *la bande des ennemis*, Máh-Ihäh-Ächke (*i* scarcely audible, *ch* always guttural). They carry long hangings of mussels and beads (*rassade*) attached, as among the men, to their temples, and a feather is fixed diagonally to the front of their heads.

3. The skunk band, *la bande de la bête puante*, Chóchkäiwi (*ch* guttural, *äi* together, *wi* very short and soft). At the back of their heads is a tuft of feathers, and their faces are painted black with a white stripe down over the nose, like a skunk.

In addition to these bands, the Mönnitarris also have a couple of independent dances.

1. Táiruchpahga (pronounced like German), the dance of the old, *la danse des vieux*. The men take part in this dance naked and completely unadorned. It is only performed by old people who have passed through everything,[5] and who no longer go to war.

2. Zúhdi-Arischi (second word very short, *r* sounds almost like *d*), the scalp dance, *la danse de la chevelure*. The women dance this, carrying the scalps on staves (see Plate 18). In their hands they hold guns, axes, clubs, staves, etc. Some men beat the drums and rattle the Schischikué. While this is going on, the men of the war party stand in a line and move their feet to the rhythm. See the description in the following chapters [1841: 302 ff. = 1843: 442 f.].

---

[4] *Hauben von Kriegsadlerfedern.* I think Maximilian means that these were eagle's feathers, which symbolized particular military achievements (cf. p. 266 n. 37 of this volume).

[5] Presumably Maximilian means Stinking Ears, men who have passed through all the age-societies (p. 258 of this volume).

Bibliography

Abou-Zeid, A. M.
    1953 A study of some age-set systems of north and east Africa. Unpublished
           B.Litt. thesis, University of Oxford.
Adamson, Joy
    1967 *The peoples of Kenya.* London: Collins and Harvill Press.
Aghassian, Michel
    1971 Bibliographie. In *Classes et associations d'âge en Afrique de l'ouest,*
           edited by D. Paulme. Paris: Plon.
Anonymous
    1962 Bij de Xavantes woeste school. *Salesiaans Nieuws,* June 1962, 21[e]
           Jaargang (No. 6): p. 43 and p. 46.
Appenzeller, J. C.
    n.d.   *Die Jahrgänger am Jubelfeste ihres fünfzigsten Altersjahres, 1825.* St.
           Gallen: Huber.
Augé, Marc
    1969 *Le rivage alladian: organisation et évolution des villages alladian.*
           Mémoires ORSTOM, 34. Paris: Office de la recherche scientifique et
           technique outre-mer.
Bahrey
    1907 *Historia gentis galla.* I. Guidi, trans. and ed. Corpus scriptorum chris-
           tianorum orientalum, ed. I.-B. Chabot et al. Scriptores Aethiopici,
           versio, series altera 3. Paris: Carolus Poussielgue.

Baker, E. C.
1927 Age-grades in Musoma District, Tanganyika Territory. *Man* 27: 221–224.
1953 Age-grades in Musoma District, Tanganyika Territory. *Man* 53: 64.
1955 *The Ba-Kuria of Musoma.* Manuscript in the National Archives, Tanzania. Microfilm in Rhodes House, Oxford (Micr. Afr. 459).
Baldé, S.
1939 Les associations d'âge chez les Foulbé du Fouta-Djallon. *Bulletin de l'Institut Français d'Afrique Noire* 1: 89–109.
Baldus, Herbert
1970 *Tapirapé, tribo tupí no Brasil Central.* São Paulo: Companhia Editora Nacional.
Banner, Horace
1952 A casa-dos-homens Górotire. *Revista do Museu Paulista,* N.S., 6: 455–459.
Barnes, John Arundel
1967 *Politics in a changing society.* Manchester: Manchester University Press.
Barton, Juxom
1923 Notes on the Kipsikis or Lumbwa tribe of Kenya Colony. *Journal of the Royal Anthropological Institute* 53: 42–78.
Bass, Althea
1966 *The Arapaho way: a memoir of an Indian boyhood.* New York: Clarkson N. Potter.
Bates, Daisy M.
1925 Organisation sociale des Birangoumat et Djouamat (Australie Occidentale). *Revue d'Ethnographie et des Traditions Populaires* 6: 27–40.
Bateson, Gregory
1932 Social structure of the Iatmül people of the Sepik River. *Oceania* 2: 245–291, 401–453.
1958 *Naven.* Stanford, California: Stanford University Press.
Baxter, Paul T. W.
1954 The social organization of the Galla of northern Kenya. Unpublished D. Phil. thesis, University of Oxford.
1965 Repetition in certain Boran ceremonies. In *African systems of thought,* edited by Meyer Fortes and G. Dieterlen. London: Oxford University Press.
Beaglehole, E. and P. Beaglehole
1938 *Ethnology of Pukapuka.* B. P. Bishop Museum Bulletin, 150. Honolulu: The Museum.
Beaton, A. C.
1936 The Bari: clan and age-class systems. *Sudan Notes and Records* 19: 109–146.
Beattie, John
1964 *Other cultures.* London: Cohen and West.
Beckwith, Martha W.
1938 *Mandan-Hidatsa myths and ceremonies.* Memoirs of the American Folk-Lore Society, 32. New York: J. J. Augustin.
Befu, Harumi
1968 Village autonomy and articulation with the state. In *Studies in the institutional history of early modern Japan,* edited by J. W. Hall and M. B. Jansen. Princeton, New Jersey: Princeton University Press.

Beidelman, Thomas O.
1960 The Baraguyu. *Tanganyika Notes and Records* 55: 245–278.
1970 [Review of Klima 1970.] *Anthropos* 65: 1055–1058.
Benson, T. G. (ed.)
1964 *Kikuyu-English dictionary.* London: Oxford University Press.
Berger, P.
1938 Die Datoga, ein ostafrikanischer Hirtenkriegerstamm. *Koloniale Rundschau* 29: 177–193.
Berlepsch, H. A.
1864 *Schweizerkunde.* Braunschweig: S. A. Schwetschke und Sohn.
Bernardi, Bernardo
1952 The age-system of the Nilo-Hamitic peoples. *Africa* 22: 316–332.
1955 The age system of the Masai. *Annali Lateranensi* 18: 257–318.
1971 Il Mugwe dei Meru (Kenya). *Africa (Rivista trimestrale di studi e documentazione dell'Istituto Italiano per l'Africa)* 26: 427–442.
Bischofberger, Otto
1972 *The generation classes of the Zanaki (Tanzania).* Studia Ethnographica Friburgensia, 1. Fribourg: The University Press.
Bohannan, Laura and Paul Bohannan
1953 *The Tiv of Central Nigeria.* Ethnographic Survey of Africa, Western Africa, 8. London: International African Institute.
Bohannan, Paul
1965 The Tiv of Nigeria. In *Peoples of Africa,* edited by J. L. Gibbs. New York: Holt, Rinehart and Winston.
Boller, Henry A.
1959 *Among the Indians.* Chicago: The Lakeside Press.
1966 The letters of Henry A. Boller: Upper Missouri fur trader, edited by R. H. Mattison. *North Dakota History* 33: 106–219.
Bouscayrol, R.
1949 Notes sur le peuple ébrié. *Bulletin de l'Institut Français d'Afrique Noire* 11: 382–408.
Bowers, Alfred W.
1948 *A history of the Mandan and Hidatsa.* Unpublished Ph.D. dissertation, University of Chicago.
1950 *Mandan social and ceremonial organization.* Chicago: University of Chicago Press.
1965 *Hidatsa social and ceremonial organization.* Bulletin of the Bureau of American Ethnology, 194. Washington, D.C.: Government Printing Office.
Bradbury, R. E.
1957 *The Benin kingdom and the Edo-speaking peoples of south-western Nigeria.* Ethnographic Survey of Africa, Western Africa, 13. London: International African Institute.
Bradley, James H.
1896 The Sioux campaign of 1876 under the command of General John Gibbon. *Montana Historical Society Contributions* 2: 140–228.
1923 Characteristics, habits, and customs of the Blackfoot. *Montana Historical Society Contributions* 9: 255–287.
Brausch, G. E. J.-B.
1951 Polyandrie et "marriage classique" chez les Bashi Lele. *Problèmes d'Afrique Centrale* 12: 86–101.

Bruner, Edward M.
1961   Mandan. In *Perspectives in American Indian culture change*, edited by
       E. H. Spicer. Chicago: University of Chicago Press.
Buchhofer, B., J. Friedrichs, and H. Lüdtke
1970   Alter, Generationsdynamik und soziale Differenzierung. Zur Revision
       des Generationsbegriffs als analytisches Konzept. *Kölner Zeitschrift für
       Soziologie und Sozialpsychologie* **22**: 300—334.
Buchler, Ira R., and Henry A. Selby
1968   *Kinship and social organization*. New York: Macmillan.
Busolt, Georg
1926   *Griechische Staatskunde*, Vol. 2. Handbuch der Altertumswissenschaft,
       4.1.1. Munich: C. H. Beck.
Cagnolo, C.
1933   *The Akikuyu: their customs, traditions and folklore*. Nyeri, Kenya:
       Mission Printing School.
Carlsson, Gosta, and Katarina Karlsson
1970   Age, cohorts and the generation of generations. *American Sociological
       Review* **35**: 710—718.
Catlin, George
1841   *The manners, customs, and conditions of the North American Indians*,
       Vol. 1. London: Published by the author.
Cecchi, A.
1886   *Da Zeila alla frontiere del Caffa*, Vol. 1. Rome: Ermanno Loescher.
Cerulli, Enrico
1922   The folk-literature of the Galla of southern Abyssinia. *Harvard African
       Studies* **3**: 9—228. Cambridge, Massachusetts: African Department of
       the Peabody Museum of Harvard University.
1929   *Etiopia occidentale*, Vol. 1. Collezione di Opere e di Monografie a cura
       del Ministero delle Colonie, 6. Rome: Sindacato Italiano Arti Grafiche.
1933   *Etiopia occidentale*, Vol. 2. Collezione di Opere e di Monografie a cura
       del Ministero delle Colonie, 16. Rome: Sindacato Italiano Arti
       Grafiche.
1938   *Studi etiopici*, Vol. 2, *La lingua e la storia dei Sidamo*. Rome: Istituto
       per l'Oriente.
1968   [Dated 1966.] Classes d'âge et rites d'initiation en Ethiopie
       méridionale. *Correspondence d'Orient, Études. Revue semestrielle.
       Centre pour l'étude des problèmes du monde musulman contemporain,
       Bruxelles.* **10**: 5—20.
Chardon, Francis A.
1932   *Chardon's journal at Fort Clark, 1834—1839*, edited by Annie H. Abel.
       Pierre, South Dakota: South Dakota State Department of History.
Charest, P.
1971   Les échelons d'âge chez les Malinké de Kédougou (Sénégal oriental). In
       Classes et associations d'âge en Afrique de l'ouest, edited by Denise
       Paulme. Paris: Plon.
Chen, Chi-lu
1965   Age organization and men's house of the Formosan aborigines. *Bulletin
       of the Department of Archaeology and Anthropology, National Taiwan
       University*, **25—26**: 93—110.
Clark, Doris
1950   Karamojong age-groups and clans. *Uganda Journal* **14**: 215—218.

Clark, William Philo
1885 *The Indian sign language.* Philadelphia: L. R. Hamersly.
Clignet, Remi
1970 *Many wives, many powers: authority and power of polygynous families.* Evanston, Illinois: Northwestern University Press.
Cooper, John M.
1957 *The Gros Ventres of Montana Part II, religion and ritual,* edited by Regina Flannery. Catholic University of America Anthropological Series, 16. Washington, D.C.: Catholic University of America.
Culbertson, Thaddeus A.
1952 *Journal of an expedition to the Mauvaises Terres and the Upper Missouri in 1850,* edited by John F. McDermott. Bulletin of the Bureau of American Ethnology, 147. Washington, D.C.: Government Printing Office.
Curtis, Edward S.
1909a *The North American Indian,* Vol. 4, *Apsaroke, Hidatsa.* Published by the author.
1909b *The North American Indian,* Vol. 5, *Mandan, Arikara, Atsina.* Published by the author.
1911 *The North American Indian,* Vol. 6, *Piegan, Cheyenne, Arapaho.* Published by the author.
1928 *The North American Indian,* Vol. 18, *Chipewyan, Cree, Sarsi.* Published by the author.
Dalby, David
1971 Distribution and nomenclature of the Manding people and their language. In *Papers on the Manding,* edited by C. T. Hodge. Indiana University Publications, African Series, 3. Bloomington, Indiana: Indiana University Press. The Hague: Mouton.
Daly, J.
1964 Boys' age groups in eastern Nigeria. *African Ecclesiastical Review* 6: 262–266.
Degri de Djagnan, R.
1967 Organisation familiale des Godie de Côte d'Ivoire. *Cahiers d'études africaines,* Vol. 7, Cahier 27, pp. 399–433.
Delord, J.
1948 L'initiation des Kondana en pays Cabrais (Togo). *Notes Africaines* 39: 27–31.
Dempsey, H. A.
1956 Social dances of the Blood Indians. *Journal of American Folklore* 69: 47–52.
Densmore, Frances
1923 *Mandan and Hidatsa music.* Bulletin of the Bureau of American Ethnology, 80. Washington, D.C.: Government Printing Office.
Dias, R. W. M.
1970a *A bibliography of jurisprudence.* London: Butterworths.
1970b *Jurisprudence.* London: Butterworths.
Dietschy, H.
1964 Altersstufen bei den Karaja'-Indianern Zentralbrasiliens. In *Beiträge zur Völkerkunde Südamerikas: Festgabe für Herbert Baldus zum 65. Geburtstag,* edited by Hans Becher. Völkerkundliche Abhandlungen des

Niedersächsischen Landesmuseums Abteilung für Völkerkunde, 1. Hannover: Komissionsverlag Münstermann-Druck.

Dobbs, C. M.
1921   The Lumbwa circumcision ages. *Journal of the East Africa and Uganda Natural History Society* 16: 55–57.

Dorjahn, Vernon R.
1959   The factor of polygyny in African demography. In *Continuity and change in African cultures*, edited by William R. Bascom and Melville J. Herskovits. Chicago: University of Chicago Press.

Dorsey, J. O.
1884   *Omaha Sociology*. Third annual report of the Bureau of Ethnology to the Smithsonian Institution, 1881–1882, pp. 211–370. Washington, D.C.: Government Printing Office.

Douglas, Mary
1963   *The Lele of the Kasai*. London: Oxford University Press.

Drabbe, P.
1940   *Het leven van den Tanémbarees*. Internationales Archiv für Ethnographie, Supplement zu Band 38. Leiden: E. J. Brill.

Dreyfus, Simone
1963   *Les Kayapo du Nord, état de Para-Brésil. Contribution à l'étude des Indiens Gé*. Le monde d'outre-mer passé et présent, I^e série, études, 24. Paris: Mouton.

Drucker, Philip
1951   *The Northern and Central Nootkan tribes*. Bulletin of the Bureau of American Ethnology, 144. Washington, D.C.: Government Printing Office.

Dundas, Charles
1915   The organization and laws of some Bantu tribes in East Africa. *Journal of the Royal Anthropological Institute* 45: 234–306.

Dupire, Marguerite
1970   *Organisation sociale des Peules: étude d'ethnographie comparée*. Paris: Plon.

Dyson-Hudson, Neville
1966   *Karimojong politics*. Oxford: Clarendon Press.

Ehrlich, Eugen
1913   *Grundlegung des Soziologie des Rechts*. Munich and Leipzig: Duncker und Humblot.
1936   *Fundamental principles of the sociology of law*. Harvard Studies in Jurisprudence, 5. Cambridge, Massachusetts: Harvard University Press.

Eisenstadt, S. N.
1954   Plains Indian age groups. *Man* 54: 6–8.
1956   *From generation to generation*. New York: The Free Press.

Elkin, Henry
1940   The Northern Arapaho of Wyoming. In *Acculturation in seven American Indian tribes*, edited by Ralph Linton. New York: D. Appleton-Century Company.

Etzioni, A.
1961   *A comparative analysis of complex organizations*. New York: The Free Press.

Evans-Pritchard, Edward E.
1940   *The Nuer*. Oxford: Clarendon Press.

Ewers, John C.
   1955   *The horse in Blackfoot Indian culture.* Bulletin of the Bureau of
          American Ethnology, 159. Washington, D.C.: Government Printing
          Office.
   1958   *The Blackfeet.* Civilization of the American Indian Series, 49. Norman,
          Oklahoma: University of Oklahoma Press.
Fajana, A.
   1968   Age-groups in Yoruba traditional society. *Nigeria Magazine* 98 (Sept.–
          Nov. 1968): 232–239.
Farina, Felice
   1965   *Nel paese dei bevitori di sangue.* Bologna: Editrice Nigrizia.
Field, Margaret Joyce
   1940   *Social organization of the Gã people.* London: The Crown Agents for
          the Colonies.
Flannery, Regina
   1953   *The Gros Ventres of Montana Part I, social life.* Catholic University of
          America Anthropological Series, 15. Washington, D.C.: Catholic Uni-
          versity of America.
Fleming, Harold Crane
   1964   Baiso and Rendille: Somali outliers. *Rassegna di Studi Etiopici* 20:
          35–96.
   1965   The age-grading cultures of East Africa: an historical inquiry. Unpub-
          lished Ph.D. dissertation, University of Pittsburgh.
Forde, Daryll
   1964   *Yakö Studies.* London: Oxford University Press.
Forde, Daryll, and G. I. Jones
   1950   *The Ibo and Ibibio-speaking peoples of south-eastern Nigeria.* Ethnog-
          raphic Survey of Africa, Western Africa, 3. London: International
          African Institute.
Fosbrooke, H. A.
   1948   An administrative survey of the Masai social system. *Tanganyika Notes
          and Records* 26: 1–50.
Fraenkel, M.
   1966   Social change on the Kru Coast of Liberia. *Africa* 36: 154–172.
Gamble, D. P.
   1955   *Economic conditions in two Mandinka villages—Kerewan and Keneba.*
          London: Research Department, Colonial Office.
Geiger, Paul, and Richard Weiss
   n. d.   *Atlas der schweizerischen Volkskunde.* Basel: Schweizerische Gesell-
          schaft für Volkskunde.
Giaccardi, A.
   1937   Le popolazioni de Borana e del Sidamo. *Rivista delle colonie,* 16:
          1549–1563.
Girard, J.
   1965   Diffusion en milieu diola de l'association du Koumpo bainouk. *Bulletin
          de l'Institut Français d'Afrique Noire, Série B, Sciences Humaines* 27:
          42–98.
Goldfrank, Esther S.
   1945   *Changing configurations in the social organization of a Blackfoot tribe
          during the reserve period (the Blood of Alberta, Canada).* Monographs
          of the American Ethnological Society, 8, New York: J. J. Augustin.

Gomila, Jacques
1971   *Les Bedik (Sénégal oriental).* Montreal: Les Presses de l'Université de Montréal.
Gomila, Jacques, and M. P. Ferry
1966   Notes sur l'ethnographie des Bedik (Sénégal oriental). *Journal de la Société des Africanistes* **36**: 208–249.
Goodenough, Ward H.
1951   *Property, kin, and community on Truk.* Yale University Publications in Anthropology, 46. New Haven, Connecticut: Yale University Press.
1956   Residence rules. *Southwestern Journal of Anthropology* **12**: 22–37.
1965   Rethinking "Status" and "role": towards a general model of the cultural organization of social relationships. In *The relevance of models for social anthropology,* edited by Michael Banton. Association of Social Anthropologists of the Commonwealth, Monographs, 1. London: Tavistock.
1970   *Description and comparison in cultural anthropology.* Chicago: Aldine.
Gray, Robert F.
1963   *The Sonjo of Tanganyika.* London: Oxford University Press.
Grinnell, George Bird
1893   *Blackfoot lodge tales.* London: David Nutt.
Guidi, Guido
1939   Nel Sidàmo orientale, i paesi del mondo. *Bolletino della Società Geografica Italiana* **76** (= Serie 7, Vol. 4): 372–384.
Gulliver, Pamela, and Paul H. Gulliver.
1953   *The central Nilo-Hamites.* Ethnographic Survey of Africa, East Central Africa, 7. London: International African Institute.
Gulliver, Paul H.
1952   The Karamajong cluster. *Africa* **22**: 1–22.
1953   The age-set organization of the Jie tribe. *Journal of the Royal Anthropological Institute* **83**: 147–168.
1958   The Turkana age organization. *American Anthropologist* **60**: 900–922.
1963   *Social control in an African society.* London: Routledge and Kegan Paul.
1965   The Jie of Uganda. In *Peoples of Africa,* edited by J. L. Gibbs. New York: Holt, Rinehart and Winston.
1966   *The family herds.* (2nd impression, with new preface and bibliography.) London: Routledge and Kegan Paul.
1968   Age Differentiation. In *International Encyclopedia of the Social Sciences,* edited by D. L. Sills, Vol. 1. New York: Macmillan and Free Press. Pp. 157–162.
Gutmann, Bruno
1926   *Das Recht der Dschagga.* Munich: C. H. Beck.
Haberland, Eike
1963   *Galla Süd-Äthiopiens.* Stuttgart: W. Kohlhammer.
Hagen, Everett E.
1961   Analytical models in the study of social systems. *American Journal of Sociology* **67**: 144–151.
1964   *On the theory of social change.* London: Tavistock.
Hahn, Johann Georg von
1854   *Albanesische Studien.* Jena: Friedrich Manke.

Hall, C. L. (ed.)
1906 Autobiography of Poor Wolf, Head Soldier of the Hidatsa or Grosventre Tribe. *Collections of the State Historical Society of North Dakota* 1: 439–443.
Hallpike, Christopher R.
1972 *The Konso of Ethiopia.* Oxford: Clarendon Press.
1976 The origins of the Borana Gada system. *Africa* 46: 48–56.
Hamer, J. H.
1970 Sidamo generational class cycles: a political gerontocracy. *Africa* 40: 50–70.
Hanks, Lucien M., and Jane Richardson Hanks
1950 *Tribe under Trust.* Toronto: University of Toronto Press.
Hanks, Lucien M., and Jane Richardson
1945 *Observations on Northern Blackfoot kinship.* Monographs of the American Ethnological Society, 9. New York: J. J. Augustin.
Harris, Rosemary
1965 *The political organization of the Mbembe, Nigeria.* Ministry of Overseas Development, Overseas Research Publications, 10. London: Her Majesty's Stationery Office.
Hart, H. L. A.
1961 *The concept of law.* Oxford: Clarendon Press.
Hartmann, Horst
1973 *Die Plains- und Prärieindianer Nordamerikas.* Veröffentlichungen des Museums für Völkerkunde Berlin, N.F. 22. Abteilung amerikanische Naturvölker, 2. Berlin: Museum für Völkerkunde.
Henry, Alexander
1897 *New light on the early history of the greater Northwest,* edited by Elliott Coues. 3 vols., consecutively paginated. London: Suckling.
Hilger, Mary Inez
1952 *Arapaho child life and its cultural background.* Bulletin of the Bureau of American Ethnology, 148. Washington, D.C.: Government Printing Office.
Ho, Ping-ti
1962 *The ladder of success in imperial China.* New York and London: Columbia University Press.
Hobley, C. W.
1938 *Bantu beliefs and magic.* London: H. F. and G. Witherby.
Hodge, Carleton T. (ed.)
1971 *Papers on the Manding.* Indiana University Publications, African Series, 3. Bloomington, Indiana: Indiana University Press. The Hague: Mouton.
Hoebel, E. Adamson
1972 *Anthropology: the study of man.* 4th ed. New York: McGraw-Hill.
Hoffmann, Hans
1971 Markov chains in Ethiopia. In *Explorations in mathematical anthropology,* edited by Paul Kay. Cambridge, Massachusetts and London: MIT Press.
Howard, James H.
1960 Butterfly's Mandan winter count: 1833–1876. *Ethnohistory* 7: 28–43.
Howell, P. P.
1941 The Shilluk settlement. *Sudan Notes and Records* 24: 47–67.

Huber, Hugo
  1973   *Marriage and the family in rural Bukwaya (Tanzania).* Studia Ethno-
         graphica Friburgensia, 2. Friboug: The University Press.
Huntingford, G. W. B.
  1951   The social institutions of the Dorobo. *Anthropos* 46: 1—48.
  1953   *The Nandi of Kenya.* London: Routledge and Kegan Paul.
  1963   The peopling of the interior of East Africa by its modern inhabitants. In
         History of East Africa, Vol. 1, edited by Roland Oliver and Gervase
         Mathew. Oxford: Clarendon Press.
  1969   *The southern Nilo-Hamites.* (Reprint, with supplementary bibliog-
         raphy.) Ethnographic Survey of Africa, East Central Africa, 8. London:
         International African Institute.
Huppertz, Josefine
  1959   Die Eigentumsrechte bei den Maasai. *Anthropos* 54: 939—969.
Imoagene, S. O.
  1969   Age group in Weppa-Wano community (Mid-western Nigeria): a cul-
         tural survival? *Ghana Journal of Sociology* 5(2): 23—29.
Ittmann, Johannes
  1955   Bemerkungen zu den Altersklassen der Duala und ihrer Nachbarn.
         Afrika and Übersee 39(2): 83—88.
Jacobs, Alan H.
  1958   Masai age-groups and some functional tasks. Paper read at the con-
         ference held at the East African Institute of Social Research, Makerere
         College, January 1958. [Mimeograph]
  1963   *The pastoral Masai of Kenya.* Mimeograph submitted to the Ministry of
         Overseas Development, London.
  1965a The traditional political organization of the pastoral Masai. Unpub-
         lished D.Phil. thesis, University of Oxford.
  1965b Bibliography of the Masai. *African Studies Bulletin* 8(3): 40—60.
  1968   A chronology of the pastoral Maasai. *Hadith* 1: 10—31.
Jeffreys, M. D. W.
  1950   Age-groups among the Ika and kindred people. *African Studies* 9:
         157—166.
Jensen, Adolf E.
  1936   *Im Lande des Gada.* Stuttgart: Strecker und Schröder.
  1941   Neuere Notizen über das Gada-System. *Paideuma* 2: 84—94.
  1942   Elementi della cultura spirituale dei Conso. *Rassegna di Studi Etiopici*
         2: 217—259.
  1952   Forschungsreise nach Süd-Abessinien. *Zeitschrift für Ethnologie* 77:
         57—61.
  1954   Das Gada-System der Konso und die Altersklassen-Systeme der Niloten.
         Ethnos 19: 1—23.
  1959   *Altvölker Süd-Äthiopiens* (editor). Stuttgart: W. Kohlhammer.
Johnson, Elden
  1965   The Tribes of the Great Plains. In *The Native Americans,* by Robert F.
         Spencer *et al.* New York: Harper and Row.
Jones, G. I.
  1962   Ibo age organization, with special reference to the Cross River and
         North-Eastern Ibo. *Journal of the Royal Anthropological Institute* 92:
         191—210.

Josselin de Jong, J. P. B. de
  1912 Social organization of the southern Piegans. *Internationales Archiv für Ethnographie* **20**: 191—197.
Julien, Paul
  n.d. *Zonen van Cham. Onder Oost-Afrikaanse Steppevolken.* Amsterdam: Scheltens en Giltay.
Kalinovskaya, K. P.
  1969 K kharakteristike sistemy vozrastnykh grupp u Galla Efiopii. *Sovetskaya Etnografiya* 1969, 4: 128—132.
  1972 K voprosu o sootnoshenii funktsij i struktury sistemy vozrastnykh grupp u Galla [Efiopiya]. *Sovetskaya Etnografiya* 1972, 4: 136—142.
  1974 Vozrastnye gruppy kak element sotsial'noj organizatsii Konso. *Sovetskaya Etnografiya* 1974, 3: 120—125.
Kaufmann, Christian
  1972 *Das Töpferhandwerk der Kwoma in Nord-Neuguinea.* Basler Beiträge zur Ethnologie, 12. Basel: Pharos-Verlag Hansrudolf Schwabe AG.
Keesing, Roger M.
  1966 Kwaio kindreds. *Southwestern Journal of Anthropology* **22**: 346—353.
Keesing, Roger M. and Felix M. Keesing
  1971 *New perspectives in cultural anthropology.* New York: Holt, Rinehart, and Winston.
Kenyatta, Jomo
  1938 *Facing Mount Kenya.* London: Secker and Warburg.
Kettel, David
  1972 What's in a name? — Age-organization and reincarnation beliefs of the Tugen-Kalenjin. University of Nairobi, Institute of African Studies, Discussion Paper, 32. Mimeographed.
Keyfitz, Nathan
  1968 *Introduction to the mathematics of population.* Reading, Massachusetts: Addison-Wesley.
Klausberger, F.
  1972 Rechtsfindung in Süd-Äthiopien (Boran- und Guǧi-Galla). *Ethnologische Zeitschrift* (Zürich) 1972, 2: 133—147.
Klima, G.
  1964 Jural relations between the sexes among the Barabaig. *Africa* 34: 9—20.
  1970 *The Barabaig: East African cattle-herders.* New York: Holt, Rinehart, and Winston.
Knutsson, Karl Eric
  1967 *Authority and change.* Etnologiska Studier, 29. Gothenberg: Etnografiska Museet.
Kokubu, N., and E. Kaneko
  1962 The tribal peoples of Formosa. *Bulletin of the International Commission on Urgent Anthropological and Ethnological Research* 5: 32—41.
Kolk, J. van der
  1924 Leeftijdsklassen op de Tanimbar-Eilanden. *Bijdragen tot de Taal- Landen Volkenkunde van Neederlansch-Indië* 80: 601—607.
Kramer, K.-S.
  1964 Altersklassenverbände. In *Handwörterbuch zur deutschen Rechtsgeschichte*, edited by Adalbert Erler *et al.* Vol. 1. Berlin: Erich Schmidt. Pp. 138—142.

Krige, E. J.
1936   *The social system of the Zulus.* London: Longmans.
Kroeber, Alfred L.
1902   The Arapaho, I, General description. *Bulletin of the American Museum of Natural History* 18: 3–35.
1904   The Arapaho, III, Ceremonial organization. *Bulletin of the American Museum of Natural History* 18: 151–229.
1908   Ethnology of the Gros Ventre. *Anthropological Papers of the American Museum of Natural History* 1: 141–281.
Kronenberg, Andreas
1961a Longarim favourite beasts. *Kush* 9: 258–277.
1961b Age sets and "bull classes" among the Topotha. *Man* 61: 89.
1972   *Logik und Leben.* Studien zur Kulturkunde, 28. Wiesbaden: Franz Steiner.
Kuls, W.
1958   *Beiträge zur Kulturgeographie der südäthiopischen Seen Region.* Frankfurter Geographische Hefte, 32. Jahrgang. Frankfurt am Main: Waldemar Kramer.
Kummer, Hans
1971   *Primate societies.* Chicago: Aldine.
Lambert, H. E.
1947   *The use of indigenous authorities in tribal administration: studies of the Meru in Kenya Colony.* University of Cape Town, Communications from the School of African Studies, New Series, 16. Cape Town: University of Cape Town, School of African Studies.
1956   *Kikuyu social and political institutions.* London: Oxford University Press.
Lamphear, John
1972   The oral history of the Jie of Uganda. Unpublished Ph.D. thesis, University of London.
1976   *The traditional history of the Jie of Uganda.* Oxford: Clarendon Press.
Lancaster, Richard
1966   *Piegan.* New York: Doubleday.
Laughlin, C. D., and E. R. Laughlin
1974   Age generations and political process in So. *Africa* 44: 266–279.
Lave, Jean Carter
1971   Some suggestions for the interpretation of residence, descent, and exogamy among the Eastern Timbira. In *Verhandlungen des XXXVIII. Internationalen Amerikanistenkongresses, Stuttgart-München 12. bis 18. August 1968,* Vol. 3. Munich: Klaus Renner.
Lawren, William L.
1968   Masai and Kikuyu: an historical analysis of cultural transmission. *Journal of African History* 9: 571–583.
Leakey, L. S. B.
1952   *Mau Mau and the Kikuyu.* London: Methuen.
Legesse, Asmarom
1963   Class systems based on time. *Journal of Ethiopian Studies* 1: 1–29.
1973   *Gada.* New York: The Free Press. London: Collier–Macmillan.

Lehmann, F. R.
1943 Terminology of age grouping. *African Studies* 2: 115–116.
Lehmer, Donald J.
1971 *Introduction to Middle Missouri Archeology.* Anthropological Papers, 1. National Parks Service, U.S. Department of the Interior. Washington D.C.: Government Printing Office.
Levine, R. A., and W. H. Sangree
1962 The diffusion of age-group organization in East Africa: a controlled comparison. *Africa* 32: 97–110.
Lewis, B. A.
1972 *The Murle.* Oxford: Clarendon Press.
Lewis, E. A.
1930– Anthropological notes, Masai and kindred tribes, Kenya and Tangan-
1946 yika. Typescript in Rhodes House, Oxford (MSS. Afr. s. 1241).
Lewis, Oscar
1942 *The effect of white contact upon Blackfoot culture.* Monographs of the American Ethnological Society, 6. New York: J. J. Augustin.
Lienhardt, Godfrey
1957 Anuak village headmen. *Africa* 27: 341–355.
1966 *Social anthropology.* Oxford: Clarendon Press.
Lindenbaum, S., and Glasse, R.
1969 Fore age-mates. *Oceania* 39: 165–173.
Linton, Ralph
1936 *The study of man.* New York: Appleton-Century.
Lloyd, P. C.
1965 The Yoruba of Nigeria. In *Peoples of Africa,* edited by J. L. Gibbs. New York: Holt, Rinehart, and Winston.
Long Lance, Buffalo Child
1928 *Long Lance.* London: Faber and Gwyer.
Lotka, Alfred J.
1928 The progeny of a population element. *American Journal of Hygiene* 8: 875–901.
1929 The spread of generations. *Human Biology* 1: 305–320.
1939 *Théorie analytique des associations biologiques,* Vol. 2, *Analyse démographique avec application particulière à l'espèce humaine.* Paris: Hermann.
Lowenthal, Richard
1972 Structural dynamics and social change. *Journal of the Steward Anthropological Society* 3: 172–188.
Lowie, Robert H.
1913 Societies of the Hidatsa and Mandan Indians. *Anthropological Papers of the American Museum of Natural History* 11: 219–358.
1915 Societies of the Arikara Indians. *Anthropological Papers of the American Museum of Natural History* 11: 645–678.
1916 Plains Indian age-societies: historical and comparative summary. *Anthropological Papers of the American Museum of Natural History* 11: 877–984.
1919 The Hidatsa Sun Dance. *Anthropological Papers of the American Museum of Natural History* 16: 411–431.

1930   Age societies. In *Encyclopedia of the Social Sciences*, edited by E. R. A. Seligman, Vol. 1. New York: Macmillan. Pp. 482–483.
1947   *Primitive society.* New York: Liveright.
1950   *Social organization.* London: Routledge and Kegan Paul.
1963   *Indians of the Plains.* Garden City, New York: The Natural History Press.

McClintock, Walter
1910   *The Old North Trail.* London: Macmillan.
1923   *Old Indian trails.* London: Constable.
1937   *Blackfoot warrior societies.* Southwest Museum Leaflets, 8. Highland Park, Los Angeles: The Museum.

MacGregor, G.
1935   *Notes on the ethnology of Pukapuka.* Occasional Papers of the Bernice P. Bishop Museum, 11 (6). Honolulu: The Museum.

Maclean, J.
1895   Social organization of the Blackfoot Indians. *Transactions of the Canadian Institute* 4 (1892–1893): 249–260.

Maconi, V.
1973   L'iniziazione ai gruppi di eta feminili presso i Karimojong. In *Festschrift zum 65. Geburtstag von Helmut Petri*, edited by Kurt Tauchmann. Cologne and Vienna: Böhlau.

Mahner, Jurg
1970   *The outsider and insider in Tigania Meru.* Cultural Division, Institute for Development Studies, University College, Nairobi. Discussion Paper No. 5. Mimeographed

Mails, Thomas E.
1973   *Dog Soldiers, Bear Men and Buffalo Women: a study of the societies and cults of the Plains Indians.* Englewood Cliffs, New Jersey: Prentice-Hall.

Mallery, Garrick
1893   *Picture writing of the North American Indians.* Tenth Annual Report of the Bureau of American Ethnology, 1888–1889. Washington, D.C.: Government Printing Office.

Malouf, Carling
1963   Crow-Flies-High (32MZ1), a historic Hidatsa village in the Garrison Reservoir area, North Dakota. River Basin Surveys Papers, 29. *Bulletin of the Bureau of American Ethnology* 185: 133–166.

Manners, Robert A.
1967   The Kipsigis of Kenya. In *Contemporary change in traditional societies*, Vol. 1, *Introduction and African tribes*, edited by J. H. Steward. Urbana, Illinois: University of Illinois Press.

Massam, J. A.
1927   *Cliff-dwellers of Kenya.* London: Seeley, Service.

Matthews, Washington
1877   *Ethnography and philology of the Hidatsa Indians.* Department of the Interior. United States Geological and Geographical Survey. Miscellaneous Publications, 7. Washington, D.C.: Government Printing Office.

Mauss, Marcel
1969   *Oeuvres*, Vol. 3, *Cohésion sociale et division de la sociologie.* Paris: Les Editions de Minuit.

Maximilian, Prince of Wied-Neuwied
1839 *Reise in das innere Nord-America in den Jahren 1832 bis 1834*, Vol. 1. Coblenz: J. Hoelscher.
1841 *Reise in das innere Nord-America in den Jahren 1832 bis 1834*, Vol. 2. Coblenz: J. Hoelscher.
1843 *Travels in the interior of North America*. London: Ackermann.
1906 *Travels in the interior of North America*. Early Western Travels, 1748–1846, Vols. 22–24, edited by Reuben G. Thwaites. Cleveland: Arthur H. Clark.

Maybury-Lewis, David
1967 *Akwẽ-Shavante society*. Oxford: Clarendon Press.
1971 Some principles of social organization among the Central Gé. In *Verhandlungen des XXXVIII. Internationalen Amerikanistenkongresses, Stuttgart-München 12. bis 18. August 1968*, Vol. 3. Munich: Kommissionsverlag Klaus Renner.

Mazlish, Bruce
1975 *James and John Stuart Mill*. London: Hutchinson.

Meek, C. I.
1950 A practical experiment in local government. *Journal of African Administration* 2(3): 21–28.

Meister, Richard
1963 *Die spartanischen Altersklassen vom Standpunkt der Entwicklungspsychologie betrachtet*. Oesterreichische Akademie der Wissenschaften. Philosophisch-Historische Klasse. Sitzungsberichte, 241. Band 5. Abhandlung.

Mercier, Paul
1968 *Tradition, changement, histoire: les "Somba" du Dahomey septentrional*. Paris: Éditions Anthropos.
1971 Les classes d'âge chez les "Somba" (Dahomey). In *Classes et associations d'âge en Afrique de l'ouest*, edited by D. Paulme. Paris: Plon.

Merker, M.
1910 *Die Masai*. Berlin: Dietrich Reimer (Ernst Vohsen).

Michels, P. J. P.
1941 *De godsdienst der Galla*. Mimeographed doctoral thesis, University of Nijmegen.

Middleton, John, and Greet Kershaw
1965 *The Kikuyu and Kamba of Kenya*. Ethnographic Survey of Africa, East Central Africa, 5. London: International African Institute.

Mills, J. P.
1926 *The Ao Nagas*. London: Macmillan.

Miner, Horace
1965 *The primitive city of Timbuctoo*. Garden City, New York: Anchor Books.

Mirkhasilov, S. M.
1963 K istorii obshchestvenogo byta Uzbekov. *Sovetskaya Etnografiya* 1963, 5: 116–121.

Moal, G. le
1971 Les classes d'âge chez les Bobo (Haute-Volta). In *Classes et associations d'âge en Afrique de l'ouest*, edited by D. Paulme. Paris: Plon.

Monteil, Charles
  1924 *Les Bambara du Ségou et du Kaarta.* Gouvernement Général de
        l'Afrique Occidentale Française. Publications du comité d'études histo-
        riques et scientifiques. Paris: Émile Larose.
Moreno, M. M.
  1938 [Review of Cerulli 1938.] *Oriente Moderno* 18: 456–458.
Morgan, Lewis H.
  1959 *The Indian Journals,* edited by Leslie A. White. Ann Arbor, Michigan:
        University of Michigan Press.
Murdock, G. P.
  1949 *Social structure.* New York: Macmillan.
Muriuki, Godfrey
  1974 *A history of the Kikuyu 1500–1900.* Nairobi: Oxford University Press.
Nadel, S. F.
  1942 *A black Byzantium.* London: Oxford University Press.
  1947 *The Nuba.* London: Oxford University Press.
Nalder, L. F. (ed.)
  1937 *A tribal survey of Mongalla Province.* London: Oxford University Press.
Needham, Rodney
  1966 Age, category, and descent. *Bijdragen tot de taal-, land- en volkenkunde*
        122: 1–35.
Neugarten, Bernice L., Joan W. Moore, and John C. Lowe
  1965 Age norms, age constraints, and adult socialization. *American Journal
        of Sociology* 70: 710–717.
Niangoran-Bouah, Georges
  1960 Le village abouré. *Cahier d'études africaines,* Vol. 1, Cahier 2, pp. 113–
        127.
  1964 *La division du temps et le calendrier rituel des peuples lagunaires de
        Côte d'Ivoire.* Travaux et mémoires de l'Institut d'Ethnologie, 67. Paris:
        Institut d'Ethnologie.
  1965 *Les Abouré: une société lagunaire de Côte d'Ivoire. Annales de l'École
        de Lettres et Sciences Humaines de l'Université d'Abidjan* 1: 37–171.
  1969 Les Ébrié et leur organisation politique traditionelle. *Annales de l'Uni-
        versité d'Abidjan. Série F. Ethnosociologie* 1: 51–89.
Nimuendajú, C.
  1939 *The Apinayé.* Catholic University of America Anthropological Series, 8.
        Washington, D.C.: Catholic University of America.
  1942 *The Serente.* Publications of the Fredrick Webb Hodge Anniversary
        Publication Fund, 4. Los Angeles: The Southwest Museum.
  1946 *The Eastern Timbira.* University of California Publications in American
        Archaeology and Ethnology, 41. Berkeley: University of California
        Press.
Norbeck, E.
  1953 Age-grading in Japan. *American Anthropologist* 55: 373–384.
Nurdzhanov, Nizam
  1956 *Tadzhikskij narodnij teatr.* Moscow: Izdatelstvo Akademia Nauk S.S.R.
Oliver, Symmes C.
  1962 *Ecology and culture continuity as contributing factors in the social
        organization of the Plains Indians.* University of California Publications

in American Archaeology and Ethnology, 48(1). Berkeley: University of California Press.

Orchardson, Ian Q.
1928 *The Kipsigis.* Typescript in Rhodes House, Oxford (MSS. Afr. s. 455).
1930– Notes on the marriage customs of the Kipsigis. *Journal of the East*
1931 *Africa and Uganda Natural History Society* 40–41: 99–112.
1961 *The Kipsigis.* Nairobi: East African Literature Bureau. The Eagle Press. [This is an abridgement by A. T. Matson of Orchardson 1928.]

Ottenberg, Simon
1971 *Leadership and authority in an African society: the Afikpo village group.* American Ethnological Society, Monograph 52. Seattle and London: University of Washington Press.

Ottenberg, Simon, and Phoebe Ottenberg
1965 Social groupings. In *The study of Africa,* edited by P. J. M. McEwan and R. B. Sutcliffe. London: Methuen.

Pakes, Fraser J.
1968 The "No-flight" societies of the Plains Indians. *The English Westerners' Brandbook* 10(4): 1–4 and 10(5): 5–12.

Paulme, Denise
1968 Pacte de sang, classes d'âge, et castes en Afrique noir. *Archives européennes de sociologie* 9: 12–33.
1971a *Classes et associations d'âge en Afrique de l'ouest* (editor). Paris: Plon.
1971b Les classes d'âge dans le sud-est de la Côte d'Ivoire. In *Classes et associations d'âge en Afrique de l'ouest,* edited by D. Paulme. Paris: Plon.
1973 Blood pacts, age classes and castes in Black Africa. In *French perspectives in African studies,* edited by Pierre Alexandre. London: Oxford University Press.

Pecci, D.
1941 Note sul sistema della gada e delle classi di età presso le popolazioni Borana. *Rassegna di Studi Etiopici* 1: 305–321.

Peristiany, J. G.
1939 *The social institutions of the Kipsigis.* London: George Routledge and Sons.
1951 The age-set system of the pastoral Pokot. *Africa* 21: 188–206, 279–302.
1975 The ideal and the actual: the role of prophets in the Pokot political system. In *Studies in social anthropology: essays in memory of E. E. Evans-Pritchard by his former Oxford colleagues,* edited by J. H. M. Beattie and R. G. Lienhardt. Oxford: Clarendon Press.

Person, Y.
1963 Classes d'âge et chronologie. *Latitudes,* numero spécial: 68–83.
1968 *Samori, une révolution dyula,* Vol. 1. Mémoires de l'Institut Fondamentale d'Afrique Noire, 80. Dakar: Institut Fondamentale d'Afrique Noire.

Philippe, René
1965 *Inongo: les classes d'âge en region de la Lwafa (Tschuapa).* Archives d'Ethnographie, 8. Tervuren, Belgium: Musée royal de l'Afrique Centrale.

Plowman, Clifford H. G.
1919   Notes on the Gedamoch ceremonies among the Boran. *Journal of the African Society* 18: 114–121.
Pollet, E., and G. Winter
1971   *La société soninké*. Brussels: Editions de l'institut de sociologie, Université libre de Bruxelles.
Prins, A. H. J.
1953   *East African age-class systems*. Groningen, Djakarta: J. B. Wolters.
Quistorp, Martin
1915   Männergesellschaft und Altersklassen im alten China. *Mitteilungen des Seminars für orientalische Sprachen an der königlichen Friedrich-Wilhelms-Universität zu Berlin*. Jahrgang 18. *Erste Abteilung. Ostasiatische Studien*, pp. 1–61.
Radcliffe-Brown, A. R.
1929   Age organization—terminology. *Man* 29: 21.
1950   Introduction. In *African systems of kinship and marriage*, edited by A. R. Radcliffe-Brown and D. Forde. London: Oxford University Press.
Raum, G. F.
1940   *Chaga Childhood*. London: Oxford University Press.
Raz, Joseph
1975   *Practical reason and norms*. London: Hutchinson.
Read, Kenneth E.
1951   The Gahuku-Gama of the Central Highlands. *South Pacific* 5(8): 154–164.
1952   Nama cult of the Central Highlands, New Guinea. *Oceania* 23: 1–25.
1965   *The high valley*. New York: Charles Scribner's Sons.
Richards, F. J.
1929   Age-organization terminology. *Man* 29: 42–43.
Rivers, W. H. R.
1924   *Social organization*. London: Kegan Paul, Trench, Trubner.
Routledge, W. S., and K. Routledge
1910   *With a prehistoric people: the Akikuyu of British East Africa*. London: Edward Arnold.
Roy, Sarat Chandra
1915   *The Oraons of Chota Nagpur*. Ranchi: Published by the author.
Ruel, Malcolm J.
n.d.   The age organization of the Kuria. Manuscript in the Tylor Library, Institute of Social Anthropology, University of Oxford.
1962   Kuria generation classes. *Africa* 32: 14–37.
1969   *Leopards and leaders*. London: Tavistock.
Saberwal, Satish
1970   *The traditional political system of the Embu of Central Kenya*. East African Studies, 35. Nairobi: East African Publishing House.
Salzmann, Zdenek
1969   *Anthropology*. New York: Harcourt, Brace and World.
Sanders, Edith
1968   *East African age-grade systems: structure and origins*. Unpublished Ph.D. dissertation, Columbia University.

Sangree, Walter H.
1966 *Age, prayer and politics in Tiriki, Kenya.* London: Oxford University Press.
Schapera, Isaac
1955 *A handbook of Tswana law and custom.* London: Oxford University Press.
Scheitlin, Peter
1829 *Das Fünfzigerfest der Jahrgängerschaft des Jahres 1779, gefeiert am 22. und 23. Tag Herbstmonats 1829.* St. Gallen: Zollikofer und Züblin.
Schoolcraft, Henry R.
1853 *Information respecting the history conditions and prospects of the Indian tribes of the United States,* Vol. 3. Philadelphia: J. B. Lippincott.
Schultz, James W.
1907 *My life as an Indian.* London: J. Murray.
1962 *Blackfeet and buffalo,* edited by Keith C. Seele. Norman, Oklahoma: University of Oklahoma Press.
Schultz, James W., and Jessie L. Donaldson
1930 *The Sun God's children.* Boston and New York: Houghton Mifflin.
Schurtz, H.
1902 *Altersklassen und Männerbünde.* Berlin: Georg Reimer.
Seligman, C. G.
1910 *The Melanesians of British New Guinea.* Cambridge: Cambridge University Press.
Simmel, Georg
1908 *Soziologie.* Leipzig: Duncker und Humblot.
Smith, Edwin W., and A. M. Dale
1920 *The Ila-speaking peoples of Northern Rhodesia,* Vol. 1. London: Macmillan.
Smith, G. Hubert
1972 *Like a Fishhook village and Fort Berthold, Garrison Reservoir, North Dakota.* Anthropological Papers, 2. National Parks Service, U.S. Department of the Interior. Washington, D.C.: Government Printing Office.
Smith, Marian W.
1960 Mandan "history" as reflected in Butterfly's winter count. *Ethnohistory* 7: 199–205.
Smith, Pierre
1971 Les échelons d'âge dans l'organisation sociale et rituelle des Bedik (Sénégal oriental). In *Classes et associations d'âge en Afrique de l'ouest,* edited by D. Paulme. Paris: Plon.
Snell, G. S.
1954 *Nandi customary law.* Kampala: East African Literature Bureau.
Snesarev, G. P.
1960 Materialy o pervobytnoobshchennykh perezhitkakh v obychayakh i obryadakh Uzbekov Khorezma. In *Materialy Khorezmskoj Ekspeditsii,* Vol. 4, edited by S. P. Tolstov. Moscow.
1963 Traditsiya muzhskikh soyuzov v ee pozdnejshem variante u narodov Srednej Azii. In *Materialy Khorezmskoj Ekspeditsii,* Vol. 7, edited by S. P. Tolstov. Moscow.

1967   On relics of men's associations among Central Asian peoples. In *Congrès international des sciences anthropologiques et ethnologiques, section 7, 1964, Moscow*, Vol. 4. Moscow.

1969   Dukhovnyj oblik uzbekskogo krestyanina. In *Etnograficheskie ocherki uzbekskogo selskogo naseleniya*, edited by G. P. Vasileva and B. Kh. Karmysheva. Moscow: Izdatelstvo Nauka.

Sofue, Takao
1962   Anthropology in Japan. In *Biennial Review of Anthropology, 1961*, edited by Bernard J. Siegel. Stanford, California: Stanford University Press.

Spagnolo, L. M.
1932   Some notes on the initiation of young men and girls in the Bari tribe. *Africa* 5: 393—403.

Spencer, Paul
1965   *The Samburu*. London: Routledge and Kegan Paul.
1973   *Nomads in alliance*. London: Oxford University Press.

Spitzer, Alan B.
1973   The historical problem of generations. *American Historical Review* 78: 1353—1385.

Spry, Irene M. (ed.)
1968   *The papers of the Palliser expedition, 1857—1860*. Publications of the Champlain Society, 44. Toronto: Champlain Society.

Stanley, S., and D. Karsten
1968   The Luwa system of the Garbiččo subtribe of the Sidama (Southern Ethiopia) as a special case of an age set system. *Paideuma* 14: 93—102.

Stewart, Frank H.
1972   Fundamentals of age-set systems. Unpublished D.Phil. thesis, University of Oxford.
1974   Mandan and Hidatsa villages in the eighteenth and nineteenth centuries. *Plains Anthropologist* 19: 287—302.
1977   The Hidatsa. In *Handbook of North American Indians*, edited by William C. Sturtevant, Vol. 13. Washington, D.C.: Government Printing Office.

Sung, Lung-sheng
1964   Preliminary report on the ethnological investigation of the Puyuma tribe of Taitung Plain, Formosa. *Bulletin of the Department of Archaeology and Anthropology, National Taiwan University* 23—24: 67—82. [In Chinese, with English summary pp. 78—82.]
1965   The organization of men's house in a Puyuma tribe—Nan-wang village. *Bulletin of the Department of Archaeology and Anthropology, National Taiwan University* 25—26: 112—144. [In Chinese, with English summary pp. 141—144.]

Szanto, Emil
1893   Agelai. In *Pauly's Real-Encyclopädie der classischen Altertumswissenschaft*, Vol. 1, edited by Georg Wissowa. Stuttgart: J. B. Metzler.

Tait, David
1961   *The Konkomba of northern Ghana*. London: Oxford University Press.

Terray, Emmanuel
1969   L'organisation sociale des Dida de Côte d'Ivoire. *Annales de l'Université d'Abidjan, Série F, Ethnosociologie* 1(2): 1—375.

Textor, Robert B.
1967 *A cross-cultural summary.* New Haven, Connecticut: HRAF Press.
Thomas, Anthony
1966 Notes on the formal education of Arusha "murran" at circumcision. *Tanzania Notes and Records* 65: 81–90.
Thomas, Elizabeth Marshall
1966 *Warrior herdsmen.* London: Secker and Warburg.
Thompson, David
1962 *David Thompson's Narrative, 1784–1812,* edited by Richard G. Glover. Publications of the Champlain Society, 40. Toronto: Champlain Society.
Trümpy, H.
1965 Jahrgängervereine. In *Festschrift Alfred Bühler,* edited by Carl A. Schmitz and Robert Wildhaber. Basler Beiträge zur Geographie und Ethnologie, Ethnologische Reihe, 2. Basel: Pharos-Verlag Hansrudolf Schwabe.
Tucker, A. N.
1967 Fringe Cushitic. *Bulletin of the School of African and Oriental Studies* 30: 655–680.
Tucker, A. N., and M. A. Bryan
1956 *The non-Bantu languages of North-Eastern Africa.* London: Oxford University Press.
1966 *Linguistic analyses: the non-Bantu languages of North-Eastern Africa.* London: Oxford University Press.
Turner, Terence S.
1971 Northern Kayapó social structure. In *Verhandlungen des XXXVIII. Internationalen Amerikanistenkongresses, Stuttgart-München 12. bis 18. August 1968,* Vol. 3. Munich: Kommissionsverlag Klaus Renner.
Uhlenbeck, C. C.
1912 A new series of Blackfoot texts from the Southern Piegans Blackfoot Reservation, Teton County, Montana. *Verhandelingen der Koninklijkl Akademie van Wetenschappen te Amsterdam* 13(1).
Vicariato Apostolico del Gimma
1938 I Conso, loro usi e costumi. *Missioni Consolata* [Turin], October 1938, pp. 152–155.
Visscher, H.
1911 *Religion und soziales Leben bei den Naturvölkern.* Bonn: Johs. Schergens.
Wagner, Günter
1949 *The Bantu of North Kavirondo,* Vol. 1. London: Oxford University Press. [Reprinted together with Vol. 2 as one volume by the same publisher under the title *The Bantu of Western Kenya* in 1970.]
Walle, Etienne van de
1968 Marriage in African censuses and inquiries. In *The demography of tropical Africa* by William Brass *et al.* Princeton, New Jersey: Princeton University Press.
Wassungu, P.
1971 Classes d'âge et initiation chez les Nawdeba (Togo). In *Classes et associations d'âge en Afrique de l'ouest,* edited by D. Paulme. Paris: Plon.

Weber, Max
    1964 *Wirtschaft und Gesellschaft.* Cologne and Berlin: Kiepenheuer und
          Witsch.
    1968a *Gesammelte Aufsätze zur Wissenschaftslehre.* Tübingen: J. C. B. Mohr.
    1968b *Economy and society.* New York: Bedminster Press.
Welbourn, F. B.
    1968 Keyo initiation. *Journal of Religion in Africa* 1: 212–232.
Whiting, John W. M.
    1941 *Becoming a Kwoma.* New Haven, Connecticut: Yale University Press.
Whyte, W. F.
    1944 Age-grading of the Plains Indians. *Man* 44: 68–72.
Will, George F., and H. J. Spinden
    1906 The Mandans, a study of their culture, archaeology, and language.
          *Papers of the Peabody Museum of American Archaeology and Ethnol-
          ogy, Harvard University,* Vol. 3, No. 4. Cambridge, Massachusetts: The
          Museum. Pp. 81–219.
Wilson, Gilbert L.
    1914 *Goodbird the Indian.* New York: Fleming H. Revell.
    1933 *Notes on the Hidatsa Indians,* edited by Bella Weitzner. Unpublished
          manuscript in the Anthropological Department, American Museum of
          Natural History, New York.
    n.d. Hidatsa age societies. Unpublished manuscript in the Anthropological
          Department, American Museum of Natural History, New York.
Wilson, Gordon McL.
    1952 The Tatoga of Tanganyika. *Tanganyika Notes and Records* 33: 34–47.
    1953 The Tatoga of Tanganyika. *Tanganyika Notes and Records* 34: 35–56.
Wilson, Monica
    1975 [Letter on the Nyakyusa.] *Africa* 45: 202–205.
Wingfield, Alys
    1948 Tribespeople of Kenya's Northern Frontier District. *The Geographical
          Magazine* 20: 351–362.
Wissler, Clark
    1911 The social life of the Blackfoot Indians. *Anthropological Papers of the
          American Museum of Natural History* 7: 1–64.
    1912 Ceremonial bundles of the Blackfoot Indians. *Anthropological Papers
          of the American Museum of Natural History* 7: 65–289.
    1913 Societies and dance associations of the Blackfoot Indians. *Anthropo-
          logical Papers of the American Museum of Natural History* 11: 359–
          460.
    1918 The Sun Dance of the Blackfoot Indians. *Anthropological Papers of the
          American Museum of Natural History* 16: 225–270.
Wissler, Clark, and D. C. Duvall
    1908 Mythology of the Blackfoot Indians. *Anthropological Papers of the
          American Museum of Natural History* 2: 1–164.
Wood, W. Raymond
    1967 *An interpretation of Mandan culture history.* River Basin Surveys
          Papers, 39. Bulletin of the Bureau of American Ethnology, 198. Wash-
          ington, D.C.: Government Printing Office.
Yegnan, Touré
    1968 Autorité familiale et autorité politique dans un village ébrié (Songon

M'bratté). *Bulletin d'information et de liaison des Instituts d'Ethno-Sociologie et de Géographie Tropicale Université d'Abidjan* 1: 2–13.

Yuan, Chang-rue
1967　The age-grade system of the Makutaai Ami. *Bulletin of the Institute of Ethnology, Academia Sinica,* 24: 123–186. [In Chinese, with English summary pp. 181–186.]

Zavattari, Edoardo
1940　*Condizioni biogeografiche et antropiche.* Reale Accademia d'Italia Centro Studi per l'Africa Orientale Italiano, 4. Missione Biologica nel Paese dei Borana, Vol. 1. Rome.
1942　Le genti del paese dei Borana. *Rivista di Antropologia* 34: 1–66.

Zoli, Corrado
1927　*Oltre Giuba.* Collezione di Opere e di Monografie a cura del Ministero delle Colonie, 1. Rome: Sindacato Italiano Arti Grafiche.

MAPS

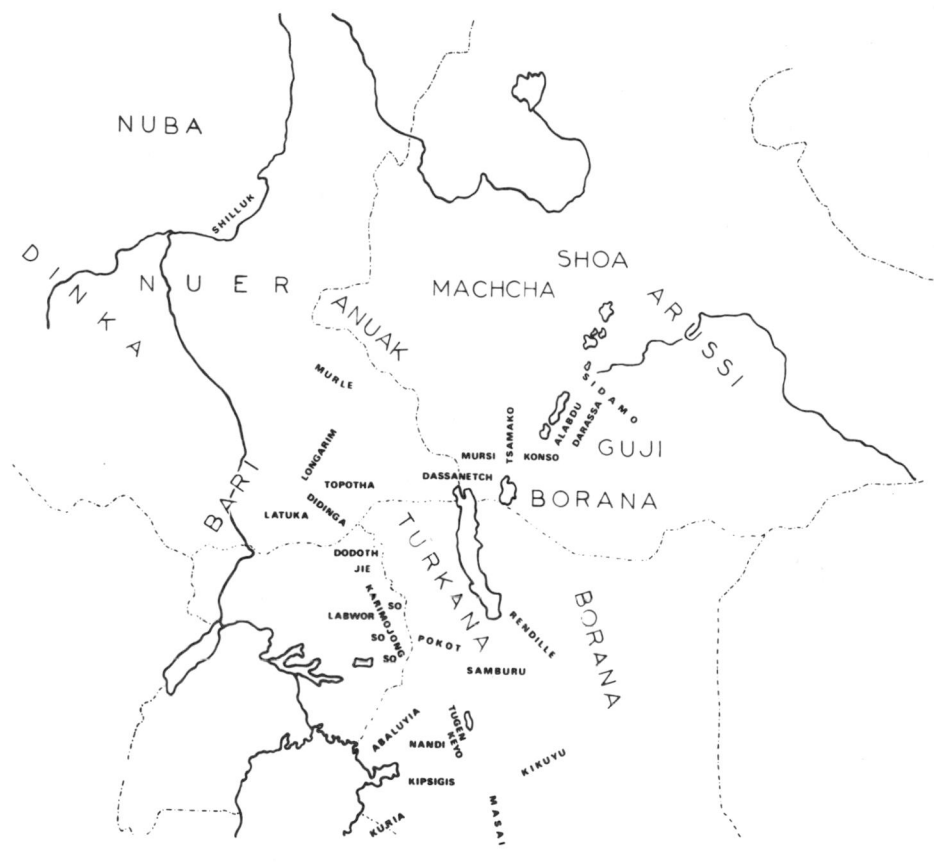

Map 1   East Africa, North.

KIPSIGIS

KURIA

M

KIKUYU

KWAYA
NGURUIMI
ZANAKI
SIZAKI
NATA
IKOMA
IKIZU
SONJO

ARUSHA CHAGGA

S

A

I

TATOGA

GOGO

BARAGUYU

NYAKYUSA

NGONI

Map 2   East Africa, South.

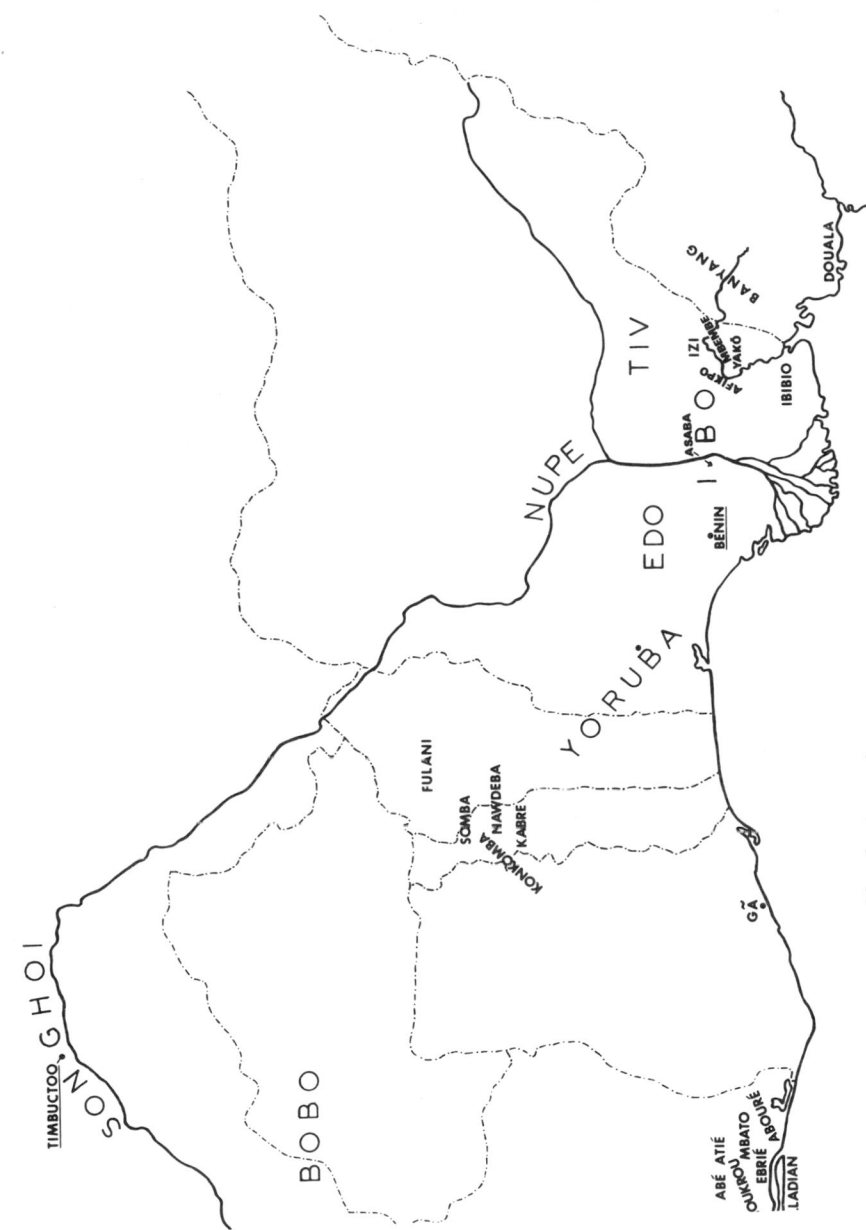

Map 3   West Africa, East. Names of towns are underlined.

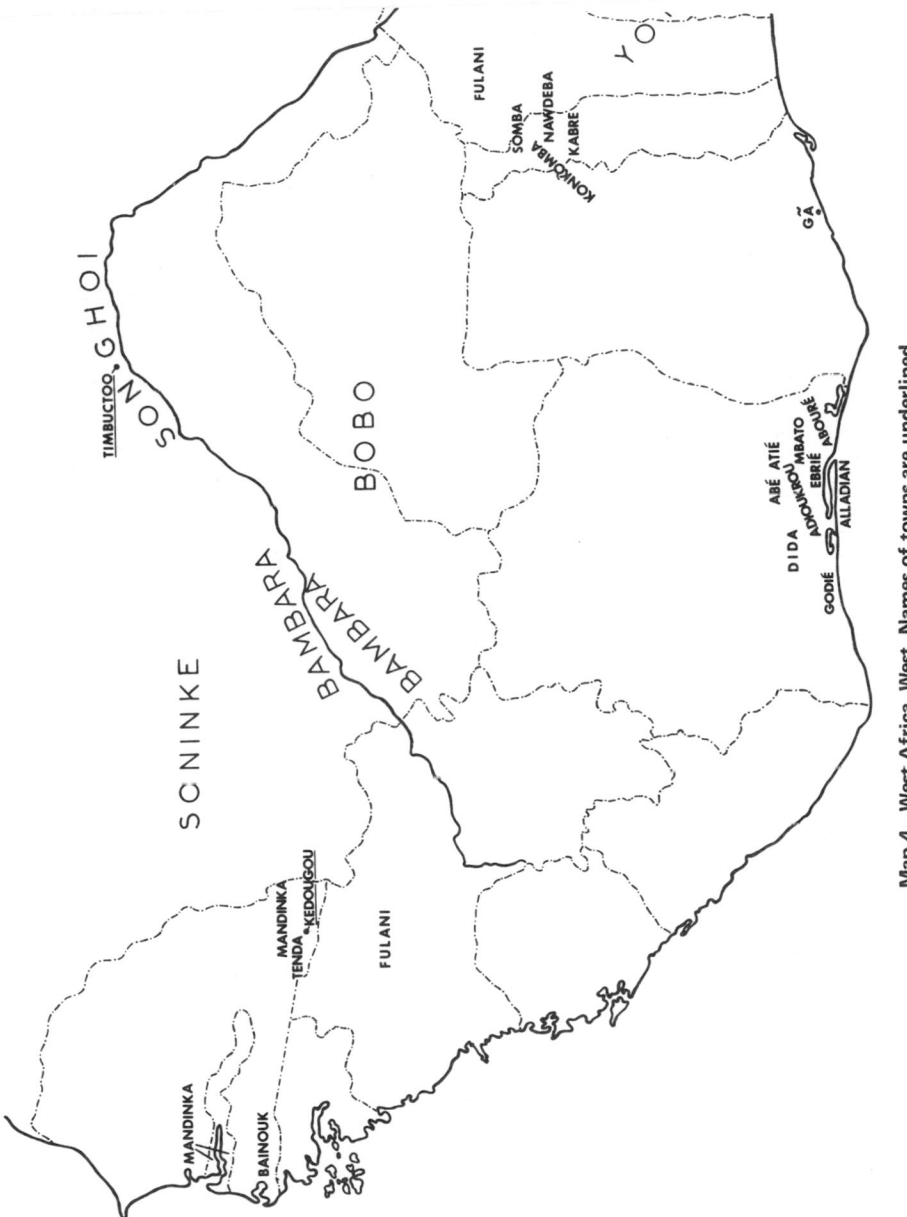

Map 4   West Africa, West. Names of towns are underlined.

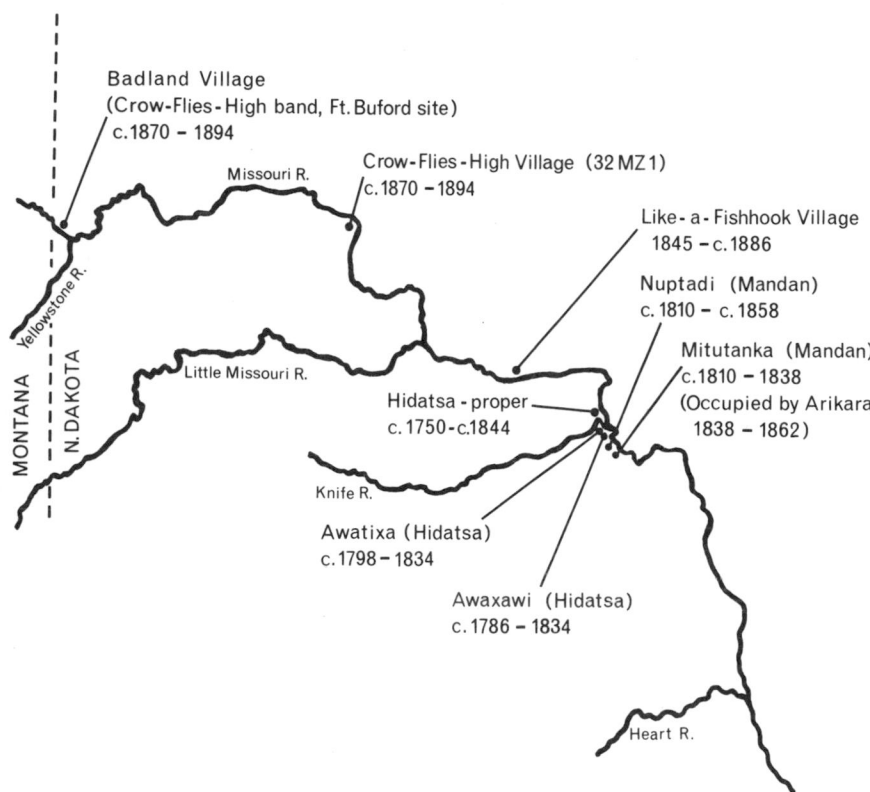

Badland Village
(Crow-Flies-High band, Ft. Buford site)
c.1870 – 1894

Missouri R.

Crow-Flies-High Village (32 MZ 1)
c.1870 –1894

Like-a-Fishhook Village
1845 – c.1886

Nuptadi (Mandan)
c. 1810 – c. 1858

Mitutanka (Mandan)
c.1810 – 1838
(Occupied by Arikara
1838 – 1862)

Yellowstone R.

MONTANA

N. DAKOTA

Little Missouri R.

Hidatsa - proper
c. 1750 - c.1844

Knife R.

Awatixa (Hidatsa)
c.1798 – 1834

Awaxawi (Hidatsa)
c. 1786 – 1834

Heart R.

Map 5 Mandan and Hidatsa villages at the time of Maximilian (1833–1834), together with three later villages. [Data from Stewart 1974.]

376

Index

THE AGE-SET MODEL

A collection of groups in a society constitutes an **age-set sequence** when the groups are governed by rules such that in that society they generate an unbounded number of groups with the following characteristics:

1. **The ordering characteristic.** There is a total ordering on the groups given by the order in which they begin recruiting.
2. **The no-overlapping characteristic.** Each group ceases permanently to recruit members before the next one starts.
3. **The two-group characteristic.** There are always at least two groups in existence.
4. **The dissolution characteristic.** No group dissolves before one that began recruiting before it.
5. **The enrolment characteristic.** There is a certain age (the enrolment age) that has the following properties:
   (i) No individual joins a group before reaching this age: it is the **minimum enrolment age.**
   (ii) Any individual who has not yet joined a group, but who is going to join one, and who has reached this age, joins a group as soon as there is one recruiting members: it is the **basic enrolment age.**
6. **The single membership characteristic.** No individual is at any time a member of more than one group.
7. **The no-resigning characteristic.** A member only leaves a group under one of the following circumstances:
   (i) When he leaves the society, or
   (ii) When the group is dissolving.
8. **The no-rejoining characteristic.** A member who has left a group because he has left the society or because the group is dissolving does not again join a group.